NUFFIELD – BP
BUSINESS AND ECONOMICS
FOR GCSE

Collins Educational
An imprint of HarperCollinsPublishers

Published by Collins Educational
An imprint of HarperCollins*Publishers*
77–85 Fulham Palace Road
London W6 8JB

© 1996 The Nuffield Foundation
Published for the Nuffield Foundation by HarperCollins*Publishers* Ltd

First published 1996
Reprinted 1997 (twice)

ISBN 0-00-328013-6

This book is copyright under the Berne Convention

The authors assert the moral right to be identified as the authors of this work.

British Library cataloguing-in-publication data
A catalogue record for this book is available from the British Library.

All rights reserved. No part of this publication may be reproduced, stored in a retrieval system, or transmitted in any form or by any means, electronic, mechanical, chemical, optical, photocopying, recording or otherwise, without the prior permission of the Publisher.

Commissioned by Emma Dunlop
Project management by Patricia Briggs
Design and typesetting by Ewing Paddock, Peartree Design Associates
Cover design and typesetting by Ewing Paddock, Peartree Design Associates
Cover photograph courtesy of the Daily Telegraph Picture Library
Edited by Brigitte Lee
Original artwork by Joan Corlass (pp. 12, 16, 19, 46, 70, 74, 80, 160, 202)
  and Julia Osorno (pp. 96, 169, 173)
Cartoons by Martin Shovel (pp. 65, 110, 164, 213)
Picture research by Thelma Gilbert and Caroline Thompson
Production by Jane Bressloff, Mandy Inness and Delphina Kitson-Mills-Jones
Printed in Hong Kong

Contents

A PRODUCT OF PARTNERSHIP ... iv
ACKNOWLEDGEMENTS ... v

UNIT 1: MAKE OR BREAK? — 1

ENQUIRY 1:	What is enterprise?	2
ENQUIRY 2:	Is there a market?	10
ENQUIRY 3:	Is it competitive?	16
ENQUIRY 4:	What is success?	24
ENQUIRY 5:	Why do firms go under?	32
CASE STUDY:	Disneyland	38

UNIT 2: WORK OR WHAT? — 39

ENQUIRY 1:	What's the point of work?	40
ENQUIRY 2:	Who's right for the job?	46
ENQUIRY 3:	Can we get more from less?	52
ENQUIRY 4:	What's the future of work?	58
ENQUIRY 5:	What does joblessness cost?	68
CASE STUDY:	Telephone exchanges	78

UNIT 3: RISK OR CERTAINTY? — 79

ENQUIRY 1:	Can profit be planned?	80
ENQUIRY 2:	Where's the money coming from?	88
ENQUIRY 3:	What is the bottom line?	94
ENQUIRY 4:	How can the odds be shortened?	102
ENQUIRY 5:	Can we ride the roller coaster?	110
CASE STUDY:	A risk or a certainty?	118

UNIT 4: BIG OR SMALL? — 119

ENQUIRY 1:	Is big better?	120
ENQUIRY 2:	What makes a firm grow?	126
ENQUIRY 3:	Is small beautiful?	132
ENQUIRY 4:	Can we control the giants?	138
ENQUIRY 5:	Why belong to the European Union?	146
CASE STUDY:	A question of scale	154

UNIT 5: CREATE OR DESTROY? — 155

ENQUIRY 1:	What makes people richer?	156
ENQUIRY 2:	Can there be more and more?	164
ENQUIRY 3:	Waste not – want not?	170
ENQUIRY 4:	How should firms behave?	176
ENQUIRY 5:	Should the government interfere?	184
CASE STUDY:	Power stations	190

UNIT 6: WINNERS OR LOSERS? — 191

ENQUIRY 1:	Who are the winners and losers?	192
ENQUIRY 2:	What makes a winner?	198
ENQUIRY 3:	Is there help at hand?	206
ENQUIRY 4:	Who trades wins?	214
ENQUIRY 5:	Richer country – richer people?	222
CASE STUDY:	A winner or a loser?	230

INDEX ... 231

A product of partnership

Many young people will seek work in industry and commerce. If they are to add value effectively, they need to understand the origins of wealth creation and be familiar with the concepts and application of business and economics. Business literacy is growing in importance, and young people are increasingly becoming involved in the management of enterprise.

The Nuffield – BP Business and Economics course has been developed in response to these needs. It is the result of an active partnership between a varied group of organisations.

- The Nuffield Foundation has a long history of funding innovative curriculum development. The independence of the Foundation has helped to ensure that the development of the course resources has been under the editorial control of the authors throughout.
- BP helped not only by funding the project, but also by providing advice and information from their experts in many departments.
- ULEAC contributed by supporting a member of the team during the syllabus development phase, as well as providing practical help with accreditation. The GCSE examination is available from ULEAC.
- EBEA members from across the country, with expertise in both business studies and economics, have contributed extensively to the syllabus development and to the resources.
- Collins Educational has worked closely with the project team to facilitate the development of the resources.

Many people helped to make this book possible. The major part of the writing was done by the project team: Stephen Barnes, Jenny Wales, Nancy Wall and David Lines. From outside the team, Keith Brumfitt and Paul Clarke made very substantial contributions, both as writers and readers. Neil Reaich and Celia Flynn also wrote and gave valuable support as classroom teachers. Peter Davies and Steve Hurd participated in the planning workshops and made helpful and trenchant comments throughout the writing process. Seamus McKenna, Helen Pritchard and Geoff Hale also helped read and comment. Patricia Briggs, Project Editor at Collins Educational, and Linda Westgarth, Administrator at the Nuffield Foundation, both provided help and support on a grand scale.

We are grateful to all the people who helped us with information and case study material. In particular, many people told us about their business ventures, sometimes in great detail. We would also like to thank Alan Fraser, Leon Oxenham, Judith Ryde, Khawer Siddiqi, Linda Trinder and Mike Turner (all members of the PGCE group at the Institute of Education, University of London) for their contributions.

It is intended that this textbook be used in conjunction with the *Teachers' Resource Pack* – also published by Collins Educational – which includes advice to teachers, photocopiable activities and software. Together, these two publications form a complete package to support the teaching of the GCSE course.

Nancy Wall
Editor

Acknowledgements

The publishers would like to thank the following for permission to reproduce photographs, artwork and cartoons in this book:

Action Images, p. 89; Paddy Allen/*The Guardian*, p. 188; AMEC plc, p. 54; Amstrad, p. 136; Clive Anderson/BBC, p. 77; Artplace, p. 203; Terry Austin Smith (Photography), p. 195; Banking, Insurance and Finance Union (BIFU), p. 29; Barclays Bank, pp. 10, 11; Baygen, p. 128; WH Bence Coachworks Ltd, pp. 106, 149; Nathan Betts, p. 206; Bic, pp. 120, 122; Big Table, p. 172; Birds Eye Wall's, p. 21/Toby Brunt, p. 139; Bluebird Toys (UK) Ltd, pp. 95, 98; Body Shop, p. 226; Tim Booth Photography, pp. 14, 47, 82; Patricia Briggs, pp. 10, 20, 100, 103, 105, 111, 112, 156, 228-9, 230; British Petroleum Co. plc, pp. 104, 105, 121, 225; Peter Brooks/*The Times*, 1995, p. 117; BT Archive Pictures, p. 78; BT Corporate Pictures, p. 78; Cadbury Ltd, p. 5; Cafédirect, p. 226; Camelot, p. 207; Charity Flowers, p. 7; Charity Projects/Mauro Carraro, p. 6/Tuppence Stone, p. 6; Chessington World of Adventure, p. 112; Collections/Michael George, p. 76; Colorific!/J. Aaronson, p. 166; Combe Grove Manor Country Club, Bath, p. 8; Gary Cook and Chris Sargent/*The Sunday Times*, 1995, p. 15; Co-operative Bank, pp. 102, 176; Dartington Crystal Ltd, p. 124; De Montfort University, p. 126; Department of Health, p. 49; Disneyland Paris, p. 38; Duckworth: from C. Falls (1961) *A Hundred Years of War*, p. 134; Dyson's Appliances, p. 128; Elms Marketing, p. 216; EMAP, p. 26; The Environmental Picture Library/Alex Olah, p. 170/David Townend, pp. 186, 215; Eolas Productions Ltd, p. 31; Eon Productions Ltd/Keith Hamshere, p. 199; Ericsson, p. 148; The Fair Trade Foundation, p. 227; Ferrosan Operations Ltd, p. 56; Allan M Finlayson, p. 90; The 5th Wave/Rich Tennant, Rockport, MA, p. 175; Grand Metropolitan, p. 179; The Ronald Grant Archive, p. 210; Graphical, Paper and Media Union (GPMU), p. 65; Greenpeace Communications Ltd/Greig, p. 180; Habitat Designs Ltd, p. 153; Robert Harding Picture Library, p. 77; Headway Hurstwood Park, p. 61; Paul Hellyer, pp. 144, 145; HELP/John Squire/Go! Disks, p. 7; Herman Miller, p. 148; Philip Hollis, p. 33; Honda (UK), p. 35; Hoseasons Holidays, p. 67; IBM, p. 132; Images Colour Library, p. 156; Imperial Chemical Industries plc, pp. 180, 224; Interactive Learning Productions, p. 28; IT/Neil Cooper, p. 77; Johnstone's Paints, p. 116; Christopher Jones, p. 93; Katz Pictures/McVay/Saba/Rea, p. 192/Rolle/Rea, p. 222/John Walters, p. 196; Kingfisher Group plc, p. 130; Kwik Fit (GB) Ltd, p. 198; Kwik Save Group plc, p. 22; Lanarkshire Development Agency, p. 143; London Borough of Richmond upon Thames/Richard Jennings, p. 9; Murdo MacLeod, p. 53; McDonalds Restaurants, p. 127; Colin McPherson/*The Independent*, p. 178; Manchester City Football Club, p. 91; Marks & Spencer plc, pp. 24, 147, 213; Media in Wessex, p. 167; Helen Mortimer, p. 10; Motorcycles Unlimited/Roland Brown, p. 34; Nanhu Indian Trading Project, Mexico, p. 226; National Union of Journalists (NUJ), p. 65; National Union of Rail, Maritime and Transport Workers (RMT), p. 29; National Union of Teachers (NUT), p. 29; NatWest Group, p. 81; Network/Jeremy Green, p. 158/Barry Lewis, p. 171/Mike Goldwater, p. 215; News International Associated Services Ltd, p. 115; Next plc, p. 200; Nissan UK Ltd, p. 158; Nokia, p. 100; North News & Pictures, p. 138; Sabine Oppenländer Associates/Karl-Heinz Hick/Joker, p. 189; Oticon, p. 175; OXFAM/Jeremy Hartley, p. 197; PA News Photo Library, p. 14/Paul Barker, p. 165/David Giles, p. 183, p. 118; Panos Pictures, p. 153/Guiseppe Bizzarri, p. 197/Nancy Durrell-McKenna, pp. 157, 192/Marc French, p. 162/Jeremy Hartley, p. 162/Zed Nelson, p. 226/Liba Taylor, p. 157/; Patak (Spices) Ltd, pp. 214, 218; Patrimonio Nacional, Madrid/The Bridgeman Art Library, p. 134; Mike Pattison Photography, p. 24; Perrier, p. 218; Tom Pilston/*The Independent*, p. 204; Pizza Hut (UK) Ltd, pp. 58–59; Polygram Records Inc, p. 140; Portmeirion Potteries (Holdings) plc, p. 123; Preston Hospital Trust, p. 104; Tony Prime/*The Telegraph* plc, 1995, p. 32; The Prince's Trust, p. 207; Psion, p. 201; QA Photos Ltd, p. 107; Rank Hovis/David Muscroft, p. 137; Rex Features Ltd, p. 21, p. 94/Martti Petonen, p. 222; Gary Rhodes/BBC, p. 154; Richmond Society, p. 156; Ritec Ltd, p. 62; Rover plc, p. 230; Derek Rowe (Photos) Ltd, p. 127; St Edmundsbury Borough Council/West Stow Anglo-Saxon Village Trust, p. 156; St John Ambulance, p. 68; H Samuel, p. 10; Save The Children, p. 7; Science Picture Library, p. 190; Roger Scruton, pp. 135, 161, 187; Sears, p. 131; Martin Shovel, pp. 65, 110, 164,

213; Jeff Smith/Caledonian Newspapers, p. 140; SmithKline Beecham/Welback Golin/Harris Communications Ltd, pp. 177, 182; Sony, p. 118; Standard Fireworks, p. 36; Still Pictures/Mark Edwards, p. 195/Julio Etchart, pp. 192, 196/Mike Schroder, p. 192/Jorgen Schytte, p. 195; Tony Stone Images/Dugald Bremner, p. 17/Simon Jauncey, p. 150/Mark Joseph, pp. 72, 140/Mitch Kezar, p. 109/Alan Levenson, p. 68/John Lund, p. 154/Mark Segal, p. 57/David Stewart, p. 14/David Woodfall, p. 186; Swatch/Beni Steiner, p. 4; Edward Sykes/*The Independent*, p. 136; Telegraph Colour Library, p. 60/Larry Williams, p. 92/Paddy Eckersley, p. 14/Paul Viant, p. 14; Tesco plc, p. 30; Tetley, pp. 194, 195; Thames Valley Enterprise, p. 66; Gwilym Thomas and Associates Ltd, p. 68; Time Communications, pp. 2, 18; Time Off, p. 204; Transport and General Workers' Union (T&G), p. 65; Transrail, p. 185; Trip/M. Barlow, p. 162/Heath, p. 157/M. Jellife, p. 162/OP, p. 162; Graham Turner/*The Guardian*, p. 174; Tyco Matchbox, p. 13; Union of Shop, Distributive and Allied Workers (USDAW), p. 29; UNISON, p. 29; Jay Ward, pp. 13, 42, 72, 88, 159, 161, 212; Kipper Williams/*The Guardian*, p. 32; Woolworth plc, p. 27; World Trade Organisation/Tania Tang, p. 221; Worthingtons Hair and Beauty Company, p. 133; Xinhua News Agency, p. 166; Zenith Windows, p. 62.

The publishers also wish to acknowledge the following sources of articles and data:

The Arson Prevention Bureau, p. 109; *The Assistant Librarian*, p. 207; Bluebird Toys (UK) Ltd, pp. 95, 97, 99; BNFL, p. 169; BP, pp. 121, 168; *Building*, p. 72, *Campaign*, p. 182; Central Statistical Office, pp. 53, 57, 58, 61, 63, 68, 69 (× 2), 71, 113, 115, 148, 215; Charity Projects, p. 6; Coopers and Lybrand, p. 2; The Co-operative Bank, p. 102; Department for Education and Employment, p. 209; Department of Health, p. 75; Department of the Environment, p. 170; Department of Trade and Industry, p. 207; DTI Small Firm Statistical Unit, p. 5; Eagle Star, p. 109; Employment Department, p. 71; *Employment Gazette*, pp. 48, 64; Euromonitor, p. 103; *Evening Standard*, pp. 138, 172, 173; Ferrosan, p. 56; *Financial Times*, pp. 54, 195; Ford Motor Company, p. 142; FT Graphite, p. 32; General Medical Council, p. 156; *The Guardian*, pp. 93, 116, 138, 140, 141, 153, 158 (× 2), 169, 174, 188, 227; HM Treasury, pp. 208 (× 2), 211 (× 2), 215; HMSO, p. 43; IDG Books, p. 175; IMF, p. 159; *The Independent*, pp. 5, 132; *The Independent on Sunday*, p. 136; Investors in People, p. 159; Kwik Save, p. 22; Milton Keynes Borough Council, p. 174; *National Institute Economic Review*, pp. 48, 56, 111, 156; NatWest Group, p. 80; *New Internationalist*, p. 171; Nokia, pp. 100, 101; *The Observer*, pp. 72, 115, 161; *Observer Magazine*, p. 53; OECD, p. 59; Oxfam, p. 197; Oxford University Press, pp. 142, 152, 156, 157 (× 2), 162 (× 3), 170, 193, 222 (× 2), 223, 224 (× 2); Portmeirion Potteries plc, p. 123; *Scottish Screen Digest*, p. 210; SmithKline Beecham, p. 177; The Tea Council, p. 194; Tesco, p. 30; *The Times*, pp. 140, 164, 165, 167, 186; Union Bank of Switzerland, p. 193; Woolworths, p. 27.

Every effort has been made to contact copyright holders, but if any have been inadvertently overlooked, the publishers will be pleased to make the necessary arrangements at the first opportunity.

Almost all the case studies in this book are real. Some businesses and people are given their real names and have genuine photographs as well. Others have been given different names to protect their identity. In these cases, the photographs are for educational purposes only and are not intended to identify the individual. The publishers cannot accept any responsibility for any consequences resulting from this use of photographs and case studies, except as expressly provided by law.

Unit 1

Make or break?

ENQUIRY 1: WHAT IS ENTERPRISE?	**2**
Why run a business?	2
Introducing enterprise, sole ownership and limited companies	
Who calls the shots?	4
Making decisions in public and private limited companies	
The charity business	6
How charities are organised	
Who plays the game?	8
Enterprise in the private and public sectors	

ENQUIRY 2: IS THERE A MARKET?	**10**
What makes a market?	10
The nature of markets and profit	
It's all to clear	12
Demand, supply and market clearing	
Target the market	14
Market segments and niches: spotting a gap	

ENQUIRY 3: IS IT COMPETITIVE?	**16**
What costs must be covered?	16
Exploring fixed and variable costs	
Will it be profitable?	18
Profits, costs and a first look at the impact of competition	
Getting it together	20
Added value, brand names and product ranges	
Compete on price or quality?	22
Competition and competitive advantage	

ENQUIRY 4: WHAT IS SUCCESS?	**24**
Is it making money?	24
Success, profit, capital employed and ROCE	
Going up or going down?	26
The nature of success: decisions and opportunity cost	
What about the workforce?	28
Employers and employees: rewards and productivity	
Whose success	30
Stakeholders and decisions: social responsibility	

ENQUIRY 5: WHY DO FIRMS GO UNDER?	**32**
What is business failure?	32
Takeover, receivership and the outcome of failure	
Did the market move on?	34
How businesses change with the market	
Has the cash run out?	36
Cash flow, liquidity and how businesses cope	

CASE STUDY: DISNEYLAND	**38**

Unit 1

Make or break?

Enquiry 1: What is enterprise?

Why run a business?

EVIDENCE

A NEW BEGINNING

Deborah Marsh and her sister Ingrid had always worked for other people in the world of public relations (PR). They recently achieved a lifelong ambition by setting up their own business. Both of them put up a share of the money to get their business started.

The objective of their company, Time Communications, is to help firms develop their image, become better known and therefore sell their products more widely.

Of course, going ahead with their plans was not without risk. When asked how they felt when the final decision was made, Deborah replied 'Dead scared!' They were not used to uncertainty. What if the phone never rang? What if no one ever came through the door? They could make estimates but did not know exactly how much they would earn.

So why did they go ahead? This was an easy question for Deborah and the words just tumbled out 'It's mine – just something inside me – I never did enjoy working for someone else – I'm in control – lots of personal satisfaction.' Her only small doubt came from the responsibility involved. 'I can't just take holidays when I want, I have to think about what's going on in the business – but then it's worth it because the world is our oyster'.

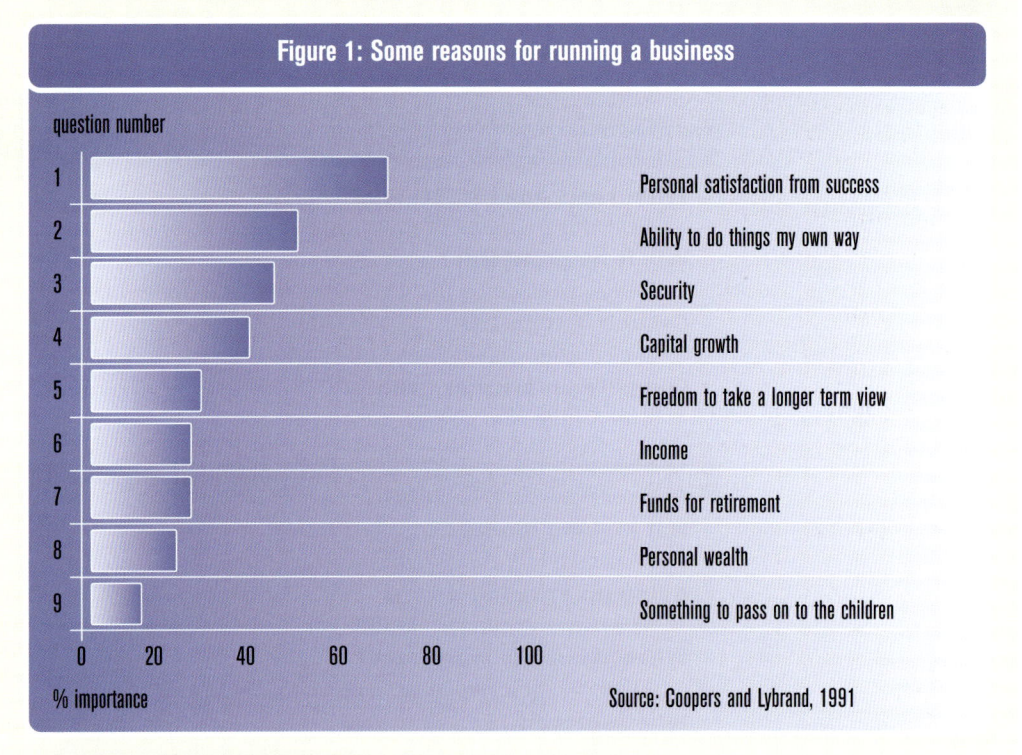

Figure 1: Some reasons for running a business

Question number	Reason	% importance (approx)
1	Personal satisfaction from success	~70
2	Ability to do things my own way	~50
3	Security	~35
4	Capital growth	~35
5	Freedom to take a longer term view	~25
6	Income	~25
7	Funds for retirement	~25
8	Personal wealth	~20
9	Something to pass on to the children	~10

Source: Coopers and Lybrand, 1991

Q1 Some people say that money is all important. Use the data in figure 1 to help you explain whether this statement is true.

Q2 What evidence is there from the story of Deborah Marsh to support this data?

THE CHALLENGE OF ENTERPRISE

Starting a business takes a spark of initiative and a great deal of time spent planning and organising. All sorts of decisions have to be made. Exactly what will the business do? Who are the customers? Will we need a shop, a factory, more people or other resources? Will the business bring in more money than it costs to run, in other words – will it make a profit? Profit is obviously important to a business. Without it, survival time is short.

Deborah Marsh, however, had many other reasons for wanting to work for herself. Figure 1 tells the same story.

A key objective of people who run their own businesses is that they are looking for the personal satisfaction that success brings. Independence is another factor. Being able to do things your own way instead of being given instructions by others is very important to many people.

Personal wealth and financial reward come lower on the list. Often, a new business pays very little to begin with. Deborah was prepared to take a drop in income in order to achieve her ambition. Fortunately, she soon started to make more than in her previous job, but this is often not the case.

EVIDENCE

'ONE DINAR! ONE DINAR!'

Mustafa lives in Tunis, the capital city of Tunisia, one of the world's richer developing countries. Although living conditions are improving and education is widespread, finding ways to earn a living can be difficult. Weighing passers-by, for one dinar a time, on an old set of bathroom scales, is just one way. It shows how, with a little initiative, many things can be put to use.

Q1 Is weighing passers-by an enterprising activity?

FORUM

Deborah and Mustafa are both involved in enterprise in different ways. Deborah has a degree in public relations but Mustafa has got only a pair of scales. Enterprise is therefore open to anyone who has a bright idea and is prepared to work at it. What sorts of skills or bright ideas have you got which might be turned to good use?

A RISKY BUSINESS

There is always an element of risk in these activities. Deborah was very uncertain about the future when she set up in business. One way to reduce the risk is to set up a company. As a **limited company**, you are protected by limited liability, which means that if the firm fails, all that is lost is the money that you have already put in. Your house and other possessions are safe. So Time Communications is known as a limited company.

The alternative for someone who is just starting out, is to become a **sole owner**. The main drawback of doing this is that you are completely responsible for all the debts. If the organization makes a loss, the sole owner can be called upon to sell their possessions to pay the debt.

ENTREPRENEURSHIP

Entrepreneurship combines a wide range of attitudes and skills which lead people to set up their own business. It may be sparked by a variety of situations. A bright idea for a new product is often a starting point. Unemployment may spur people into action as they decide to set up a company to sell their skills.

Deborah has expertise in public relations which she is selling effectively. Mustafa has spotted a gap in the market and with his bathroom scales, has set up his own small enterprise. Both of them are demonstrating entrepreneurship.

KEY TERMS

Entrepreneurship means being prepared to take risks and having the flair and skills needed to set up and run a business or other organization.

A *sole owner* is an individual who runs a business and is personally responsible for any losses incurred.

A *limited company* is an organisation which gives its owners or shareholders protection so that they can lose only the money that they have already put in.

Unit 1 — Make or break?

Enquiry 1: What is enterprise?

Who calls the shots?

EVIDENCE

WHAT MAKES SWATCH TICK?

Switzerland was once the world's leading watch producer, but by 1980 Japan had taken over and the Swiss were left with only 10 per cent of the market. Something had to be done to turn the situation around.

The survival of the watch industry was vital to the Swiss economy as it provided many jobs. A leading industrialist, Nicholas Hayek, researched the situation and proposed a scheme.

The two biggest watch-producing firms merged and created SWATCH – 'S' for Switzerland added to the word 'watch'. Nicholas Hayek took charge of the new company. He knew that the industry had to be innovative if it were to be saved.

After much market research a gap in the market was identified. The public wanted an inexpensive, good quality, quartz analogue watch. The evidence showed that people liked the traditional watch face. Fortunately, a major Swiss bank was prepared to finance the new product.

The new SWATCH was developed by team effort: technicians, designers and marketing specialists worked closely together to produce a distinctive product. Everyone involved became motivated to think and act innovatively. New and advanced technology enabled the company to produce a one-piece watch to match the design brief.

SWATCH watches were completely different from any other watch because they were designed to be a fashion accessory, not simply a watch.

SWATCH has been an incredible marketing success. The watches have fashion appeal and new models are designed and released frequently. Price has been relatively stable at around £25, but several designs in limited editions have become collectors' items – some worth hundreds, if not thousands, of pounds. There is even a SWATCH collectors club, and many consumers own, on average, three different models.

Q1 Why do several departments often work together in the design and development of new products?

Q2 Why is the market research important to the development of new products?

Q3 Who was involved in making the decision to produce a SWATCH?

Q4 Why was the bank interested in the development of SWATCH?

Q5 Why was SWATCH so successful?

FORUM

How popular are SWATCH watches in your class? Carry out a quick survey of your class – who has a SWATCH watch? Do they own more than one? If so, how many? What are their opinions of SWATCH watches? What will SWATCH do to ensure that their watches are popular in ten years' time?

WHO MAKES THE DECISIONS – IN PRIVATE COMPANIES?

Decision making in small organizations usually depends on a handful of people. SWATCH is a **private limited company** – just like Time Communications, but on a much larger scale. The shares in a private limited company are often owned by family and friends and are not available to the general public.

The decisions in SWATCH are made by a small group of **shareholders** led by Nicholas Hayek, who set up the company. The shareholders, of course, depend on the assistance of many others who provide information about finance, production, marketing and the other processes involved in the business.

WHO MAKES THE DECISIONS – IN PUBLIC COMPANIES?

Cadbury's chocolate is produced by Cadbury Schweppes, which is a **public limited company**. The difference between this company and the two previous examples is that any member of the general public can buy shares. As a result, the firm may be owned by many thousands of shareholders. There are far too many of them to be involved in the day-to-day decision making of the company. Decisions such as those involved in opening plants in Russia, Poland or China would be made by the board of directors, who would take the advice of experts.

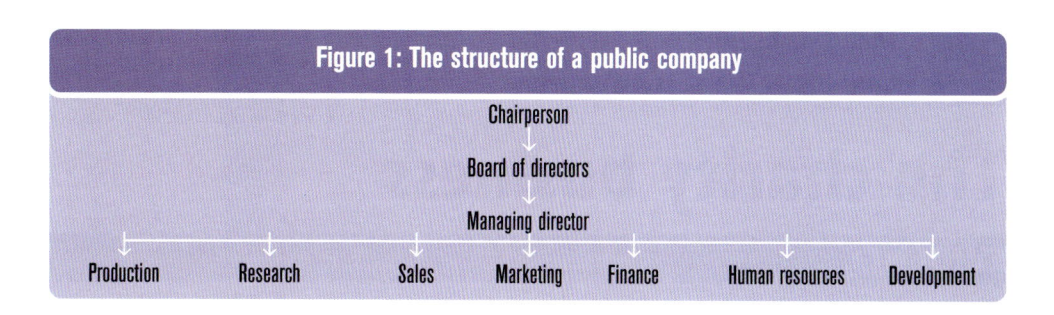

Marks & Spencer plc, British Telecom plc and National Westminster Bank plc are all public limited companies. Just like Cadbury Schweppes, they are owned by shareholders who appoint a chairperson, a managing director and a board of directors to oversee the decision making of the company.

The main objective of such companies is to make a profit for the shareholders. At the annual general meeting (AGM) the shareholders are given the opportunity to question the actions of the board of directors.

Public limited companies also have the advantage of limited liability, just like Time Communications and SWATCH.

Figure 1: The structure of a public company

Chairperson → Board of directors → Managing director → Production, Research, Sales, Marketing, Finance, Human resources, Development

EVIDENCE

WHERE NEXT?

Cadbury's new operation in Russia is proving a great success, with Russians consuming a million bars of Cadbury's chocolate a day. Production has started in Poland and will also start this year in a new plant in China.

Source: *The Independent*, 9 March 1995

EVIDENCE

The importance of individual businesses can be measured in different ways. One way is to look at how many people they employ. The first line of data in table 1 shows organizations that do not employ anyone because they are run by the people who own them. The rest range in size from the corner shop to major international companies.

Table 1: Measuring businesses

Size (number of employees)	Number of businesses	Number of employees
0	2,589,416	3,017,000
1–20	897,521	4,282,000
100–500	13,628	2,695,000
over 500	3,205	7,530,000

Source: DTI Small Firm Statistical Unit, 1993

Q1 How many businesses are there in the UK?

Q2 How many people work in businesses in the UK?

Q3 Draw a pie chart showing the proportion of people who work in firms of each size.

Q4 There are about 13,000 public limited companies in the UK. If they are the largest companies in the country, estimate how many people work for them.

Q5 Find out the names of six public limited companies in addition to those named in the text.

KEY TERMS

Shareholders are individuals or organisations which own a share of the company.

The shares in a *public limited company (plc)* are available to any purchaser. Shareholders are protected by limited liability.

The shares of a *private limited company* can be bought only with the permission of the other shareholders.

Unit 1 — Make or break?
Enquiry 1: What is enterprise?

The charity business

EVIDENCE

Comic Relief stars Lenny Henry and Billy Connolly

COMIC RELIEF

Comic Relief is run by an organization called Charity Projects, which is responsible for fund-raising projects to help disadvantaged people in the UK and in Africa. Comic Relief, which began in 1985, is its largest project.

CHARITY PROJECTS

Charity Projects helps disadvantaged people by:

- raising new money from the public;
- informing and educating;
- allocating funds in an effective and responsible way;
- ensuring that all fund-raising costs are covered by sponsorship so that every penny raised goes to charity.

Source: Charity Projects Annual Review, 1993–4

Q1 What techniques does Comic Relief use to raise money?

Q2 Why is it so effective?

Q3 Comic Relief would like a fresh idea for its next fund-raising venture. What would you suggest?

Q4 Why do you think that your idea would be a successful fund-raiser?

CHARITIES AND ENTERPRISE

Charity appeals like Comic Relief's 'Red Nose' day are a result of the enterprise of a number of different people, not least the well-known comedians who put their reputation to work to raise funds. Their objectives are to raise enough funds, or a **surplus**, to use for helping others. This is clearly different to a business enterprise, which sets out to make a profit for its owners.

Charities have other special features. The management of the work is overseen by a group of **trustees** – volunteers with a reputation as responsible citizens. They have a range of experience in both charity and business activities. Charity Projects trustees include Lenny Henry, the comedian, and Paul Jackson, managing director of Carlton Television.

While charities have different aims and methods of organization, they still need to be business-like in their methods. Here are some examples:

- Businesses and charities both have to work in a competitive world. Comic Relief doesn't want to compete with other charities, but it is competing for our attention; the organizers want us to send money as a result of their eye-catching posters and TV campaigns.
- Charity Projects and Comic Relief have to register as charities and must produce annual accounts that are available for anyone to see.
- Charity Projects wants to manage its organization as efficiently as possible. It has specialist departments such as finance and administration. In 1993–4 it bought a new computer network, set up a new system of financial management and invested money to pay for the publicity for fund-raising activities.

EVIDENCE

Age Concern launched a flowers-by-post gift service along with three other national charities. The emphasis is on a quality service for consumers who expect a good product, whether bought from a charity or a commercial business.

Save the Children, and many other charities, sell vast quantities of Christmas cards which they advertise widely by sending out catalogues to their massive mailing lists.

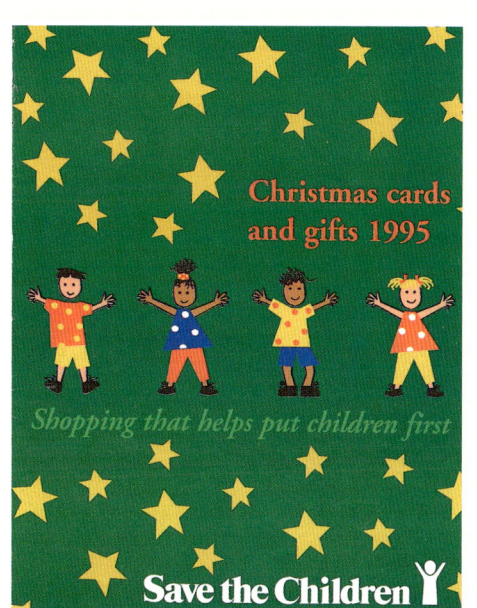

War Child's *Help* was recorded by bands who have donated their time and talent to make an album. This quickly raised £1 million to help Bosnian war victims. Securing a steady flow of income is more difficult.

Q1 In what way are these organizations being enterprising?

Q2 Who is each one competing with?

Q3 If Age Concern's initiative is successful, what advantage does it have over the other two activities?

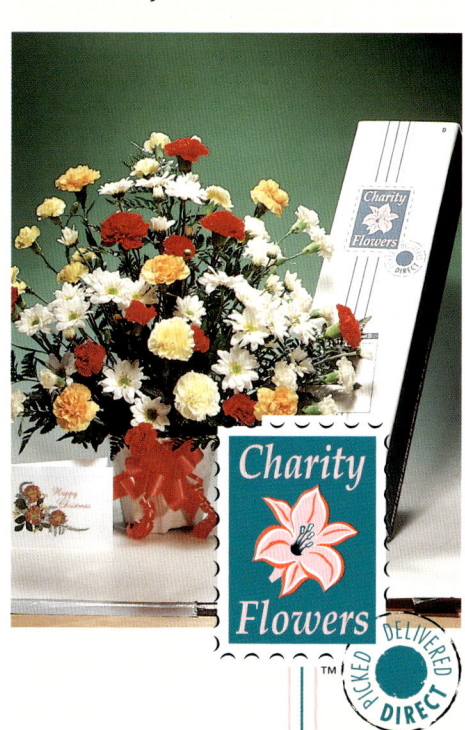

'THE BUSINESS OF CHARITY IS GETTING TOUGHER'

The title of this section is a quotation from an organizer of a national charity. Recent developments involving the National Lottery have not made life easy for charities. One charity estimated that donations to charities have fallen by £61 million since the lottery's launch.

The competition for funds is growing steadily more intense. As a result, charities are becoming more and more innovative in the tactics they use to persuade us to give. In fact, many are no longer simply expecting us to give, but are looking for ways to persuade us to buy from them. In doing this, they are in competition with many large companies. Charities have different aims from those of businesses, but they may still use business-like methods.

CHECKPOINT

Q1 What are the similarities and differences between organizations such as Comic Relief and a commercial soft drinks business?

Q2 What charities and fund-raising activities, if any, do you, your friends, or your family support?

Q3 Has your support changed? If so, why?

Q4 In what ways do these organizations appear to compete with one another?

FORUM

A charity that raises money to help the elderly has asked for advice about a joint venture with a big commercial drugs company. A share of the profits would go to the charity in return for putting the charity logo on drug packets. What would be your advice to the charity?

KEY TERMS

A *charity* is an organization set up to raise funds and support other people or a cause.

A *surplus* is the balance from the income of a charity after all costs have been paid.

A *trustee* is a person trusted to manage a charity for the benefit of others.

Unit 1

Make or break?

Enquiry 1: What is enterprise?

Who plays the game?

EVIDENCE

BATH SPORTS AND LEISURE CENTRE

Bath City Council believes that a good standard of leisure provision is essential to the quality of life of local people. It wishes to promote a wide range of leisure opportunities through its own leisure department, which runs, among other things, the Bath Sports and Leisure Centre. The centre has a wide variety of facilities which cost, on average, £2 to use. They include:
- sauna
- health and fitness rooms
- swimming
- squash
- badminton
- crèche

The sports centre is in the heart of the city and provides a service to many groups as well as the general public:
- parents with young children
- school groups for swimming
- youth groups
- retired groups
- disabled groups
- swimming clubs
- triathlon club.

COMBE GROVE MANOR COUNTRY CLUB LTD

Combe Grove Manor Country Club occupies a large area of land in beautiful countryside. It is built around an old country house with extensive views and is easily accessible by car. Membership is limited to 1,400 in order to maintain high standards of service. The company sees its staff as a very important resource in its effort to create a special atmosphere for customers. Recently, the demand for membership has matched the places available. This has allowed the club to maintain its prices as well as offering better facilities. Membership of the club now costs over £600 per year.

The Country Club offers all the facilities that are available at the Sports Centre in addition to target golf, indoor and outdoor tennis, a restaurant and a hotel.

Combe Grove Manor Country Club is owned by Jack Chia Ltd, a Singapore-based business with a diverse range of interests including engineering and sweet manufacture. Jack Chia Ltd aims to provide profits for its shareholders.

Q1 In what ways are the facilities offered by Combe Grove Manor Country Club similar to, and different from, those offered by the Bath Sports and Leisure Centre?

Q2 Compare the objectives of the Sports and Leisure Centre and the Country Club.

Q3 In what ways are both organizations being enterprising?

Q4 If the Bath Sports and Leisure Centre closed down, what would happen to the availability of sports facilities in the area?

OBJECTIVES

Organizations in the same line of business may have different objectives according to their ownership. Combe Grove Manor Country Club, like other companies, is owned by its shareholders, and is therefore in the **private sector**. Companies must place profit high on their list of objectives in order to satisfy their shareholders, who are looking for a return on their shares.

Anything that is run by the government at either local or national level is said to be in the **public sector**. As the Sports and Leisure Centre is run by Bath City Council it is a public-sector organization. The objectives of public-sector organizations are often different from those in the private sector.

A key objective of a private-sector organization is to satisfy its shareholders. It generally does this by making a profit. Without profit, a company will cease to exist because people who hold shares expect to receive a return on their money.

A key objective of a local council is to satisfy local residents. If it fails to do so, the political party that controls the local council will lose the next election.

The local council receives funds from:
- local residents in the form of the council tax;
- local businesses in the form of the business rates;
- central government.

It must make decisions about how much tax to take from the local community and how the money should be spent. In order to spend more on leisure, it will have to spend less on other things, or increase the amount of tax that people pay. In total, central government provides about half of the money that local government spends.

EVIDENCE

RICHMOND COUNCIL

Q1 Make a list of the services provided by Richmond Council. Put them in order according to how much they cost.

Q2 In what way do the objectives of the Council differ from those of a private-sector organization?

Q3 If the Council decides to spend more on leisure services, where will the money come from to meet the increased costs?

DELIVERING SERVICES

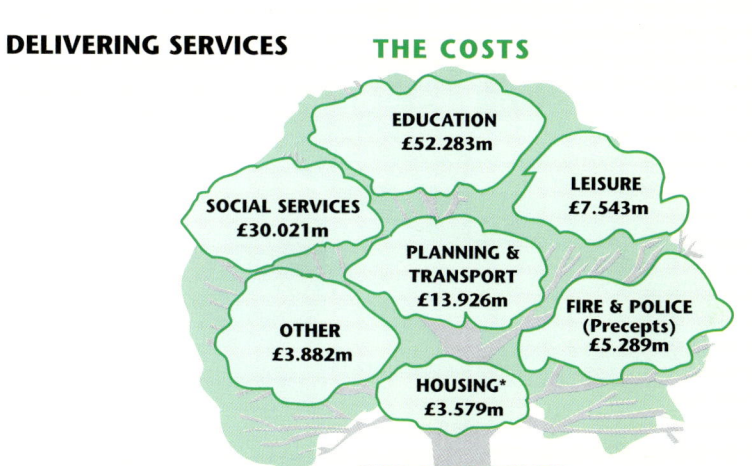

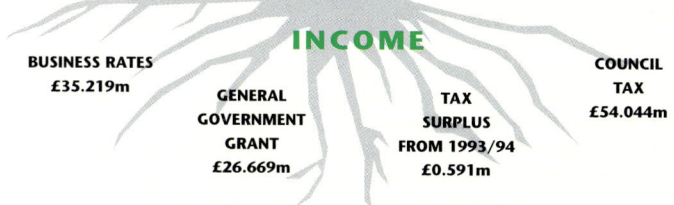

THE COSTS

- EDUCATION £52.283m
- LEISURE £7.543m
- SOCIAL SERVICES £30.021m
- PLANNING & TRANSPORT £13.926m
- FIRE & POLICE (Precepts) £5.289m
- OTHER £3.882m
- HOUSING* £3.579m

OUR OBJECTIVES

Helping people to meet their needs and expectations

To communicate clearly and coherently with the community

To increase participation by decentralising decision making to the most effective local level

To preserve and enhance our distinctive and valued environment

INCOME

- BUSINESS RATES £35.219m
- GENERAL GOVERNMENT GRANT £26.669m
- TAX SURPLUS FROM 1993/94 £0.591m
- COUNCIL TAX £54.044m

* The cost of council housing is excluded as it is not charged to council tax.

FORUM

A council-run sports centre makes a loss of £200,000 but provides a service to its citizens. A survey shows that only 10 per cent of the local population have used the centre on more than one occasion in the last year. The loss of £200,000 means that all 20,000 local households pay an extra £10 a year in council tax. What is your opinion of this and what do you think, if anything, should be done?

KEY TERMS

The *private sector* includes all organizations that are owned by individuals or shareholders.

The *public sector* includes all organizations that are owned or run by either the local council or the government.

Unit 1 — **Make or break?**
Enquiry 2: Is there a market?

What makes a market?

EVIDENCE

WHERE'S THE MARKET?

If you want to buy a watch, where would you go? The pictures give you some clues, but there are many more alternatives. The one thing all of them have in common is that they are ways in which buyers and sellers come together. They don't have to meet one another in person; communication by telephone, fax, computer links or post works just as well. Wherever buying and selling is carried out, there is a **market**.

The word market, therefore, has a much broader meaning than the one we are used to. It is not just the stalls along the street or in the square – a market includes any location or any method of communication that brings buyers and sellers together.

Markets are not just about selling **goods** – items such as watches or vegetables that you can carry away with you. There are also markets for **services**, things that you might want done for you, such as a haircut, or a repair to a car. Some of these services can be obtained in a high street shop, or you might arrange something over the telephone.

EVIDENCE

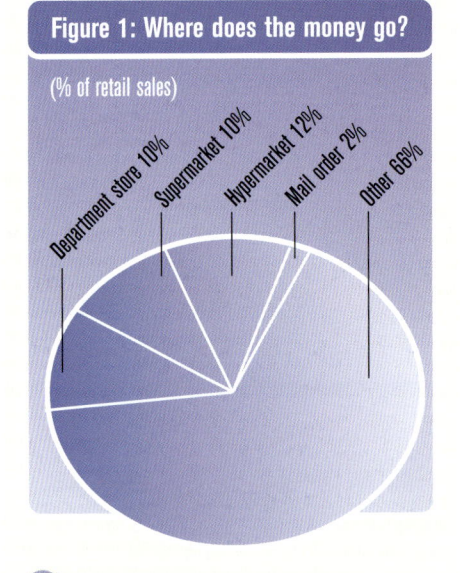

Figure 1: Where does the money go?

(% of retail sales)

Department store 10% Supermarket 10% Hypermarket 12% Mail order 2% Other 66%

Q1 The category called 'Other' accounts for 66 per cent of shopping. What will it include?

Q2 Where does your family do its shopping? Is the pattern the same as the average figures in the chart?

WHAT'S THE DEAL?

What brings people together in a market? Those with something to sell want to meet others who want to buy. But what actually makes the sale take place? **Price** is the key. The seller will offer the product so long as the price covers the cost of production and profit. The buyer will make a purchase as long as the price seems to represent good value for money.

In any market, both buyer and seller seek a gain. This is easy to understand when you think of people swapping. Say you swap one of your own CDs for one of your friend's CDs. It is obvious that you value your friend's CD more highly than you do your own. Likewise, she values your CD more highly than she does her own. By swapping, you both make a gain. When you buy a product in the shops, the idea is the same. You are 'swapping' money for the product. You would rather have the product; the shopkeeper would rather have the money. When the price is right, it's a deal.

The seller will go on trying to sell the product as long as the price covers

EVIDENCE

GO SURFING IN BARCLAY SQUARE!

You no longer need to leave your computer to go shopping. In a surf around Barclay Square you can book a train to Paris from Eurostar, buy presents from Toys 'R' Us or Argos, wine from Sainsbury's, or something extraordinary from the Innovations catalogue.

Barclay Square is a site on the Internet that has been set up by Barclays Bank. It rents space to other companies that sell both goods and services direct to the public.

Having made your selections, you can use your computer keyboard to pay by credit card, as Barclays Bank has devised a scheme to ensure that such payments can be made securely.

Q1 Who are the buyers and sellers in Barclay Square?
Q2 What are the advantages of shopping in this way?
Q3 Why might you be unwilling to shop like this?

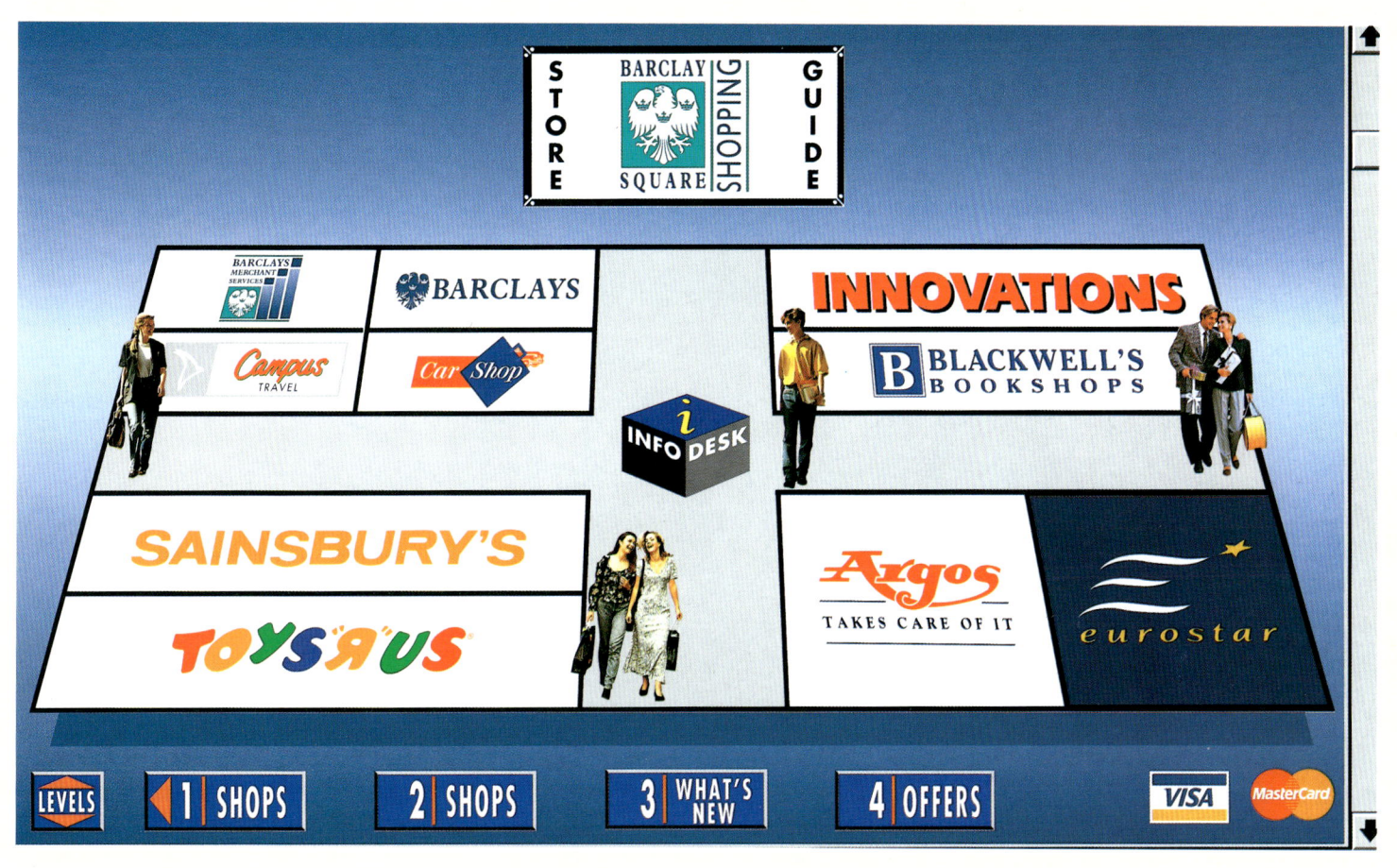

---

the cost of making it available, and leaves a **profit**. The buyer will go on buying as long as the value to be had from the purchase seems worth the price to be paid.

FORUM

How might technology change markets in the future? Give examples. Do you think the data in figure 1 will be different in ten years' time?

CHECKPOINT

Are the following providing goods or services?

- washing machine repairer
- clothes shop
- vet
- accountant
- computer salesperson
- mobile disco
- travel agent
- jewellers

K KEY TERMS

A *market* is any location or process that brings buyers and sellers together.

Price is the amount of money that is given in exchange for a product.

Goods are anything you buy which are natural or manufactured products.

Services involve buying the skills of another person.

Profit is the difference between the price and the cost of making a product available.

Unit 1 — *Make or break?*
Enquiry 2: Is there a market?

It's all to clear

EVIDENCE

Towards the end of a drizzly afternoon, the market stall is still piled high with strawberries. They won't last another day and the stallholder does not want to pack them back into the van and return them to his lock-up. Only a dozen punnets have gone so far. What is the best solution? There are still plenty of people about, so there is no shortage of potential customers. The stallholder decides to cut the price... perhaps 20p off? That makes them 80p. Things start to move more quickly – but not fast enough. An hour or so later only another twenty punnets have been sold. Two for the price of one seems to be the only answer (40p). It cuts the profit but at least it clears another fifty punnets over the next hour and keeps the customers happy. Now he has only twenty punnets left over.

Q1 What happens to the amount that people want to buy as the price is reduced?

Q2 Draw a graph to show how many punnets of strawberries are sold as the price falls.

Q3 What should the stallholder do if he wants to sell the last twenty punnets?

DEMAND AND PRICE

When the stallholder wanted to clear his stock, he reduced the price. In doing this, he is assuming that people will buy more when the price falls. In other words, consumers **demand** more when the price is lower. There are two reasons for this:
- people who are buying strawberries already may buy more strawberries instead of another fruit as the price falls;
- people who could not afford strawberries at the higher price can now start to buy them.

Of course, this works the other way round. When the price goes up, sales will fall because some people will buy fewer and others will be unable to buy any at all. Consumers demand less at higher prices.

SUPPLY AND PRICE

High prices make businesses want to produce and sell more. The higher the price, the bigger the incentive they have to increase the amount for sale. Price is therefore acting as a signal to both the consumer and the seller. Low prices encourage consumers to buy, while high prices encourage firms to produce more.

GETTING THE PRICE RIGHT

If the price is too low, firms will run out of stock. If it is too high, they will have a lot left over. Getting it just right doesn't often happen, but when it does:
- consumers can buy all they want at that price;
- firms can sell all they want at that price.

This price is known as the **market clearing price** because it is the point at which the amount that consumers want to buy balances exactly with the amount that producers want to sell. When it occurs, the market is said to clear. As the price of strawberries showed, it may take some time and several price adjustments before the market clearing price is found.

CHECKPOINT

Q1 On a graph plot the lines showing how much customers will demand at each price and how much producers will supply at each price.

Q2 What is the market clearing price?

Q3 What happens to the amount demanded and supplied above the market clearing price?

Q4 What happens to the amount demanded and supplied below the market clearing price?

Q5 Will the price stay above the market clearing level for long?

Table 1: Strawberries – demand and supply

If the price of strawberries is (no. of punnets)	Customers will want to buy (no. of punnets)	Sellers will want to supply
20p	50	10
40p	40	20
60p	30	30
80p	20	40
£1	10	50

THE DEMAND AND SUPPLY DIAGRAM

In any market people make the decision to buy or sell because they are happy with the price. If the price is too high, buyers will not buy and if it is too low, sellers will not sell.

This can be shown simply by plotting two lines on a graph. Strawberries have been used as an example so far, but the same can be done for anything that you might buy. The example in figure 1 is for compact discs.

The demand curve shows how much people will buy at each price and the supply curve shows how much producers are prepared to sell at each price. The point where they cross shows the price at which the two agree and can therefore make a deal.

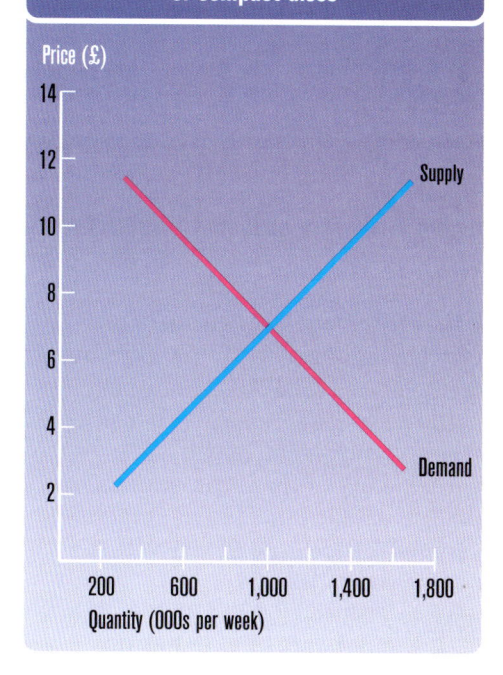

KEY TERMS

Demand is the amount of a product that customers want to buy at a particular price.

Supply is the amount of a product that producers want to supply at a particular price.

The market clearing price is the price at which the amount that customers want to buy is exactly the same as the amount that producers want to sell.

Figure 1: The demand and supply of compact discs

EVIDENCE

Heat wave keeps Brits at home

Millions of package holidays left unsold

Empty beds on the Costas

One Christmas almost every child in the country wanted Tracy Island – a key part of the essential Thunderbirds equipment. Long before the festive season arrived, all stocks were sold. Parents were even seen fighting over the boxes when an occasional delivery arrived. The item was priced at £29.99.

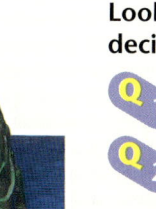

Look at each piece of evidence and decide:

Q1 What has happened in each of the three situations?

Q2 Should the price rise or fall to reach the market clearing price?

Q3 What might the supplier decide to do next time?

Unit 1 — *Make or break?*
Enquiry 2: Is there a market?

Target the market

EVIDENCE

WHO ARE THE BUYERS? WHAT DO THEY WANT?

When trying to decide what sort of watches to make, Swiss manufacturers identified the following groups of customers: active, sporty pre-teens, young trendsetters, or any other combination of these categories. From the mix of age and lifestyle, producers can predict the type of watch that people would buy.

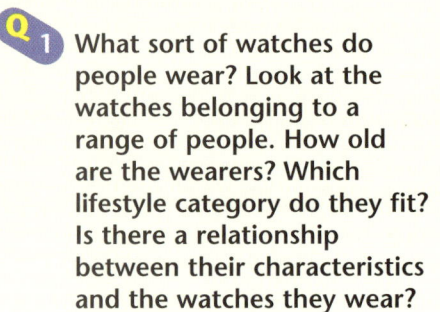

Q1 What sort of watches do people wear? Look at the watches belonging to a range of people. How old are the wearers? Which lifestyle category do they fit? Is there a relationship between their characteristics and the watches they wear?

age groups: pre-teens, trendsetter 16-24, 24+

lifestyle: cool and clean, active and sporty, young and trendy, classic

MARKETS AND THEIR SEGMENTS

The market for watches is just like an orange – it divides into segments. There are all sorts of watches for sale that are designed for people with different needs and tastes. You're unlikely to see the Prime Minister, for example, wearing the latest, loudest SWATCH watch. People in such positions are likely to prefer a more classic style.

The market for watches is divided up by age and lifestyle. This is the pattern for most markets.
• How old are you?
• Are you male or female?
• What social class are you?
• Where do you live?
• How do you spend your free time?

Your answers to these questions will help to define the sort of products that you will buy – or which market segment you fall into. This information helps firms to develop and market products that aim at particular groups of people. **Market segmentation** means that the market can be divided up in this way.

IS THERE A GAP IN THE MARKET?

An innovative firm will match the consumer categories to the types of product that are on the market. If there is no product in one category and the firm decides to develop one, it may have a winner on its hands. First, however, it must investigate whether a new product will be profitable. If there are not enough customers in this particular segment, it will obviously not be worth going into production.

Such gaps in the market are described as **market niches**. In developing a car for the elderly, Ford may have found a very successful market niche. Before it goes into production, the company will need to know whether people will buy the car. If the over-sixties all enjoy fast travel, they will be prepared to sacrifice convenience for style and start to buy the latest sports car! Researching the market is therefore crucial to the success of a new product.

EVIDENCE

FORD SPOTS A GAP IN THE MARKET

By the turn of the twenty-first century there will be 11 million people in the UK over the age of 55. No one has ever thought about making a car specially designed for this age group. Ford looked at the existing market segments and realized that something was missing. Its new car has been christened the 'Ford Wrinkly' or even the 'Oldsmobile'! It will have swivelling seats for easy access, a magnified rear view mirror and radar-assisted parking.

Q1 In what way does this car meet the needs of the group of people for whom it is designed?

Q2 Why is Ford interested in producing a car for this group of people?

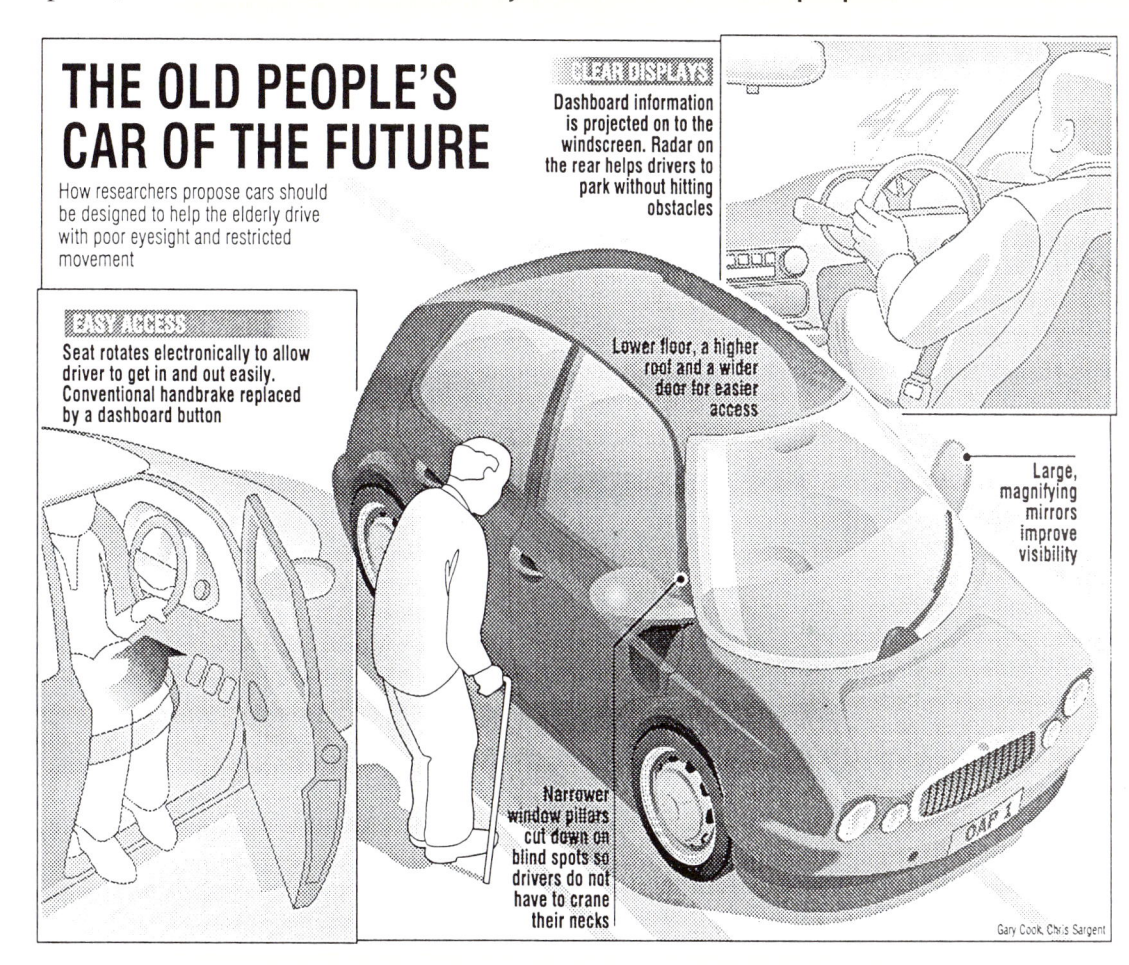

THE OLD PEOPLE'S CAR OF THE FUTURE

How researchers propose cars should be designed to help the elderly drive with poor eyesight and restricted movement

EASY ACCESS
Seat rotates electronically to allow driver to get in and out easily. Conventional handbrake replaced by a dashboard button

CLEAR DISPLAYS
Dashboard information is projected on to the windscreen. Radar on the rear helps drivers to park without hitting obstacles

Lower floor, a higher roof and a wider door for easier access

Large, magnifying mirrors improve visibility

Narrower window pillars cut down on blind spots so drivers do not have to crane their necks

Gary Cook, Chris Sargent

FORUM

Name some places near where you live where you can go to eat out. What sort of food is on offer at each place? How expensive is it? What types of people tend to eat there? Try to identify the market segments for places to eat in your area. Can you identify a gap in the market that might be a business opportunity?

CHECKPOINT

Q1 Use examples to explain what is meant by market segmentation.

Q2 How is the market for trainers segmented?

Q3 To what extent is the market for package holidays segmented?

Q4 What is a business opportunity?

KEY TERMS

Market segmentation is the division of markets according to different types of customer in order to develop products that meet people's needs.

A *market niche* is a gap in the market which a firm might want to fill with a new product.

Unit 1 — **Make or break?**
Enquiry 3: Is it competitive?

What costs must be covered?

EVIDENCE

Gina and Steve started their mobile disco 'ManicMixers' with £960 they had borrowed from Steve's mum and a £750 bank loan. They used the money to buy some lights and an effects unit, records and CDs, turntables, a CD player, an amplifier, and a couple of speakers that they've never yet managed to run at full volume. Steve's mum didn't want to charge any interest, and they pay her back at £40 a month. They have to pay the bank £40 a month over two years. This didn't seem very much when they first started, but it has kept Gina and Steve under pressure to get bookings. Over the summer they don't get so many, although they still have to keep repaying their loans. They use Steve's van to get to each venue, usually in a pub or a hotel.

They reckon on spending an average of £20 for each booking to cover the cost of petrol, wear and tear on the van, and breakages. They often have to replace the bulbs for the lights. The van's suspension has never been very good, so the equipment gets bounced around. Gina and Steve aim to pay themselves £50 per month each, but it doesn't always work out. The money comes in handy, but neither of them would consider trying to make a living out of it.

Q1 What costs do Gina and Steve have to meet even when they have no bookings?

Q2 What are their other costs?

LOOKING AT COSTS

It costs a lot to keep even a small business going. Some of these costs still have to be met even if the business stops producing or serving customers. The owner of the business might take out a loan to buy equipment or to improve the building. Loan repayments will stay the same regardless of whether there are many customers or none at all. This kind of cost is called a **fixed cost**. Other costs go up or down with the number of customers. A shop has to buy more from its wholesaler if it starts attracting more customers. This kind of cost is called a **variable cost** because it varies as the number of products or the amount of service provided by the business changes.

Fixed and variable costs added together give **total costs**. Figure 1 shows how fixed costs are constant while variable costs grow with output.

Figure 1: Fixed, variable and total costs

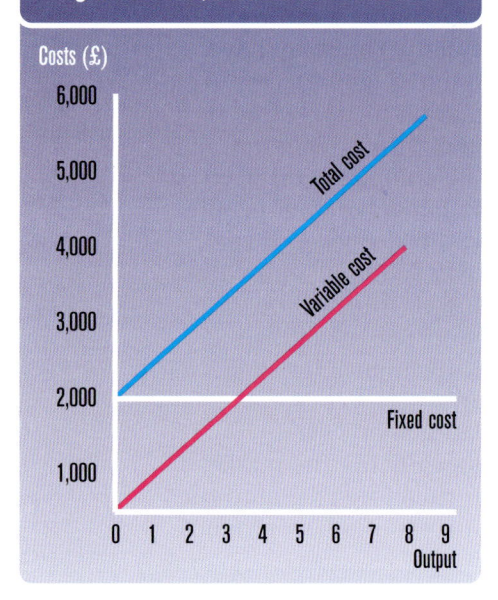

Businesses vary a great deal with regard to whether they have high or low fixed costs. The level of fixed costs in relation to output is very important. If a business has high fixed costs and its output is low, it will be in danger of going out of business. For example, if a garage sells only a couple of cars in a month, the fixed costs of paying off loans, maintaining the building and paying staff will have to be spread over just two cars. It is unlikely that the garage

EVIDENCE

TALL PINES

Doris has been growing flowers at Tall Pines for forty years. She has a small greenhouse where she raises the seedlings, and two fields where she grows chrysanthemums for the autumn and daffodils for the spring. She also grows some vegetables, and has a few Christmas trees. She has a small tractor for cultivating the ground. At busy times she has help from Emma and Mick. Mick drives the tractor and goes to the market with the flowers, and Emma helps with planting and picking. Doris does the rest of the work herself.

Q1 What items will be fixed costs for Doris?

Q2 What items will be variable costs?

Q3 Doris competes successfully with much bigger growers. Can you see how she might be able to do this?

CHECKPOINT

Fill in the table showing Gina and Steve's fixed, variable and total costs for the month, depending on whether they get two, three, four or five bookings in that time. Include the money they pay themselves as a fixed cost.

Draw a graph of their fixed, variable and total costs, with bookings on the horizontal axis and costs on the vertical axis.

Bookings	Fixed costs	Variable costs	Total costs
2			
3			
4			
5			

could earn enough from the sale of only two cars to cover all these costs.

A window cleaner will have low fixed costs: a ladder, an old van and an insurance policy will be the main ones. An oil company has very high fixed costs because it needs drilling rigs, pipelines and delivery tankers. A street vendor has almost no equipment, and therefore very low fixed costs. In general it is easier to set up in business if the fixed costs are low.

ARE WAGES FIXED OR VARIABLE?

Gina and Steve regarded their pay as fixed, provided they got enough bookings. In some businesses, the wage bill will vary with output: if more people have to be taken on in order to increase output, then their wages will be a variable cost. It depends on the circumstances.

K KEY TERMS

Fixed costs are those costs of production which have to be paid regardless of the level of output.

Variable costs are the costs of production which will rise with the level of output. They include raw materials and any other inputs needed to make the actual product.

Total costs are fixed costs + variable costs.

Unit 1 — Make or break?
Enquiry 3: Is it competitive?

Will it be profitable?

EVIDENCE

WILL TIME COMMUNICATIONS BE PROFITABLE?

When Deborah Marsh set up Time Communications (see p. 2) she took a big risk: she might have got very little business at all. She was prepared to take a cut in salary, but how long could she survive if she could not get enough to live on?

She needed to be able to cover the cost of her office space and equipment, and to pay Ingrid and the two office assistants. And she needed enough to live on herself.

How could she be at all confident? She had to believe that the business could generate enough sales revenue to cover all these costs and leave a profit at the end. But she knew that she had her own qualifications and past experience in PR. She also had something extra: she could offer customers specialist knowledge of ethnic minority markets.

This meant that Deborah soon had a number of contracts which involved communicating with these markets. She does not just advertise the product, she works to create an image of the company which will bring it to the forefront of people's minds.

Landing a number of contracts does not on its own make a business profitable, of course, but it is a good start.

Q1 If Deborah finds she isn't working flat out and has time to take on more contracts, should she charge a lower price?

Q2 What else might Deborah do to get more business?

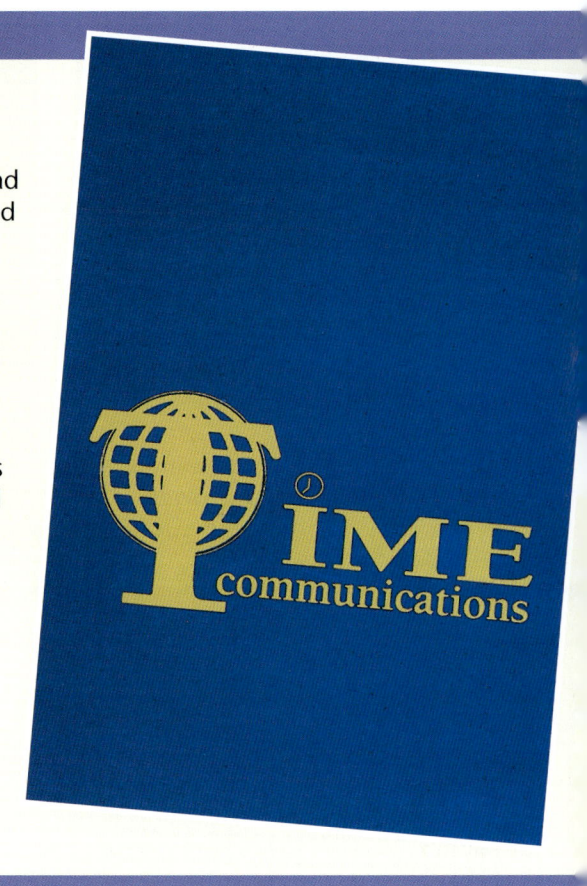

PRICE

In looking at her business prospects, Deborah had to consider a number of things. First, what price would she charge for her services? This needed to be a price that would, in the long run, cover her costs. It also needed to be a price that would compare reasonably with the charges of other competing firms, otherwise she would be unlikely to attract much business.

Once price is decided, then the **sales revenue** depends on the number of contracts Deborah can get. In general, sales revenue is equal to the price multiplied by the quantity sold.

CALCULATING PROFIT

Profit is found by adding up all the sales revenue and all the costs. The difference between the two is the profit made.

Although profit is not always the most important factor in going into business, there has to be enough of it in the long run to make it worth keeping the business going.

Profit rewards entrepreneurs for using their judgement and taking risks. A big risk may mean big profits, but it may also mean **losses**. The risks Deborah is taking are not, in fact, especially large. She is well qualified and experienced, and she understands the market in which she is working. Her start-up costs are reasonable.

A film company that decides to make a film with an unknown director is taking much more of a risk. The film might be a box office flop. This is one reason why many film companies are big: they have the financial resources to take risks. Small film companies do survive, but they seldom make big-budget films because they don't have the financial resources to do so.

PROFIT AND COMPETITION

The business that can produce something clearly of better value than its competitors' product can usually be sure to make a profit. As long as 'ManicMixers' (see p. 16) disco is seen as being good value and good fun, it will have no trouble getting bookings. Of course, this

18

means getting the price right, because if it is too high the disco will not seem to be good value. It also means that care must be taken to ensure that the disco is well organized.

KEEPING COSTS DOWN

If the business can find a way to cut costs, it may be able to reduce its prices. This will make the product more attractive to customers. Sales may rise and so may revenue. Or prices might be left as they are, in which case there will be more profit. Either way, it is clear that cutting costs is often a good idea.

Some costs are hard to cut. A bakery can't cut the costs of its ovens, but next time it buys new ones, it might be able to get ovens which use energy more efficiently and so save on electricity bills. It may also be able to find ways of using employees more effectively, so that fewer are needed. It may be able to bulk buy its flour and other ingredients so that costs per loaf are lower.

CHECKPOINT

Q1 Use the information on Gina and Steve's costs on the previous page to calculate their total costs when they get four bookings per month.

Q2 Gina and Steve charge £80 for a disco. What will their sales revenue be for the month?

Q3 With four bookings, what will their profit be for the month?

Q4 Is there any way in which Gina and Steve could increase their profit? Explain your answer.

Q5 Supermarkets try to cut costs and increase profits all the time. Think of as many ways of doing this as you can.

FORUM

Does £50 per month give Gina and Steve a reasonable amount of money for the time they spend on the disco? How many bookings would they need for the profit to reward them adequately? Do people who go into business on their own always get paid what they would earn if they were working for someone else?

KEY TERMS

Sales revenue is price multiplied by sales.

Profit is total sales revenue minus total costs. Profit is the reward for risk-taking.

Losses occur when sales revenue is less than total costs.

Unit 1 — Make or break?
Enquiry 3: Is it competitive?

Getting it together

EVIDENCE

CLEAN UP AND ADD VALUE

Vanish started life as a soap bar. It became a successful product because it removed difficult stains – even the worst grass stains on cricket trousers! The company that produced it added value by making the soap from a range of raw materials, and packaging it in a way that appealed to shoppers.

Having become well established in the home-washing market, the company decided that it wanted to develop the product. What could it do to attract customers and persuade them to pay a higher price without adding greatly to the costs of production?

First of all they put the soap into a Stain Stick format. The cricket trousers could then be scrubbed without getting your hands wet. This product sells for £1.99, compared with £1.49 for the bar of soap. They both contain 75 grams of soap and the additional packaging for the Stain Stick might cost an extra few pence. By adding just a little to the cost, the company has succeeded in adding more value for the customer.

In a further step, the product was developed into a Concentrated Stain Gel. This time it was put in a tube with a brush on the end, giving even more scrubbing power. Again, the development added more to value than to cost, so the company had another success on its hands.

Q1 What gave the original product its value in the shops?

Q2 What made the two new products worth more than the original soap bar?

Q3 Suggest some examples of other products which are sold in different versions and at different prices.

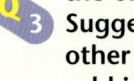

Q4 Why might this strategy increase the number of customers that buy the company's products?

ADDING VALUE

Vanish is a manufactured product, so the company uses physical and human resources to make it. The cost of the resources used is less than the value the customers put on the soap, in whichever form they buy it. All successful businesses **add value** in this way. They put effort into transforming the product so that its value to the consumer becomes as great as they can make it. In creating and developing a product, all companies must add value if they are to make a profit on a continuous basis.

Firms which provide services will also add value. A hairdresser combines the physical resources of the salon with the skills of the people who work there in order to add value – the greater the skills, the greater the value.

VALUE THE BRAND

There are all sorts of strategies for adding value. It may be done by improving the product, as Vanish did, or value may be added by creating an image with which people want to be associated.

Calvin Klein jeans cost twice as much as a pair of Levi's and several times as much as a pair of ordinary jeans. They may cost a little more to make than the ones that you find in Marks & Spencer, for instance, but certainly not as much as the price would suggest.

By creating a name which gives a message, it is possible to add value because people are prepared to pay extra to be seen wearing or using such products. If the product is marketed successfully, the customer will believe that it is worth more to them than other, similar products. Sometimes a company will have several **brand names** which it will use to sell different product ranges.

EVIDENCE

DESIGNER JEANS

How do brand names add value? The brand name can be combined with an eye-catching advert which makes buyers feel they are getting an image as well as a product.

The advert for Calvin Klein jeans says something about the wearer – young, sexy, attractive – and it is this image that is attracting the buyers; they are prepared to pay for it.

Q1 How is Calvin Klein adding value?

Q2 Many products besides Calvin Klein jeans use brand names, which may have a powerful effect on consumers. Make a list of the ones you can think of.

Q3 Brand names are not only about image. They may be about reliability or any other important product feature. For each of the brand names you have thought of, say what the brand is supposed to be noted for.

CHECKPOINT

Wall's, the ice-cream company, sells many products under its own name but it also sells a superior range under the name of Ranieri. All the marketing suggests that it is Italian in origin. The packaging claims 'Gelato alla panna e al tiramisu' which translates as 'Velvety smooth tiramisu ice cream'.

Q1 Why does Wall's go to the expense of producing and marketing this alternative range of ice cream?

FORUM

If you buy Levi's, or Calvin Klein jeans even, why do you spend the extra? Do you eat Heinz Baked Beans or Kellog's Cornflakes? Are you sure that the supermarkets' own brands are not just as good?

KEY TERMS

Added value is the difference between the costs of inputs into a product and the value placed on that product by the market.

Brand names create an identity for the product and highlight the ways in which it is different from competing products.

Unit 1 — Make or break?
Enquiry 3: Is it competitive?

Compete on price or quality?

EVIDENCE

KWIK SAVE

Kwik Save is Britain's largest chain of discount food stores with over 800 supermarkets across the country. The company faces competition from European-owned discounters (e.g. Netto and Aldi) as well as from the major superstores such as Tesco, Sainsbury's and Safeway.

Kwik Save is highly successful and has been expanding over the past five years. It makes a very small profit on each item sold. Yet overall its profits have doubled during that time. What is the company's secret?

'Kwik Save keeps its prices permanently discounted by holding costs to the minimum and by concentrating its effort on the fastest selling brands, varieties and sizes.'

Source: *Kwik Save Annual Report and Accounts,* 1994

Q1 How does Kwik Save survive in a highly competitive market?
Q2 How can Kwik Save make big profits when only a small amount of profit is made on each item sold?

COMPETITION

Where markets operate, firms compete and customers have a choice. Even the managers of the most successful enterprise must be on their guard and continually check that the competition is not getting too close. Kwik Save is always aware there is Tesco; McDonalds must never forget Burger King.

The ability of a firm to attract and retain customers is called **competitiveness**. We have seen that every business must provide consumers with the sense of good value for money and at the same time leave themselves a margin for profit. This can be difficult enough, but it is even harder when a firm's rivals are doing their best to lure its customers away. It is therefore understandable that firms try to find something special about themselves and use this as a way of attracting customers. This special feature is called **competitive advantage**.

The two most straightforward routes to competitive advantage – and hence competitiveness – are:
- to offer low prices and acceptable quality
- to offer acceptable prices and high quality.

Of course, the ideal formula would be low prices and high quality. Unfortunately, cost usually rises with quality and so puts a squeeze on profit. Kwik Save chooses to compete mainly on price. This is not to say that it sells poor quality food. It offers 'acceptable' or average quality but at very competitive prices. This is achieved by bulk buying standard lines and fitting shops cheaply in low-cost locations.

EVIDENCE

THE GOURMET

For over thirty years Bruce Bannerman and his wife have been the owners and managers of The Gourmet delicatessen and outside caterers. Almost everything that makes Kwik Save profitable, The Gourmet does not do. When asked about price, Mr Bannerman says ' I don't make anything of it.' But where The Gourmet does compete is on quality: foods are carefully selected, very varied and most attractively presented. The idea of quality is then taken further, as customers all receive personal service, and many are known by name. Individual needs can be met in a friendly and unhurried atmosphere.

Despite being surrounded by competition from supermarkets, The Gourmet not only survives but prospers.

QUALITY

Offering the customer distinctive quality is an alternative route to competitiveness. This does not mean that price is irrelevant. Quality can offer special attractions, but customers will still expect good value.

Indeed, distinctive quality or rock-bottom prices are just two different ways of providing customers with competitive value for money. Each approach appeals to a different segment of the market. Kwik Save attracts people on low incomes while, in contrast, The Gourmet appeals mostly to customers enjoying high incomes which allow them to spend more on quality.

Of course there are many different combinations of price and quality that can also be competitive. Sainsbury's claims to offer good quality food at low prices. In reality it cannot match the prices of Kwik Save or the quality of The Gourmet, but its quality is high enough and its prices low enough to make Sainsbury's highly competitive.

Nothing in business stands still. A competitive advantage is difficult to gain but easy to lose. Kwik Save pride themselves on low prices, but there are always competitors waiting to attack their market share with even better value for money. The company therefore works constantly to cut its costs further and to meet changing customer needs. Mr Bannerman at The Gourmet also studies the special wishes of his customers and must keep ahead of a new delicatessen that has opened in the same town.

CHECKPOINT

Q1 'Top quality – lowest prices!' What are the strengths and weaknesses of this as the slogan for a large store?

Q2 How might a large competitor 'plot' to attack Kwik Save's market share?

Q3 How might a large or a small competitor plan to take The Gourmet's customers?

FORUM

Competitiveness means different things in different industries. How do car manufacturers compete with one another? How do newspapers compete?

KEY TERMS

Competitiveness means the strength of a firm's position in the market measured by market share and profitability. It reflects the value for money provided by the firm's products.

Competitive advantage is the means by which a firm's appeal to the market is made both distinctive and defensible.

Unit 1 — Make or break?
Enquiry 4: What is success?

Is it making money?

EVIDENCE

MARKS & SPENCER

In 1862 a young Russian refugee – Michael Marks – arrived in Yorkshire and began selling haberdashery from a simple tray round his neck. Some twelve years later he had a chain of stalls and formed a partnership with Tom Spencer. Today Marks & Spencer (M & S) is a leading British retailer of clothing, foods and household goods. There are 283 stores in Britain and a further 85 worldwide. Sales in the year to 1995 amounted to £6,800 million, or £18.5 million per store (that's about £60,000 per store per day).

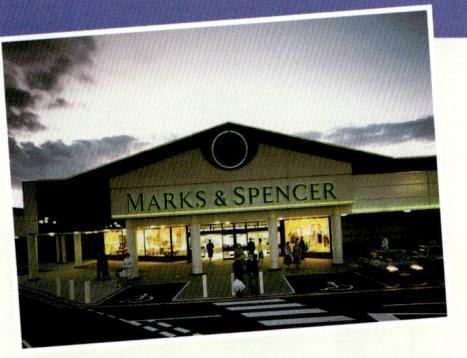

Table 1: Profit at Marks & Spencer (£ million)

	1995
Sales revenue	6,806
Costs	5,910
Net profit	896

Source: company data

MEASURING PROFIT

Marks & Spencer stores occupy some of the most valuable high street (and out-of-town) sites in Britain. Yet the firm manufactures nothing itself. However, it does add value to the output of its suppliers – with whom the company has a very close relationship. M & S selects the right products, organizes and schedules production, controls quality and arranges deliveries to the stores. It is then expert in creating a shopping experience that persuades the customer to choose Marks & Spencer – and the well-known St Michael brand.

Although the company has a huge sales value – or turnover – it also faces heavy costs. We have seen that the difference between sales revenue and costs is profit. The figures for M & S are shown in table 1.

The size of the gap between sales and costs is obviously vital and is a big clue to the health of any company. The measurement becomes even more useful when profit is expressed as a proportion or percentage of the selling price. This value is called the **profit margin**.

Think about a shop paying 40p for chocolate biscuits and selling them at 50p per packet. The profit is 10p out of 50p sales revenue, or:

$$\frac{10p}{50p} \times 100 = 20 \text{ per cent.}$$

For M & S the same calculation is:

$$\frac{\text{Profit}}{\text{Sales}} \times 100 = \frac{896}{6,806} \times 100 = 13.2 \text{ per cent}$$

For a large retailer in a very competitive market, this is an excellent result.

EVIDENCE

RICHER SOUNDS PLC

Julian Richer is well named. Still only 36, he is owner and chairman of Richer Sounds, now the largest retailer of specialist hi-fi equipment in Britain. The enterprise, launched in 1978 by Richer (then aged just 19) with a single store at London Bridge, is now a chain of 23 shops across the UK.

The information in table 2 suggests that the company is certainly making money.

Table 2: Profit at Richer Sounds (£ million)

	1993	1995
Gross sales	£17.8 million	£24.9 million
Net profit	£2.2 million	£2.7 million
Profit margin	12.3%	10.8%

Source: company data

GETTING RICHER

Both Richer Sounds and Marks & Spencer are profitable companies. Yet their total profits in the year to 1995 are very different. Richer Sounds made nearly £2.7 million against Marks & Spencer's profit of £896 million. Does this mean that Marks & Spencer is more profitable? The best answer is that this is an unfair comparison, as M & S is a much larger company. When profit margins are compared, there is little difference: Richer Sounds is on 10.8 per cent, M & S on 13.2 per cent.

But both companies are using scarce resources that have a value. As well as people – labour – they employ capital. This includes all the buildings, plant and machinery. It is possible to add up the value of everything the firm owns, and look at profit as a proportion of it. This measurement is called **Return on Capital Employed (ROCE)**:

$$\text{ROCE} = \frac{\text{net profit}}{\text{capital employed}}$$

The value for M & S in 1995 is:

$$\frac{£896 \text{ million}}{£3,736 \text{ million}} \times 100 = 24.0 \text{ per cent}$$

This is a good rate of return compared with other leading companies.

For Richer Sounds, however, the ROCE is:

$$\frac{£2,683,000}{£2,689,000} \times 100 = 99.8 \text{ per cent}$$

This is an outstandingly high value and would probably be hard to maintain if the company grows larger.

You will have noticed that we are using the term **net profit**. There are several different definitions of profit because there are different ways of measuring it. The key terms explain the difference.

CHECKPOINT

Look carefully at the company data for the year to 1994 in table 3. (A negative figure for profit means that a loss was made that year instead of a profit)

Q1 Calculate the profit margin for each company and arrange them in corresponding rank order.

Q2 Calculate ROCE values for each company and arrange again in rank order.

Q3 Can you suggest reasons for any differences between positions for the companies?

Table 3: Net profit and capital employed (£ million)

Company	Business	Sales	Capital employed	Net profit
British Steel	Steel	4,303	4,588	– 95
Kwik-Save	Supermarkets	2,651	377	127
Pilkington	Glass products	2572	2567	132
SmithKline Beecham	Consumer goods	6,164	3,497	1,303
Trafalgar House	Construction	3,879	1,376	– 276
Zeneca	Pharmaceuticals	4,440	2,759	729

Source: *Times 1000*, 1995

KEY TERMS

Gross profit is the difference between the cost of buying the products and the revenue earned from their sale.

Net profit is the amount of profit earned from producing and selling a product or service, once all the input costs have been deducted.

Profit margin is net profit as a percentage of the value of sales.

Capital employed is the value of all the buildings, machinery and equipment used in producing the goods or services made by the business.

ROCE is net profit divided by capital employed. This gives an idea of how successful the business has been in spending its money on equipment and factories.

Unit 1 — *Make or break?*
Enquiry 4: What is success?

Going up or going down?

EVIDENCE

GOING UP?

EMAP is a publishing company with its head office in Peterborough. Since the 1980s it has been one of the fastest-growing and most successful firms in the media business.

Table 1: EMAP sales and net profit (£ million)

	1987	1989	1991	1993	1994
Sales	117	233	269	318	547
Net profit	13	32	30	41	68

Source: company data

The company owns a vast range of newspaper and magazine titles including *Smash Hits*, *Just Seventeen*, *New Woman*, *Elle* and *Match*. Staff numbers have grown from 4,200 in 1991 to around 7,000 by 1995. They work in more than 350 small creative teams and are strongly encouraged to take responsibility and to feel important within the company.

Q1 Calculate the percentage change in EMAP's sales and profit in 1991, 1993 and 1994.
Q2 Why do you think EMAP's sales are growing?
Q3 Can the company continue to grow at the rate achieved in 1994?

PROFIT AND COMPETITIVENESS

Profits for the current year are important, but a company's prospects for the future also matter. Over the past five years at EMAP the ROCE value has averaged about 20 per cent. How else can we judge a firm's likely success? Much depends on its competitiveness within the relevant market. An enterprise competes well when it is able to offer customers better than average value for money. One route is to ensure low costs and low prices. Richer Sounds (see p. 24) does this. An alternative is to offer distinctive quality for which customers are willing to pay a higher price.

EMAP controls its costs carefully and manages to develop publications that are distinctive and good quality in their market. Giving good value for money over time earns a favourable reputation among customers and this goodwill is valuable in itself.

Holding on to competitiveness – and success – depends for any business on the quality of management. Key decisions about the use of resources are made by directors and the team of managers. An ability to get these decisions right is crucial to business success.

EVIDENCE

GOING DOWN?

The first Woolworths store opened in the USA in 1889. The chain opened its first store in Britain in 1909. Soon there was a branch of Woolworths in every large town and by the 1960s there were a thousand British stores. But the company drifted out of date and eventually poor performance led to the sale of the UK stores to British management in 1982. Today the company's 780 stores are owned by Kingfisher plc, a retail group that also includes B&Q, Comet and Superdrug.

During the 1980s and early 1990s the fortunes of Woolworths were revived as the new managers concentrated on entertainment, gifts and confectionery, childrenswear and toys. But by 1994 progress had moved into reverse. Profits and margin fell steeply: table 2 shows that Woolworths was on the slide again.

Table 2: Woolworths' net profit (£ million)

1991	1992	1993	1994	1995
245.4	233.6	77.8	74.5	51.4

Source: company data

SUCCESS

Business success depends not on profit in one year, but on a stream of (increasing) profit over time. Woolworths had made mistakes in its choice of products to stock. But the chain also faced the blast of competition from other specialist stores such as Toys 'R' Us, Argos, Mothercare and Our Price Records.

The company's **share price** reflects what investors think of its prospects for the future. As Woolworths profits fell – and Comet began to make losses – the value of Kingfisher shares slumped. At the peak in 1993 the shares had been worth 773p each, but two years later they were selling for only 399p.

DECISION TAKING

Success depends on good decision taking. This in turn requires the gathering of all the relevant information. It is also useful to think carefully about alternatives. One way of doing this is to consider the **opportunity cost**: this is what the business loses when it decides against an alternative course of action. The opportunity cost of Woolworths' choice of products was the profit it might have made if it had chosen differently. Every decision has an opportunity cost, even on the personal level: for you, the opportunity cost of going out tonight might be not having your homework done tomorrow.

CHECKPOINT

When you are not involved in the running of a business it is difficult to know whether a business is succeeding or not. Even when you work for a business, either part time or full time, it is sometimes hard to know if the business is a success. If you wanted to work out whether a business was succeeding, what sort of information would you need? Add to the following list of signs of success and failure:

Sign of success	Sign of failure
e.g. sales staff earn large commissions	e.g. customers return products that are faulty

KEY TERMS

The *share price* is the price at which the ordinary shares of a company are bought and sold.

Opportunity cost is what a person or a business might have had if the next best course of action had been chosen.

Unit 1 — Make or break?
Enquiry 4: What is success?

What about the workforce?

EVIDENCE

INTERACTIVE LEARNING PRODUCTIONS (ILP)

In 1986 a team began work at Newcastle University to develop systems for learning which used new computer technology. For four years the team worked to combine video, audio, still images, text and graphics into exciting 'packages' that would help people of all ages to learn about new subjects. These are based around computers, CD-ROM, laservision and touchscreens.

By 1990 the original six researchers were ready to form a company. Interactive Learning Productions (ILP) achieved rapid success and became the fastest-growing and probably the largest multimedia producer of its kind. Learning packages are made to order for the school and college market and for firms in the fields of training, product information and public relations.

Today ILP employs 65 staff, including management, programmers, package designers and research staff. Sales were worth £500,000 in 1990 and are now soaring past £3.5 million. Everyone is strongly committed to the firm's success and employees often work into the night to hit crucial deadlines. **Rewards** from work are exciting career chances and good salaries – plus a regular bonus based on company success, personal performance and contribution to the overall enterprise.

Q1 ILP has created many jobs. How was it able to do this?

Q2 Why would you expect the staff to be strongly committed?

PEOPLE MATTER

So far we have been looking at business from the point of view of business owners and business managers. But firms also depend on their workforce; the men and women who are their employees or staff. In fact, human resources are often the biggest source of added value and the key to a firm's competitiveness. At ILP it is the quality of staff that decides the quality of the product.

In a wider sense any firm has customers only because other firms have provided those people with employment and paid them an income. The wages and salaries paid by one firm are spent somewhere on the products of another firm.

So the individuals who make up a workforce are important. As a resource, people are obviously special, with feelings, expectations and rights. Like many firms, ILP knows that employees work more efficiently when they feel they have a stake in the business. In some companies – such as Asda – staff are actually given shares as a bonus. But the 'stake' of employees is often also some emotional loyalty to the firm and a commitment of their working life. A job is more than a weekly or monthly pay slip; it is about financial security in the future, about satisfaction in achievement and sometimes about ambition.

INDUSTRIAL RELATIONS

In some businesses, the workforce will belong to a **trade union**. The union will often have a close relationship with the employer, because it can negotiate collectively for all its members. It may be able to get improved working conditions or pay for its members, and it will help to protect them from unfair dismissal, i.e. the loss of their jobs for no good reason.

Some successful businesses take care of their employees so well that they do not bother to join a union. Others may have a very positive and productive relationship with their employees' unions, which helps the business to work efficiently. Some businesses perform poorly because conflicts arise and the relationship between management and unions is difficult.

PRODUCTIVITY AND SECURITY

The success of ILP has meant personal success for its growing number of employees. But no business and no job is totally secure. The tide of success can always turn. Demand for the product may fall, leading to difficult decisions about jobs. The key to success is maintaining competitiveness, so that sales remain strong. This in turn means that everyone in the business needs to produce as efficiently as possible. We call output per person employed **productivity**. When this is growing, prices can be kept from rising and people can be paid more as well. But even then, the fact that people are striving to become more productive may mean that fewer people are needed to do the job.

CHECKPOINT

A computer retailer employs three sales representatives, all of whom are successful. The business is aware of the productivity of each member of staff and keeps a check on sales. In the past three years the business has recorded the data shown in figure 1.

If the business had to lose one of the sales staff, who would you suggest should be dismissed? Explain how you made your decision. Would it help in making the decision if other sorts of information were available? What kinds of information might help?

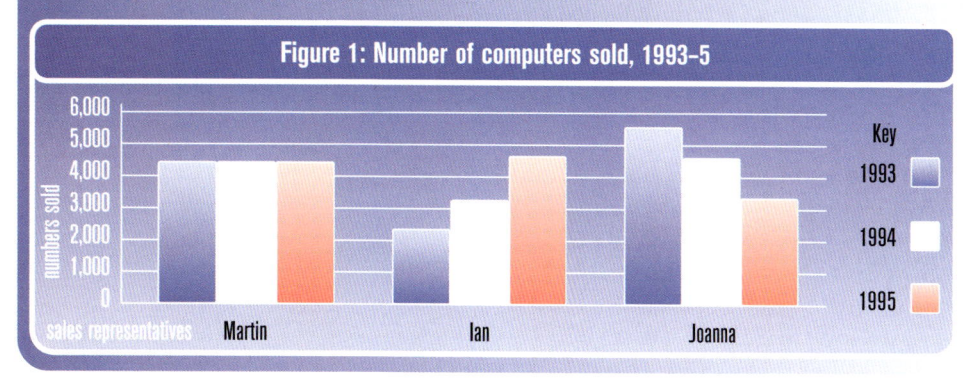

Figure 1: Number of computers sold, 1993–5

FORUM

When a business is successful, it seems as if everyone benefits. This is not always the case. In some businesses financial success means that the workforce can be replaced with computers and robots. For the workforce, who have worked hard to ensure this financial success, the loss of jobs because of the new technology seems a harsh reward.

What incentive is there for workers to work hard in this situation? Do you think it is fair for workers to lose their jobs because of their own success?

KEY TERMS

Rewards include any benefit earned as a result of one's job, e.g. wages, luncheon vouchers, an interest-free travel loan.

Trade unions are organizations that work on behalf of a group of employees in one industry or profession, e.g. National Union of Teachers, and Unison.

Productivity measures the value of goods or services produced by each employee in a business.

Unit 1 — Make or break?
Enquiry 4: What is success?

Whose success?

EVIDENCE

TESCO PLC

In April 1995 it was officially announced that Tesco had at last overtaken its arch rival, Sainsbury's, to become Britain's biggest grocer.

The supermarket giant was founded in 1932 by Jack Cohen. One of his first products was tea from a supplier called T.E. Stockwell. These initials – T.E.S. – were hurriedly combined with COhen – hence TESCO. The company has expanded ever since and especially quickly in the 1990s, with sales increasing rapidly, as table 1 shows.

Table 1: Tesco's sales, 1991–5 (£ million)

1991	1992	1993	1994	1995
6,346	7,097	7,581	8,347	9,655

Net profit is up, too: from £388 million in 1991 to £642 million in 1995. Clearly this progress will please the directors and senior managers. But perhaps Tesco is more than a set of financial results? Who else – apart from the directors and managers – is involved?

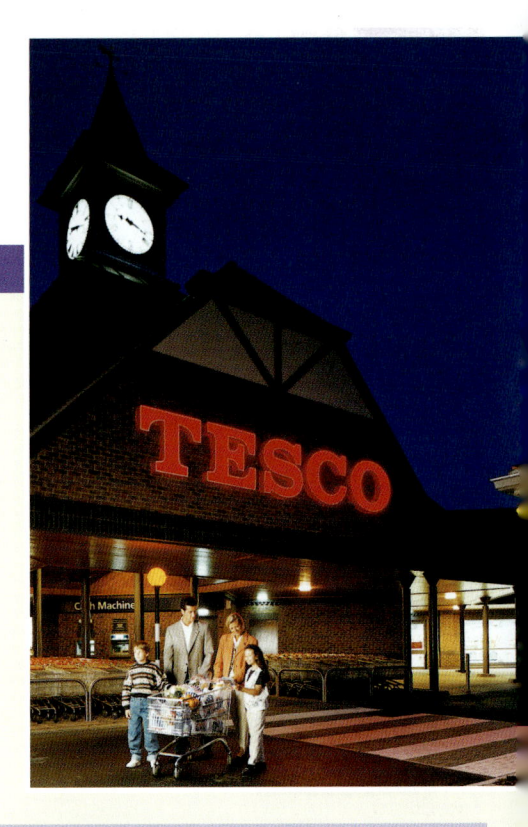

A quick answer would be, almost everyone. Look at the following facts. Tesco has:

- 132,000 shareholders;
- 10 directors (chairman: Sir Ian MacLaurin);
- about 700 managers;
- 69,000 employees, among whom 30,000 own shares in the company;
- 519 stores, serving most of the UK (since the purchase of William Low);
- over 10,000 companies that supply it with goods;
- a duty to pay business rates to, and observe the planning regulations of, about 71 different local councils;
- 11.4 per cent of the total groceries market, meaning that around 10 million people in Britain shop at Tesco regularly or occasionally.

STAKEHOLDERS

Sir Ian MacLaurin, the nine other directors and the management team control Tesco. The business is actually owned by the 132,000 shareholders. These include 30,000 of the 69,000 employees who depend for their livelihood on being employed by Tesco. Many of the 10,000 suppliers would go out of business if they lost the Tesco contract, making their own staff dependent on the supermarket chain. Then there are the **creditors**, to whom Tesco owes money.

Business rates paid by Tesco are a vital source of revenue for many local councils. And millions of families rely on Tesco as their main source of food and household goods. In addition, the company aims to advance the well-being of the communities among whom its stores are located.

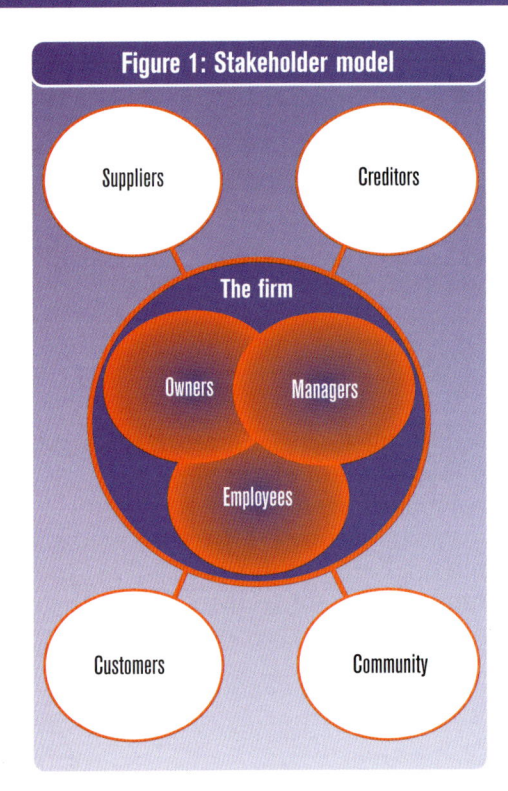

Figure 1: Stakeholder model

Suppliers — Creditors — The firm (Owners, Managers, Employees) — Customers — Community

Finally, it pledges itself to protect the environment. Tesco and many other businesses put a high priority on their **social responsibility** to the community as a whole and to the environment.

Each of these groups who have some 'stake' in Tesco (or any other company) are called **stakeholders**. This does *not* mean that they are shareholders (although shareholders *are* stakeholders). All the stakeholders are related in a kind of web in which each group is dependent in some way on the other.

Most major public companies now accept that they have duties to all their stakeholders. However, it is impossible to please everybody all of the time. To survive in the market Tesco must remain profitable and this may sometimes mean taking some tough decisions.

EVIDENCE

REMOVING A MOUNTAIN

This is exactly what Redland Aggregates, a large Surrey-based mining company, wants to do. In 1993 it applied for permission to sink Britain's largest super-quarry on the Scottish island of Harris.

The case has been debated widely, especially in Scotland. Redland argues that it does care about the environment and is taking the necessary precautions. But the issue has such importance to the different stakeholder groups that it has been necessary to hold a government-run public enquiry. This aims to balance the conflicting arguments and reach a decision that is fair, taking all the stakeholder claims into account.

It will not be possible to please everyone. If the quarry is built, then Redland will get access to the stone and jobs will be created, but there will be an environmental cost. If the quarry is refused, the environment will be undisturbed, but Redland will have to find stone at higher cost and there will be no new jobs.

Site of the proposed quarry on Harris

Q1 How will Redland benefit from the quarry?
Q2 How does Tesco benefit from building a new supermarket?
Q3 How will Tesco's stakeholders react to a new supermarket?

COSTLY DECISIONS

In a sense, all decisions carry a cost. Think through your own choice of subjects for GCSE. In some cases, by choosing one subject, you were excluded from taking another. The loss of your second choice was the 'cost' of your first choice. So, in taking any decision, the loss of the 'next-best choice' should be recognized. As we have already seen (on p. 27), this loss is called the opportunity cost of a decision.

In the case of the mountain, a decision not to build the quarry would carry an opportunity cost in terms of lost wealth and jobs not created.

FORUM

List all the groups of people who might have an interest in the quarry decision. For each group of stakeholders, say which way they will want the decision to go, and explain how they might argue their point of view. Put the arguments to others in the group so that you can see how interests may conflict.

KEY TERMS

Creditors are people to whom the business owes money.

Stakeholders are people who have an interest in the success of a business.

Social responsibility is the responsibility of the business to the local community.

Unit 1 — Make or break?
Enquiry 5: Why do firms go under?

What is business failure?

EVIDENCE

TAKE THAT?

One of the last marketing campaigns at the Athena chain of poster shops was based around the 1994 teenage idols, Take That. Some of the shops were looking rather sad and run down by then. None of the young Christmas customers that year knew that Athena was broke. Yet on 10 January 1995 the doors of the 131 shops closed for the last time, with the loss of 600 jobs.

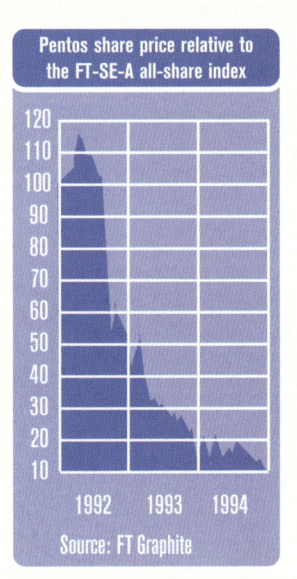

Pentos – the company that owned Athena – pointed out that in the final six months the chain lost £5 million on sales of £16 million. This represents a negative net profit margin of 31 per cent. At the time of its collapse Athena's debts amounted to £10 million – little of which would ever be repaid. Meanwhile, the Pentos share price fell to 11½p after a high of 170p.

There were probably two main reasons for the Athena collapse. First, the rents agreed for the shops in the 1980s were far too high: fixed costs were a heavy burden. Second, the Athena chain – founded in the 1970s – had depended on a mass teenage market. By the 1990s that market was declining in size and had divided into many smaller segments.

DEALING WITH FAILURE

All firms have to make efficient use of the scarce resources they control. Even for Marks & Spencer or Tesco there is no 'right' to be in business. In many towns Athena will already have been forgotten.

The commonest sign of weak performance is falling sales. Often the company is losing market share to competitors. Profits start shrinking. This means less money to maintain and develop the business and less money to reward the shareholders. The firm's ROCE value will also decline and the value of the shares is likely to plummet.

These events all signal change. Directors and managers may try hard to cut costs, or improve quality, or respond to changes in customers' tastes.

For a firm where the managers are unable to regain a competitive advantage and the downward spiral continues, there are several possible outcomes. Key directors may resign (or be sacked) and a new management team may be appointed. This provides a second chance for the firm to solve its problems.

Another possibility is a **takeover** offer from another firm. This means that the whole enterprise changes ownership. However, there is usually a drastic shake-up of the business. Parts or branches of the business may close or be sold again.

The most serious outcome of all is 'going bust', or passing into **receivership**. When a firm cannot settle its bills and can raise no further loans from the bank, then the directors lose control and the business passes into the hands of a receiver appointed by the courts.

The task of a receiver is to ensure repayment of the company's debts. If possible, part or all of the business will be sold as a 'going concern'. The new owners can make a fresh start and the company stays in business, often raising more money than it would have done had it decided to sell the property and equipment.

EVIDENCE

A CHAPTER CLOSED

Dateline: 28 February 1995. The board meeting at Pentos – the company that had abandoned Athena – had already been postponed four times. Now it was due to start at 3 p.m. But the delays continued. Finally, at 9 p.m., the chairman, Sir Kit McMahon, opened the meeting. He announced that Pentos, the owners of Dillons and Hatchards bookshops, could not continue in business and would move into receivership.

Events continued through the night. Accountants KPMG were appointed receivers at 3 a.m. The following morning the shops were closed. Yet by the afternoon they were open again, now owned by the entertainment giant Thorn-EMI, who had already bought them straight from the receivers.

Pentos was no more. Founded in 1972 and built up into an empire with annual sales of over £240 million, its shares were worth 146p in 1991. On the day before the final collapse they were down to 4½p. The directors and senior managers were out of a job.

CHECKPOINT

Look carefully at table 1.

Table 1: Companies entering receivership, 1983–93	
1983	14,038
1984	14,327
1985	15,546
1986	15,080
1987	12,045
1988	9,939
1989	11,028
1990	15,649
1991	22,626
1992	25,251
1993	21,417

Source: *Economic Trends*, HMSO, 1995

Q1 Suggest a range of reasons for business failure. What are the most common reasons?

Q2 Why do you think the number of companies that 'go under' might change over time?

FORUM

'There is nothing to regret about firms going bust. Just as in nature the fittest survive, so it is in business. Customers decide the fate of firms by buying or not buying their products. Bankruptcies just show that the market is working.' What do you think?

KEY TERMS

When a firm is unable to pay its debts, the courts have power to appoint a receiver (often a firm of accountants) to sell the business whole or in parts so that its debts may be repaid. The firm then goes into *receivership*.

A *takeover* occurs when one firm buys enough shares in another firm to ensure control over its decisions.

Unit 1 Make or break?
Enquiry 5: Why do firms go under?

Did the market move on?

EVIDENCE

TRIUMPH OR TRAGEDY?

Triumph Motorcycles produced its first primitive machine in 1902. Based around Coventry and Birmingham, it was known for high-quality bikes. In 1951 the company was bought by BSA (Birmingham Small Arms) Ltd. During the 1950s there was little challenge to the powerful British motorcycle industry at home or abroad. BSA was British and British was best.

But there were ominous changes in the market. Increasing traffic congestion made motorcycles attractive for getting around in built-up areas, while more women were beginning to buy. But the new demand was mainly for cheap, low-power machines quite unlike the oily monsters most associated with the Triumph name.

At this time, Yamaha, Kawasaki, Honda and Suzuki were building modern, large-scale and highly efficient factories. These firms had carefully studied the needs of customers in Japan and abroad. By the early 1960s over 50 per cent of the British low-powered market had been lost to imports – mainly from Japan.

KEEPING UP WITH THE CUSTOMER

Although the total market size was expanding, BSA's market share contracted. This is shown by the shift in demand in figure 1.

One of the commonest causes of business failure is losing sight of the market – the needs and desires of customers. BSA believed its British product was best but by the 1970s the British market had switched to Japanese makes.

When any product is selling well, there is a natural tendency for managers to take their eyes off the customer in the belief that they know best. This was probably a key mistake at Pentos. It certainly happened at BSA.

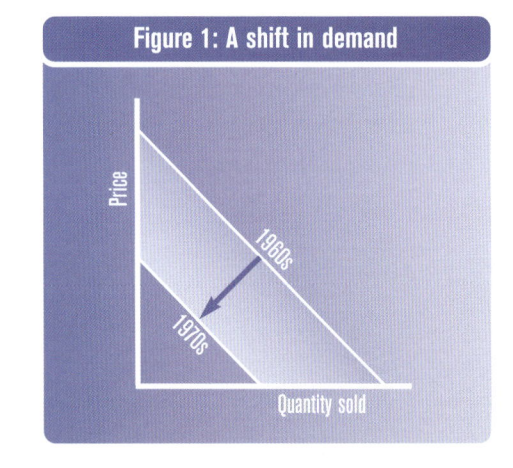

Markets never stand still. Because people and ways of life are always changing, every business must keep up with (or ahead of) those changes. If one firm doesn't, another will. Tired, traditional products can be beaten by new ideas.

Figure 1: A shift in demand

EVIDENCE

THE SEQUEL

Triumph never really fought back. The Japanese had the advantage of a large home market. Small bikes – like the famous Honda 50 – could be produced in large numbers and exported at very competitive prices. Instead Triumph placed its faith in the power market and its superiority in performance and design. New launches were made in the late 1960s, including the famous Trident in 1969. But the counterblast from Japan – and especially from Honda – was devastating. The Japanese machines might have lacked the classic English good looks, but they had electric starters and reliable engines. Redesigning the range in the 1970s made matters worse. The changes were very expensive and added to fixed costs in altering capital equipment. The production lines were seriously delayed by shortages of new parts and lack of skilled staff. Deliveries of bikes were then late, leaving another hole in the market which the Japanese could fill. Serious losses now threatened the enterprise. Despite management efforts to reduce costs, in 1973 BSA crashed through its bank borrowing limit; its shares were immediately suspended.

STAYING COMPETITIVE

What caused demand for Triumphs to fall so sharply while the demand for Japanese machines surged forward? For a **world-class** firm, competitiveness depends either on low costs and prices, or a quality product that consumers widely value. In the low-power market, Triumph lost its cost advantage. In the high-power market it lost because consumers' tastes changed: they ceased to value the distinctive qualities of Triumph bikes. Both these failures meant that Triumph was losing its market.

There is pressure in this situation to sell output by cutting price, but if costs don't fall then profit suffers. The real lesson here is that businesses can exist only if they are competitive. It follows that managers must protect (or increase) their source of competitiveness. This means keeping the whole focus of the firm's attention on the customer. Any failure in this task and the market will move on.

CHECKPOINT

Q1 Thinking about Triumph,
- why did they fail?
- what might they have done to avoid failure?

Explain as fully as you can.

Q2 Here are three lines of business:
(a) butchers in the high street;
(b) suppliers of mobile phones;
(c) operators of cross-Channel ferries.

In each case:
- indicate how you would expect demand to have changed since the 1980s and suggest some reasons;
- sketch a diagram showing your predicted change;
- recommend any steps that seem to you sensible for a firm in this line of business.

EVIDENCE

TRIUMPH AGAIN

Triumph continued to be a very troubled business. Eventually the old factory closed down, but another company bought the name. It built a new factory in Leicestershire based around Japanese production methods. In 1990 the Triumph New Trident was launched and by 1995 the company was second only to Honda in the UK's growing power market.

KEY TERMS

A *shift in demand* is a change in the quantity of a product demanded at each and every price.

World-class firms are those with a strong competitive advantage in all major markets.

Unit 1

Make or break?

Enquiry 5: Why do firms go under?

Has the cash run out?

EVIDENCE

FIREWORKS

Standard Fireworks Ltd sells most of its stock for Guy Fawkes night in November each year. This means that 80 per cent of its income arrives during this month. Unfortunately the company has costs to pay during the whole year. In this situation the company expects to have an overdraft from March to October each year. Calculating cash flow is very important as it helps the business to plan for the whole year.

Q1 Is it a problem for the business if most of its income arrives in one month?

Q2 How might Standard Fireworks earn income throughout the whole year?

Q3 What other types of business do not receive their income on a regular basis?

Q4 In general, what will happen if the income the business expects to receive is delayed?

CASH MERRY-GO-ROUND

All businesses have money going out on a regular basis. In an ideal world a business would prefer its income to be coming in on a regular basis. In this way there is never a problem with cash. Unfortunately this does not always happen. Figure 1 shows the ideal situation whereby businesses can use the money they receive from selling their products to pay all their bills.

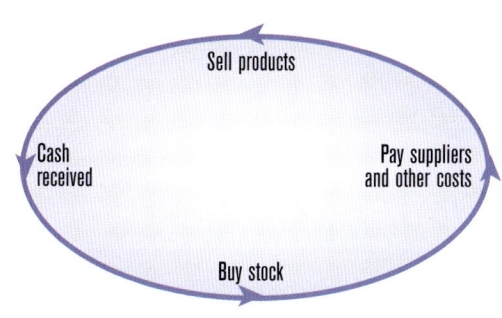

Figure 1: The cash merry-go-round

Businesses can show their **cash flow** by using a simple chart or a set of numbers. These approaches, shown in table 1 and figure 2, help the business to get an instant picture of its situation. The numerical method is the more popular as it gives precise information, rather than an impression.

Table 1: Cash flow (£)

	Month 1	Month 2	Month 3
Income	2,000	1,500	2,500
Payments	1,500	1,400	3,000
Balance	500	100	−500

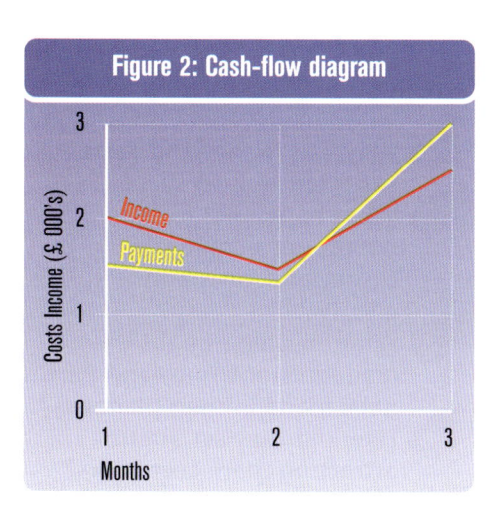

Figure 2: Cash-flow diagram

WHY DO BUSINESSES NEED CASH?

Businesses regard profit as one of their important indicators of success. Profit is important, but it is not the only financial information that should be considered. Businesses have to look at their day-to-day finances to check that they can pay the bills. For example, a business that sells something for a good profit, but cannot collect the money from the customer, will have problems. Even though the sale looks profitable, if the customer is unable to pay or has 'bounced' the cheque, then the seller could have difficulties paying his or her own bills.

CHECKPOINT

J and S Painters and Decorators have used a simple cash-flow system for the past three years. They have found that it helps them to plan for the uncertainties they anticipate in the future. Table 2 shows how the information was presented in their 1995 cash flow.

Calculate their predicted cash flow for 1996 using the following information. (This could be done on a spreadsheet.)

Q1 Indoor income rises by 20 per cent each season.
Q2 Outdoor income rises by 10 per cent each season.
Q3 A new trainee is appointed at a cost of £2,000 per season.
Q4 Materials costs become 25 per cent of the income received.

Table 2: Cash flow for J and S Painters and Decorators, 1995 (£)

	Spring	Summer	Autumn	Winter
Indoor work	3,000	2,000	6,000	14,000
Outdoor work	7,000	12,000	3,000	0
Total income	10,000	14,000	9,000	14,000
Wages	6,000	6,000	6,000	6,000
Materials	2,000	2,800	1,800	2,800
Other expenses	1,000	1,000	3,000	3,000
Total costs	9,000	9,800	10,800	11,800
Balance	1,000	4,200	−1,800	2,200

Not having enough cash to pay the bills is called a **liquidity** problem. It will usually involve the business in borrowing, probably by using an **overdraft** facility with a bank. This will have a **credit limit**, and the bank may refuse to lend anything above that amount. In any case there will be **interest** to pay on the borrowed money.

Preparing a budget for the month or year allows the business to plan ahead. This is important as there may be times when it will inevitably need to borrow money or cut down on spending. It is much better to know about this in advance rather than facing a surprise.

KEY TERMS

Interest is the amount that has to be paid to have a loan or an overdraft. It is usually expressed as a percentage of the amount borrowed, e.g. 8 per cent.

Credit limits set the maximum amount that can be borrowed from a bank or other lender.

An *overdraft* is an agreed amount that can be borrowed from a bank or other lender.

Cash flow gives a record of all the money coming into and going out of a business within a period of time.

Liquidity is the ability of a business to pay its bills when they arrive. A liquidity problem occurs when the business is not able to pay its bills.

Unit 1: Make or break?
Case study

Disneyland Paris

Minnies go FREE*. Ha Ha Ha Ha.

Kids stay free at Disneyland Paris.*
What a great time to take le Shuttle!

*One child (3 - 11 years old inclusive) free per paying adult.

Until April 4th 1996, valid only on "Disneyland Paris packages" under certain conditions, offer does not include vehicle transportation cost. See your travel agent and reservations or call Disneyland Paris Direct on 0990 03 03 03

Disneyland Paris changed its name from Eurodisney at the beginning of 1996.

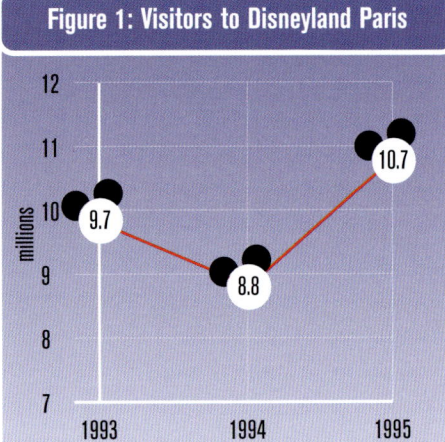

Figure 1: Visitors to Disneyland Paris

millions
- 1993: 9.7
- 1994: 8.8
- 1995: 10.7

Source: *L'Essential du Management*, February 1996

Q1 Why was Disneyland Paris expected to be a success?

Q2 What happened to the number of people visiting Disneyland Paris between 1993 and 1995?

Q3 What mistakes might the managers of Disneyland Paris have made in their planning?

Q4 How did they set about attracting more customers?

Unit 2

Work or what?

ENQUIRY 1: WHAT'S THE POINT OF WORK?	40
Will you swap? *Division of labour, specialisation and exchange*	40
Work into wealth *Employment, motivation and rewards*	42
What reward? *Exploring peoples' motives for working*	44

ENQUIRY 2: WHO'S RIGHT FOR THE JOB?	46
Does the job fit the person? *Job descriptions: matching people*	46
Getting the right person *Earnings, qualifications and scarce skills*	48
How to get the job *Essential and desirable criteria, CVs and discrimination*	50

ENQUIRY 3: CAN WE GET MORE FROM LESS?	52
Does money motivate people? *Performance-related pay, differentials and motivation*	52
Managing people *Human resource management: teamwork and communication*	54
What can machines do? *Investment and productivity*	56

ENQUIRY 4: WHAT'S THE FUTURE OF WORK?	58
What kinds of jobs? *The changing structure of the labour market*	58
Work away from the workplace? *Teleworking, voluntary and domestic work*	60
Is it important to be flexible? *Adaptation in the labour market*	62
What do trade unions do? *How trade unions have developed*	64
A workforce for the future *Lifetime learning and training targets*	66

ENQUIRY 5: WHAT DOES JOBLESSNESS COST?	68
Sign in or sign on? *Who are the unemployed?*	68
Why don't I have a job? *Unemployment and the individual*	70
Is there a market for jobs? *The labour market: changing demand and supply*	72
What a waste ... *The costs of unemployment to society*	74
What can the government do? *Unemployment policies in four countries*	76

CASE STUDY: TELEPHONE EXCHANGES	78

Unit 2 Work or what?
Enquiry 1: What's the point of work?

Will you swap?

EVIDENCE

PAVILION MOTORS LTD

Ten people work at Pavilion Motors. Besides Geoff in the photo, there are two other mechanics. Then there is Ray, who does bodywork, which includes welding and painting. Charlie is the repair shop foreman. Jim buys and demonstrates second-hand cars. Liz does the accounts and office work. Spencer runs reception, makes up bills and orders spares. Finally there is Russ, the manager, and his wife Eva, who together own all the shares.

Geoff adds value every day by repairing cars. The company charges customers for Geoff's labour. Geoff receives the greater part of this added value as wages. The remainder covers other costs and leaves some profit for the company. Geoff finds that he can add most value by working as a mechanic, so he earns more that way. A few years ago he worked in a supermarket warehouse, but the work was unskilled and his hourly rate was much lower.

Q1 How does Pavilion Motors add value?

Q2 Suppose Liz and Ray were to swap jobs. How much value would each of them add? Would the company be successful?

Q3 Explain why Geoff was paid less at the supermarket warehouse.

SPECIALIZATION

Each person at Pavilion Motors has a different role and knows his or her own job. Geoff wouldn't touch bodywork and hasn't got Ray's qualifications. Ray can weld anything, but hates paperwork. Jim is a born salesman and loves cars, but likes to keep his hands clean. The total labour of running Pavilion Motors is divided among ten people. The splitting of one big task into a number of smaller, different jobs is called the **division of labour**.

In effect, the staff at Pavilion form a team. Each person does the job that he or she is best at doing. This is called **specialization**. By specializing, each member of the team produces more. The company can increase its added value because the members of the team are all doing the things they do best.

EXCHANGE

Jody's choice of specialization is the job of hairdresser. She adds value by providing a service to customers and receives wages in return. Now suppose that her car fails its MoT. Pavilion Motors specializes in MoT repairs and it could well be Geoff who spends half a day working on Jody's car. And when she pays the bill, she would, in effect, be paying Geoff's wages.

This is an important idea. In a sense, Jody and Geoff have reached a deal, or done a 'swap'. If Jody spends her time adding value by hairdressing, then Geoff will spend some of his time mending her car – and adding value. The link between them is **money**. Jody earns wages that she uses to pay Pavilion's bill. Pavilion is then able to pay Geoff's wages, which he will spend on what he wants – including hairdressing.

In the real world Jody and Geoff do not know each other. Money enables them to swap their skills without the need for personal introductions. When individuals in a job add value, they do not need to swap *that* value in exchange for each

EVIDENCE

UPPERCUTS

Jody Wells is an experienced hairdresser at a large salon, close to the centre of town. After leaving school, she qualified at the Technical College and this is her second job. She is paid £225 for a 36-hour week, which is more than her older sister makes as a chambermaid at the White Hart Hotel. Jody drives to work in her own car.

'The customers are often interesting and I still like hairdressing. But it gets boring 7 hours a day, 5 days a week. And you never seem to sit down. One day I'd like to set up my own salon in the village where I live.'

of their own needs. Instead they receive money that can be used to buy – or swap for – anything they like.

Unlike, for example, a book token or a WH Smith's token, money is a 'whole world' token that is acceptable everywhere in exchange for anything. The knowledge that rewards will be paid in money enables people to do the specialized jobs that result from the division of labour. In a typical week Jody spends her wages on over 80 different items. In a small way she is helping to pay the wages of all the thousands of people whose work she is buying in a week.

KEY TERMS

Division of labour is the splitting of a task into smaller, more specialized jobs where the worker repeats a given sequence of operations.

Money is anything that is generally acceptable as payment in exchange for goods or services. In today's world, this means coins and banknotes as well as accounts with banks and building societies.

Specialization means that a person (or machine) performs a particular task which he or she (or it) is well suited to doing.

FORUM

Suppose there were no division of labour and, instead of specializing, people did everything for themselves. Money would then be unnecessary. What exactly would this world be like? Would people benefit from their lack of financial problems?

Unit 2 Work or what?

Enquiry 1: What's the point of work?

Work into wealth

EVIDENCE

EXMOOR PINE LTD

The company employs 40 skilled manual staff at its modern factory on the edge of Exmoor. A wide range of simple 'country-style' furniture is produced and sold to trade and retail dealers in the West Country and further afield.

THE JOB

Experienced furniture-maker required for varied work in medium-sized family firm. 40-hour basic week. Further training available.

THE REWARDS

£5.00 per hour basic wage. Occasional overtime likely. Profit-related bonus.

Three weeks' paid holiday. Subsidized staff restaurant.

EMPLOYMENT AND REWARDS

How does an employer decide how much to pay? The production manager at Exmoor Pine Ltd employs expensive skilled carpenters because they are a key source of added value. However, he does not wish to pay more than the value added by the job. Equally, the workers will expect at least as much as they could obtain in another job.

The benefit of the workers to the company depends on their skill and **motivation**. Skills include the expertise needed to do the job well and personal qualities such as honesty or friendliness. If employees are well motivated they will work with energy and commitment. This increases the value they add.

An employer will try to assess skills and likely motivation at an interview, but, initially at least, will pay only the 'going rate' for the job. If there is a strong demand for carpenters and a limited supply, then rewards will tend to be high. But if either demand falls or the supply of qualified people increases, then rewards will tend to be lower.

In other words, there is a **labour market** in very much the same way as there is a market for anything that can be bought and sold. In fact, labour is a service which – like any other – has its 'price'. This price is called wages or, more accurately, a **rewards package**, which includes **fringe benefits** such as pension contributions, a car and holidays.

It is important to remember that, as in any market, both the buyer and the seller must be satisfied. The 'buyer' or employer needs the value added by the employee to be greater than the cost of the rewards. The 'seller' or employee needs the rewards to be as good as, or better than, those that could be obtained in another job.

EVIDENCE

MAKING A MOVE

Chris MacDonald was a teacher of art and design at a secondary school in Kent. After eight years he decided to put his skills to a new use. In 1994 he moved with his family to Brighton and opened a workshop/showroom, where he makes and sells unique ornaments constructed from old-fashioned household goods. His raw materials include old radios, record-players, toasters and clocks. He adds value by applying practical skills and vivid imagination.

SELF-EMPLOYMENT

Being employed means selling labour – and its effect in adding value – to an employer. The alternative is to sell your own labour – and added value – direct to the final customer. Chris MacDonald has stopped selling labour to Kent County Council and now sells his labour direct to the customers in his Brighton shop. He is therefore **self-employed**.

Self-employment can be risky as the individual is the entire business and, like any business, he or she can fail. It is also likely to be hard work involving long hours. But the rewards can be high, too. Self-employed people set their own rate of pay according to what they can afford. There is freedom and challenge in the work and a chance to fulfil personal ambition.

CHECKPOINT

The numbers of self-employed people have increased over the past 15 years. The proportion of those in employment who are self-employed tends to be highest in rural areas and lowest in large urban centres.

Table 1: Employment and self-employment, 1979–94 (millions)

Year	Total employed and self-employed	Self-employed
1979	22.7	1.9
1982	21.4	2.2
1985	21.4	2.6
1988	22.3	3.0
1991	22.2	3.4
1994	21.5	3.3

Source: *Monthly Digest of Statistics*, HMSO

Q1 What might account for the change in total employment?

Q2 (a) How has the proportion of self-employed people changed over the period 1979–94?
(b) Suggest some possible causes for this change.

Q3 Why do you think the rate of self-employment differs between urban and rural areas?

KEY TERMS

Employment means working for an individual or organization in exchange for regular payment.

Fringe benefits (often called 'perks') are rewards provided by an employer other than wages or salary, e.g. pension rights, holidays or a car.

The *labour market* includes everyone who wants to work in exchange for money and other rewards, and all the employers who want to hire people.

Motivation is about how keen and committed a person is in performing a task or job.

A *rewards package* is the total pay and fringe benefits received by the holder of a job.

Self-employment means that a person works in his or her own business and receives payment from it.

Unit 2 — Work or what?

Enquiry 1: What's the point of work?

What reward?

EVIDENCE

C.H. BRANNAM & CO. LTD

The pottery was founded by Charles Brannam in 1879, with its factory in Barnstaple, North Devon. It remained in the Brannam family until 1980, when the pottery was sold to its present owners. The business has now moved to new premises and is expanding through the success of its *Mr Brannam Houseware*.

About half of the company's 65 employees work on the manufacturing process itself. There are three 'throwers' and three 'assistant throwers', who are highly skilled craftsmen and women working by hand. They produce between 1,000 and 2,000 pieces each week. A further five staff have semi-skilled jobs working the 'jolly', which is a partly mechanized process with a total output of 2,500–4,000 pieces per week. Finally, four workers operate the 'pollards', which are clay-moulding machines able to produce 15,000 to 18,000 simple pieces each week. A typical piece of *Mr Brannam* pottery sells for £10 in the shops.

OUTPUT

The value that employees can add depends on the quantity and quality of their **output**. Quality is particularly important at Brannam's, where a high level of craftsmanship is involved. But the market must not be forgotten. Output is worth nothing unless it has a buyer. What gives it value is the price for which it can be sold.

The value of employees' output depends on the demand for the firm's product. Suppose that sales of Brannam's pottery began to fall steeply. Unsold stock would pile up. The company could simply cut back the weekly quantity of products made. This would solve the stock problem and reduce output. But it would also mean that fewer employees would be needed. The workforce might be cut or hours might be reduced.

Alternatively the company could cut prices. This should win back the lost sales, but would reduce sales revenue. Since the same work is now adding less value, there might be a cut in wages or fringe benefits.

EVIDENCE

THE WAGE FOR THE JOB

The rewards for production workers at Brannam's reflect the forces of demand and supply in the local labour market. The hand throwers have skills that take years to acquire. They are paid according to their output, with wages likely to be around £250 to £500 per week. This rate is high because demand for their skills is strong (they represent a vital source of added value) and supply of such craftsmen is very limited.

By contrast, the operators of the 'jolly' and the 'pollard' earn only around £150 per week.

All staff get three weeks' paid holiday every year in addition to bank holidays. Fringe benefits include a pension scheme, a subsidized restaurant, free overalls and a free coach service to the factory.

Q1 Why do the hand throwers add the most value?

Q2 Why do you think Brannam's provide fringe benefits as part of their rewards package?

MONEY AND FULFILMENT

Are money and fringe benefits all that people gain from their work? Some people enjoy the social life at their place of employment. Others say that their job is worthwhile or that it brings personal fulfilment. Certainly for many people a job is about much more than money or benefits. Often a job gives a person a sense of identity. Interestingly, some of the big winners on the National Lottery have decided to keep their jobs.

These non-financial rewards of employment can affect the level of wages or salaries. Nursing is clearly 'worthwhile' but poorly paid. Bookshops often employ young, well-qualified staff who like their job but receive low wages. On the other hand, people with dangerous work or unsocial hours – oil-rig workers, for example – are usually paid quite well.

It seems that when work carries invisible rewards such as pleasant or glamorous surroundings, then more people want the job and money rewards may be lower. But if the work carries invisible drawbacks such as an unpleasant environment, then people need attracting to the job with the compensation of money rewards that are higher.

CHECKPOINT

How would you expect the value of rewards at Brannam's to be affected by:

Q1 increased sales?

Q2 the introduction of labour-saving new technology?

Q3 another major pottery factory opening in North Devon?

FORUM

Why does Brannam's not pay its machine operators £500 per week? Is it right for skilled workers in demand to receive much higher rewards? The chairman of Tesco plc receives £1,010,000 per year. Can this be explained as high demand for a highly skilled person?

KEY TERM

Output refers to goods and services produced by an enterprise from its inputs of scarce resources.

Unit 2: Work or what?
Enquiry 2: Who's right for the job?

Does the job fit the person?

EVIDENCE

A PERSONAL VIEW

Rebecca worked as personal assistant to the human resources manager of a medium-sized company. She had good qualifications and was prepared to work for reasonable pay. What her boss, Mrs Green, really needed was someone who could take care of all the paperwork relating to the employees of the firm. This would leave her to deal with specific problems, particularly those involving recruitment.

However, part of Rebecca's job was to deal with employees coming into the office with problems. They might have been off sick, or they might have had complaints about their contracts of employment. Rebecca was immensely sympathetic and spent time listening to all the problems. She began to get seriously behind with her paperwork. Mrs Green asked her to spend less time talking, but Rebecca felt that it was important to hear what people had to say. The disagreement between them went on and, after a while, Rebecca started looking for another job.

Q1 What was Mrs Green's problem with Rebecca's approach to her job?

Q2 Could Rebecca be helping the company by listening to people's problems?

Q3 Do you think Mrs Green should try to persuade Rebecca not to move on?

Q4 Mrs Green has to write a job description to help the person who will replace Rebecca. What sorts of things will she need to include?

A JOB DESCRIPTION

Defining what a particular job is about is not always easy. But fitting the right person to the right job means being able to describe the nature of the job, and deciding what skills and qualities the person must have. Often a job becomes much more clearly defined when there is a need to recruit someone to fill it.

To help applicants most employers prepare a **job description**. This sets out the nature of the things the person will have to do. Sometimes an employer will also write a **person specification**, outlining the particular skills the person must have in order to do the job well. These skills will be not just those that can be obtained with qualifications. They will include personal skills such as the ability to work in a team, or to deal tactfully with members of the general public.

You can get an idea of the kind of qualities many employers are looking for by looking through the 'Situations Vacant' pages of a newspaper.

MATCHING PEOPLE

It is not always easy to know from a job advertisement what skills and experience an employer wants. Employers have a list of criteria to help them decide who is the best person to appoint. The criteria make clear the important qualities that the successful applicant should have. They are divided into the essential criteria and the desirable criteria. All candidates have to match up to the essential criteria for the job if they are to be considered, but they do not have to meet all the desirable criteria. The essential criteria are not just qualifications, but also personal qualities and skills.

Even when people are trying hard to find a job, they may not be

EVIDENCE

THE PERSON AND THE JOB

Michael Jenkins has recently completed his A levels and has one year's work experience in his family's restaurant. He can drive and lives at his parents' home, five miles from the centre of town. He is interested in computers and wants a career, not just a job.

Winston Brooks has just finished his degree course in business management and is looking for a suitable career that will allow him to use his skills and expertise. He is very flexible as to the type of job he is prepared to take, though he is interested in working with people.

Charles Smith is a qualified chef and has worked in local restaurants for the past eight years after leaving school at 16 with seven GCSEs. He has decided to change the direction of his career and is looking for something that will be a new challenge.

Q1 Who do you think is most suited to each of the two jobs?

Q2 Why do you think he is the most suited?

PANEX — SALES ADMINISTRATOR
Salary: £11,000

PANEX is a Danish-owned market leader in non-stick bakeware for commercial bakers, supplying the baking industry world-wide. Several of the major UK supermarket groups are among our customers.

PANEX LTD is looking for an office-based Sales Administrator to help our small but rapidly expanding operation to develop its UK business. The job will include all aspects of marketing, sales and customer contact. As part of a small team, your duties will be wide-ranging and varied. We are looking for a responsible person, with initiative and flexibility. The successful candidate will have excellent organisational abilities and good written and spoken English.

If you are interested, please write with full CV and current salary details.

Administration Clerk
Salary: £8,755 – £10,815

We require an Administration Clerk to join our professional Customer Services team, providing administrative support to our first-class Call Centre with a staff of 70+ personnel. The qualities and skills required are:

- an ability to work on your own initiative and to prioritise workload;
- excellent keyboard skills and experience of using modern office technology;
- a positive and friendly attitude; and
- a flexible approach to current and newly developing practices.

Previous experience of a support role in a similar environment would be an advantage. For further details and an application form please telephone 01234 100 2000.

WARWICKSHIRE CABLE COMMUNICATIONS

---

successful. This is sometimes because there are no jobs available, but at other times it is because those looking for work do not have the right skills and experiences to meet the employers' needs. There is a market for jobs. People seeking work supply their time and effort, and employers demand people with the necessary skills and experience. The skills in supply and the skills demanded have to be the same for someone to find a job. You can be unemployed if your skills, qualifications and experiences do not match up exactly to what is required.

FORUM

Are qualifications really necessary? Some people leave school with few qualifications but still manage to be successful in their career. How do you think they have managed to do this? Has it all been luck?

KEY TERMS

A *job description* outlines the work involved in the job, including the tasks and responsibilities the person will have.

A *person specification* explains the qualities, skills and attitudes the applicant should have in order to be able to do the job.

Unit 2 Work or what?
Enquiry 2: Who's right for the job?

Getting the right person

EVIDENCE

SCARCE SKILLS

Although many people are unemployed, there is still a shortage of people with particular skills. Some engineering skills are in short supply, as are many skills involving new technologies. Table 1 shows how many employers think skill shortages are a problem. Quite a number of them would expand faster if they could get the kinds of people they want.

Table 1: Percentage of employers reporting difficulties recruiting skilled people, 1988-95

Year	1988	1989	1990	1991	1992	1993	1994	1995
% of employers	23	23	14	4	4	4	8	10

Source: *National Institute Economic Review*, 1995

Q1 What do the figures suggest about the problem of skill shortages in 1995?

Q2 What can employers do to attract people with scarce skills?

Q3 Explain what you would expect to happen to the pay of people with scarce skills.

ARE QUALIFICATIONS IMPORTANT?

One way to get the right person is to take great care in writing the job description. Another is to ensure that the qualifications required are appropriate to the job. Qualifications may show what a person actually knows already about how to do the job: usually these are known as **vocational qualifications**. Alternatively, qualifications may be just a way of identifying someone who has a particular kind of general education: these are **academic qualifications**. These may be of little practical use in the job, but they may indicate that the person has some ability to learn new tasks or ideas and work with accuracy, efficiency and insight.

If employers can't find the sort of people they are looking for, they can train people themselves. But from their point of view, training costs money. They may prefer the government to organize training schemes.

EVIDENCE

AVERAGE EARNINGS

An index number is an easy way of comparing figures with one another. In figure 1, average earnings for all occupations have been set at 100. The figures for each occupation show how much above or below the average their earnings are. For example, managers and administrators earn 43 per cent more than the average, while plant and machine operators earn 20 per cent less than the average.

Q1 How much less than the average is earned in clerical occupations?

Q2 Why are professionals paid more than people with craft skills?

Q3 If there is growing demand for restaurant meals, what would you expect to happen to the earnings of chefs? Will more people want to become chefs?

Figure 1: Average earnings according to occupation
(Average earnings, all occupations = 100)

Source: *Employment Gazette*, November 1993

Nursing requires lengthy training but is not generally highly paid.

Nursing

IT MAKES YOU THINK.

IS MONEY IMPORTANT?

There is an old saying that goes like this: pay peanuts, get monkeys. We have already seen that people have many reasons for working besides money, and some jobs are deeply satisfying even though not very well paid. However, sometimes it makes sense to pay more in order to attract a person with exactly the right skills and personal qualities. Equally, having recruited that person, it may be important to pay enough to ensure that he or she doesn't leave.

Figure 1 shows that different groups of people can command different rates of pay. In general, though not always, a longer training period means higher pay. People need the extra pay to compensate for lost earnings while they were undergoing training. From the employer's point of view, someone who adds more value is worth higher pay.

PERSONAL SKILLS

Getting a job is not just about having the right qualifications; employers are keen that individuals have the skills and attitudes they know are important to their business. Some of these skills you learn alongside studying for your GCSEs, but other skills are sometimes hard to acquire and demonstrate to employers.

For some jobs, having the right skills and experience is more important than having the right qualifications.

CHECKPOINT

Do you have the required skills? The following questions will allow you to decide your views on getting a job.

- **Q1** How important is work to you?
- **Q2** How successful would you want to be at work?
- **Q3** What do you do in your spare time?
- **Q4** Do you enjoy working as part of a team?
- **Q5** How important is it to earn a high wage from your first day at work onwards?
- **Q6** How much training are you prepared to do?
- **Q7** How important is it for you to get further training after leaving school?
- **Q8** What skills do you think you will need in your first job?
- **Q9** Have you got any of these skills now?
- **Q10** How prepared are you to move home to get the right sort of job?

Try to think of the impression you would give to employers if they were able to see your truthful answers to these questions. Are you presenting an image that you are happy with?

FORUM

Should a solicitor earn more money than a nurse?

KEY TERMS

Academic qualifications are those that can be achieved by studying school subjects which have no special connection with particular types of work.

Scarce skills exist when the demand for people with certain qualifications is greater than the supply.

Vocational qualifications relate to particular types of work and prepare people for specific occupations.

Unit 2 — Work or what?

Enquiry 2: Who's right for the job?

How to get the job

EVIDENCE

A JOB WITH THE COUNCIL

The job of Office Administrator in the Housing Services Department at Birmingham City Council has been advertised and the following are the requirements:

ESSENTIAL CRITERIA

- Appropriate knowledge
- Relevant skills
- Relevant experience

DESIRABLE CRITERIA

- Confidence
- Helpful approach to people
- Ability to work without supervision
- Willingness to take part in training
- Commitment to the council's Equal Opportunities Policy
- Willingness and ability to keep up to date with housing issues

People from a variety of backgrounds could apply for this post because it does not require a certain number of GCSEs, A levels or a degree. You could meet the criteria in a number of ways without having formal academic qualifications.

OFFICE ADMINISTRATOR

Package:	Attractive salary
Location:	Central Birmingham
The job:	We require someone to provide administrative support to our Housing Services Department. The successful candidate will have excellent word-processing skills, a keen eye for detail and a confident telephone manner. The need to meet regular tight deadlines requires a flexible attitude, a good sense of humour, enthusiasm and the ability to work on your own initiative. Duties will include post, filing, photocopying, and some reception duties. An awareness of current housing issues will be a definite advantage in working on the range of administrative projects in the department. Some training will be provided.

Please send your cv, with starting salary requirements.
We operate an equal opportunities policy.

CURRICULUM VITAE

Name: ELAINE HOWORTH

Date of Birth: 15.09.77

Address: 12 Kingston Lane
Acton
Middlesbrough ME4 8HY

Telephone: 01492 453421

Education: 1990–1996: John Bright College, Acton

Qualifications:
GCSEs:
English Language (B)
Mathematics (B)
Science (C)
Geography (A)
Business Studies (B)

Work Experience:
I have completed two work placements, each of two weeks:
1995 – at a local newsagent
1996 – at a childcare centre

I have also worked for my parents in their restaurant during my school holidays. I have worked in the kitchens, as a waitress, and I have helped with the accounts. In all of these roles I have been able to work accurately to tight deadlines.

Interests:
I play basketball for the college team and help coach at a local sports club.

Additional information:
I am learning to drive.
I can use a variety of computer software for IBM machines.
I am a good organizer and am able to work unsupervised.

References:
A referee from the school   A personal referee

Q1 What are the essential criteria mentioned in the job advertisement?

Q2 Could a school-leaver meet the criteria?

Q3 How do you think you could meet the criteria without having formal qualifications?

EXPLAINING YOURSELF

The **curriculum vitae (CV)** is a record of your achievements to date. It gives employers an idea of the sort of person you are as well as recording your successes. A CV should be:
- brief
- relevant to the job you apply for
- a way of selling yourself
- truthful
- interesting for the reader
- sending the right 'signals' to the employer.

The CV shows that you have the skills that an employer wants. You should stress the skills you have acquired through your experiences, rather than just listing what you have done. In this way it is possible to show what you can do as well as what qualifications you have.

INTERVIEWS

If you were interviewed for the job of laboratory assistant advertised in the Evidence, you would be unlikely to have to answer questions on science; your qualifications will speak for themselves. The interview is much more likely to concentrate on finding out more about what sort of person you are, what approach you have to work, how well you work in teams, whether you can show initiative, whether you are ambitious, and so on. In this way the employer tries to build up a picture of how you would fit in with other members of staff and what training needs you will have.

Some employers use other methods to find out if you're a suitable person to join their business, for instance:
- an aptitude test, which measures your ability to reason, interpret and analyse information; or
- a personality questionnaire, which tries to find out what sort of person you are.

EQUAL OPPORTUNITIES

Under the law everyone has rights as well as responsibilities. You cannot face **discrimination** in employment on the grounds of sex or race. The Sex Discrimination Act 1975 states that employers must not discriminate directly or indirectly on the grounds of sex or marital status. The Race Relations Act 1976 states that it is unlawful to discriminate on the grounds of colour, race, nationality, ethnic origin or national origin. Despite these laws, many employers still discriminate. If they did not, men and women and people of varying ethnic origins would all get equal pay for equal work. They don't. Some people have difficulty getting a job because there is prejudice against them.

EVIDENCE

Q1 Someone who has just left school at 18 might consider applying for the job in this advertisement. As well as the scientific requirements, what other skills and experience would be required for this post?

Q2 If you were to apply for this job, what sort of questions would you expect to be asked at interview? Do you think you could answer these questions?

Leminster Science is a leading organisation in laboratory analysis and environmental consultancy, and enjoys an outstanding reputation for quality and innovation.

Laboratory Assistant

Based in South Yorkshire   £7,500 – £10,000

We are seeking a young person, possibly a school-leaver, to join the Trace Metal Analysis section at our Sheffield Laboratory. Reporting to a Senior Scientist, you will be responsible for undertaking analysis, maintaining NAMAS accreditation standards, and assisting other members of the team. You should be educated to A-level standard in science, and be computer literate. Full training will be provided.

If you feel you have the necessary attributes for the above role, please send your letter of application and CV to Miriam Watson, Personnel Manager, Leminster Science Ltd, Premier House, York YO2 1BS.

LEMINSTER SCIENCE

EVIDENCE

Mr Rewcastle worked for a large supermarket chain, which had strict rules about the length of hair. Men's hair had to be short but women could have long hair and tie it back. Mr Rewcastle offered to tie his hair back but he did not want to have it cut. He was dismissed.

Mrs Baker returned to work after a break of six years, during which period she looked after her two children. At interview she was asked about how much time off she would need if her children were ill. Do you think a man with children would be asked this question?

Mr Sharifi, a British subject of Iranian origin, was rejected for three jobs with a local council. Despite his relevant degree qualifications in science, he was not given an interview, and he brought a case for race discrimination.

FORUM

Many people think they cannot get a job without experience, and they cannot get experience without a job. How do you think you will overcome this problem?

K KEY TERMS

A *curriculum vitae* is a record of your achievements to date.

Discrimination occurs when one person is treated differently from another.

51

Unit 2 — Work or what?
Enquiry 3: Can we get more from less?

Does money motivate people?

EVIDENCE

GETTING A BONUS

Garth is in charge of technical support at a conference centre in central London. He works with Richard, who is responsible for getting bookings for the centre.

They have a target for the revenue they get over a three-month period from organizations booking conferences. When they get enough bookings to bring in 5 per cent extra revenue, over and above the target, they get a bonus of £300 each.

Garth is not directly responsible for getting the bookings, but he does have to ensure that clients have all the technical equipment and help they need. Their requirements are often complex. They may want to display delicate images on a single computer screen in a way that can be seen clearly by up to a hundred people. Garth has to be able to set up all kinds of equipment and ensure that everything works perfectly on the day. He has to keep up to date with technical developments all the time. If anything goes wrong, the client is unlikely to use the conference centre the next time. So Garth's performance is critical to the success of the conference centre.

Garth and Richard both see the £300 bonus as a reward for commitment to the job.

Q1 The bonus is for the success that Garth and Richard achieve together. What can they each do to earn the bonus?

Q2 Garth earns about £950 per month. This has to cover everything for himself, his wife and his daughter. Will the bonus £300 earned over three months be enough to motivate him?

PEOPLE AND MONEY

Most people feel the need to work. Many will work to ensure that their standard of living is higher than it would be if they were on benefits. Some will work very hard to get a high standard of living. But the link between money and motivation is complicated.

Besides money, there are other things that can help to motivate people to work efficiently. However, money is still an important factor for most people.

One way to motivate people is with **performance-related pay**. Garth's bonus is an example of this. Another approach is to pay **commission**; this usually applies to sales staff, who may be paid according to the level of sales they achieve.

In general, we think of performance-related pay as giving a person an incentive to work hard or well. **Incentives** need to be designed in such a way that they do not become automatic but actually make people try harder.

Differences in pay for different people are called **differentials**. Differentials give people an incentive to get more training or more varied experience. They then become more efficient or productive in the way they work. Table 1 on the next page gives some examples of differentials. (The figures are in 1994 prices so that allowance is made for inflation.)

EVIDENCE

DIFFERENTIALS

Q1 Do differentials stay the same? Compare the three years in table 1.

Q2 Does training lead to higher pay? Give evidence from table 1.

Table 1: Weekly earnings (£) at 1994 prices

Occupation	1986	1991	1994
Waiter/waitress	151	161	157
Cleaner	179	181	180
Bricklayer	235	248	252
Nurse	216	298	316
Teacher (secondary)	322	390	427
Mechanical engineer	423	493	511
Solicitor	418	590	569
Doctor	592	669	746

Source: *Social Trends*, Central Statistical Office, 1995

KEY TERMS

Commission is a payment to a salesperson made on the basis of the amount of the product sold.

Differentials are the differences between pay in different occupations and in grades within an occupation. They will usually reflect differences in skill or responsibility.

Incentives encourage people to act energetically and work harder or more effectively.

Performance-related pay involves paying people more if they produce more or do their job better.

EVIDENCE

A NEW CAREER

Twenty-four years ago, Jane Heape, then a nurse, and her husband, a chartered surveyor, left the south of England for a new life in Scotland. Today she is one of the most successful hill-farmers in Britain. Her Corglass herd of pedigree goats is renowned for the cashmere wool it produces, and her Ballindalloch goat's cheese is sought after all over Britain. 'One doesn't farm to make money,' she says, 'one does it because one wants to. But farming has changed, and the modern farmer has to have a business-like brain to keep his or her head above water. One learns about modern methods of management from the press and television and from talking to people, and then adapts them.

'Farming can be stressful, but I think life would have been more stressful if we hadn't become farmers. We make our own decisions, the work is rewarding and interesting, and the farm is a fantastic place to live. We haven't made our fortunes, but feeling that one is making a contribution to the farming industry and rural life in Scotland is more important than making money.'

Source: *Observer Magazine*, 21 March 1993

Q1 Make a list of all the things that may motivate people to work harder or more effectively, including the ways mentioned on these pages as well as any others you know of.

Q2 Which of the motivators you've listed will apply to
(a) a farmer;
(b) a nurse;
(c) a waiter;
(d) a bricklayer; and
(e) a solicitor?

53

Unit 2 — Work or what?

Enquiry 3: Can we get more from less?

Managing people

EVIDENCE

WORKING TOGETHER

Amec Process and Energy builds oil-drilling platforms on Tyneside. In the office, a poster on the wall shows a hard-hatted Kevin Keegan urging: 'Let's make sure that Newcastle United isn't the only team on Tyneside that's going places.'

Teamwork, the football manager's message goes, gets results. 'All it takes is honesty, integrity, responsibility, reliability and continuous development.'

Until recently, Amec had a 3,000-strong workforce. When there was plenty of work employees might work a 60–70-hour week with very high earnings. But relations between management and employees were not good. There was a short-term view that concentrated on making as much money as possible without planning for the future. And payments for overtime were costly.

Now demand for big drilling rigs has shrunk and there is very strong competition in the market for smaller rigs. The workforce is down to 500. New managers have introduced a radical new pay and conditions package. The employees are split into two groups, both working full time. One works from Monday to Thursday, the other from Friday to Sunday.

Union leaders argued that, with so many colleagues unemployed, it was morally right to reduce excessive overtime working. Many of the workforce will lose money and just 58 per cent of them voted in favour of the new agreement. But Amec should get more orders.

Under the new agreement, old ways of working have been abandoned. Employees will be organized in teams. Communications are being improved with the introduction of briefing sessions for all. Shop stewards (trade union representatives of the employees) are being involved in the negotiations with BP, the customer.

Managers and employees recognize that this new **culture** of commitment will work only if new orders can be won. Only then can jobs be created. But the new measures will cut costs and make Amec more competitive, so the chances are good.

Source: adapted from *Financial Times*, 7 August 1995

Q1 Why did the number of jobs at Amec fall to 500?
Q2 What usually happens when a business finds itself with fewer orders for its product?
Q3 What is Amec doing to improve the situation?
Q4 What is meant by the term 'a culture of commitment'?

HUMAN RESOURCES

A business that decides it wants to organize itself more efficiently can work on a whole range of things. Amec agreed a new pay package and new ways of working together. It also tried to improve communications within the organization.

Other measures might include training programmes, increasing the flexibility of the workforce and working to improve quality. Usually these things turn out to be related and that is why they may often be implemented as part of a package.

Sometimes people who are working in well-equipped factories find that their jobs are boring and repetitive. The management might consider **job enrichment**, thinking about how jobs can be made more interesting.

TEAMWORK

The traditional approach to factory work was to have most people doing repetitive and uninteresting tasks, managed by a foreman. A different approach is to organize people into teams, each with responsibility for its own work. This allows for some job enrichment: if people have a range of skills, they will be able to do a number of different tasks, rather than keep repeating the same process. Also the team members are responsible to one another, not just to their employers. Co-operation is essential. And the good ideas of individual team members can be used to improve the production process.

QUALITY CONTROL

Traditionally, manufacturers employed inspectors who looked for faulty items. Now it is usual for everyone to be involved in the process of quality control. In this way, people work better because they understand what the quality requirements are. Quality is often an absolutely essential part of being competitive, and getting effective quality control can mean the difference between success and failure for the business. Quality control is often part of the function of a team.

COMMUNICATION

When employees do not know why they are being asked to do certain things, they may not be very co-operative. When they understand the reasons they can work together better. Efficient businesses place a high priority on effective communication with employees.

TRAINING

Effective human resource management usually means giving good training. **Continuous improvement** has become part of the culture of many firms. This means that training becomes a regular feature of working life. Good teamwork, quality control and communication also need commitment to training. Learning new skills and new technologies is essential to staying competitive.

MATCHING PEOPLE TO THE NEEDS OF THE BUSINESS

Human resource management uses ways of working that motivate employees to do their best by ensuring that they feel involved in the process. It also works to ensure that people have the skills. Although we have looked at human resource management mainly in the context of manufacturing, it can be just as important when the product is a service.

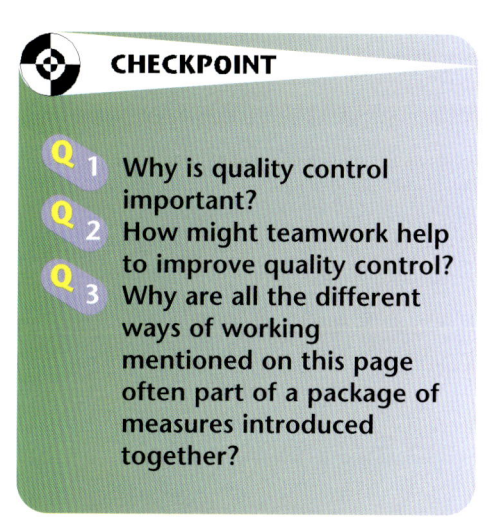

CHECKPOINT

Q1 Why is quality control important?
Q2 How might teamwork help to improve quality control?
Q3 Why are all the different ways of working mentioned on this page often part of a package of measures introduced together?

FORUM

Think of all the business strategies mentioned here. Which are good for the individual employee? Which are not so good? Are they just ways of making a bigger profit? Or are they in everyone's best interest?

KEY TERMS

The corporate *culture* is the collection of attitudes shared by people who work in the business. It may be positive or negative.

Job enrichment involves finding ways of making a job more rewarding, for example by giving a person more responsibility.

Quality control refers to the processes by which a business tries to ensure that faulty goods or poor service are avoided.

Continuous improvement is an important objective for many businesses that are committed to improving quality in the long run.

Unit 2 — Work or what?
Enquiry 3: Can we get more from less?

What can machines do?

EVIDENCE

MAKING VITAMIN PILLS

Ferrosan makes vitamin tablets and pills in Lewes, East Sussex. The company has invested heavily in recent years. For example, its new packaging machine automatically puts pills into blister packs and then into boxes. All the employees need to do is to keep the machine supplied with pills and packaging materials, and to remove the packages of boxes at the end. The machine's little rubber suckers do the rest.

Output has grown, but so has demand. Food supplement sales are rising, and the result is that the business has taken on more people, even though some jobs are now done by machine. Between 1989 and 1994, the firm spent £2.4 million on **investment** in new equipment.

Table 1: Output at Ferrosan

Year	Sales	Employees
1989	£11.9 million	98
1994	£19.3 million	148

Q1 Why might the market for food supplements be growing?

Q2 How has Ferrosan responded to the increase in demand for vitamin pills?

Q3 How are Ferrosan employees likely to feel about the increase in sales? Will the investment in new equipment worry them?

MAKING PEOPLE MORE PRODUCTIVE

There are a number of ways to help people produce more at work. One very important way is to invest in machinery. If people have more or bigger or better machines they will be able to produce more. Robots are an example of the kind of machines that do this. Computers are another: they can make both office workers and factories more efficient. The same number of people can create more output. A JCB operator is able to dig far more metres of trench in a day than a man with a spade.

An increase in output per person employed is called an increase in **productivity**. Figure 1 shows index numbers for productivity. The figures for 1990 are set at 100. What figure 1 shows us is that productivity on average has grown for the whole economy, and it has grown even faster in manufacturing. It is fairly easy to increase productivity when making things like cars or washing machines. It is harder to find ways in which machines help to increase the output of services such as hairdressing or restaurant meals. You probably wouldn't want your hair cut by a robot. So although productivity is growing in the service sector, it is growing more slowly.

When businesses increase productivity they will usually be able to cut their costs. This may mean that they can cut prices, too. This will help them to compete with other companies. A price cut would also mean that customers would be able to afford more of the product. Or they might have more money left over for other things. Either way, their standard of living would improve.

When people can produce more, their employer may be willing to pay them more. This is another way in which increasing productivity may improve standards of living.

Investing in more machines may mean that some people lose their jobs. But if the market is growing, the staff may still be needed.

Figure 1: Output per person employed 1990 = 100

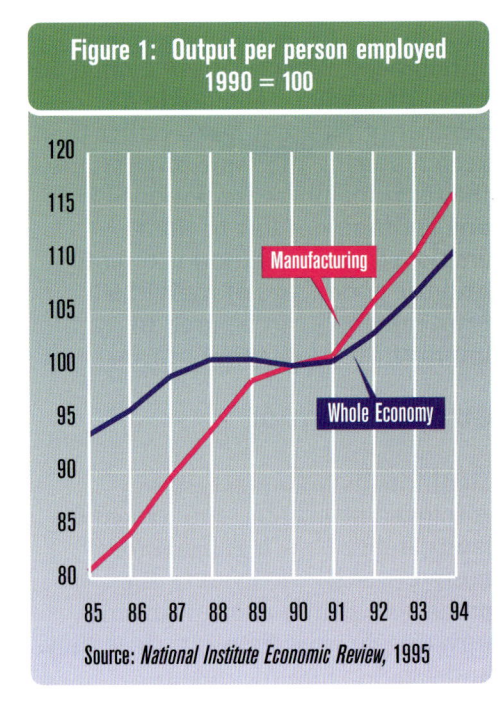

Source: *National Institute Economic Review*, 1995

56

EVIDENCE

In recent years, car makers have spent much money on investment in their factories. Ford, Rover, Vauxhall, Nissan and all the major producers have bought larger, more efficient machinery. They have invested in robots and machines with arms that weld metal parts together, spray paint, or help to assemble the finished product. They have also used computers to speed up and co-ordinate production.

In the picture above, you will see that there are not many people around. Machines can take the place of people in the production process. Equally, they enable each individual employee to produce more.

Table 2 shows that sometimes it is possible for an industry to invest more, enabling its employees to produce more. Of course there may be other reasons why output rises. But, in general, when people have more or bigger or better machines, they can produce more.

Table 2: Employment and output in the UK car industry

Year	Employment	Output (number of cars and commercial vehicles)
1984	281,000	1,133,731
1989	264,000	1,625,672
1993	200,000	1,568,991

Source: *Annual Abstract of Statistics*, Central Statistical Office, 1995

Q1 Work out how many vehicles, on average, each person employed in the car industry was able to produce in a year, in 1984, 1989 and 1993.

Q2 What will happen as a result of the changes?

Q3 Do you know of any local businesses that have bought more machinery? What happened to the number of people employed?

KEY TERMS

Investment means spending money now, for example on machines and buildings, which will mean more money coming in in the future.

Productivity is output per person employed. It can also be output per machine.

FORUM

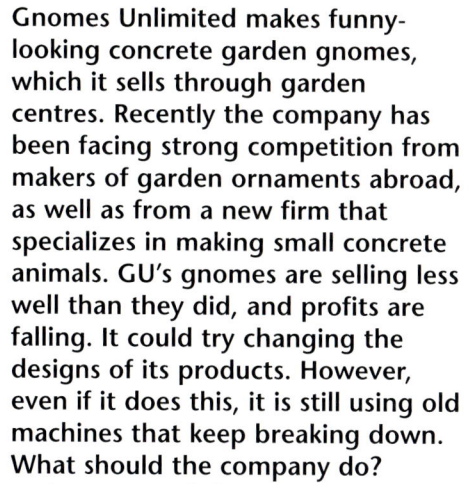

Gnomes Unlimited makes funny-looking concrete garden gnomes, which it sells through garden centres. Recently the company has been facing strong competition from makers of garden ornaments abroad, as well as from a new firm that specializes in making small concrete animals. GU's gnomes are selling less well than they did, and profits are falling. It could try changing the designs of its products. However, even if it does this, it is still using old machines that keep breaking down. What should the company do?

In groups of three, each take one of the following roles: GU's managing director; a representative of the workforce making the gnomes; and the driver of the lorry used to make deliveries to garden centres. Think out the best course of action from the point of view of the person concerned, then discuss each proposal. Are they all likely to agree?

Unit 2 — Work or what?
Enquiry 4: What's the future of work?

What kinds of jobs?

EVIDENCE

A MIXED STORY

More people work part time than ever before. There is growing demand for people who are prepared to be flexible about the hours they work. The government thinks that flexible working will lead to more jobs. However, the reality is that flexible working can be an uncertain business. For instance:

- some workers employed by Pizza Hut find out only on a Saturday the times they are required to work the following week;
- some retailers favour zero-hours working; this means that staff are given no guaranteed hours, but have to wait for a phone call to let them know when they are needed;
- at Marks & Spencer, part timers make up 80 per cent of the workforce, with flexibility as the key to match staff to peaks and troughs in demand.

Staff at Marks & Spencer get a full week's notice if extra hours are required to be worked. For M & S, and other companies who handle part-time working well, labour flexibility has advantages for both employer and employee.

However, people working in conditions similar to those at Pizza Hut will find the attractions of the flexible labour market harder to appreciate.

Table 1: People in full-time and part-time work (millions)

	Males Full time	Males Part time	Females Full time	Females Part time
1984	13.2	0.6	5.4	4.3
1994	12.9	1.0	6.1	5.3

Source: *Social Trends*, Central Statistical Office, 1995

Q1 Which groups of people are likely to be looking for part-time work?
Q2 Why is it possible to get people to accept uncertain hours of work?
Q3 What advantages does part-time work have for the employer?
Q4 How much has part-time working increased from 1984 to 1994? What percentage is this?
Q5 What was the change in the total number of jobs available between 1984 and 1994?

CHANGE IN THE LABOUR MARKET

Table 1 shows that there has been a major change in the level of part-time working.

That is not the only change. The workforce has grown: up from 27.5 million in 1986 to 29 million in 1995.

Another major trend involves changes in the type of output produced. This has affected many industrial countries in a similar way. Employment in traditional heavy industries such as coal, steel and shipbuilding has shrunk. Meanwhile, job opportunities in services have grown. This is called **structural change**.

There are three sectors in the economy. Agriculture, forestry, fishing, mining and quarrying are all part of the **primary sector**. They involve getting raw materials from the earth's resources. Manufacturing is the **secondary sector**; it takes raw materials and makes them into other products. The **tertiary sector** consists of services.

As economies grow, fewer and fewer people are needed to work in the primary sector. The raw materials needed can be produced by a much smaller number of people, using machines, which over time get bigger and do more. All the industrial countries have now found that fewer people are needed to work in manufacturing. Investment in capital equipment has meant that more goods are produced by fewer people. This process began in the 1960s and moved fast in the 1980s and 1990s.

A massive shift in jobs to the service sector has taken place, with retailing, leisure, hotel and catering, finance, insurance and banking all creating jobs. Since 1979 over 2 million jobs have been lost in manufacturing, while 2.4 million have been created in the service sector. Employment in banking, insurance and finance increased by 55 per cent in nine years over the period 1979–88. Table 2 shows how these trends have affected three major nations.

This major restructuring of the UK labour market has effectively removed some of the traditional male strongholds of employment. Many of the jobs created in services, particularly those that are part time, suit women rather than men.

MORE WOMEN WORKING

A third trend involves the increasing participation of women in the labour force. There are a number of reasons for this. Although women are still generally paid less than men in similar work, their pay has risen, and that means that the opportunity cost of not working has risen. Also, opportunities to work have improved: employers looking for sources of cheaper labour have created more opportunities for part-time work.

EVIDENCE

Q1 Which country has shown the biggest increase in employment in services between 1974 and 1992?

Q2 Which groups of people have been most affected by these changes?

Table 2: Employment by sector in the UK, USA and Japan as a percentage of total employment

	1974	1984	1992
UK			
Agriculture	2.8	2.7	2.2
Industry	42.2	32.9	27.8
Services	55.1	64.4	70.0
USA			
Agriculture	4.2	3.3	2.9
Industry	32.5	28.5	24.6
Services	63.4	68.2	72.5
Japan			
Agriculture	12.9	8.9	6.4
Industry	37.0	34.8	34.6
Services	50.1	56.3	59.0

Source: *Labour Force Statistics*, OECD, November 1994

CHECKPOINT

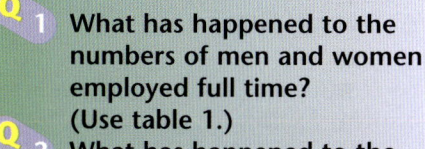

Q1 What has happened to the numbers of men and women employed full time? (Use table 1.)

Q2 What has happened to the number of part-time jobs employing men and women?

Q3 Think about the impact that these changes have had on individual families. What important effects will the changes have had?

FORUM

Manufactured products are often cheaper or better than they used to be, partly because people have been replaced by machines. This has resulted in falling employment in manufacturing. Who gains and who loses from this?

KEY TERMS

The *primary sector* includes agriculture, forestry, fishing, mining and quarrying: all involve the use of natural resources.

The *secondary sector* includes all manufacturing.

The *tertiary sector* includes all services.

Structural change involves the shift of resources from one use to another, for example from agriculture and manufacturing into the service sector.

Unit 2 — Work or what?
Enquiry 4: What's the future of work?

Work away from the workplace?

EVIDENCE

WHERE ARE WE GOING NEXT?

Think of the directory enquiry service provided by British Telecom. Do you imagine a huge room with banks of computers, rank upon rank of operators with headphones, phones ringing and clicking keyboards? The reality is very different. BT has recently completed trials in which enquiries are handled by people working from their homes. Each person, or homeworker, is provided with a telephone and a personal computer with a video camera fitted to the screen. This not only enables supervisors to check on performance levels, but it also means that homeworkers can communicate with one another so they feel less isolated.

Q1 What are the advantages of homeworking from BT's point of view?

Q2 How are employees likely to feel about these developments?

Q3 Draw up a list of industries where homeworking in the way described above is most likely to be effective.

Q4 What other sorts of work are done in the home?

WORKING FROM HOME

Working from home is nothing new. Some people have always 'lived over the shop' while others, for example artists, work freelance at home. But new computer and telecommunications technologies have made it possible to do office jobs at home. This type of homeworking, where individuals are in contact with their management team through phones, video conferencing and computers, is known as **teleworking**.

Homeworking has advantages. It can create jobs in remote areas and offer new opportunities for single parents, people with disabilities or the long-term unemployed. Teleworking may also promote exports; when a firm has many overseas clients in different time zones, customer satisfaction is likely to be increased by the availability of person-to-person contact outside office hours.

For employers such as BT, teleworking offers a number of attractions. It enables them to retain people with scarce skills, or those who want to spend more time with their families. Employers can make use of specialist skills on an occasional basis to accommodate changes in the availability of work. Teleworkers are generally thought to be more productive, more loyal, more likely to produce better quality work and less likely to be absent than are office-based staff. The company may also save on **overheads** (office costs).

Another way that companies have found of achieving this is by **hotdesking**; this means that a desk and its attached technology become the shared property of a group of people who work mostly at home, but who need an office base sometimes.

VOLUNTARY WORK

The contributions of people who do **voluntary work** for particular charities or for schools or hospitals are given no money value in the government's statistics, but they play a major part in improving the quality of many people's lives. We do at least know how many people undertake this kind of work (see table 1).

EVIDENCE

HEADWAY HOUSE

Every day, 18 people who have suffered head injuries gather at Reedens, an old house with a big garden, for rehabilitation. Some have physical disabilities, others serious memory loss which prevents them from working. At Reedens they learn new skills, make bird tables for sale, play games and go swimming, among many other activities. Their families also get a break from caring for them, while the individuals have a chance to get out, meet people and do something constructive. Reedens employs a qualified supervisor, but almost all the work is done by volunteers.

Table 1: Percentage of people doing voluntary work, 1992

Males	Females
21	27

Source: *Social Trends*, Central Statistical Office, 1995

Q1 List all the different kinds of voluntary work you can think of.

Q2 In what ways are volunteers at Reedens making someone better off?

Q3 What does the information in table 1 suggest about the importance of voluntary work to society?

WORKING IN THE HOME

Work around the home includes caring for children, or relatives who are elderly or disabled, keeping house, cooking and so on. Many people do their own home improvements, too. This kind of work also is not included in the government's statistics, and a person doing these things full time is said to be **economically inactive**. The fact remains that many useful and valuable tasks are being performed by people, even though they receive no payment in return.

Society as a whole benefits, for example, when someone goes to visit his or her elderly mother to make sure she is alright and has all she needs. That person is saving the government money that would have to be spent if there were no one there to help. This kind of work goes unrecognized in the national statistics for output, even though it has real value.

FORUM

Savewell, a leading building society based in the South-East, has recently agreed to merge with a smaller building society based in Bradford. Efficiency savings are essential and the new company cannot afford to maintain two head offices. However, each office has many skilled employees and an excellent customer services network which needs to be retained. What options does the new company have?

KEY TERMS

Economically inactive describes a person who is not in paid employment or who is registered unemployed.

Homeworking means doing paid work from home.

Hotdesking means that workstations are available in the office for use by anyone who normally works at home, but who needs office space from time to time.

Overheads are the costs of running offices, canteens and car parks, and include rent, rates, insurance and anything else not directly related to the costs of making the product. Overheads are also known as fixed costs.

Teleworking means using telecommunications to work away from the company's office base.

Voluntary work is unpaid work for an organization.

Unit 2 — Work or what?
Enquiry 4: What's the future of work?

Is it important to be flexible?

EVIDENCE

ZENITH WINDOWS

Zenith Windows is a large company that produces replacement windows. It has invested heavily and has found ways to develop its products in order to make them even more attractive to potential customers.

One new development is the application of 'Clear-shield' to the glass. This is a unique system developed by a British company, Ritec, which has received the Prince of Wales Award for Industrial Innovation and Production. With the application of 'Clear-shield', the glass acts like the surface of a non-stick pan, so that as dirt, grit and grime land on the glass, most of it simply falls off. This means that the glass keeps its clarity and is much easier to clean. It also resists staining and discoloration.

Q1 In which kinds of buildings might 'Clear-shield' glass be particularly useful?

Q2 Which groups of people are likely to gain, and which are likely to lose, from the introduction of 'Clear-shield' glass?

ADAPTING TO CHANGE

In the past the UK was a major producer of ships, steel and coal. This is no longer the case, and most of the people who were employed in these industries have been forced to seek work elsewhere. These changes in the structure of industry have resulted in what is called **structural unemployment**, as people have found it difficult or impossible to find new jobs. This process of changing employment continues all the time and, as new technologies are developed, it is likely to speed up.

As can be seen from the evidence, Zenith's flexibility and ability to change ensure that it continues to maintain its **share** of the replacement-window **market**, and it may actually increase it. But where does this leave the workforce? As far as Zenith's employees are concerned, it should result in a much more secure future, and it may even result in the creation of more jobs if demand for Zenith windows grows.

Other people in the labour market will have a different experience. If Zenith's share of the market increases, other replacement-

EVIDENCE

EDUCATION

Young people today recognize the changing trends in the job market and the need to be flexible, and are remaining in full-time education longer. Table 1 shows the stay-on rates for students aged between 16 and 18.

Q1 Will the trend towards staying in education after the age of 16 continue?
Q2 What sort of changes might encourage people to get more education?
Q3 How can academic qualifications make people more flexible?

Table 1: Stay-on rates for students aged 16–18 (%)

	1983	1993
Full time	33.8	52.5
Part time	19.5	14.7
Total	53.3	67.3

Source: *Annual Abstract of Statistics*, Central Statistical Office, 1985 and 1995

---

window companies' sales may decrease and they may have to make some of their staff **redundant**.

Zenith's windows are made from plastic (UPVC) and not wood. If demand for plastic windows grows, there may be a substantial decline in the demand for wooden window frames and for the carpenters who make them. UPVC windows are 'maintenance free'; there is already a decline in the number of painters and decorators employed, and this decline will continue. Finally, with the advent of 'Clear-shield', demand for the services of people who clean windows may also decline.

Both companies and individuals must be prepared to be flexible in their attitudes towards the working environment and the job market. In the future an individual may have to change occupation as many as three or four times during his or her working life as the pace of change increases.

If people are to be flexible and change their jobs when necessary, they must be mentally ready and prepared, and have the ability to retrain and adapt. For this purpose qualifications, both academic and vocational, are extremely important.

FLEXIBILITY

A flexible labour force is one in which people are able to move into another occupation if they are made redundant. It is also one in which employers are able to hire the people they need, when they need them. We have already seen that some part-time workers may be very uncertain about what hours they will work, and therefore about what pay they are likely to receive. Sometimes people are hired temporarily, and so their jobs are very insecure. By law, employees must be given a **contract of employment** within 13 weeks of starting the job. Employers who want to keep to a minimum their obligations to the person hired may take them on just for a short time. This makes the labour force flexible, but it also creates problems for people who want stable employment.

It is easier for employers to create jobs in a **flexible labour market**, but some of the jobs may be of limited benefit, especially to people who have dependants to support.

FORUM

There are other industries where changes have affected jobs rather as they did in the replacement-window industry. List those you can think of. What effect have these changes had on the local community?

KEY TERMS

A *contract of employment* is a written agreement between employer and employee setting out the pay and conditions of the job.

Flexible labour markets enable employers to find the kind of people they need to employ, and to employ them in ways that keep costs down.

Market share is the quantity sold by the company as a percentage of total sales for the product during a given period.

Redundant means no longer required because the job has ceased to exist.

Structural unemployment occurs when people are made redundant from an industry where employment is declining, and they are unable to find another job.

Unit 2 — Work or what?
Enquiry 4: What's the future of work?

What do trade unions do?

EVIDENCE

PEOPLE AT WORK

Pete left school without any qualifications and went to work at a scotch whisky bottling plant. After a while he became the drummer with a band that began to enjoy some success. Because of this Pete needed to take more and more time off from his full-time job. Before long, the company decided he had asked for too much and dismissed him. Pete went to his trade union for advice and then sued the company for unfair dismissal. He was awarded some compensation.

Caroline taught in a comprehensive school. One evening she went home, leaving her new jacket on the back of her chair. Next morning the jacket had vanished. Caroline was insured through her union, and eventually she got a cheque to cover the cost of a replacement.

Nearly every year, Unison negotiates with the National Health Service (NHS) on behalf of its members to ensure that they get a pay increase at least sufficient to cover price increases. Many of Unison's members are quite poorly paid and would find it hard as individuals to pressurize a big employer such as the NHS to pay more. By joining together, the employees have some impact.

Q1 Why do employees need the protection of a trade union?
Q2 What is happening to union membership?
Q3 Can you think of any other services that a trade union can give to its members?

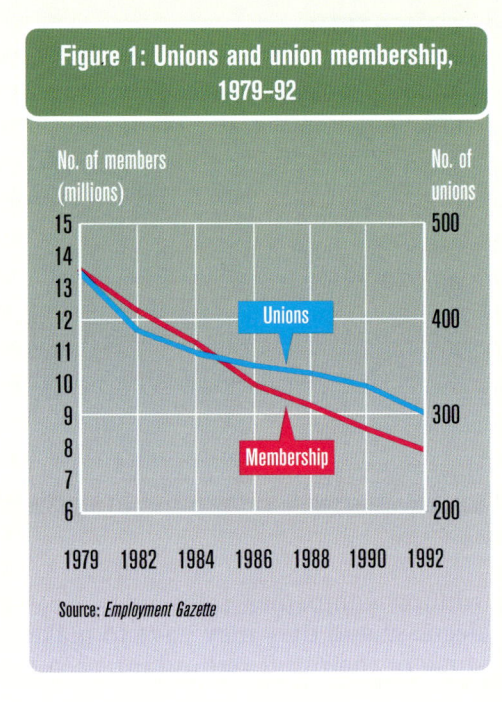

Figure 1: Unions and union membership, 1979–92

Source: *Employment Gazette*

HISTORY

In the past, many people experienced dangerous working conditions and very low pay. From the 1860s onwards, many were able to join trade unions and to negotiate with employers through **collective bargaining**. This meant that union officials could negotiate improvements in members' pay and working conditions.

The trade unions also helped to form the Labour Party. This in turn meant that in time parliament passed **employment laws** that gave employees protection. The membership and influence of trade unions continued to grow until the early 1980s. Then the Conservative government responded to public anger over strikes and introduced laws restricting the unions' activities.

In recent times, rising unemployment and a decline in the manufacturing industries that formed the traditional base of the unions have reduced union membership. The increase of part-time jobs and the number of women working has also had an impact on union membership. In the past neither of these groups have been strong supporters of trade unions. What is more, the 1980s saw an increase in the number of people working in small businesses, which are not usually unionized. For all these reasons, union membership fell from 1979 onwards.

In response, unions have tried to improve their image by making their services more appealing and relevant to today's world. They offer their members loans, mortgages and insurance, and some also provide credit cards and discount shopping cards.

TRADE UNIONS NOW

There are four types of union. General unions represent workers in a range of industries, e.g. the TGWU (Transport and General Workers Union), whose members include drivers, warehouse workers, hotel employees and shop workers. Craft unions represent workers who share a particular skill, e.g. the GPMU (Graphical, Paper and Media Union), whose members are workers in the printing, paper, publishing and media industries. Industrial unions represent people in a particular industry whatever their skill, e.g. the NUM (National Union of Mineworkers). White-collar unions represent clerical and professional workers, e.g. the NUJ (National Union of Journalists), whose members are journalists in print and broadcast media.

Unions are concerned to support their members when they are made redundant. For this purpose some unions provide grants for college courses or arrange programmes of **retraining** in areas such as electronics or computing. They also provide representation for members in cases of redundancy, grievance, disciplinary hearings and legal action, for example on equal pay.

As employment becomes more flexible, the unions see an increasing role in offering advice and support in the areas of employment contracts, pensions and employee rights. Some have expanded their legal service to cover advice on general issues such as family law and debt. They also aim to encourage employers to train and develop their employees. Unions believe that the way forward is a 'social partnership' between employer and the unions.

FORUM

Jim James has worked for International Plastics for 15 years. Jim joined the company straight from school and therefore knows no other employment. Unfortunately, the plant is to close due to lack of business. What could Jim's trade union do to help him?

KEY TERMS

Collective bargaining occurs when the trade union and employer negotiate in order to reach an agreement that both find acceptable.

Employment laws are laws passed by the European Union, and parliament, that set out rules of behaviour for employees, employers and trade unions with regard to employment.

Retraining is the process of developing new skills, when existing skills are no longer needed.

Unit 2 **Work or what?**
Enquiry 4: What's the future of work?

A workforce for the future

EVIDENCE

THAMES VALLEY ENTERPRISE

Thames Valley Enterprise (TVE) is a **Training and Enterprise Council**, or TEC. TECs exist to co-ordinate the government's training programmes in a geographical region, and to provide links between employers and colleges. Like other TECs, TVE provides a large range of services in its area. These are a few:
- Youth Training, which leads to vocational qualifications for young people.
- Skilltrain, which creates opportunities for unemployed adults to learn new skills.
- The Enterprise Allowance, which gives financial support and business advice to people going into self-employment in their first year of trading.
- **Investors in People**, which provides a national standard that recognizes the contribution of individual businesses to the continuous development of their employees' skills.

The role of TVE is 'to help the region become more competitive and increase its productivity by raising local skills and encouraging better business performance'.

Q1 Why is it important to get as much training as possible?
Q2 What happens to people who leave education as soon as possible and then find that they want to get more skills later?

GETTING MORE FLEXIBLE

Clearly it is no longer realistic to think of everyone having one job for life. So, how should people respond?

Flexibility is necessary, so that as one career opportunity fades or disappears, another one takes its place. Easy to say – not so easy to do!

The key to flexibility is more and better education, or training that is not specific to a particular job. People must have the basic skills of literacy and numeracy. Other skills are also important, such as communication and the ability to work with others.

People without skills find it very difficult to get a job. Research undertaken by the Labour Party in 1995 found that over 250,000 people under the age of 25 have never had a job or a place on a training scheme. Those without jobs are concentrated amongst those with few or no qualifications. When these young people do find work it is often temporary or part-time employment, dishing up pizzas or hamburgers during anti-social hours.

THE ANSWER?

People are talking about **lifetime learning**: this means being retrained, or returning to college or university for more qualifications. Much is already being done by TECs and individual businesses to help people train and retrain, but unfortunately it seems that far more needs to be done if the problem is to be solved. Unemployment is expected to remain above 2 million well into the 21st century, which means that a lot of people need opportunities that they are not yet getting.

In a recent report Britain ranked 40th out of 48 nations for its motivation to retrain, and came 39th for equal opportunities regardless of background (source: *The Guardian*, 21 October, 1995). So, appropriate training needs to be offered to many more people.

FORUM

Over the last few years there has increasingly been a division between those people who leave school well qualified and those who do not. The ones with few qualifications often become unemployed for a long time or get short-term or part-time work which is usually poorly paid. What do you think the likely consequences might be for the country and the economy of having a significant number of people with few prospects of getting a lasting, satisfying career?

EVIDENCE

EDUCATION AND TRAINING TARGETS

The government has set a number of targets in order to ensure that the UK has a more highly trained and skilled workforce as it moves into the 21st century. NVQs stand for National Vocational Qualifications. NVQ2 is equivalent to five GCSEs at grades A–C, and NVQ3 is equivalent to two A-level passes.

The targets are divided between Foundation Learning Targets, which specify the targets for young people entering the workforce, and Lifetime Learning Targets for everyone, including firms, which are encouraged to become recognized as 'Investors in People'.

Q1 Why do you think the government has decided to specify education and training targets?
Q2 How many people in your class intend to stay in full-time education after Year 11?

KEY TERMS

Investors in People is a scheme that recognizes businesses which make a real effort to train their workforce on an ongoing basis.

Lifetime learning is the process of gaining more education and training throughout one's working life.

Training and Enterprise Councils aim to offer training and provide links between employers and colleges.

EVIDENCE

HOSEASONS

Hoseasons is a well-established company that offers boating holidays in the UK. At its headquarters the 200 full- and part-time staff all receive extensive training. Induction courses help to train new recruits. Job-specific training is routine for everyone. Hoseasons was one of the first companies to get accreditation from Investors in People; this recognizes the fact that its employees will be able to develop their skills continuously.

Q1 What advantages will Hoseasons get from making training a high priority?
Q2 Some people argue that it is not in the interests of individual employers to train and retrain their workforce. Why is this? What can be done about it?

NATIONAL TARGETS FOR EDUCATION AND TRAINING

'Developing skills for a successful future'

AIM

To improve the UK's international competitiveness by raising standards and attainment levels in education and training to world-class levels through ensuring that:

1. All employers invest in employee development to achieve business success.
2. All individuals have access to education and training opportunities, leading to recognised qualifications, which meet their needs and aspirations.
3. All education and training develops self-reliance, flexibility and breadth, in particular through fostering competence in core skills.

TARGETS FOR 2000

Foundation Learning

1. By age 19, 85% of young people to achieve 5 GCSEs at grade C or above, an Intermediate GNVQ or an NVQ level 2.
2. 75% of young people to achieve level 2 competence in communication, numeracy and IT by age 19; and 35% to achieve level 3 competence in these core skills by age 21.
3. By age 21, 60% of young people to achieve 2 GCE A levels, an Advanced GNVQ or an NVQ level 3.

Lifetime Learning

1. 60% of the workforce to be qualified to NVQ level 3, Advanced GNVQ or 2 GCE A level standard.
2. 30% of the workforce to have a vocational, professional, management or academic qualification at NVQ level 4 or above.
3. 70% of all organisations employing 200 or more employees, and 35% of those employing 50 or more, to be recognised as Investors in People.

Unit 2 — Work or what?

Enquiry 5: What does joblessness cost?

Sign in or sign on?

WHO ARE THE UNEMPLOYED?

This question appears to be straightforward and the answer seems easy, too: anyone without a job. Yet if you study the pictures the answer is anything but easy. Is a worker who works just four hours a week employed or unemployed? Is a chef to be included during the quiet winter months when fewer tourists are around? Is it only paid employment that counts? What about a person working to maintain a home and a family so that others in the household can work?

What happens in the winter?

What will he do for the rest of the day?

Who else could do this job?

Is there a wage for this job?

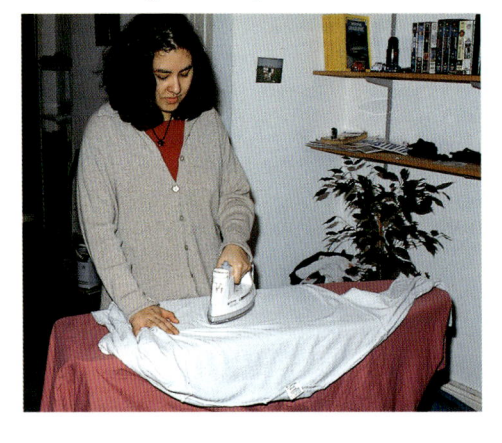

From the point of view of the economy as a whole, people who aren't working are not contributing to the country's output. If they are unemployed, opportunities are being wasted to make more goods or to provide more services.

People who stay at home to look after others are often very busy, but their work is not included in the government's figures. They are not counted as unemployed unless they want to work and are receiving benefits.

The **unemployment figures** that are produced every month show how many people are actively seeking work and claiming benefit. There are other methods of counting the unemployed that give a different result. The evidence entitled 'What is the real jobless total?' explains an alternative strategy.

EVIDENCE

WHAT IS THE REAL JOBLESS TOTAL?

Is the total 2.3 million, 2.5 million – or even perhaps 3, 4 or 5 million? There are people who would lay claim to all these figures. The issue comes down to how you count them.

Political parties have motives for exaggerating the figures in one direction or the other. Counting the number of benefit claimants is fine, as long as you don't keep changing the rules for making claims. Excluding school leavers from being eligible reduces the number of claimants, but does it reduce the number of unemployed? Similarly, does putting men over 60 into 'early retirement' bring the number of jobless down?

The Labour Force Survey, on the other hand, surveys 60,000 households and includes people who are unemployed but who cannot claim benefit. Many people would like to work, but if their spouse is already earning, they don't bother to sign on because they will not receive any financial support. It also includes the number of people who are working part time rather than full time.

Above all, it is essential to have a system that is both accurate and reliable so that governments can make decisions about the state of the economy.

Q1 Compare the two measures of unemployment in 1986, 1990 and 1993.

Q2 Which measure is more stable?

Figure 1: Two ways to count unemployment

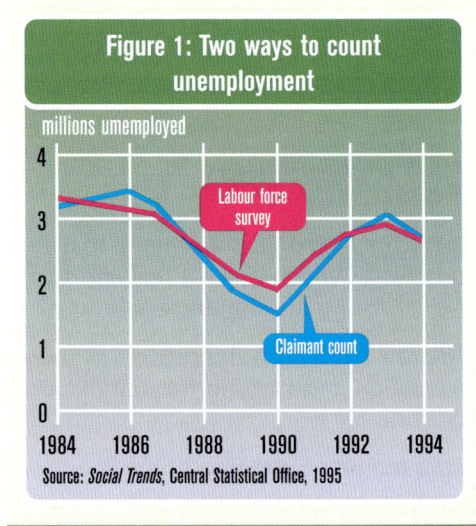

Source: *Social Trends*, Central Statistical Office, 1995

EVIDENCE

YOU ARE MORE LIKELY TO BE UNEMPLOYED IF ...

Some groups of people are more likely to be unemployed than others. Table 1 breaks the population up according to age and gender. Some clear differences can be seen.

Q1 To what extent are young men more likely to be unemployed than older men?

Q2 To what extent are young men more likely to be unemployed than young women?

Q3 To what extent are young women more likely to be unemployed than older women?

Q4 Draw a graph showing unemployment for 16–19-year-old males and females.

Q5 What might help to reduce the figures for young people?

LONG-TERM UNEMPLOYMENT

Q1 Approximately what proportion of all unemployment is long-term unemployment?

Q2 When all unemployment falls, does long-term unemployment fall as much?

Q3 Why might it be difficult to get the long-term unemployed back to work?

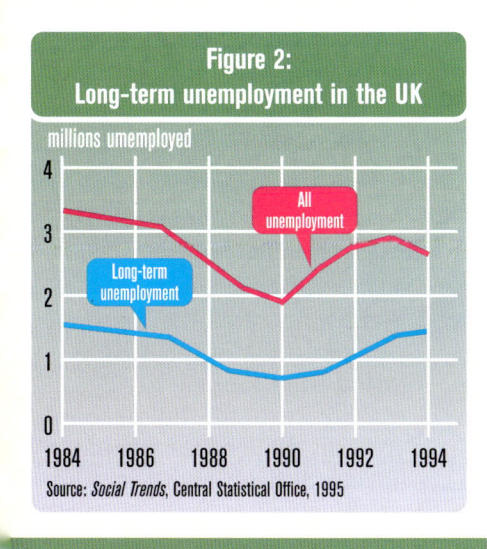

Table 1: Unemployment rates by age and gender (%)

	1991	1992	1993	1994
Males				
16-19	16.5	18.7	22.0	21.0
20-29	12.3	15.3	16.4	14.8
30-39	7.8	10.4	10.3	10.2
40-49	5.8	7.8	8.8	7.6
50-64	8.4	10.4	11.9	11.0
65 and over	5.9	4.9	4.6	3.7
Females				
16-19	13.2	13.8	16.1	16.1
20-29	9.4	9.4	10.2	9.3
30-39	6.9	7.2	7.0	7.0
40-49	4.9	5.0	4.7	4.7
50-59	5.1	5.0	5.6	5.6
60 and over	4.4	3.1	3.9	3.0

Source: *Social Trends*, Central Statistical Office, 1995

Figure 2: Long-term unemployment in the UK

Source: *Social Trends*, Central Statistical Office, 1995

FORUM

If there were a national emergency that required the maximum possible work from everyone, who do you think could be persuaded to provide extra hours? What prevents these people working in a normal situation?

FORUM

If you were working in a benefits claim office, what rules would you make to decide who could and could not receive unemployment benefit?

KEY TERM

The *unemployment figures* produced by the UK government count as unemployed those people who are actively seeking work and claiming benefit.

Unit 2 **Work or what?**
Enquiry 5: What does joblessness cost?

Why don't I have a job?

EVIDENCE

JAMIE (AGE 24)
'I never did my GCSEs. I'd been ill a lot that year and never finished the course work. It didn't seem worth doing the exams. The only proper work I've ever had was selling ice creams in Blackpool one summer – but of course, that didn't last long.'

CHRISTOPHER PARKER (AGE 47)
'The bank installed cash machines and closed some of its branches. They didn't need so many people after that. I thought I had a job for life, but it didn't turn out like that.'

DR KASHIF SINGH (AGE 59)
'This isn't the first time I'm out of a job. It's happened twice before. Sometimes the firm has just cut back on research and development. On other occasions, I've been employed on a specific project and when it's finished, I have to find something else.'

ANNE WEATHERBY (AGE 35)
'I'd love to go back to nursing and earn my living, but since I've been divorced I can't afford to pay for child care.'

Q1 Christopher Parker lost his job because of changes in technology. What other jobs have disappeared in this way?

Q2 In what lines of work do people often find themselves between jobs?

Q3 In what other types of jobs are there people whose position is similar to Anne Weatherby's?

Q4 Make a list of all the reasons you can think of for people losing their jobs.

Q5 Make a list of all the reasons you can think of for people having difficulty getting a job.

WHAT ARE THE REASONS?

Jamie, Christopher, Kashif and Anne were all jobless for very different reasons. In Jamie's case, he had left school without any qualifications. In today's competitive job market, it is difficult to find employment without some evidence of achievement.

Table 1: Young people meeting national targets for education and training, 1994

	Qualified to NVQ level 2	Qualified to NVQ level 3
England	63.7	38.5
Wales	60.2	36.4
Scotland	69.3	49.3
N. Ireland	66.8	39.2

Source: *Regional Trends*, Central Statistical Office, 1995

This is one reason why more and more students take up opportunities for further education (see table 1).

Christopher Parker had lost his job because technology had changed and therefore his services were no longer required. He has also been affected by the bank's need to remain competitive. Many firms have restructured their organizations by reducing the number of managers in order to reduce costs.

Dr Kashif Singh's age is against him. Adverts for jobs often state that applicants must be under a certain age. The age in question will vary according to the job, but it is often very difficult for anyone over 50 to find employment.

Finding continuous employment has also been difficult for Dr Singh. Like many others he has often found himself spending some time unemployed while searching for the next job.

Anne Weatherby would like to work and has skills that are in demand, but as she won't earn very much as a nurse, meeting the bills for child care would be beyond her. As a result she stays at home and relies on state benefits.

As there is constant change in the structure of the economy, people in all sorts of lines of work have found themselves out of a job. The pattern varies across the country, but the shift in output from manufacturing to services has affected many people in areas where heavy industry used to exist.

Unemployment often results from there being too little demand for the skills of an individual. If there are many people available who have the right skills, employers will be able to pick and choose, so anyone who doesn't quite match requirements will have less chance of employment.

EVIDENCE

Table 2: Proportion of employees receiving job-related training, by age and gender

	1984	1992
Males		
16-19	25.2	26.8
20-24	15.3	19.4
25-29	12.5	17.2
30-39	9.8	15.0
40-49	6.3	12.8
50-59	3.3	4.7
60-64	2.0	2.9
All males aged 16-64	9.7	14.4
Females		
16-19	16.4	19.9
20-24	11.7	18.9
25-29	10.2	16.1
30-39	8.9	15.2
40-49	6.1	13.8
50-59	3.5	8.4
All females aged 16-59	8.5	14.7

Source: Employment Department

Q1 What has happened to the proportion of people being trained?

Q2 Who receives more training, males or females?

Q3 Has training for males risen more than training for females?

Q4 What effect do you think training has on:
(a) the employee: and
(b) productivity?

FORUM

Use the newspapers on CD-ROM to find further reasons for unemployment. Try combining unemployment with technology, banks, nurses, wages and abroad, or any other categories you can think of. Use 'and' rather than 'or'. Look for the words in the same paragraph or article – not next to one another.

CHECKPOINT

Use the following headings and try to classify the causes of unemployment that have been mentioned here.

- Changes in the structure of the economy
- Temporary
- Discrimination
- Seasonal

Unit 2 — Work or what?
Enquiry 5: What does joblessness cost?

Is there a market for jobs?

EVIDENCE

BRICK WALL

Reports from inside the construction industry last week said rates of pay for skilled bricklayers in London and the South East have risen 25 per cent since the New Year. Brickies, apparently, are resorting to practices not seen since the heady days of the late eighties when they took their skills from job to job on a daily basis.

The bad news is that, despite the loss of 450,000 jobs since 1989, there is a shortage of skilled brickies.

Why? Because the industry and the Government have not trained enough people and the net result is that, as activity picks up, the shortage of skilled labour will drive up wage rates.

Source: *The Observer*, 17 April 1994

Q1 What has happened to wages in the bricklaying trade?

Q2 Why?

Q3 What would have helped to avoid these changes?

EVIDENCE

ORDERS DOWN 8 PER CENT ON YEAR

The value of total new orders received by building contractors fell by 8 per cent compared with the same time last year, and within that there was a 19 per cent fall in orders for private housing. This would force many redundancies in the industry. These cuts also meant that the industry's training targets were slashed by one-third because there are insufficient on-the-job training places for existing recruits.

Source: adapted from *Building*, 13 October 1995

Q1 What is the likely effect on wages of this decline in the construction industry?

Q2 In the longer term, how will the reduction in training places affect wages?

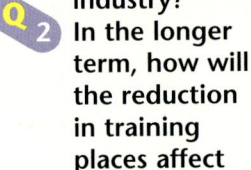

THE LABOUR MARKET

The first article shows how wages can rise when there are not enough people to do a particular job. Demand and supply works in just the same way for people as it does for anything you might buy in the shops. Demand for labour is influenced by the demand for the end product. The more houses that people want, the more bricklayers will be required.

In this case, if more bricklayers are needed and there are not enough to meet this change in demand, people will have to pay more if they want to build a house. In figure 1, the shift of the demand curve to the right shows how this takes place. As more people want to build houses, more bricklayers are needed, but because there are not enough, employers have to pay more to attract additional workers.

WHAT IF DEMAND FALLS?

If demand for labour falls, then the process is reversed and wages will tend to fall, or at least grow more slowly. The construction business often has unemployed people because demand for new buildings varies over time.

AN EXPLANATION FOR UNEMPLOYMENT?

If people have been unemployed for some time, it is possible that the reason is that the going wage rate is higher than employers want to pay. Suppose the current level of wages is above the rate at which the market clears. This is the situation in figure 2. What would happen if wage rates fell? Lower wages would encourage employers to take on more people, and unemployment would fall.

However, this may not happen. If you have the wrong skills, whatever the wage levels, no one will want to employ you. If you live in a place where no new jobs are being created, there are no opportunities to find work at any wage.

In this situation a country needs different strategies for dealing with unemployment.

Figure 1: Supply and demand in the labour market

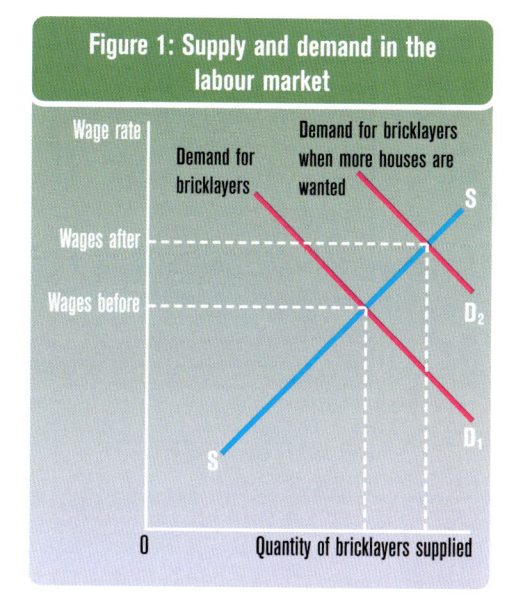

Figure 2: Wages fall, employment rises?

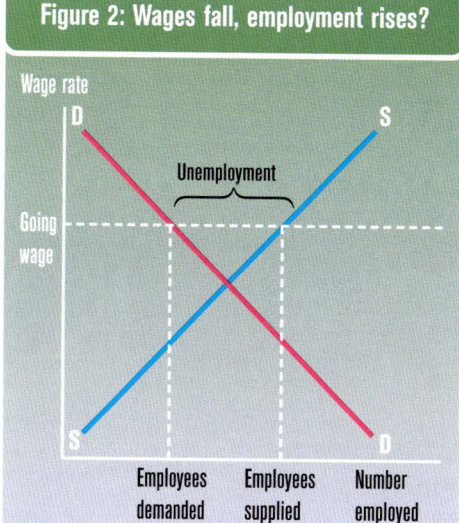

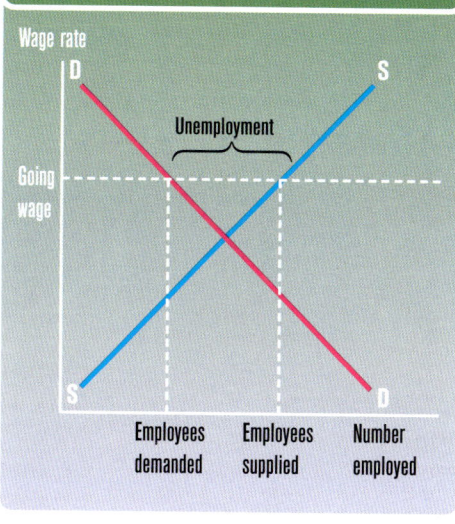

EVIDENCE

WHERE ARE THE JOBS?

Q1 In which areas of the UK is the demand for labour low?

Q2 In which areas is the demand for labour high?

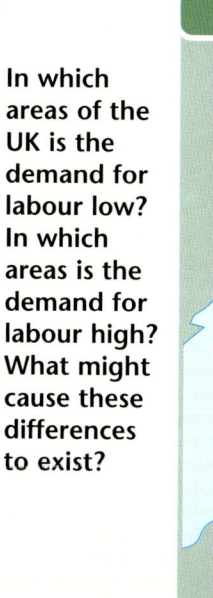

Q3 What might cause these differences to exist?

Figure 3: Unemployment in the UK, January 1995

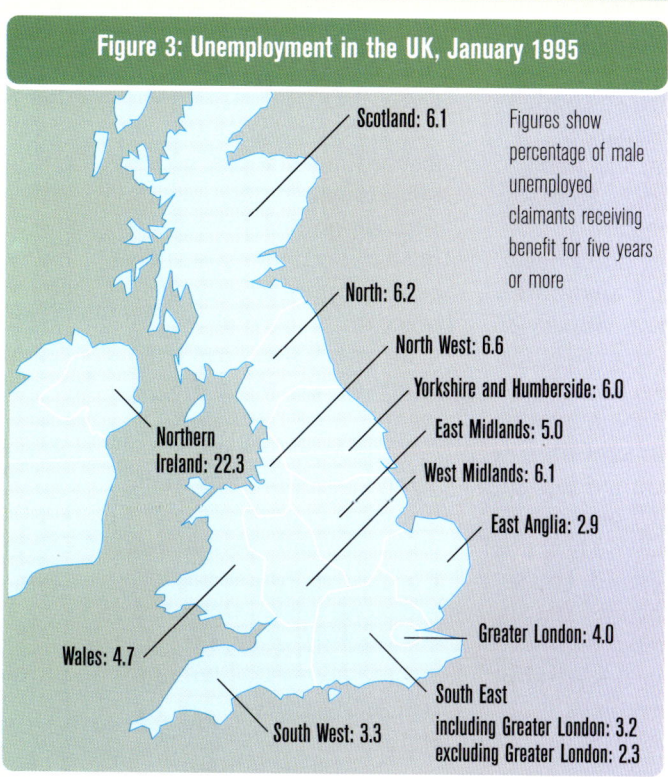

Figures show percentage of male unemployed claimants receiving benefit for five years or more

- Scotland: 6.1
- North: 6.2
- North West: 6.6
- Yorkshire and Humberside: 6.0
- East Midlands: 5.0
- West Midlands: 6.1
- East Anglia: 2.9
- Northern Ireland: 22.3
- Wales: 4.7
- South West: 3.3
- Greater London: 4.0
- South East including Greater London: 3.2 excluding Greater London: 2.3

CHECKPOINT

Draw a diagram to show what happens to bricklayers' wages when the building industry goes into decline.

KEY TERM

All those people who want to work are the supply of labour. All who want to employ them are the demand for labour. The two together make up the *labour market*.

Unit 2 — Work or what?
Enquiry 5: What does joblessness cost?

What a waste ...

EVIDENCE

Remember the people we met on page 70? We now continue their stories.

JAMIE (AGE 24)

'Most people would probably call me a waster. I call myself unfortunate. My school days were spent in Nottingham. Dad was an alcoholic and hadn't held down a job for years. Mum did her best to manage, but there were six of us and we were all a handful!

'I left home and assumed I'd find a job in the big city – that was eight years ago. It didn't work out. I lived rough, stole, begged and even had to be treated for TB. I didn't think anyone got that any more. Finally I did a stint inside.

'Now I sell *The Big Issue* and I've managed to sort myself out a bit. I suddenly realized that I couldn't go on the way I was for the rest of my life. I've got an old van and I sleep in that. I've started making a few honest pennies. Who knows what the future will bring?'

CHRISTOPHER PARKER'S SON, MICHAEL (AGE 16)

'When Dad lost his job he became very moody. The whole family put on an act whenever he was around – we tried to pretend everything was normal. The atmosphere was tense, we couldn't relax.

'It happened so suddenly we couldn't prepare ourselves for it. The bank closed his branch. So many people use the cash machines, they don't need to visit the bank any more. Computerization works well for some, but not for others.

'Fortunately, Mum had a job as a secretary in a local company. That kept the family going. I tried to stay away from the house as much as possible. My school work really suffered. Louise was worst affected – she did badly in her mock exams. She passed her A levels, but only just scraped into university.'

ANNE WEATHERBY (AGE 35)

'My children, Sarah and Richard, are still very young. I was divorced only recently and live on benefits – my ex-husband is unemployed and can't support the kids. It's going to be hard at Christmas when I can't afford all the things they want.

'The local hospital is always advertising for staff, but what with the cost of child care and the shift work, it would be impossible for me to go back. I don't like living off the state. I feel I've wasted all my training and my skills are becoming outdated.'

DR KASHIF SINGH (AGE 59)

'I was first made redundant four years ago. I worked as a Scientific Research Officer at British Aerospace. I had always thought that my job would be secure. I felt rejected and useless. It's difficult to describe the hurt that I felt.

'My wife, Kayuri, was so encouraging. She continued with her part-time work at the doctor's surgery. I used my redundancy money to pay off the mortgage and we saved the rest for "emergencies".

'I've had a variety of short-term jobs since, but I'm 59 now and I won't get anything full time. But I'm kept busy – I am Chairman of Governors at the local comprehensive school. I'm also a Justice of the Peace.

'I've learned not to worry so much about money and I have discovered that there's more to life than work!'

WE ARE ALL WORSE OFF ...

Not only does unemployment deprive a family of its livelihood, it also deprives the country of a valuable asset. If Jamie, Christopher, Kashif and Anne were working, they would be adding to the total output of the country, which is known as the **gross domestic product** (GDP). Unemployment therefore reduces the GDP. Also, if they were in work they would be paying taxes. The government loses these as well as having to pay **unemployment benefits**.

Three out of four of these people have qualifications that are not being put to good use, so the government's investment in education and training is being wasted.

WHAT DOES THE INDIVIDUAL LOSE?

Being unemployed affects the individual person, his or her family, and society as a whole. It is hard to understand why you've lost your job and it can lead to a wide variety of problems, as the evidence shows.

Living on benefits puts an individual into the poorest 20 per cent of society. In fact, most of the people in that group are on benefits. There is evidence to show that there is a strong link between poverty and ill health. Figure 1 shows that babies from poor families are less likely to survive than those from richer families. In the graph the population is divided up by social class. The unemployed are generally included in social classes 4 and 5, which are the semi-skilled and unskilled groups.

Education can also be affected. Children may have nowhere to do their homework and, if they are missing school through illness, they will find it hard to catch up. Once families are trapped in unemployment, it can be very hard to escape.

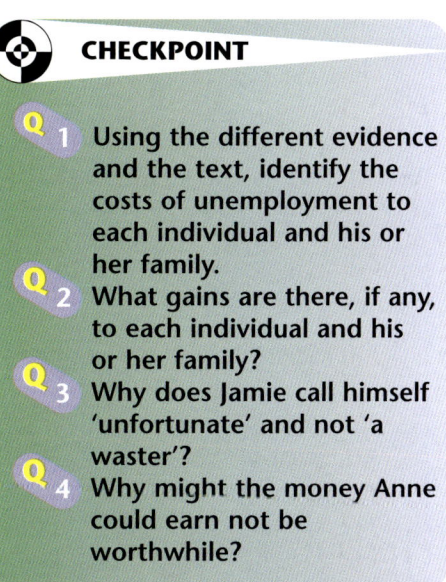

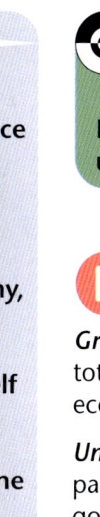

Figure 1: Infant death rates (by social class) in England and Wales, 1979–93

Death rate per 1,000 live births

Source: *Variations in Health*, Department of Health, 1995

CHECKPOINT

Q1 Using the different evidence and the text, identify the costs of unemployment to each individual and his or her family.
Q2 What gains are there, if any, to each individual and his or her family?
Q3 Why does Jamie call himself 'unfortunate' and not 'a waster'?
Q4 Why might the money Anne could earn not be worthwhile?

CHECKPOINT

List all the ways in which unemployment wastes resources.

KEY TERMS

Gross domestic product (GDP) is the total amount of all output in the economy in one year.

Unemployment benefit is the money paid to unemployed people by the government. This has been renamed 'the jobseeker's allowance'.

FORUM

What could be done to help Jamie? If he is going to get a job, what does he need? How might such help be provided?

Unit 2 **Work or what?**
Enquiry 5: What does joblessness cost?

What can the government do?

EVIDENCE

Government committed to increase unemployment benefit

New training schemes set up for young unemployed

Unemployment benefit cut to get people back to work

Job creation schemes for areas of high unemployment

INCENTIVES FOR YOUNG PEOPLE TO STAY AT SCHOOL

Q1 Explain how each of these strategies would help the unemployment situation.

Q2 What effect would each one have on government spending?

WHAT ARE THE SOLUTIONS?

Governments throughout the world are faced with the problem of unemployment. The headlines refer to government policies that might be used to get people back to work. In some countries few benefits are given in the hope that people will take whatever work is going. At the other extreme, some governments create jobs for everyone.

The evidence shows how very different countries have dealt with the problem.

All solutions have costs. Governments have to decide what is more important. Some may view unemployment as the most serious problem they face, while others have different objectives.

EVIDENCE

NEW ZEALAND: HELP YOURSELF

In 1990 the New Zealand government decided to cut the support it gave to the needy in an effort to save money, reduce taxes and encourage people to find jobs rather than depend on state handouts. Unemployment is down and there has been an increase in economic growth, but there are more people in poverty. In Wellington people queue outside charity shops giving away free food parcels, there are more homeless and families can be seen searching for food among rubbish bags outside supermarkets.

Q1 What has happened to:
(a) the level of unemployment; and
(b) the number of people living in poverty?

Q2 What has happened to the standard of living of people who found jobs?

EVIDENCE

CUBA: JOBS FOR ALL

Clive Anderson made a light-hearted TV documentary about Cuba, where the government decides what will be made and sold. Clive entered a motorway service station. There were no cars in the car park and the café was empty of customers. Clive ordered food from one of the four staff behind the counter. He was told that there was no food. He then ordered a drink, but was told that there were no drinks. This is an example of **underemployment** in a poor economy.

Q1 Who pays for the wages of these staff?
Q2 Are they likely to be well paid? Give reasons for your answer.
Q3 Do you think that the people working in the café have much job satisfaction?

EVIDENCE

TUNISIA: A RANGE OF SOLUTIONS

In Tunisia, the government pays people to do a number of necessary jobs such as street cleaning and laying pipes. These jobs are done with simple tools rather than using machines. Wages are low. By employing many people to do these tasks, the government is making more jobs available.

Tunisia also provides education for all children and is therefore helping to develop a better workforce for the future.

Q1 The government of Tunisia is paying people to keep them in work. How does this compare with New Zealand and Cuba?
Q2 In what ways will education help people to be employable in the future?
Q3 How will this help the country?

EVIDENCE

BANGLADESH: JOBS FOR A DEVELOPING COUNTRY

The country's population of 120 million is expected nearly to double by the year 2025. So job creation is a major concern in Bangladesh. At present, most people live in the countryside; the majority have no land.

Geoff Wood works for an organization that helps the country to develop. He has to be imaginative in his approach to creating more jobs: funds are limited. Small-scale projects based on individual villages have helped modernize farming. This has created jobs as more crops have to be planted, harvested, processed and marketed. The organization provides training and lends money to help people set up small businesses.

Successes include fish farms, irrigation services, rice processing, making honey, rearing goats and chickens, silk production and many others. The poor often work as groups, and some opportunities are taken by women. Geoff believes that this gives the rural poor additional strength when bargaining for higher wages or lower rents from their landlords.

Q1 What jobs are created by modernizing farming in Bangladesh?
Q2 How will these new jobs help the economy to grow?

LOOKING TO THE FUTURE

All these countries have different strategies for overcoming unemployment. The choices that are made will often depend on the political views of the government.

Many countries have now decided that high-quality education and training are key factors in making a country competitive in world markets. This encourages companies to expand and therefore creates more jobs.

FORUM

Businesses can set up anywhere in the world. In deciding where to locate production, what important factors will influence the decision makers?

K KEY TERM

Underemployment occurs when people have jobs but there is not enough work to fill their time.

Unit 2 Work or what?
Case study

Telephone exchanges

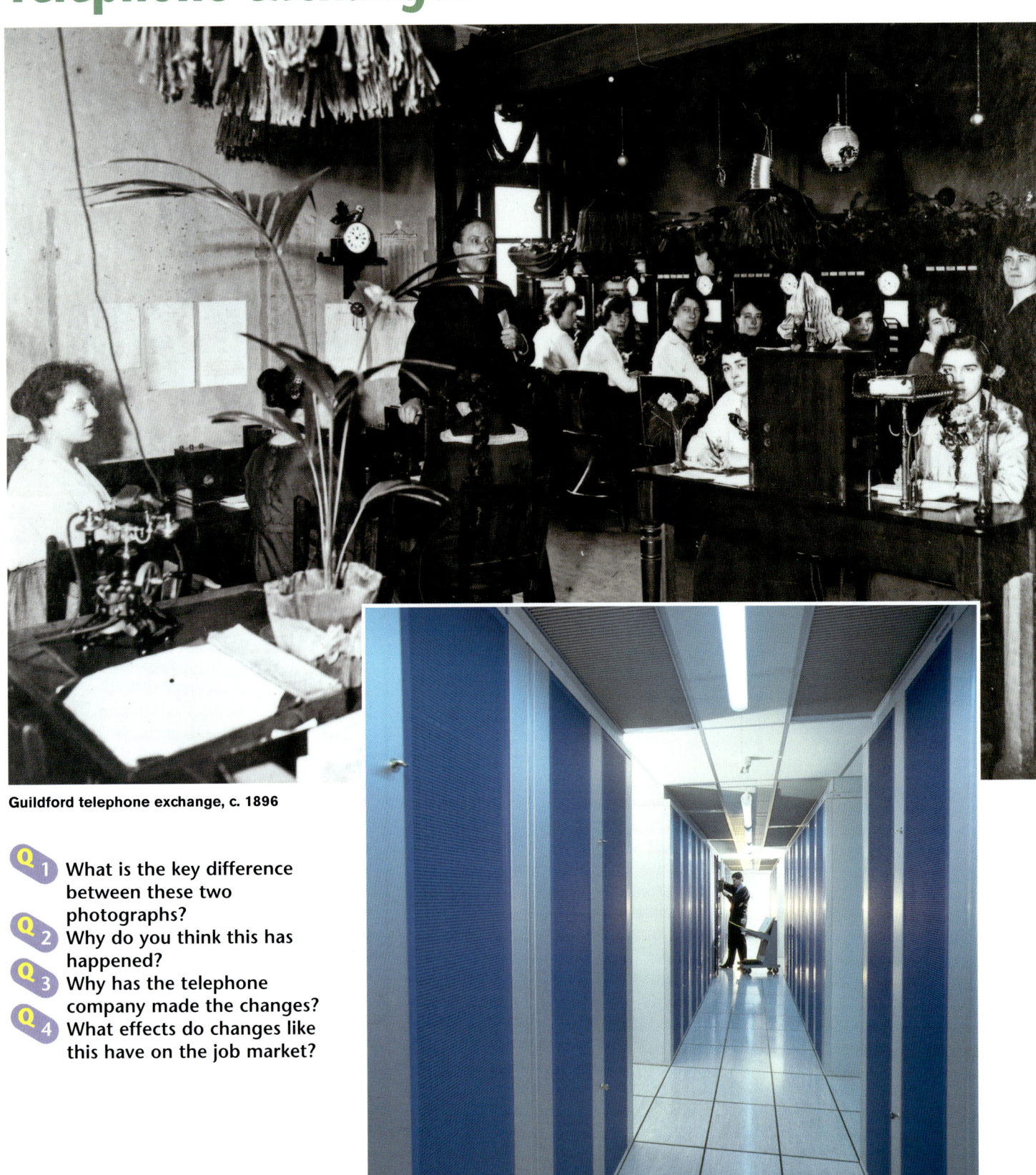

Guildford telephone exchange, c. 1896

Madley Communications Centre, 1992

Q1 What is the key difference between these two photographs?
Q2 Why do you think this has happened?
Q3 Why has the telephone company made the changes?
Q4 What effects do changes like this have on the job market?

Unit 3

Risk or certainty?

ENQUIRY 1: CAN PROFIT BE PLANNED?	80

Talking of profit — 80
Making a business plan

What is the plan? — 82
Exploring budgets, assets and the marketing mix

How much? — 84
Setting a price: cost-plus or competition?

Breakthrough? Breakdown? Breakeven? — 86
Calculating breakeven output

ENQUIRY 2: WHERE'S THE MONEY COMING FROM?	88

Have we got enough? — 88
Financing the business from internal sources

Who will help us? — 90
Borrowing and the costs of finance

Starting up — 92
Different ways of getting the business going

ENQUIRY 3: WHAT IS THE BOTTOM LINE?	94

How can we account for profit? — 94
Building up a profit and loss account

Striking a balance — 96
Making the balance sheet balance: T-form

Holding the balance — 98
Vertical balance sheets

Can numbers tell a story? — 100
Who needs to know? What the accounts mean

ENQUIRY 4: HOW CAN THE ODDS BE SHORTENED?	102

Consulting the customer — 102
Market research: all the sources

Catching the customers — 104
Thinking about marketing strategies

Can the cash keep flowing? — 106
Costs and cash-flow forecasts

Buying peace of mind — 108
How insurance can reduce risks

ENQUIRY 5: CAN WE RIDE THE ROLLER COASTER?	110

On the roller coaster — 110
All the features of the business cycle

Riding the roller coaster — 112
How businesses cope with the cycle

Prices Prices Prices — 114
Prices and inflation

Can the government rule the roller coaster? — 116
Economic policies

CASE STUDY: A RISK OR A CERTAINTY?	118

Unit 3 — Risk or certainty?

Enquiry 1: Can profit be planned?

Talking of profit

EVIDENCE

SANDWICH EXPRESS

Scene: The edge of an East Midlands village about 10 miles from Leicester. Jackie Harwood, Elaine Watton and Keith Ingham are sitting round the kitchen table at Jackie's mum's house on a dark November evening.

Jackie: 'I reckon we can sell them for £1.25 on average. Filled French sticks will be a bit more than that. It's what you call a gap in the market. We can go to the factories, warehouses and offices. I've only found two factories with their own canteen. Most people bring their own food. And a lot of lunch breaks are less than an hour.'

Elaine: 'When you're working out on the industrial estates, there's hardly anywhere to go for lunch. I've already talked to one personnel manager and he said we can park round the back and sell five-course lunches if we like. Thought he was being funny.'

Keith: 'Elaine and I have found a possible van. It's an H-reg Daihatsu. "Exceptional for year", it said in the ad. Offers on £1,200. Also Bridge Bakery are keen to be suppliers. I thought their prices were OK and they do good French bread.'

Jackie: 'The catering unit on the old airfield is definitely vacant. We can have it at £400 a month but it needs refitting. Looks horrible at the moment. Talking of which, I checked The Café des Sports and the food's grim. The place is full of cigarette smoke and very expensive.'

Keith: 'We'll get menus printed, order forms and a timetable for deliveries. Everyone I know thinks it's a great idea. We can't go wrong.'

Q1 Do you have a clear picture of how Sandwich Express will make a profit? What else would you want to know?

Q2 'We can't go wrong.' What would you say in reply?

HOW TO BE SURE

It is one thing to talk about a profit but another to make one. Every business venture needs a 'vision' or mental image of success. But real business is about the use of scarce resources. This has a cost and carries a risk. Will the product sell in a competitive market? After the expenses are paid, will there still be profit?

There is never any certain answer to these questions. All business tends to be risky. But think of an expedition to climb a mountain. That is also risky. Yet mountaineers reduce the risk by planning: teams, routes, schedules, provisions and emergency back-up. Business planning is based on exactly the same idea.

Sandwich Express may be successful but there is no guarantee. Jackie and her team needed to begin on some very careful research and planning.

EVIDENCE

SOME QUESTIONS TO ASK...

- What will be the product?
- Who are the customers?
- How large is the market?
- How strong is the competition?
- How will the product be promoted?
- How will the market be reached?
- What is the price?
- What are the prospects for growth?
- What are the legal constraints?

Source: adapted from *The Business Start-up Guide*, National Westminster Bank and Durham University Business School

BUSINESS PLANNING

The first step in business planning is to connect the vision with the market. All too often, one person's enthusiasm for a product is not shared by the people who may buy it. The process of finding out what people want and how much they are prepared to pay is called **market research**. The results of interviews and questionnaires should help to shape the planned product so that it fits the real picture of market demand.

In particular it is essential to study the competition. What will make the product special and distinguish it from similar products offered by competitors? Such a feature is called a **unique selling point** (USP) and helps to establish the firm's competitive advantage.

Once these things are decided, the team will be able to start work on a business plan. As well as describing the key features of the product, the business plan should cover:
- how to price the product;
- how to promote the product;
- where to sell the product.

Like any preparation for the future, a business plan has to make estimates and assumptions about what will happen over the months ahead. The estimates for sales, revenues, costs, profit and financial needs are called a **budget** and usually cover a period of 12 months.

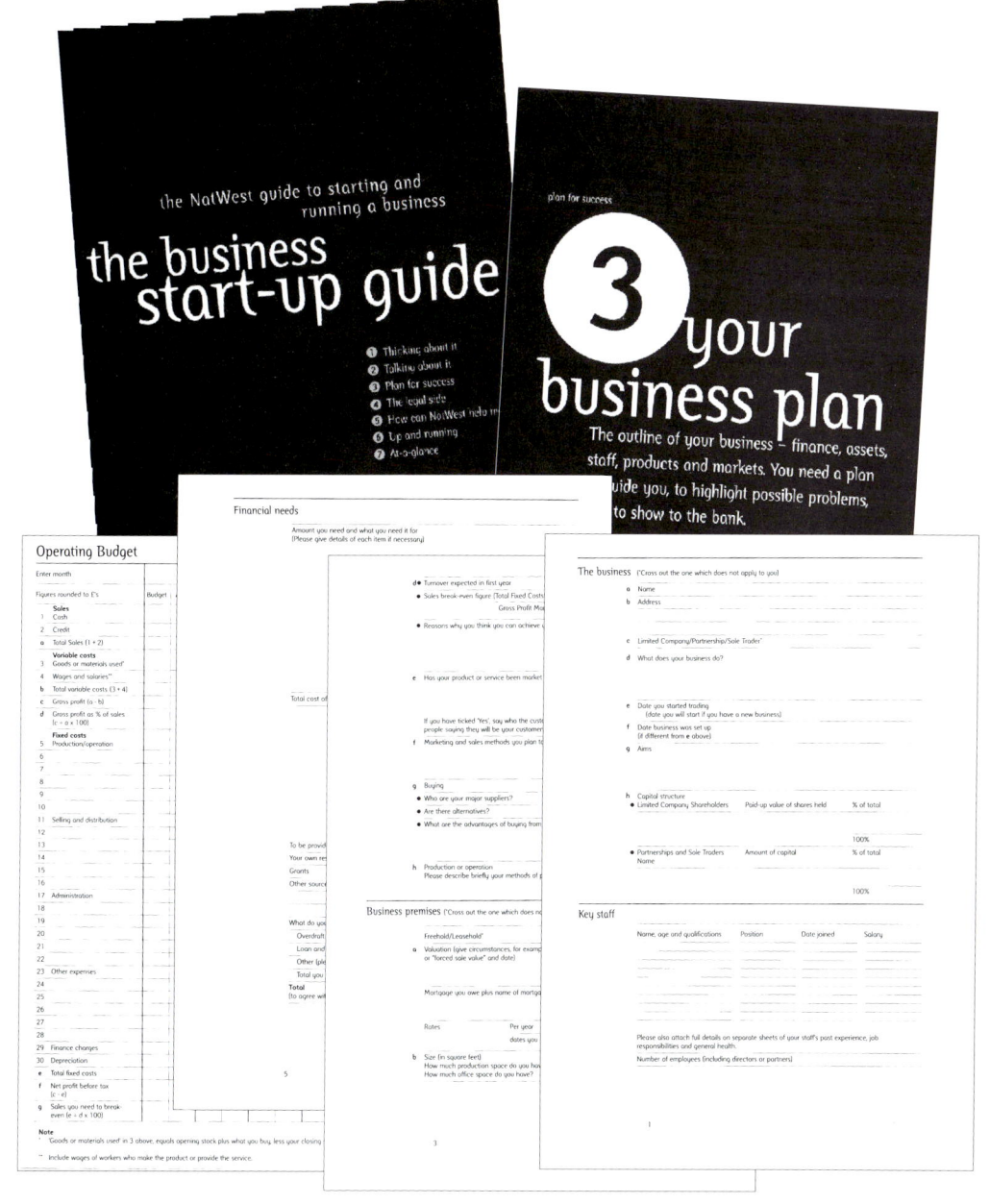

CHECKPOINT

WHAT'S WRONG?

The Drummonds own and run a bakery in a small Shropshire town. They are now losing customers to the new superstore that has opened on the by-pass. Mrs Drummond's answer is to convert a storeroom into a café offering lunches and teas. It will need a £5,000 loan from the bank but she feels that her regular customers will appreciate sitting down for a chat and a bite to eat.

Give Mrs Drummond your detailed advice:
- Is she right to think that customers will like a café?
- What will happen if she is wrong?
- Is there any way she could attract her customers back without needing such a large loan?

FORUM

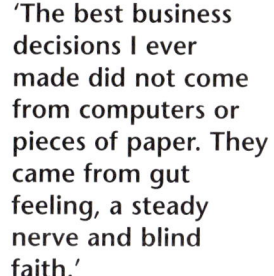

'The best business decisions I ever made did not come from computers or pieces of paper. They came from gut feeling, a steady nerve and blind faith.'
Owner of a successful antiques business.

How would you reply?

KEY TERMS

A budget is a forward-looking financial plan and is likely to include a cash-flow forecast.

Market research is the process of collecting, collating and interpreting information about the market for a product.

A *unique selling point* (USP) is a particular feature in the product or service that a firm offers its customers that sets it apart from competitors.

Unit 3 Risk or certainty?
Enquiry 1: Can profit be planned?

What is the plan?

EVIDENCE

SANDWICH EXPRESS – PUTTING TOGETHER A BUSINESS PLAN

1 THE BUSINESS
Name will be Sandwich Express. The main business activity will be the production and sale of sandwiches and other refreshments. The objective for the first 12 months is to establish a secure customer base and to cover all costs including wages. The aim is to establish an expanding and profitable business based on quality and customer loyalty.

2 KEY STAFF
Jackie Harwood, aged 24, who will be general manager and in charge of sales.

Keith Ingham, aged 25, who will be responsible for transport, stores, finance and legal affairs.

Elaine Watton, aged 22, who will control production.

All staff will help with production and sales as necessary.

3 PRODUCT RANGE
Sandwiches, toasted sandwiches, French sticks, and hot and cold drinks. Available to order and over the counter. Supplied by van.

4 MARKETING
The menus will be distributed to target workplaces. Menu collection will be by van every morning when breakfast snacks will be sold over the counter. Orders will then be relayed to the kitchen by mobile phone. Distribution will be over the lunch period, from 11.30 a.m. to 1.30 p.m.

Our survey shows that there are at least six substantial employers ready to co-operate. The customers are likely to be people of all types and backgrounds; young women working in factories and offices will be particularly important at lunchtime, and the breakfast trade will need to cater for early morning workers with big appetites.

With low overheads, prices can be very competitive yet still allow real quality.

The USPs will be quality and convenience. The sandwiches will be generously filled with good ingredients. They will arrive fresh and to order.

WORKING THINGS OUT

The basic business activity needs to match the skills or interest of the owners. As well as a broad aim, it is important to have specific objectives and these are made more exact through the budget projection.

The quality of staff is often the deciding factor in the success or failure of a business venture. It is vital that each person's responsibilities are clear and that they have sufficient skills for the job. The business plan needs to provide detailed information on this.

Marketing is likely to be the least well prepared part of a business plan, although it may turn out to be the most important. There is a particular danger of 'wishful thinking', where the real needs of customers have not been properly researched, nor has the strength of competition been recognized.

An effective marketing programme will have a number of strands: together these are known as the **marketing mix**. There will be careful attention given to the nature of the **product**. There will also be a plan for **promotion**, which includes all kinds of advertising and packaging. **Price** is important, too: fixing the price too high or too low will spell disaster. Finally, attention must be given to **place**: the way the product is distributed. Together these four elements in the marketing mix are known as the **4Ps**.

EVIDENCE

SANDWICH EXPRESS
– THE BUSINESS PLAN CONTINUED...

Q1 What might be included in the administrative costs?

Q2 What is the profit margin?

---

5 PREMISES, EQUIPMENT AND VEHICLES
Catering unit to be rented at £400 per month. Equipment, fittings and utensils will cost £1,500.

6 FINANCIAL NEEDS
£1,000 to be provided by each key member of staff. A loan of £2,000 to be requested from the Co-operative Bank.

7 BUDGET (MONTHLY FOR NEXT 12 MONTHS)

Assumptions

Sales (per week)
1,200 sandwiches (all types) at average £1.25 each = £1,500

Sales (per month)
£1,500 × 4 = £6,000

Costs include:
Wages at £200 per week or £800 per month
Materials at average £0.45 per sandwich inc. packaging
Rent at £100 per week or £400 per month (an administrative cost)

	£	£
Projected sales revenue		6,000
less cost of sales		
Supplies and materials	2,160	
Labour costs (3 × £800)	2,400	4,560
Gross profit		**1,440**
less overheads		
Rent	400	
Administrative costs	600	1,000
Operating profit		**440**

COVERING ALL THE ANGLES

The budget outlines the current, day-to-day costs and revenues. It does not include the capital investment that is needed when the business starts up.

Many small firms rent rather than buy premises. This avoids the need for finding a large capital sum and allows flexibility as the business develops. The financial needs of Sandwich Express are therefore limited to the purchase of equipment and the money necessary to run the business from day to day. Things of value that are owned by the firm are called **assets**.

The budget is based on estimates. Sales revenue could easily be lower or higher than expected. This is where good market research helps. Costs are more predictable but most expenses can increase or turn out to be higher than expected.

In reality, a business plan needs to be much more detailed than the example above. Even then it cannot guarantee business success. But it can reduce risk. Among firms failing after one year, the great majority do not have a proper business plan. A plan is also a valuable basis for management and control.

CHECKPOINT

The sales at Sandwich Express turn out to be 10 per cent lower than expected.

Q1 How likely do you think this outcome is?

Q2 What would be the effect on the company's profit and on their profit margin?

FORUM

Sandwich Express intends to show this business plan to the bank when applying for its £2,000 loan. As the bank manager, what comments would you have?

KEY TERMS

Assets refer to everything owned by a firm that has a money value.

The *marketing mix* is the combination of product, promotion (e.g. advertising), place (distribution) and price that is designed by a firm to achieve its sales target. It is often remembered as the *4Ps*.

Promotion includes all kinds of advertising, free gifts and other incentives to purchase.

Place refers to the distribution channels which may be used to market a product. Different ways of retailing are possible, including mail order, for example.

Unit 3 Risk or certainty?

Enquiry 1: Can profit be planned?

How much?

EVIDENCE

THE CHOCOLATE BOX

The Chocolate Box is a small shop in a country town near Hereford. Its owners, Tom and Betty Ginn, sell chocolates, local crafts and greetings cards.

'We concentrate on quality and personal service,' says Tom, 'but we can't ignore price.'

'Generally our mark-up is 50 per cent,' explained Betty, 'but it's nearer 80 per cent on cards and 100 per cent on the crafts.'

Asked about supermarkets, Tom says: 'They're only fairly small here and we don't worry too much about their prices. We offer something different.'

PRICE AND VALUE

We have already seen that some products sell mainly on quality and others mainly on price. Petrol often sells on price: most people can't tell the difference between one brand and another, so they stop where the petrol is cheapest, unless they are in a hurry, when they may be prepared to pay a bit more for convenience. Belgian chocolates, on the other hand, sell on quality. They are expensive anyway, and having decided to buy them, many people will not think too much about the price.

However, even where buyers are wanting quality, they still care about price. In any market, price affects:
- the buyer's value for money
- the seller's profit.

If the price is low, the buyer gets better value for money but the firm gets less profit. It may still make good sense for the firm, because a high level of sales will be the outcome. (Remember Kwik Save, with its small profit on a high level of sales?) In contrast, Tom and Betty Ginn get a high level of profit on cards. People are willing to pay the price in order to get a card that appeals to them. Finding the right price depends very much on the type of product and the situation in which it is sold.

COST-PLUS PRICING

Although in some countries people bargain, in Britain customers expect to be told the price. So how does a firm set its price? One approach is called **cost-plus pricing**. Suppose a card costs Betty 50p. She expects to make 100 per cent profit, so the amount to be added on is 50p, giving a price of £1.

The percentage that is added on to costs is called a **mark-up**. This is not the same as a profit margin. In this example the margin is 50p also, but to calculate the margin we take profit as a percentage of sales, and that is 50 per cent. So the mark-up is 100 per cent, while the profit margin is 50 per cent.

Mark-ups are a very convenient way to set prices. The percentage can be varied to take account of what customers are prepared to pay. Betty found customers were prepared to pay more for cards than for other things, so she simply set a higher percentage mark-up.

EVIDENCE

CLIFF END BED AND BREAKFAST

Cliff End is a tall Victorian villa where a bed and breakfast business is run by Rachel and David Pooley.

'It really is at the cliff end,' explains Rachel. 'There are five other people doing B&B in Cliff Road and we're the last.'

When asked about how they set prices, David smiles. 'We don't set them. They're set for us. There's what you might call a going rate for B&B in this town – about £15. Cliff Road has good sea views so it's £16 per person. All six of us charge more or less the same. We tried £17.50 per night for a month last year but being last in the road, we never stood a chance. Three-quarters of the rooms were empty.'

Q1 Do Rachel and David Pooley have any choice about their pricing policy?

Q2 What other kinds of business can you think of which might find that there is a 'going rate' for their product?

Q3 What is the difference between Tom and Betty Ginn's way of pricing their products, and Rachel and David's?

COMPETITIVE PRICING

Using mark-ups suits some businesses. With others, pricing has to start with the competition. This is usually essential when there is little difference between the products of competing firms. Bed and breakfast in the same road is one example. Petrol in the same town or area of a city is another.

Firms find out about one another's prices. Often a survey is made of the prices of similar products, and a price is chosen that is very close to those of the other firms. This is called **competitive pricing** because the price is competitive with those of alternative sales outlets. Prices tend to get pushed down towards 'rock bottom', i.e. a point very close to what it costs the business to supply the product.

Each firm is tempted to protect or expand its market share by slightly undercutting its competitors. This makes other firms want to retaliate by cutting their prices. The outcome is good for the customer but profits will be low.

To solve this problem, a business may try to persuade customers that its product has special features that make a slightly higher price worth paying. For example, Cliff End emphasizes its home cooking and its baby-sitting service. In effect these are the Pooleys' unique selling points. But with similar products in competitive markets, it is difficult to raise prices very far above the 'going rate'.

CHECKPOINT

Granny's Kitchen produces fudge and sells it to shops in 200g bags. The current budget shows variable costs running at 60p per bag with projected output at 1,000 bags per month. Fixed costs on a monthly basis are estimated at £200. The business applies a 60 per cent mark-up.

Q1 How much do shops pay per 200g bag?

Q2 How might Granny's Kitchen respond if a local rival began selling similar fudge to shops at 99p per 200g bag?

FORUM

'Firms can talk about quality. But in the end it is price that sells. Trimmings never made a turkey.'

Do you agree?

KEY TERMS

Competitive pricing means the business uses prices of similar products as the basis for setting its own price.

Cost-plus pricing means deciding price on the basis of total cost plus a percentage profit.

Mark-up is a percentage addition to the cost of a product that determines its selling price and profit element.

Risk or certainty?

Unit 3

Enquiry 1: Can profit be planned?

Breakthrough? Breakdown? Breakeven?

EVIDENCE

MEMORY MUGS

A disused brewery is not where you would expect to find a pottery, but that is where Mo Hammid has his small workshop. Here he makes mugs that are individualized for each customer. Designs and lettering are carefully applied to order. Some people want the name of a child or relative. Others want an event commemorated – birthdays, weddings, anniversaries.

Because the mugs are customized, Mo charges a standard price of £7.50. The variable costs involved – materials, power and labour – work out at £4.50 per mug. Overheads or fixed costs are heavy and run at about £300 per month. A maximum of 200 mugs could be made in any month.

Q1 What is Mo's unique selling point?

Q2 How could you calculate the number of mugs that must be sold so that the business exactly covers its costs, making no loss and no profit?

Q3 If 160 mugs are produced and sold every month, what will be the total profit?

BREAKEVEN

It is important for any business to have a clear picture of how output and sales will affect profit or loss. In particular, it is significant to know the level of sales necessary to avoid any loss. This is called the **breakeven point**. These calculations are often included in a business plan as an extension of the budget.

Fixed and total costs for Memory Mugs are shown in figure 1.

The broken line to the right is labelled 'capacity'. This means that the maximum number of mugs that the pottery could produce in one month is 200. So far the diagram or 'model' only tells us about money leaving the firm. The next step is to add a line representing sales revenue, or money coming into the firm. This is the level of sales multiplied by price and is called **total revenue** (TR). If a single price is charged, the line is easy to draw. If zero products are sold, revenue will be zero. The TR line therefore always starts at the origin. If the maximum output is sold, then the total revenue will be 200 x £7.50 = £1,500. This provides the second point for the TR line shown in figure 2.

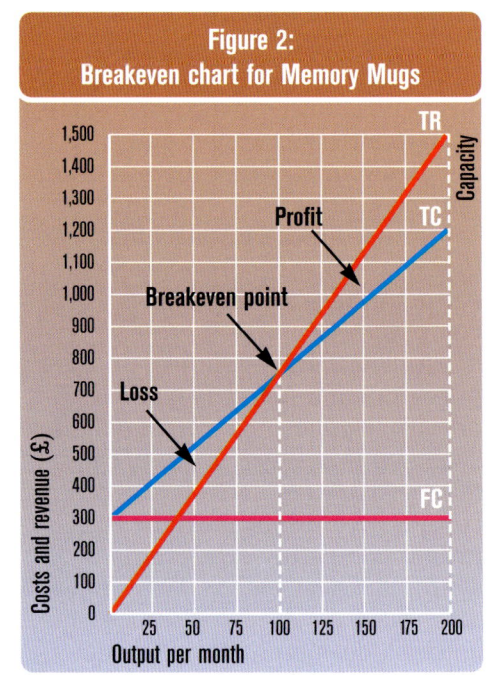

Look closely at the wedges marked 'profit' and 'loss'. While total cost (TC) is more than total revenue, a loss must be the result. Once total revenue is more than total cost, then a profit will be made. At the point where TR = TC, there is no profit or loss: this is the breakeven point. Supposing current sales are 160 mugs per month. Total revenue is greater than total cost, sales are above the breakeven level, and a profit is made.

Figure 1: Memory Mugs: fixed costs (FC) and total costs (TC)

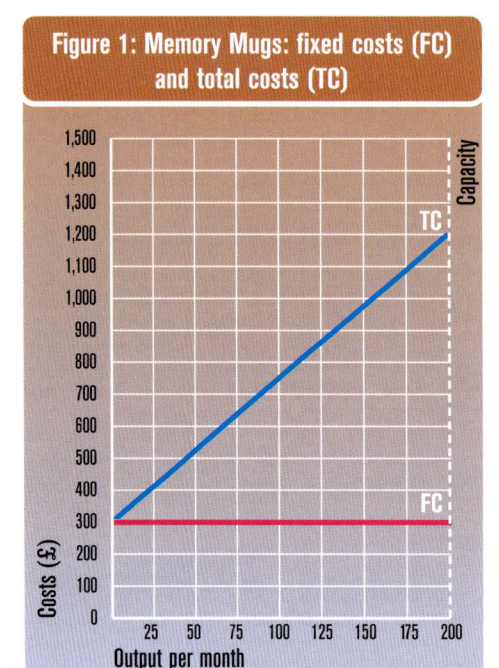

Figure 2: Breakeven chart for Memory Mugs

86

EVIDENCE

Bad news for Memory Mugs has arrived in the post. The owners of the old brewery want a sharp increase in the rent. Mo's fixed costs are likely to rise to £360 per month. As a result, the breakeven level of output will rise and profit will fall.

What is the best course of action? One possibility is an increase in price. Suppose that the mugs were priced at £8.50? Would this protect profits?

Q1 At the current price of £7.50, what would be the new monthly profit after the rise in fixed costs?

Q2 If price were increased to £8.50 and sales were unaffected, what would be the new profit?

Q3 In practice, would sales be unaffected?

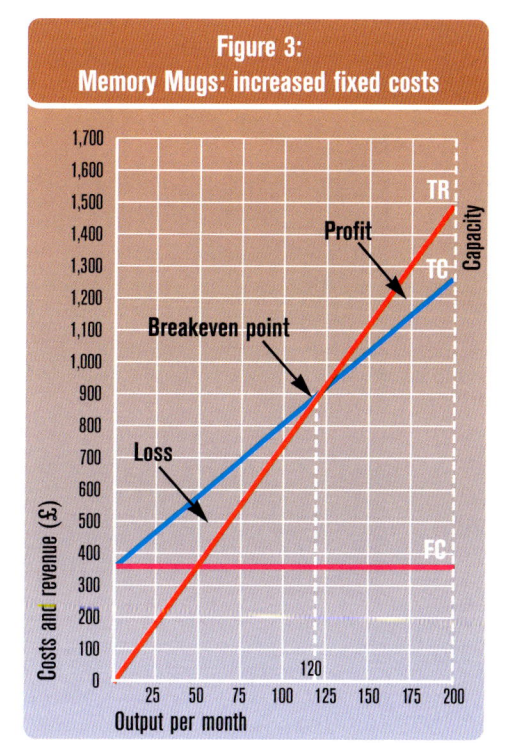

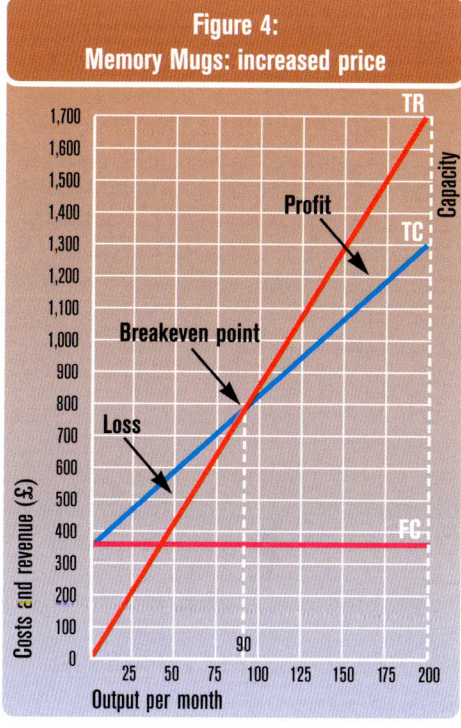

CHECKPOINT

Arctic Ices has monthly overheads of £1,200. The variable costs of producing an ice cream are 30p and the current selling price is 60p. Last month the company sold 3,000 ices.

Comment carefully on the company's performance. What steps do you think the sales manager should consider?

KEY TERMS

Breakeven point occurs where total cost is equal to total revenue.

Total revenue is the number of items sold multiplied by the selling price.

Figure 3: Memory Mugs: increased fixed costs

Figure 4: Memory Mugs: increased price

AN INCREASE IN COSTS

A breakeven chart is ideal for exploring problems of this type. The effect of an increase in fixed costs is to 'jack up' the firm's cost structure. The fixed cost line is now drawn at £360 instead of £300 per month. Variable costs are unaffected but total cost now starts from a £360 baseline. See figure 3.

The breakeven point has shifted. This means that the profit wedge starts later and is 'thinner' at Mo's original output of 160 mugs per month.

AN INCREASE IN PRICE

The effect of increasing price to £8.50 can now be explored. In figure 4 the total revenue line pivots upwards and now has a steeper gradient.

TR at zero sales is still zero but TR at 200 sales is now 200 × £8.50 = £1,700. The profit wedge starts earlier and is 'fatter' again. Mo's breakeven point has moved back to 90 mugs and profit is up sharply at higher levels of output.

Many other changes can be explored on a breakeven chart. Business managers can project the likely effects of changes in the costs or prices of their products. However, a breakeven chart is only as good as the data on which it is based. In the real world costs do not move in a straight line, while the output of a firm will not necessarily all be sold at any given price.

Unit 3 — **Risk or certainty?**

Enquiry 2: Where's the money coming from?

Have we got enough?

EVIDENCE

Paul and Patti Goldsmith own their own cane furniture business. They started trading in 1982 from a small shop in an arcade in Leicester. The business became very successful in the 1980s and they were able to move to a larger shop in 1990. They would now like to open a second shop in another part of Leicester. In 1990 they had financed the move by increasing the mortgage on their house, but they are reluctant to do this again. Both Paul and Patti saw many of their fellow traders go bankrupt in the early 1990s when interest rates increased and they don't want to borrow money from the banks.

FINANCE FOR SMALL BUSINESSES

All businesses want to invest from time to time. They may want to set up new production facilities or a sales outlet. They may be developing a new product or improving their organization. But all these things have to be paid for and finance will have to be obtained. Sometimes funds can come from inside the firm itself.

All businesses have assets: these include anything that provides benefits over a period of time. A business that has retained profits from earlier years has cash assets, which can be used immediately for spending on new projects. These retained profits are known as an **internal source of finance**; it will be easier to raise finance when profits are good. But for small businesses the amount of money available from retained profits may be limited – 90 per cent of the UK's businesses are small and employ fewer than ten people; they are mostly sole owners (sometimes known as sole traders).

ASSETS AND LIQUIDITY

Many small businesses suffer from having assets that cannot easily be changed into cash. In other words, they may be successful but there just isn't a lot of cash to invest. Another way of putting this is to say that the business does not have enough **liquidity**.

Small businesses are often owed quite large sums of money by their **debtors**. Debts are an asset that can be turned into cash. But if the company has had to pay its bills before its debts have been paid, it may be very short of cash. So getting the debts paid may be a good way to increase liquidity and raise finance.

CHECKPOINT

Paul and Patti's business suffers from customers who sometimes do not pay for the furniture they have bought. They have been offered help from a finance company, which has suggested giving Paul and Patti 80 per cent of all the money they are owed. The finance company will then try to get the money owed from Paul and Patti's debtors. If the company can get more than 80 per cent of the outstanding debt, then Paul and Patti will receive half of this extra money.

Table 1: Profit and loss?	
Cost of making the furniture	£12,000
Money owed to Paul and Patti	£20,000
Amount offered by finance company	£16,000

Paul and Patti could receive an additional £2,000, if the finance company is successful in recovering all the £20,000 that is outstanding.

Q1 What sources of finance may be available to Paul and Patti?

Q2 What advantages and disadvantages do you think each of the different sources of finance might have?

Q3 Looking at the figures in table 1, do you think it is a good idea for Paul and Patti to accept the offer from the finance company?

EVIDENCE

In 1994 Manchester United plc made £11.4 million profit. This money was used to finance investment in new players and a new stand, and also to pay dividends to the shareholders. This £11.4 profit was partly due to the club's winning the Premier League Championship for the second year in succession, the FA Cup and the Charity Shield. Not all football clubs are so financially successful and many well-known clubs have difficulty raising the finance they need to fund their investments.

Q1 How could a less successful football club raise finance using its own resources?

Q2 Compare the situations of Paul and Patti and Manchester United. In what ways are they different?

FORUM

If you borrow money from someone else for your business, whether from a bank or a friend, you have to pay interest. This means there is a cost involved in borrowing money. Are there any costs involved if you use your own money to expand the business?

KEY TERMS

Debtors are people and organizations that owe the business money.

Dividends are part of the profits made by the company and paid to shareholders.

Internal sources of funds come from the operations of the business, e.g. past profits.

Liquidity is the ability of the business to change assets into cash quickly. A factory is not a liquid asset but debtors may be.

OTHER INTERNAL SOURCES

It is sometimes difficult for businesses to raise finance from internal sources that depend on retained profits. Companies can decide to pay lower **dividends** to shareholders and keep back more of the profits for expanding the business. This can be risky as the shareholders may not be happy with smaller dividends and may be tempted to sell their shares. If a number of shareholders in a public limited company sell their shares then the price of the shares will fall, reducing the value of the business. So any move to reduce dividends needs to be explained carefully to shareholders.

A football club can consider selling one of its players. This is really the sale of an asset, which is a possibility for all businesses trying to raise finance. Some businesses can sell some of their assets and rent them back. In this way they can still use the assets, such as a factory or a football ground, but have the benefit of a large sum of cash. The business will, of course, have to pay a charge for continuing to use the asset.

Unit 3

Risk or certainty?
Enquiry 2: Where's the money coming from?

Who will help us?

EVIDENCE

EXPORT SUCCESS

Allan Finlayson owns and runs a small business which gives advice to clients on how to sell their products in overseas markets. He works from his home on the southwest coast of Scotland. At present his small sales team of three can cope with the needs of existing clients. The business was established in 1988, and the owner is now thinking about expanding as a number of new customers are seeking his advice. Any expansion would mean adding an extra room to the house, from which the business operates. Although there is space in the garden for this work to take place, Allan is uncertain whether it is a good idea.

Q1 What factors should Allan take into account before deciding to expand the business?
Q2 In general, why do businesses try to expand?
Q3 Are decisions to expand affected by what sources of finance are available?
Q4 Does it make any difference that Allan works from home?

EXTERNAL SOURCES OF FINANCE

The decision to expand depends partly on the costs of financing the expansion. When businesses do not have enough of their own savings from past retained profits, they are forced to look to **external sources of finance**. This may mean issuing shares or taking out a **bank loan**.

Taking on a loan involves **risks**. Who will lend the money? Are the repayments affordable? Will the business investment be profitable? What happens if the business cannot repay the loan? For a sole owner there is an additional worry: what happens if he or she is ill? This uncertainty is part of the normal worry of running a business. There are ways of reducing some risks. Forecasting and planning ahead will help decide whether a particular investment is a good idea. Many organizations that lend money, such as banks, will help small businesses to plan ahead to see if they can afford to take the risk.

Having decided to borrow money for an investment, all businesses need to ensure that the loan meets their requirements. Not only should the business consider how much to borrow, but it should also consider the **interest rate**, how long it will be before the loan has to be repaid, and what security is needed by the lender.

CHECKPOINT

Table 1: Two schemes for financing expansion

Amount borrowed in 1995 (£)	Repayments each year (including interest)					
	1996	1997	1998	1999	2000	
20,000	5,000	5,000	5,000	5,000	5,000	Scheme 1
20,000	6,000	6,000	6,000	6,000		Scheme 2

We looked above at whether Allan Finlayson should expand his business. The bank has offered him two ways of financing the expansion of the business and has sent him the information in table 1.

What should Allan consider when trying to decide which of the two bank loans is better for his business? What would you advise him to do?

EVIDENCE

In 1994 Manchester City Football Club, a public limited company, reported a £6 million loss on its activities. One of the consequences of this loss was that shareholders did not receive a dividend in 1994. To overcome the financial problem and inject some more money into the club, the business decided to:
- borrow £3.25 million; and
- issue a large number of extra shares.

Q1 What would happen if the club continued to make losses in future years?

Q2 How does Manchester City's situation compare with that of Allan Finlayson?

CHECKPOINT

Borrowing money can be an expensive business. Sometimes there are too many risks involved and the costs are too high to make it worthwhile expanding a business. Look at the following data and explain whether you think it is a good idea for Churchill's Newsagents to expand the business.

Buying and fitting a new shop will cost £200,000 and this should increase the profits by £20,000 per year, provided the new shop is as successful as the other outlets. Churchill's is considering using part of the 1995 profits to buy this new shop. The alternative is to leave the money at the bank where the interest rate is currently 6 per cent.

Profit for Churchill's Newsagents in 1995 £300,000

FORUM

Large businesses, which are well established, can often borrow money at a lower rate of interest than small businesses because of the risks involved. How does this affect small businesses?

THE COSTS OF FINANCE

Very few businesses can finance all their growth and development from their own money. They often seek help and assistance from a range of external sources. Small businesses can take advantage of **overdraft** facilities, bank loans and **hire purchase** arrangements, though with all these interest must be paid out of future sales revenue. Whatever the source of loan finance, there are the costs of repaying the loan as well as the interest charges.

Larger companies have access to the same external sources of funds as small businesses. Public limited companies can also raise money by issuing shares to existing or new shareholders. Although normally shareholders expect a dividend every year, if the business makes a loss in one year, a dividend need not be paid. Interest is payable however poor the profits may be. Also, with shares there is no need to repay the amount raised.

KEY TERMS

A *bank loan* is a long-term loan from the bank that is always agreed in advance.

External sources of finance provide funds which come from outside the business, e.g. a bank loan.

Hire purchase involves a business or an individual buying an asset over a long period. Each month a regular payment is made until, by the end of the period, the whole amount is paid and the business owns the asset.

Interest rates give the annual cost of a loan, e.g. 12 per cent of the loan has to be paid each year as a charge for borrowing the money.

An *overdraft* is a temporary loan from a bank. This allows the business to borrow exactly the amount needed at any one time, up to an agreed limit.

Risk is a measure of the likely success of a business venture or initiative.

Unit 3 — Risk or certainty?

Enquiry 2: Where's the money coming from?

Starting up

EVIDENCE

HAIR CONNEXIONS

Starting your own business involves challenges, particularly if you do not have your own money to use as **start-up capital**. Samantha Golding opened her own studio, Hair Connexions, in March 1993, having received financial support from the Prince's Youth Business Trust. Following her own market research she thought there was potential for a hair salon specializing in hair extensions. In her first year of trading turnover was £24,000, with a projected increase for future years. Of course, she had to convince the Trust that her plans were realistic.

Q1 What other sources of finance might have been available to Samantha?

Q2 What sort of skills will be needed to ensure that the business succeeds?

GETTING HELP

Getting someone to trust you and put money into your new idea is not easy. Despite this, thousands of people have set up their business, often without any security or **collateral**. There are organizations that are prepared to help you set up in business. Most of these organizations will charge you for lending you the money – after all, they are in business, too.

Some organizations, like the Prince's Youth Business Trust, which has helped over 25,000 disadvantaged young people with starting up and developing their own business, do not aim to make a profit from their activities. Financial help is also available from some government schemes such as Business Links, organized in collaboration with the local Training and Enterprise Councils in England and Wales. Even when you have gathered the finance together, it still takes a lot of effort, hard work and determination to get your business to succeed.

LIMITED LIABILITY

Any new business, if it is a company or a co-operative, has limited liability. This allows the shareholders or members to know that the amount they can lose, if all goes wrong, is limited to the amount of money they invested. This makes this type of business more popular for people thinking of investing in someone else's business. Every business, whether a sole owner, co-operative or company, needs profit to continue, not least because the owners expect a return from their investment.

People invest in companies mainly to earn a share of the profit. As well as receiving the dividend payments, shareholders hope that the value of their shares will rise as the company becomes more successful. There are therefore two ways that shareholders can benefit from having shares: the dividend and a rise in the value of the shares.

Shares in public limited companies are sold on the **Stock Exchange**. The value of these shares is listed every day in the financial pages of the national newspapers. This allows the shareholders to decide which shares to buy and when to sell so as to gain a profit. People who work for the Stock Exchange are able to make a profit by buying and selling shares on behalf of other people. They sell shares at a higher price than they paid for them. These people, called marketmakers, ensure that shareholders are always able to sell their shares whenever they want. So shareholders can always be sure that they can sell their shares if they need the money.

FORUM

Whenever a company becomes bankrupt the shareholders are not liable to pay the debts of the business. This is the advantage of limited liability. Why is limited liability an important feature of business organization?

EVIDENCE

OUT OF THIS WORLD

In November 1995 a new retail co-operative supermarket was launched in Bristol. The ethically based retailer aims to provide for the UK population that 'cares'. The product range has been chosen to meet six ethical principles: healthy eating; animal welfare; human welfare; environmental concerns; fair trade; and community development. The finance for this new venture in retailing was raised by the issue of shares to over 2,000 people; by contributing they become members of the co-operative.

A co-operative is owned by the people who work in a business or buy the products it sells. This type of business ensures that everyone has a say in how the business is organized and run. The owners, called members, all expect to make a profit. In the case of Out of This World, the managing director of the co-operative sums up its approach: 'Profit is important to Out of This World. It is not a primary objective but it is an essential condition of success.'

Source: adapted from *The Guardian*, 18 November 1995

Q1 What are the advantages of using a share issue to launch a business?

Q2 Why do you think this business has set up as a co-operative?

Q3 Would this type of approach have been of any use to Samantha Golding?

CHECKPOINT

Draw up a list of all possible sources of internal and external finance, showing which are appropriate for small and which for large businesses. Explain the advantages and disadvantages of each source of finance for (a) the business that needs the funds, and (b) the person or organization that provides the funds.

KEY TERMS

Collateral is security provided by a business just in case the business is unable to repay its loan, e.g. you may borrow some money against the security of the factory or office premises.

Start-up capital is the money originally invested in the business.

The *Stock Exchange* is a market for second-hand shares, where buyers and sellers arrange to exchange shares.

Unit 3

Risk or certainty?

Enquiry 3: What is the bottom line?

How can we account for profit?

EVIDENCE

OASIS

When Oasis appeared at Earl's Court in 1995 the concerts were the largest ever indoor shows in Europe. Tickets very quickly sold out. Quite clearly they were huge successes, not only for the band but also for their managers and promoters.

During 1995 Oasis became one of the biggest acts on the British music scene. A sell-out concert tour, a hit album and Top Ten singles, plus numerous appearances on radio and TV, all helped to generate a huge income – or revenue – for the band.

Q1 What *types* of cost would Oasis need to subtract from their revenue in order to calculate their profit? Give one example of each.

Q2 If you were a member of a band, how important would it be to you to make a profit?

PUTTING THE FIGURES TOGETHER

Like any enterprise, Oasis wants to make a profit. This means that over a period their revenue must exceed their costs.

What exactly generates revenue for the band? If you wanted to estimate Oasis's revenue from the Earl's Court concerts you might start by multiplying the average ticket price by the number of tickets sold. Then you would add the revenue from other concerts.

Add in sales of recorded music. For each CD or cassette sold, Oasis receive a royalty payment. There is revenue from T-shirts, mugs, calendars and other merchandise that carries the band's name and logo. There are fees received for TV and radio appearances. Together these would show total sales revenue or turnover.

What are the costs that will need to be subtracted before profit can be found? For the Earl's Court concert there would be the costs of printing the tickets, hiring Earl's Court and getting out the publicity. Going on tour involves costs such as the transport of equipment and the wages of road crews and electricians. Making albums and singles means using expensive studios and fees for producers and sound engineers. Merchandise must be purchased before the Oasis logo can be added. When all of these variable costs have been subtracted from total revenue, we have the band's **gross profit**.

It is fairly obvious, however, that there are other costs that must be taken into account. Like all bands, Oasis have teams of people who help to manage and promote them, and they have to be paid all the year round. Their telephones and the buildings in which they work cost money all the time, regardless of whether Oasis are playing a concert or not. These costs are overheads, fixed costs that must be paid regardless of sales. Once we deduct overheads from gross profit we are left with operating profit. This is best remembered by thinking that **operating profit** is all the revenue less all costs associated with running the operation.

All the time, looking over the shoulder of the business is the tax man! The Inland Revenue collects **corporation tax** from companies just as it takes income tax from people. So, once the operating profit has been worked out, tax has to be paid before what is left can be divided up between the owners.

Of course, accountants normally want to calculate profits for the whole year. This means adding up all the income earned in that period, and deducting all the costs. When all the subtotals have been included, this creates a **profit and loss account**.

In practice, the profit and loss account for a business as complex as Oasis would be difficult to describe briefly. The Evidence looks at Bluebird Toys. Figure 1 shows their profit and loss account and explains some of the terms.

K KEY TERMS

Corporation tax is the amount of tax companies pay on their profits.

Gross profit is sales revenue minus the costs of the actual production process (the variable costs).

Operating profit is the amount left after the costs of the actual production process and overheads have been taken away from sales revenue.

A profit and loss account shows all of a firm's revenues and costs over a period of time, usually one year.

EVIDENCE

Bluebird is a UK company that designs, makes and markets toys. It has grown into an international business, with factories in Hong Kong and mainland China as well as at Merthyr Tydfil in South Wales.

Over 60 per cent of Bluebird's sales are overseas, mainly in North America. Its leading brands are Polly Pocket and Mighty Max.

The toy business is highly competitive. In 1994 Mighty Morfin Power Rangers came on the market. They were a real challenge for Mighty Max. Even so, sales increased by 44 per cent overall, with an increase of 55 per cent in overseas sales and 30 per cent in the UK.

Increasing sales do not necessarily mean increased profits. Only by drawing up a profit and loss statement for the year will the company and its shareholders know if it has succeeded or not.

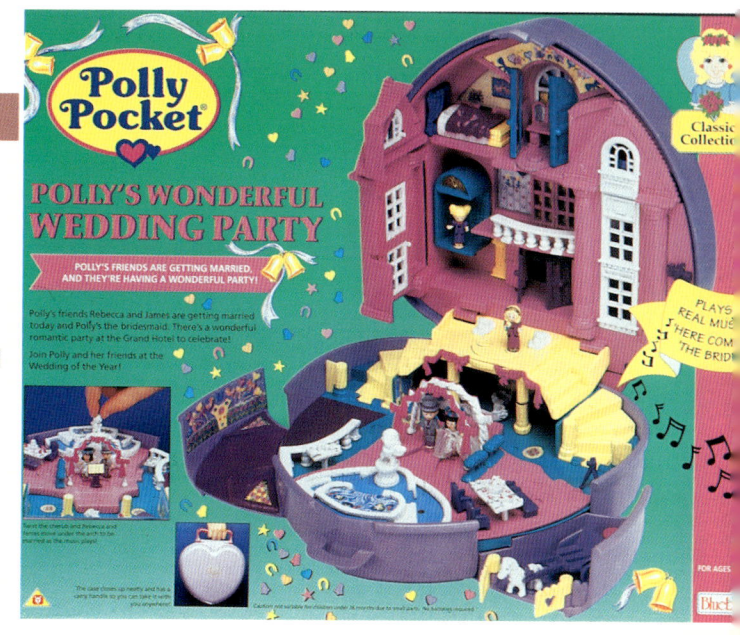

A profit and loss account shows the result of trading over a period, usually the year that has just gone by. This is the profit and loss account for Bluebird for 1994.

This shows Bluebird's performance in 1994. The figures are shown in thousands of pounds, so sales revenue is actually £99,416,000, not £99,416.

The cost of sales are the costs directly related to making and selling the products. All negative figures are in brackets to show that they should be taken off the figures that are above them.

Sales revenue is the amount of income Bluebird has earned from its sales over the year.

Overheads are costs that cannot be directly related to the production process.

Gross profit shows the difference between the costs of making or buying a product and the revenue from selling the product.

Operating profit is the amount left after the costs of the actual production process and overheads have been taken away from sales revenue.

Very often companies have other sources of income or expenditure that are not directly related to sales, such as interest which has to be paid on loans.

Like individuals, companies have to pay tax. This tax is called corporation tax.

After all the expenses have been paid, what is left of sales revenue can be either distributed to the shareholders – who own the company – or retained within the company for future expansion. Shareholders may be happy to see much of the profit after tax being retained, if this is better for the company, and for them, in the long run.

Figure 1

PROFIT AND LOSS ACCOUNT
for the year ended 31 December 1994

	£,000
Sales revenue	99,416
Cost of sales	(65,151)
Gross profit	34,265
Overheads	(14,923)
Operating profit	19,342
Interest receivable	847
Interest payable	(526)
Profit before taxation	19,663
Tax	(6,432)
Profit after taxation	13,231
Dividend	(3,533)
Retained profit	9,698

Source: Company accounts

CHECKPOINT

Q1 What was Bluebird's profit margin in 1994?

Q2 Which items in the profit and loss account would you use to help you decide whether the business was successful?

Q3 What might the retained profit be used for?

Q4 What other information would you want to have to help decide whether Bluebird was successful?

Unit 3 — Risk or certainty?
Enquiry 3: What is the bottom line?

Striking a balance

EVIDENCE

Bluebird is able to use the money that has been invested in the company by its shareholders. It also makes use of money borrowed from its bankers.

How is all this money actually used? The company occupies buildings on several valuable sites. It has bought machinery, computers, vehicles and other equipment. In addition, there is money tied up in stock, money owed to the company and money in their account at the bank.

Q1 Suppose Bluebird takes out an extra bank loan to pay for a new moulding machine. How would this affect the scales?

Q2 Explain simply why the scales in the picture must always balance.

BALANCE SHEETS BALANCE

Each year an **accountant** visits the firm to check the company's finances. The accountant who goes into the firm can make two lists. The first of these is headed 'Where did the money come from?' and the other answers the question 'Where is the money now?'

The first list shows the money the business has raised. We can distinguish two sources of money. First, there are the **shareholders' funds**. This is the money that the owners paid for their shares (**share capital**) plus all the profits retained in the business from previous years. Second, there is the money that has been borrowed. This is called **liabilities** because the firm is liable to repay its debts. We can divide the liabilities into long-term liabilities (due to be repaid in more than twelve months) and short-term liabilities (due to be repaid in less than twelve months). Shareholders' funds and liabilities are both given sub-totals, while the grand total tells us the amount of money that is financing the business.

The second list shows what has happened to the money. Every business enterprise owns many different items of value. We can separate these items into two clear groups. The first group includes items like buildings or machines that stay in the firm over a long period: these are called **fixed assets**. The second group consists of items like stock or cash that move through the business over fairly short periods: these are called **current assets**. The two groups are each listed with a sub-total. The grand total then tells us the value of all the assets in the business.

As we have asked the questions 'where did the money come from?' and 'where is the money now?', the total amounts of money are obviously the same. These two lists together are called a **balance sheet**, precisely because both lists, or two sides, always balance. This type of balance sheet, as shown in figure 1, is set out in **T-Form**.

Figure 1

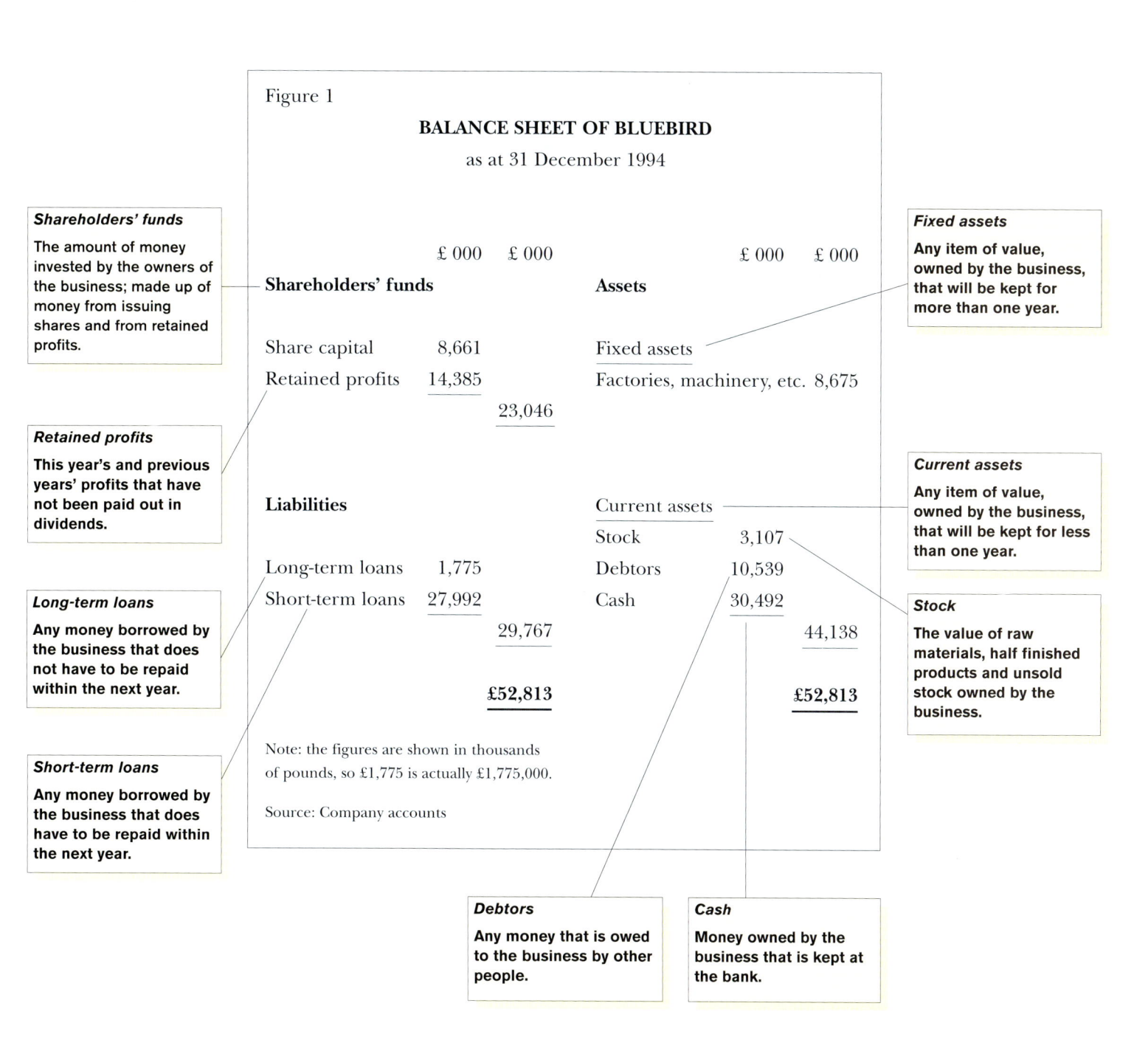

BALANCE SHEET OF BLUEBIRD
as at 31 December 1994

	£ 000	£ 000		£ 000	£ 000
Shareholders' funds			**Assets**		
Share capital	8,661		Fixed assets		
Retained profits	14,385		Factories, machinery, etc.	8,675	
		23,046			
Liabilities			Current assets		
			Stock	3,107	
Long-term loans	1,775		Debtors	10,539	
Short-term loans	27,992		Cash	30,492	
		29,767			44,138
		£52,813			**£52,813**

Note: the figures are shown in thousands of pounds, so £1,775 is actually £1,775,000.

Source: Company accounts

Shareholders' funds
The amount of money invested by the owners of the business; made up of money from issuing shares and from retained profits.

Retained profits
This year's and previous years' profits that have not been paid out in dividends.

Long-term loans
Any money borrowed by the business that does not have to be repaid within the next year.

Short-term loans
Any money borrowed by the business that does have to be repaid within the next year.

Fixed assets
Any item of value, owned by the business, that will be kept for more than one year.

Current assets
Any item of value, owned by the business, that will be kept for less than one year.

Stock
The value of raw materials, half finished products and unsold stock owned by the business.

Debtors
Any money that is owed to the business by other people.

Cash
Money owned by the business that is kept at the bank.

CHECKPOINT

Using the information above, rearrange the following numbers to create a balance sheet in the T-Form style. Show each of the four sub-totals as well as the grand totals.

Penge Plastics Ltd

Short-term liabilities	50,000
Debtors	23,000
Stock	6,000
Shareholders' funds	123,000
Machinery	56,000
Retained profits	45,000
Long-term liabilities	110,000
Factory	230,000
Cash	13,000

KEY TERMS

An *accountant* is a qualified individual who is responsible for checking the accuracy of a firm's financial statements.

A *balance sheet* is a legally required document showing a firm's assets, liabilities and capital. This must be produced at least once every year.

T-Form is the name given to the way of presenting a balance sheet with capital and liabilities on the left-hand side and assets on the right-hand side.

(Other key terms are defined in figure 1.)

Unit 3 Risk or certainty?

Enquiry 3: What is the bottom line?

Holding the balance

EVIDENCE

Bluebird is a public limited company. This means that shares can be bought and sold on the Stock Exchange by anyone who thinks they are worth it at the quoted price. Deciding whether they are worth it or not usually means looking at the firm's Annual Report and Accounts. This will include the profit and loss account, the balance sheet and a good deal of information that will be contained in the Notes to the Accounts and various reports.

Although Bluebird's balance sheet on page 97 was drawn up in the T-form, for technical reasons it is now required by law that public companies write the figures all in one column. This is called the vertical form of account, and is shown in figure 1.

Q1 Bluebird is now very profitable but in the early 1990s, when trading conditions were very difficult, it made large losses for two years in a row. How can a firm survive when it makes such losses?

Q2 What other information would you want to have, in addition to Bluebird's balance sheet, if you were going to assess Bluebird's performance?

VERTICAL FORM

It is important to remember that the vertical Balance Sheet uses exactly the same data as the T-form. The only difference is in the layout. However, the vertical pattern does show additional totals that help to assess the health of the company's finances.

On a day-to-day basis all firms need to pay for such items as raw materials, power and wages. A firm unable to pay these bills will go out of business – even though, in the long run, it may actually be profitable. It is important for managers, therefore, to be able to check that the firm has sufficient current assets to meet such needs.

Current assets move or circulate through the business over a short period. Some of these resources can be paid for using short-term loans (called **current liabilities**). The difference between current assets and current liabilities is called **working capital**. Working capital is shown in Figure 1.

You will remember that the balance in a T-form balance sheet is:

Shareholders' funds + All liabilities = **Total assets**

A vertical balance sheet also balances, for the same reason, but with current liabilities subtracted:

Shareholders' funds + Long-term liabilities = **Total assets less current liabilities**

The name given to shareholders' funds plus long-term loans is **capital employed**. We have seen that an important measure of a company's performance is Return on Capital Employed and thus the correct value for use in the formula is found in the balance sheet.

Finally look again at the share capital. The profits retained from earlier years are called **reserves**. This is money belonging to the shareholders that has been invested in the company. Surprisingly, it does not mean that the money is held 'in reserve'.

Although the figures in Balance Sheets appear to be precise, they are not. No one knows for sure how much Bluebird's factory, or its machinery are worth. Only if they were sold would that ever be known. Of course, estimates can be made, but accountants will have different opinions. In the same way, managers will have different opinions about employee relations or attitudes within the firm.

This means that accounting is not an exact science: there is no single right answer about how accounts should be drawn up. There are legal requirements and regulations, but there is also room for a great deal of variation. If you look at the accounts of several different public companies, you will find that they fit the general rules set out above, but they will also show several differences. Many people would like them to be easier to understand, so that ordinary members of the public would be able to interpret them.

Figure 1   **BALANCE SHEET OF BLUEBIRD**
as at 31 December 1994

	£ 000	£ 000
Assets		
Fixed assets		8,675
Current assets		
Stock	3,107	
Debtors	10,539	
Cash	30,492	
	44,138	
Total assets		52,813
Liabilities		
Short-term loans		
Amounts falling due within one year	(27,992)	
Working capital		16,146
Total assets less current liabilities		24,821
Long-term loans		
Amounts falling due after more than one year		1,775
Shareholders' funds		
Share capital		8,661
Retained profits (reserves)		14,385
		24,821

Source: Company accounts

Annotations:

- *The balance sheet is always given a precise date.*
- *The figures are shown in thousands of pounds, so the value of fixed assets is £8,675,000.*
- ***Working capital** is the difference between current assets and current liabilities. These are the funds needed by the company for day-to-day business.*
- ***Total assets less current liabilities** balance shareholder's funds and long term liabilities. Current liabilities are short term loans that must be repaid within one year*

FORUM

Companies are often sold for prices far above the value shown on their balance sheet. What factors might explain this difference? Could a firm have advantages which cannot be valued as assets on its balance sheet?

KEY TERMS

Key terms are defined in figure 1.

99

Unit 3 — Risk or certainty?
Enquiry 3: What is the bottom line?

Can numbers tell a story?

EVIDENCE

DODGY BUSINESS

Mr Hewlett has been a tax inspector with the Inland Revenue office for the past eight years. He and his colleagues see themselves as private investigators. They use a company's profit and loss (P&L) account and balance sheet as a starting point for their investigations into possible tax evasion. Kingsway Motors are a recent example. Mr Hewlett happened to notice that the cost of sales figure was very high in comparison to similar motor traders. Expenses such as power and wages were also unusual. Mr Hewlett believed that a visit to the premises was justified, as he guessed that personal expenses were being covered by the business and that the tax declaration might be suspect. The brand new Porsche parked outside the office and the owner's home address were sufficient to start a full investigation.

Q1 Everyone who works has to declare their income to the Inland Revenue. Find out how often, and when.

Q2 What is the name of the tax that an individual pays? What is the name of the tax that a company pays?

Q3 Why is it important to ensure that these taxes are paid?

EVIDENCE

NOKIA

Nokia is an international company that manufactures mobile phones and has its headquarters in Finland. Just a few years ago it was involved in making a number of different products, but gradually these activities have been cut back.

The 1994 accounts give the figures, shown in table 1.

Table 1: Nokia	
Finnish markka (millions)	
Net sales	30,177
Costs and expenses	−26,581
Operating profit	3,596
Profit after tax and interest	2,995
Total Assets	27,849
Source: company accounts	

FINDING OUT THE FACTS

Any set of published accounts tells a story, but the story that is told will be different depending on the individual reading it. There are a number of different groups of people who will be interested in studying a company's P&L account and balance sheet.

It is, of course, quite possible that the interests of these separate groups may conflict. A period of recession may lead the company to lower production levels, reduce overtime, make staff redundant and close some factories. A shareholder or investor might view this as good practice. The trade unions and employees would see the same decision as a failure.

WORKING IT OUT

These figures in table 1 tell us very little, especially as they are in a foreign currency. Nevertheless, by looking a little further into the accounts we can start to uncover some interesting facts. For instance, in 1994 Nokia earned a profit margin of 11.9 per cent.

Now the figures are starting to tell us something. A profit margin of nearly 12 per cent is good for a manufactured product of that sort.

Clearly Nokia had a good year in 1994, but by looking at the figures in table 2 we can get even more useful information.

It is clear that the company has emerged from a serious position in the early 1990s by getting rid of the operations that were not central to its business.

GETTING THE WHOLE PICTURE

Reading the accounts enables us to ask the right questions, but there are others that we would have to ask in order to complete our picture of Nokia's performance. These would include:

- how well did other telecommunications companies do in 1994?
- how badly did they do in 1991?
- how well did Nokia do compared to other Finnish companies in the same business sector?
- how well did Nokia do compared to other Finnish firms of an equivalent size?
- how well did Nokia do compared to companies in other countries?

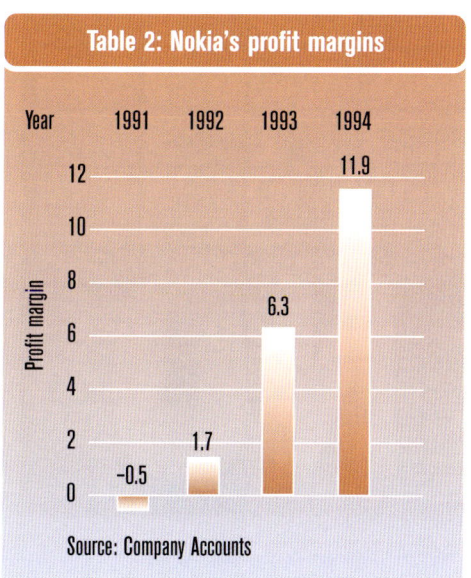

Table 2: Nokia's profit margins

Year	1991	1992	1993	1994
Profit margin	−0.5	1.7	6.3	11.9

Source: Company Accounts

If we could answer these questions we would have quite a full picture of the state of the business. However, interpreting the accounts can never provide a complete review of the business. It may face opportunities and threats, which may be technological, political or economic. The accounts say nothing about these, or about industrial relations, or the morale, skills and training of the management and workforce. What they offer is a snapshot of a firm's financial health which may or may not be a fair reflection of its long-term position.

CHECKPOINT

Look back at the accounts for Bluebird. What can you say about its performance from the information given in the accounts? Then compare the figures with those of another company you know about. What can you say about (a) profit margins and (b) retained profit? If total assets less current liabilities are growing, what does it mean?

WHO READS THE ACCOUNTS?

The Government
The Inland Revenue will want to be sure that the state is collecting the correct amount of tax from the business and that the accounts are a true reflection of the company's business activities.

Shareholders
are concerned about whether they will receive a good dividend, whether the share price is likely to rise and whether their investment is secure.

Investors
who are trying to decide which companies' shares they should buy will study the financial statements for any clues as to where they are most likely to make profits.

Managers
are generally interested in whether the company is operating efficiently. Are they making the right decisions? Are they likely to receive a performance bonus? Just how much did their directors earn this year?

Employees
are very concerned about the security of their jobs. If a company is doing well they are less likely to be made redundant and more likely to get a pay rise.

Trade Unions
will always have employees' interests at the top of their agendas. Knowing more about the company can also help unions to work together with management. High company profits but no offer of a pay increase may be a recipe for industrial action.

Banks
which have made long-term loans to the company have a strong interest in the accounts.

Creditors
are people such as suppliers to whom the company owes money. Their prime considerations are getting paid and securing further orders. If a company's results are poor they are less likely to receive the money owed to them.

Take-over bidders
are other firms with an interest in taking control of the company by buying its shares. They look for activities and assets that could be economically combined with their own. Hanson operates in this way, promoting its own growth by buying into other firms and managing them more effectively.

Customers
who have made purchases of durable goods may like to check that the company is still going to be in business in the next few years in case spare parts or after-sales service are necessary. Many customers will be other businesses, which will expect to have a long-term relationship with the company.

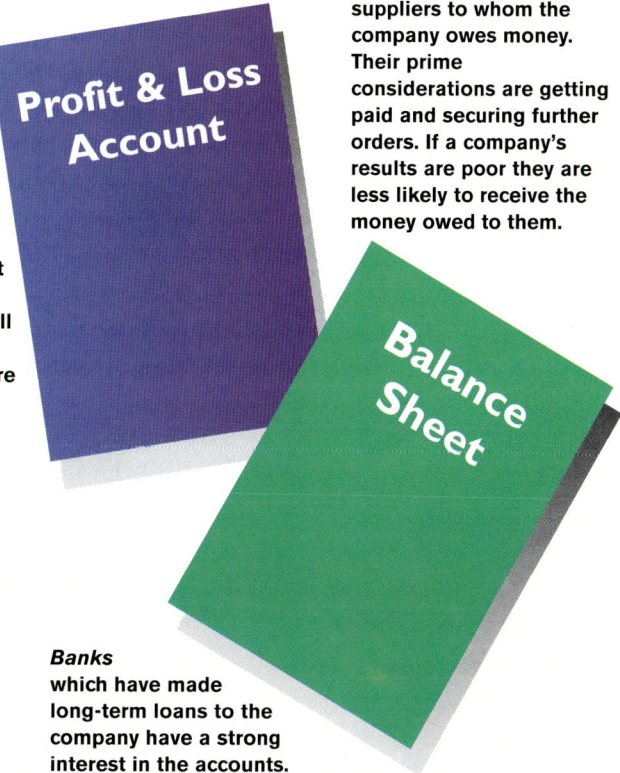

Unit 3 **Risk or certainty?**

Enquiry 4: How can the odds be shortened?

Consulting the customer

EVIDENCE

CHECKING THE NICHE

The Co-operative Bank is a small organization compared with Barclays or the Midland. It searched for a niche in the market which would identify it clearly as being different from the others. On looking at existing customers, the management thought that they might be more concerned about the environment and ethical issues than most. But how could they be sure?

The pictures above and the following quote come from their advertising leaflets, so something must have convinced them!

'Our ethical policy has been developed with the support of our customers. If you share our customers' concerns about such issues as the environment, human rights and the exploitation of animals, we invite you to join The Co-operative Bank.'

This is a very bold statement for any bank to make. Would existing customers be driven away by such a powerful message? Were there people out there who cared enough to change their banking habits?

Why did the management of the bank decide to take this line? The quotation says 'with the help of our customers', which gives us a clue.

Q1 What do you think the bank did in order to make the decision?

USING MARKET RESEARCH

The Co-operative Bank used market research techniques to decide whether an ethical policy would be appropriate. Market research is used by many firms that want to plan future strategy as it can help to identify the need for product development, new market niches and customer needs. New products are often tested by asking potential customers what they think. This is a way in which firms reduce the risk factor when making decisions.

Qualitative research uses interviewing to find out people's views and opinions, often in some depth. Generally this does not provide enough material to make decisions.

To be convinced, most companies like to see some numbers. The Co-operative Bank used quantitative methods, such as questionnaires, to find out what percentage of potential customers supported its ethical policy.

ASKING QUESTIONS

Much of the work of market researchers involves asking questions. They may be asked in person or on paper. Have you ever bought something that has a questionnaire attached to the guarantee form? Asking questions is not as easy as it seems. The process is full of pitfalls. Here are some of the rules.

- A questionnaire must be short or there must be a reward for doing it.
- Questions must be straightforward.
- Put the questions in the right order. Some may depend on others.
- Take care with sensitive issues such as income, health or gender.
- Decide on the best type of question: multiple choice; Yes, No, Don't know; open-ended questions (for when people have time to answer).
- A pilot survey will show if the questionnaire works.

EVIDENCE

WHAT DID THE BANK DO?

Qualitative research: the bank talked to small numbers of people in some detail – both customers and non-customers. This gave it an opportunity to probe people's views in depth.

The resulting comments ranged from:

'You can't bank with someone and say "Oh well, my money goes into this and I don't care".'

to

'The Co-operative Bank's ethics might not be my ethics.'

Quantitative research: people were surveyed to put numbers to the views.

RESULTS FROM CUSTOMER SURVEYS:

- 84 per cent thought the bank should have an ethical policy.
- 5 per cent thought ethical issues had nothing to do with banking.

THE ISSUES THAT MATTERED MOST WERE:

• Human rights	90 per cent
• Arms exports to oppressive regimes	87 per cent
• Animal exploitation	80 per cent
• Environmental damage	70 per cent
• Fur trade	66 per cent
• Manufacture of tobacco products	60 per cent

Q1 The bank used questionnaires for the quantitative research. Why can these be tricky to get right?

Q2 Did the evidence provide support for the plan?

Q3 What concerns might the bank have had about going ahead?

DESK RESEARCH

Market research does not always involve talking to customers or potential customers, which is known as **primary research**. Desk research is often used in order to find out about trends in the market for a product. This will mean turning to government data such as Family Spending, which is published every year, or to material produced by specialist market research organizations that collect information about many products and services.

CHECKPOINT

FORECAST SALES OF SAVOURY SNACKS, 1992–7

£ million at 1992 prices

	1992	1993	1994	1995	1996	1997
Crisps	835	838	840	843	847	852
Extruded snacks	525	533	539	546	550	554
Nuts	140	145	150	153	155	156

Source: Euromonitor

Q1 These data are available from Market Research, a magazine which is published monthly. What sort of research would its users be carrying out?

Q2 How would it help the makers of Quavers to plan the future?

Q3 What other information would they want before planning new ranges?

KEY TERMS

Desk research uses information that has been collected by other organizations, such as the government or specialist market research organizations.

Primary research gives first-hand information about the market.

Qualitative research involves interviewing people to find out their views and opinions.

Quantitative research involves carrying out surveys to give numerical information.

Unit 3 — Risk or certainty?
Enquiry 4: How can the odds be shortened?

Catching the customers

EVIDENCE

WHY BP?

Q1 Why does BP need to carry out marketing activities?
Q2 Why do petrol companies often use stamps or tokens as an incentive?
Q3 Why have petrol stations become mini-supermarkets?
Q4 Do you think that price is important to petrol buyers?

WHY MARKETING?

Companies spend millions of pounds every year on marketing. They employ people in their own marketing departments and buy the services of advertising agencies to plan their campaigns.

If all this money is being spent, there must be some powerful objectives. The first is to be more competitive than others in the same industry. That is easily said but more difficult to achieve, because marketing is not just about persuading people to buy once – it is about persuading customers to come back again and again. To do this, a firm has to look carefully at the messages from market research and try to meet the needs of its customers.

These needs are not just about packaging and advertising, but also about the nature of the product itself and its back-up services.

Using a successful marketing mix with a good product, attractive packaging and advertising (promotion), the right price and all the necessary back-up should win customers and increase – or at least retain – customers. Good marketing reduces the risk of failure.

EVIDENCE

WHAT ARE THE NEEDS?

Cath Galaska is Director of Marketing for the Preston Hospital Trust. Her job involves encouraging greater use of the hospital services. As GPs usually make the choice of where their patients are treated, Cath spends much of her time finding out about their needs.

Patients don't like long waits for appointments and queues when they get there. They don't like doctors who don't explain gently what the problem is. GPs want swift responses from the hospital, so that they know what is going on.

Cath's job is not the creation of zappy adverts or promotions but the careful matching of the services provided by the hospital to the requirements of patients and doctors.

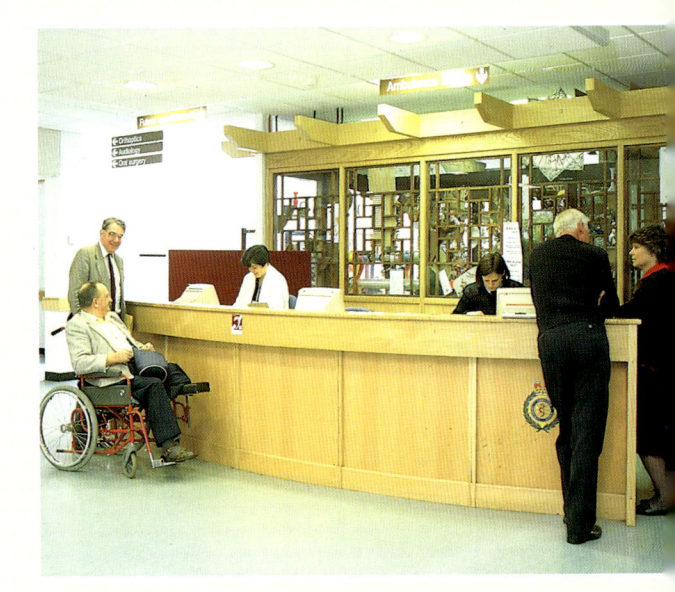

If she is not successful, patients will complain to their GPs and the hospital will lose the business.

Q1 What makes a good marketing mix for a hospital?
Q2 Why does the hospital need a marketing department?

STRATEGIES FOR SELLING

The 4Ps give us the range of strategies which businesses use to get their products to sell. 'Promotion' involves advertising as well as vouchers and other schemes to build loyalty. 'Product' involves ensuring that the product range meets the needs of everyone who may buy. 'Price' is important, too: we have already seen that if the customer feels the product is not good value, there will be no sale. 'Place' may affect sales, if buyers are to have every possible opportunity to obtain the product conveniently.

ADVERTISING

Advertising has a variety of forms and functions. It informs and persuades. BP and Preston Hospital Trust will use both techniques. BP and other oil companies have used television advertising to inform us about how they look after the environment, since this helps to protect the image of a company that might be thought of as harmful. The hospital will inform GPs of the services that they provide.

Persuading people to buy once is relatively easy. Persuading them to buy the second time is much more difficult. If products do not live up to the claims, people won't buy again.

A marketing manager will have to select the appropriate location for adverts. Television is very expensive but does reach millions of people. Newspapers and magazines are cheaper but will cover the market less effectively unless the product is a very specialist one. Many of BP's products are used as raw materials to make other things, so there would be no point in advertising widely. The trade magazine for the industry would be the appropriate place.

SALES PROMOTIONS

Promotional activities may be aimed at building loyalty. The promotion in the petrol station involved collecting stamps that can be exchanged for a variety of entertainment products. Once a collection has begun, the customer will return to BP stations in order to gather enough stamps to receive a video, CD, radio or even a television.

Many companies have devised strategies that entice customers to return. Tesco, for example, have cards that give customers discounts. The more they spend, the greater the percentage that they save.

PRODUCT RANGE

The **range of products** which a company provides is also an important aspect of the marketing strategy. Once only few petrol stations sold unleaded petrol because few cars could use it. Now it would be disastrous not to provide it.

Shampoos are a good example of a product with a very wide product range. Hair may be dry, greasy, permed or coloured, need frequent washing or have dandruff. Shampoos, therefore, must meet all these needs alone or in combination and maybe even add a conditioner!

WHAT STRATEGIES WILL WE USE?

The marketing team will have to decide the appropriate mix of strategies to use for each product. Each strategy will have a cost, so, in making a decision, the probable added sales must be weighed against the cost. There is no point in spending millions on a campaign if the effect on sales is insignificant.

CHECKPOINT

What does your local supermarket do to meet the needs of its customers? What strategies does it use to persuade you to return?

FORUM

'Marketing is all a waste of money. Television adverts cost millions. Couldn't the money be used better another way?' If this is true, why do firms continue to have large marketing budgets?

KEY TERMS

Advertising is either informative or persuasive. It uses newspapers, television and other media as a means of encouraging people to buy a product.

Product range is the full list of the products offered by a firm.

Unit 3 — Risk or certainty?
Enquiry 4: How can the odds be shortened?

Can the cash keep flowing?

EVIDENCE

FIT FOR A PRINCE

Terry is one of two shareholders who own and manage W.H. Bence Coachworks Limited. The company converts vans and lorries into mobile libraries, exhibition units, specialized ambulances and any other vehicle the customer wants. Terry knows that it is important to turn round work quickly because W.H. Bence has to pay for all the materials and the wages before receiving any money from its customers. To overcome part of the problem, the customer always provides the vehicle to be converted. Terry received an order from a Saudi Arabian prince to convert six trailers into luxury mobile palaces. The contract, lasting six months, would be worth over one million pounds. Landing a big order like this can cause problems and Terry hesitated about accepting it. He would have to gaze into his crystal ball. How much money would he need and where would he get it from? Terry entered the details into the company's spreadsheet showing the cash coming in and going out over the next six months. He then knew he could not wait six months before he received any money from the prince. However, he managed to get the prince to give W.H. Bence fortnightly staged payments of £100,000 each. After this Terry went to his bank to see if they would extend his £200,000 overdraft.

Q1 Why does Terry insist on the customers providing their own vehicles?

Q2 Why might Terry not accept the order from the prince?

Q3 Terry did accept this order, but how do you think he found the money to pay his bills over the next few months?

Q4 Why does using a cash-flow forecast reduce the risk of failure?

CASH FLOW

Cash is needed to pay bills such as materials, rent, wages and interest charges. The cash merry-go-round (page 37) shows that money goes out before it comes in. If bills can't be paid the business will go bust. W.H. Bence will insist on being paid no later than 28 days after delivery. For this reason Terry refused to do business with TML in connection with the Channel Tunnel. TML would pay only 96 days after receiving converted vehicles. A business that does not pay its bills when agreed is likely to make cash-flow problems for others.

By making **cash-flow forecasts**, businesses will reduce the risk of going bust because they are planning for their needs and making decisions about whether they can afford to go ahead with projects. However, predictions or forecasts do not mean accuracy. Many things can go wrong.
- Your sales might be lower or higher than expected.
- Your suppliers might raise their costs.
- Bank interest rates may rise or fall.
- Production problems may mean you have delays in meeting deadlines.
- You may have to increase wages to keep your workforce.
- The customer may be late in paying you.
- Your customer may go out of business.

It is wise to keep monitoring the cash flow, especially if sales are different from those expected. Of course, it is possible for sales to be greater than expected and then it would be feasible to reduce the bank loan and therefore pay less interest. Even so, if orders increase, costs will too, so new orders are not always good news. Many firms have gone under when expanding too fast.

EVIDENCE

WILL THERE BE LIGHT AT THE END OF THE TUNNEL?

Eurotunnel was set up in 1987 to run a transport service under the English Channel. TML, a consortium of construction companies, was contracted to build the tunnel.

Even if things had gone to plan Eurotunnel would not have received any income from fares until 1994. However, Eurotunnel's cash-flow forecasts have had to be repeatedly revised because building costs soared, the opening of the tunnel was delayed by 18 months, and fierce competition from the ferries forced expected fares down.

The £10 billion cost of the tunnel is more than double the original estimate and a shortfall of cash forced Eurotunnel to borrow £8 billion from a group of over 200 banks. Revenue from users of the tunnel is not yet enough to cover even the £700 million yearly interest on the bank debt. That's £2 million per day!

In September 1995 Eurotunnel and the banks agreed that no interest would be charged for 18 months to allow Eurotunnel some breathing space. Eurotunnel still have to find £260 million to run services and maintain the tunnel. Without this agreement Eurotunnel would be forced into **liquidation**, unable to pay its debts.

The best forecast is that Eurotunnel will break even by 2003, but some believe it will not cover its costs until 2040.

Q1 Building has finished, but Eurotunnel still has costs. What are these?

Q2 How can companies such as Eurotunnel be so inaccurate in their predictions?

Q3 Eurotunnel is financed for £2 billion by shareholders and a loan of £8 billion from banks. Why is this ratio a risk?

Q4 Who would be the losers and who the winners if Eurotunnel went bust?

CHECKPOINT

Estimate your own cash-flow needs over the next two weeks and show how you intend to cover them.

KEY TERMS

Cash-flow forecasts are used to look ahead to check that there is enough money coming in to cover payments that have to be made.

Liquidation occurs when a business closes down, usually because it cannot pay its debts.

Unit 3 — Risk or certainty?
Enquiry 4: How can the odds be shortened?

Buying peace of mind

EVIDENCE

WHAT ARE THE RISKS?

Brian Drury runs a small business with ten staff who repair electronic equipment, much of which has been returned to mail order companies. The work is carried out in a warehouse unit set in an industrial estate on the edge of a West Midlands city. There can be over 100 video recorders worth £150–£200 each on site during a busy week. The company can be delivering up to 20 video or music systems at a time. These items are worth a lot of money when in good repair. Brian protects his business and his workers by paying for **insurance** cover.

Q1 What risks does Brian need to insure against?
Q2 Why will he pay for insurance cover?

EVIDENCE

BRIAN'S INSURANCE POLICIES COVER:

- **Employer's liability**
  Brian has a legal responsibility for all his workers in case they suffer injury at work. If the employer is at fault the insurer will pay the bills.

- **Business liability**
  To cover any risks of damage or injury to customers or to the public, for example, faulty repairs which harm a customer.

- **Goods in transit**
  To cover the video recorders, etc. against theft or damage when they are being delivered.

- **Goods in stock**
  To cover the goods in the warehouse from theft, fire, flooding, etc.

- **Cars and vans**
  The law says that all motor vehicles must be insured in case they are involved in an accident.

EVIDENCE

WHAT IS THE COST?

The cost of insurance is not just the **premium**, the amount that Brian pays for cover. The insurance company has rules about the security of the building. If the business does not follow the rules, there will be no payments to cover the damaged or stolen property. In order to insure his business, Brian has had to:
- put bars of a specified thickness on all windows;
- install a specialist alarm system linked to a telecommunications network;
- give the local police a list of all key holders and guarantee that someone will go to the site if the alarm rings;
- lock all the doors of the building and the van when unattended.

REDUCING THE RISK

There are many risks in running a business. Will there be customers to buy the goods? Will the costs of the business suddenly increase? What if there is a fire at work? The first two have to be faced without support, but there is help available for the last.

Owners of businesses can pay someone else to take over the risk of accidental damage or of theft. If there is an accident, the insurance company pays for the cost of repairs or replacement of damaged goods claimed by the business owner.

The business owner will see the insurance cover as value for money if the peace of mind is worth more than the yearly premium.

EVIDENCE

Arson to cover theft: damage £48.8 million

One of the largest and most costly fires resulted from a blaze in a bonded warehouse. The fire began in racks of boxed electronic equipment and spread rapidly. Over a period of months the warehouse had suffered regular theft of video recorders and it was thought the fire was started deliberately to cover the thief's tracks.

Source: The Arson Prevention Bureau, 1992

EVIDENCE

TRADESTAR – THE BUSINESS INSURANCE

- All your insurance needs in one policy.
- Running a business in today's competitive environment is a big challenge and if things go wrong, it is important to have the right insurance.
- The 'Tradestar' policy is a special package to meet everyday needs with optional extras for those who need more.
- Compulsory section: trade contents (including business interruption).
- Liabilities (including health and safety at work cover).
- Extra available: goods in transit, buildings, legal expenses, all risks.

Q1 Why is 'business interruption' an important part of the policy?
Q2 What is likely to happen to business insurance premiums after a year in which there were many claims for fire and theft?
Q3 What might keep premiums down?

Source: adapted from *Tradestar prospectus*, Eagle Star, 1995

WHY SELL INSURANCE?

Insurance companies, like any other business aim to make a profit. They can offer insurance because they understand the risks involved. But they have to balance the risks against the premiums and the claims. To do this, they have to make some careful calculations and answer some tricky questions:

- What is the chance of fires, thefts or any of the other risks insured actually happening?
- What is the cost of running the business?
- What will other companies charge for cover?
- What are customers willing to pay?

Insurance companies work on the principle that only a small proportion of customers will make claims. The premiums are used to meet all the company's costs and pay for the claims. Anything that is left over will be profit. In a bad year, the claims might outstrip the premiums.

Many different kinds of risks can be covered – from loss of goods in delivery to a play that has to be cancelled because the leading actors are ill. Some insurance companies work together to cover giant risks such as the loss of an oil tanker or a space shuttle.

FORUM

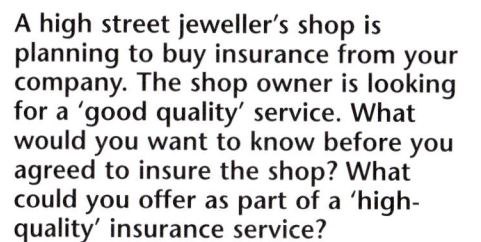

A high street jeweller's shop is planning to buy insurance from your company. The shop owner is looking for a 'good quality' service. What would you want to know before you agreed to insure the shop? What could you offer as part of a 'high-quality' insurance service?

KEY TERMS

Insurance is an arrangement for payment of a sum of money in the event of loss or injury.

An *insurance policy* is the contract that identifies what is and is not covered by the insurance.

The *premium* is the charge made for the insurance cover. It is usually paid monthly or yearly.

Unit 3 — **Risk or certainty?**

Enquiry 5: Can we ride the roller coaster?

On the roller coaster

EVIDENCE

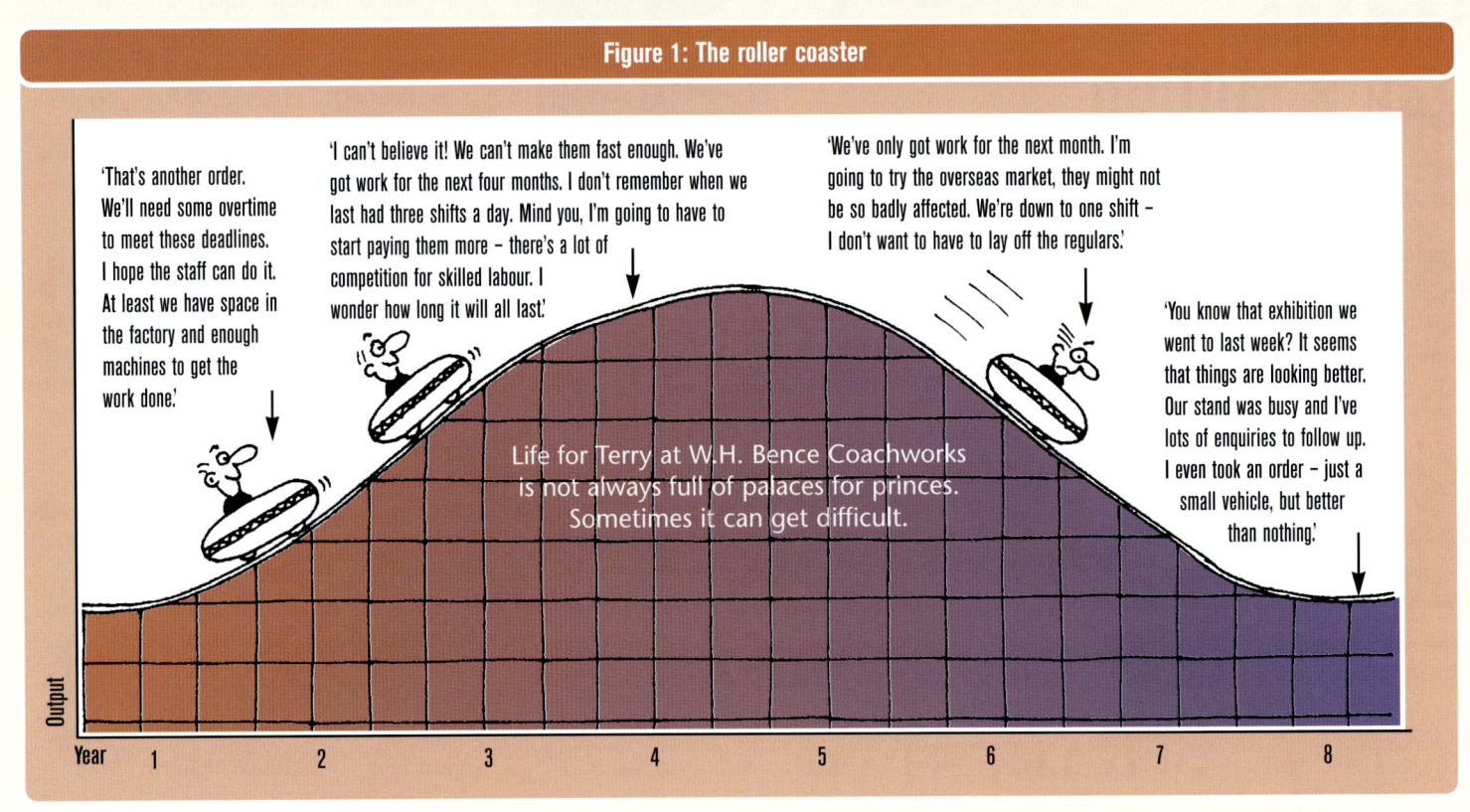

Figure 1: The roller coaster

'That's another order. We'll need some overtime to meet these deadlines. I hope the staff can do it. At least we have space in the factory and enough machines to get the work done.'

'I can't believe it! We can't make them fast enough. We've got work for the next four months. I don't remember when we last had three shifts a day. Mind you, I'm going to have to start paying them more – there's a lot of competition for skilled labour. I wonder how long it will all last.'

'We've only got work for the next month. I'm going to try the overseas market, they might not be so badly affected. We're down to one shift – I don't want to have to lay off the regulars.'

'You know that exhibition we went to last week? It seems that things are looking better. Our stand was busy and I've lots of enquiries to follow up. I even took an order – just a small vehicle, but better than nothing.'

Life for Terry at W.H. Bence Coachworks is not always full of palaces for princes. Sometimes it can get difficult.

Output / Year 1 2 3 4 5 6 7 8

Q1 Why will 'a lot of competition for skilled labour' mean that Terry has to pay people more?

Q2 If other companies are in the same situation, what effect is each of these situations going to have on unemployment?

Q3 What might persuade firms to start to order new vehicles?

CYCLES

The **business cycle** is a normal feature of any economy. It reflects the level of economic activity. The downward path is known as a **recession**, or, if it becomes really intense, a **slump**. The upward path is referred to as a **boom**.

THE SLIPPERY SLOPE

Businesses are affected by each stage of the cycle, some more than others. W.H. Bence is particularly sensitive because the firm depends on other companies' marketing plans and local authorities' spending decisions. When money is tight, these are often the first things to be cut.

Equally, when things start to improve, orders will increase. W.H. Bence depends on orders from other companies, but firms that depend on the consumer are affected in just the same way. The florist in the Evidence on the next page demonstrates how people's spending patterns change.

During the downturn or recession in the economy, unemployment will increase, so people will feel uncertain about their future. Those without jobs will obviously reduce their spending, but uncertainty makes everyone cautious, so people may try to build a nest egg – just in case.

EVIDENCE

THINGS ARE BLOOMIN' DIFFICULT

'What a good year I had in 1990. Since then it's been hard to make a living out of the flower business. People buy flowers when they are feeling well off and they don't seem to have done recently. They used to spend £25 on a bouquet with ribbons – now it's just a £5 bunch of flowers. Even brides will phone round for the best prices these days!

'We've tried to keep the quality right and this has made the profit margins very tight. I don't know how much longer the business can survive. I have to pay the wholesalers immediately, but my account customers delay and delay – for as much as three months.

The newspapers keep talking about "green shoots". I think they mean that there are some signs that things might be improving. I do hope so – I could do with whole bunches of flowers, not just green shoots!'

Q1 Why do people buy flowers when they are feeling well off?

Q2 What effect does the payment pattern of account customers have on cash flow?

Q3 What might be happening in the economy if there are 'green shoots'?

CHECKPOINT

Output % change

	UK	Germany	US	Japan
1984	2.0	3.3	6.8	5.1
1985	4.0	1.9	3.2	5.0
1986	4.0	2.2	2.9	2.6
1987	4.6	1.4	3.1	4.1
1988	4.9	3.7	3.9	6.2
1989	2.3	3.6	2.5	4.7
1990	0.6	5.7	1.2	4.8
1991	-2.1	1.7	-0.7	4.0
1992	-0.5	1.9	2.6	1.3
1993	2.2	-0.8	3.0	-0.5
1994	3.9	3.7	4.2	0.8

Source: NIER, April 1995

Q1 Plot the data showing changes in output in each country.

Q2 Can you see the pattern of the business cycle?

Q3 Which years saw the top of the boom and the bottom of the recession in each country?

Q4 Did each country have booms and recessions at the same time?

THE BOOM

During the recovery, firms produce more and the economy grows. As orders increase, firms take on more people so unemployment falls. Spending power increases and demand rises. The economy begins to boom. It seems to make a rosy picture, but if people start to want more than companies can produce, the scene starts to change. What happened at the coachworks as more and more orders came in? They had to pay higher wages. What effect does this have on the cost of producing new vehicles? It goes up. Here we have the beginnings of inflation. Prices start to rise and products may become uncompetitive. Demand falls because other countries may be able to make things more cheaply, so we go over the top and down the slippery slope of recession.

FORUM

Look at the shops, offices or factories in your neighbourhood. Have any opened or closed recently? Are there other reasons or is it as a result of the business cycle?

KEY TERMS

Boom is the part of the business cycle in which output rises.

The business cycle shows the regular pattern of upturns and downturns of the level of output in the economy.

Inflation is a sustained rise in prices.

Recession is the part of the business cycle in which output falls.

Slump is a severe form of recession.

Unit 3 — Risk or certainty?
Enquiry 5: Can we ride the roller coaster?

Riding the roller coaster

EVIDENCE

CUTTING YOUR CLOTH ...

Terry at W.H. Bence says that the company adjusts to meet the circumstances. More orders, more people – less orders, less people. The company looks for other ways to cut costs as well. Cameras are cheaper than a guard at night and its insurance is cut to the minimum.

KEEPING AHEAD OF THE GAME

Attendance at Chessington World of Adventure has defeated any economic predictions. It has risen steadily year by year. In 1980, Chessington was just a zoo with a fun fair. Now it has become one of the country's foremost leisure attractions, with a range of rides designed to terrify the bravest! By investing in new equipment, Chessington has kept the customers coming through the gates.

Although more people visit, they don't always spend more once inside. There are shops throughout the complex and retailing is a major part of the business. Whenever there is a sign of decline, the product range is looked at and changed as necessary.

SURVIVAL STRATEGIES

As we saw in the previous section, (see pp. 68-9) the downturns and upswings of the economy can affect businesses in different ways. As a depression turns into a slump, it becomes more difficult for firms to survive. The strategies that companies will use to escape the effects will depend on the type of business they are in. Much depends on their capacity to adapt.

All four examples here survived by adapting to the changes that were taking place in the economy. They did so by
- cutting costs
- spreading risks
- changing the product to outstrip the market.

Small organizations often have more difficulty surviving recession because they are less creditworthy. Banks are more willing to lend to large companies because there is greater certainty that they will be repaid. Many small businesses have gone into liquidation when the bank has decided that the overdraft has grown too large and demanded repayment. Surviving firms are usually those that see a problem coming and look for a solution – weaknesses are identified and opportunities spotted, threats are therefore minimized and strengths built upon.

FORUM

What is happening where you live? Look in the local shops and in the paper. Are they closing, advertising for more staff, laying people off or having sales of surplus stock? What else tells you how firms are reacting to changes in the economy?

SPREADING THE RISKS

Norbert Dentressangle set up a haulage business in France in 1978. The company has continued to grow and now the trucks are seen throughout Europe. Keep an eye open for them next time you are on a motorway.

Ray McCord, the UK managing director, explains the company's success in riding the business cycle in the following way: 'If recession hits one country in Europe, others are still doing well. If the haulage of raw products falls, then that of packaged products will probably increase. It tends to balance out.'

The combination of this spread of risks across a range of products and countries, and the search for growth, has enabled Norbert Dentressangle's company to grow and develop through a difficult period of recession.

PRICES DOWN – DEMAND UP

When the recession bit hard, life grew very difficult for the clients of Nick and Pat Harvey, who run a small accounting business near Croydon in Surrey. If the clients went out of business, so would Nick and Pat. Their services were a high proportion of costs for some of the small firms they dealt with, so, in Nick and Pat's words, 'we decided to lower our prices to help keep the customers' costs down and hopefully enable them to "weather the economic storm". By doing this we think we showed our customers that we valued and cared about them. We did lose some accounts, but only a few. We won some, too. It was cheaper for some firms to buy our services rather than continue to employ their own accounts staff.'

Q1 What strategy did each organization use to overcome the problems of recession?

Q2 How might they deal with a boom?

Q3 Why are small businesses particularly at risk in recession?

CHECKPOINT

Table 1: Number of new firm registrations less deregistrations, 1986–93

Year	
1986	27
1987	41
1988	68
1989	80
1990	55
1991	3
1992	-42
1993	-28

Source: *Regional Trends*, 1995

Q1 Plot the data, putting the years on the horizontal axis.

Q2 Compare the pattern with the graph you drew of the UK growth rate on page 69. Is there a relationship between the business cycle and the number of new firms being created and existing firms closing down?

FORUM

How might the government help to make life less difficult for firms?

KEY TERM

Company registrations are made with the Registrar of Companies, who keeps a record of all the companies that exist in the UK.

Unit 3 — **Risk or certainty?**

Enquiry 5: Can we ride the roller coaster?

Prices Prices Prices

EVIDENCE

THE ROUBLE RACE

'When I tell people what I earn, I always give them the figure in dollars. Roubles don't mean much because they fall in value every week. When I go shopping, I know that everything will cost more so it's very hard to budget. If I have the money and we need something, I don't give it a second thought. I buy straight away because I may not be able to afford it next week.

'Inflation is rising so fast that prices are often quoted in US dollars because no one knows how much anything will cost in roubles tomorrow. Even adverts for fruit juice in the local paper use dollars.

'My salary hasn't gone up nearly so much as prices, so life gets harder week by week.'

Marina, *Perm*, Russia, November 1995

Q1 Why are prices quoted in dollars?

Q2 What has happened to Marina's standard of living?

PRICES AND PEOPLE

Prices in Russia have been rising rapidly since 1989. Inflation peaked in 1992 at 1,353 per cent. In general, wages have stayed much the same. The obvious effect of this is that people can buy less than they used to. If juice costs 85 cents, as the advert shows, and a low rent is about 20 dollars, a Russian income of 100 dollars won't go very far.

Inflation on this scale makes life very uncertain because people can't plan ahead. The instinct is to spend whatever money you have because it may be worth less tomorrow.

There have been cases of hyperinflation throughout history. In Germany, in the 1920s, people used wheelbarrows to carry money to the shops because, as its value fell, more and more was needed in order to buy even a loaf of bread.

Even when inflation is rising less rapidly, at perhaps 10 per cent a year, it can make life difficult for people. Those who have retired and are living on a pension which doesn't increase every year will find that they can buy 10 per cent less each year.

People who have borrowed money enjoy inflationary times because the value of their debt will fall. If, however, you have saved money and put it in the bank or building society, you will be less happy because the value of your savings will fall.

EVIDENCE

NEWSPRINT PRICE RISE THREATENS DAILY PAPERS

The cost of paper, known as newsprint, is rising as demand increases with the global industry coming out of recession. Most national newspapers negotiate their prices for newsprint on a yearly basis. They face rises of between 15 and 20 per cent.

The Mirror has already fractionally reduced its size, cutting costs by millions of pounds a year. Other papers may be forced to raise their prices.

'During the recession the market was oversupplied and prices were down. Since the recession, demand has increased and we can sell more advertising, so we need more pages. We have to have the paper, so the manufacturers can charge what they like', says one national tabloid title executive.

Source: adapted from *The Observer*, 30 October 1994

Rising paper prices was one of the factors that led to the closure of the Today newspaper in November 1995.

Q1 Why should the cost of newsprint rise as the recession ends?

Q2 What effect will cutting the size of the paper or putting up prices have on a newspaper's profit margins?

Q3 Could the newsprint manufacturers really 'charge what they like'?

PRICES AND BUSINESS

Inflation creates a very uncertain environment for business as well as people. If companies do not know what will happen to the price of their inputs, it is impossible to set accurate prices for their output. If you cannot set accurate prices, you do not know how many will be sold, so you do not know what resources you will need nor how much profit you will make.

If you are selling in overseas markets, life can be even more difficult. Other countries may not be suffering from inflation to the same extent, so prices may not be rising as fast. As your products become more expensive because of inflation at home, they will become less competitive abroad.

If prices are rising, there will be pressure from employees for wages to rise. Inflation means that their standard of living is falling because the money does not go as far. A rise in wages increases the cost of production for the company and it may then have to increase prices, which causes more inflation. The effect, therefore, is that prices tend to spiral upwards.

MEASURING INFLATION

Inflation can be measured in all sorts of ways. The costs of inputs are measured on a monthly basis. This gives advance warning about what will happen to prices because the price firms have to pay for their inputs will probably affect the price of the end product at a later date. 'Factory gate prices', which show the price of goods when they leave the factory, give the next stage of information.

The data used most frequently is the Retail Price Index (RPI). This is compiled by surveying the prices of a range of goods and services that people buy on a regular basis. This is often referred to as 'a basket of goods'. Each item is given a weighting according to how important it is in the spending of the average household. Rents and mortgages are therefore a large proportion, whereas salt would be small.

Every month prices are recorded all over the country in different kinds of shops. This means that the RPI reflects the national average for people who are doing their shopping in large supermarkets as well as the corner shop.

KEY TERM

The *Retail Price Index (RPI)* is the main measure of inflation in the UK. It shows changes in the price of the average person's shopping.

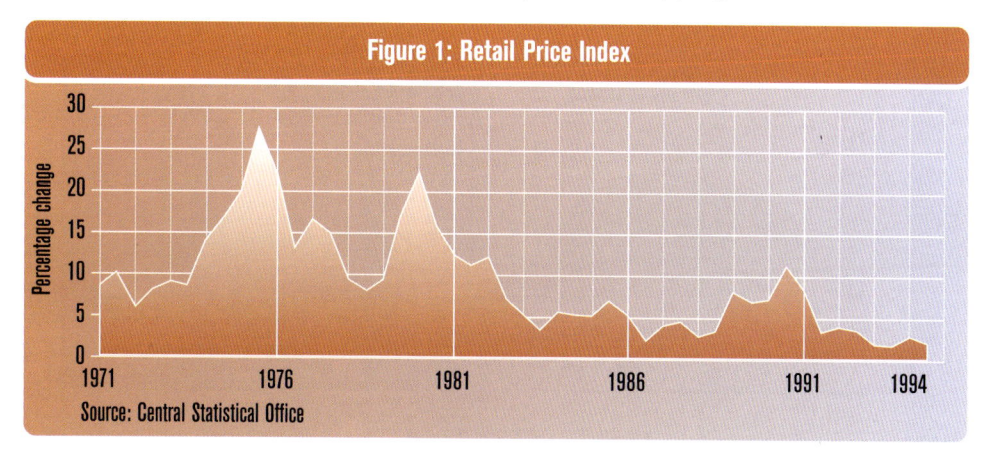

Figure 1: Retail Price Index

Source: Central Statistical Office

Unit 3 Risk or certainty?

Enquiry 5: Can we ride the roller coaster?

Can the government rule the roller coaster?

EVIDENCE

WAITING FOR THE NATION TO REDECORATE

Ian Rowe sees his company as a good indicator of changes in the fortunes of the economy. Johnstone's Paints is the third biggest supplier to the UK's painters and decorators.

'Confidence is very important to our industry', says Ian, marketing manager of Johnstone's. 'Painting and decorating can be easily affected by the signals given out by governments.'

Customers of all kinds are uncertain of the future and are unwilling to spend money on new building or refurbishing projects.

As far as Ian is concerned, the threat of losing customers is greater than any worries about rising prices. He thinks his customers are willing to spend more after years of gloom, but they need a signal from the government that the future is bright. Lower interest rates would encourage more spending and investment.

Source: adapted from *The Guardian*, 12 January 1994

Q1 What part of the business cycle do you think the economy is in?

Q2 What is likely to be happening to unemployment?

Q3 Ian Rowe would like the government to reduce interest rates. How would this help?

Q4 What else might a government do to have similar effects?

WHAT'S TO BE DONE?

In the Evidence, Ian Rowe is asking the government to help the country move out of recession. On other occasions, there are pleas for the government to control inflation. There is no hope that the government can remove the business cycle altogether, but it often aims to reduce the effects. Catching events before they reach extremes often makes them easier to solve.

DEALING WITH RECESSION

At the bottom of a recession a government wants to encourage people and firms to spend money. Every pound that is spent means that more is bought, so businesses need to employ more people to provide these extra goods and services. More jobs mean more spending, so demand starts to rise and the economy starts to climb out of recession.

WHAT STRATEGIES MIGHT IT USE?

- Tax cuts would leave people with more to spend.
- More government spending would increase demand.
- Reduced interest rates would encourage businesses and consumers to borrow and invest.

If any of these schemes are going to work, people have to be convinced that things will get better and the economy is going to grow. Expectations are very important as no one will spend money if they are worried about whether they will have a job next week. No firms will make expansion plans if they think that no one will buy their products.

Figure 1: Government and the business cycle

(Path of the economy; Government attempts to reduce the effects of the business cycle; Output vs Time)

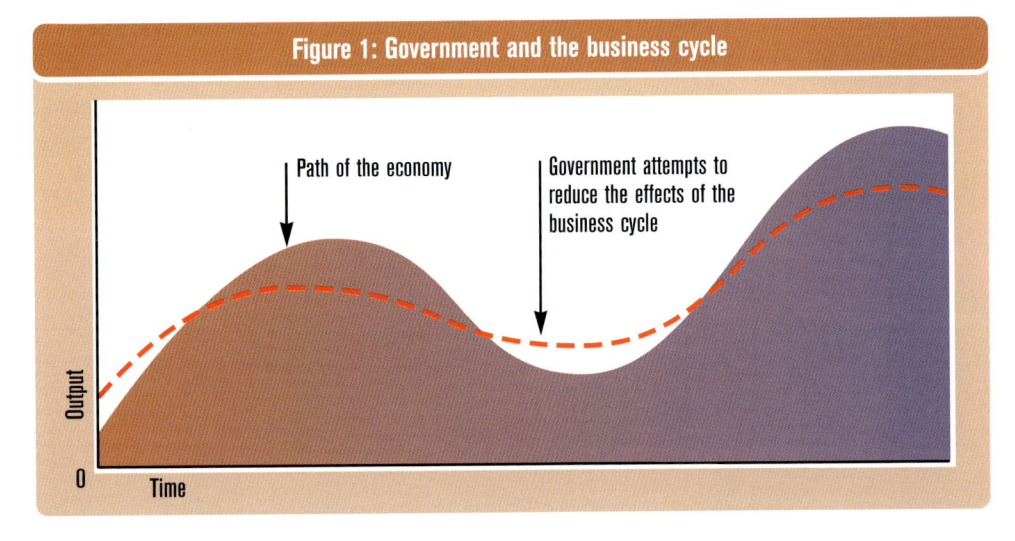

116

WHAT TO DO IN A BOOM

At the top of the cycle, in a boom, the situation is quite different. People are all buying too much. The government will want to persuade us to cut our spending so that demand falls and prices stop going up. To achieve this, the government will use the strategies already listed, but in reverse:

- Increases in taxation will cut spending.
- Cutting government spending will reduce demand.
- Raising interest rates will discourage firms from borrowing more.

However, making the right decision about what is to be done is not at all straightforward. There are likely to be times when advisers disagree about the best government action. It is often difficult to decide exactly whereabouts in the business cycle the economy is at any time. This complicates matters further. The only guidance that the government has is what has been done before. No one has a crystal ball that can look into the future, yet if the government gets it wrong it can do more harm than good.

MAKING BUDGET DECISIONS

The Chancellor of the Exchequer has the responsibility of guiding the government's economic policy. The yearly Budget announcement provides the framework for taxes and government spending for the following year. The Budget also has to fit in with the government's longer-term plans which may have targets for economic development in the future.

The pressures on a Chancellor to interpret correctly the many different indicators of business activity are immense. The Evidence above shows some of the contradictory views.

Any Chancellor receives this mix of both advice and criticism. Economists have differing views of how the economy works and politicians have differing views of what is important. Whatever is announced in the Budget will reflect the political opinions of the party in power and will not please everyone.

EVIDENCE

ADVICE AND CRITICISM

'Tax trimmer Chancellor plays safe'

'Thanks for nothing!'

"YOU KEN NOT BE SERIOUS!"

'Chancellor opts for caution on tax cuts'

'The UK is experiencing "Goldilocks" growth: neither too hot, nor too cold. Some tax cuts could help to boost spending.'

'Output grew in the second part of this year, but there are still areas of weakness in retail sales, industrial production and housing. Lower interest rates would encourage investment and borrowing.'

'Prices are rising and manufacturers are facing significant cost pressures. Interest rates should be kept steady.'

FORUM

Find out what measures the present government is using to encourage business activity. How effective do they appear to be? What changes might be recommended?

KEY TERMS

The *Budget* is the annual statement made by the Chancellor of the Exchequer in which taxation and government spending for the following year are announced.

The *Chancellor of the Exchequer* is the member of the government responsible for the country's finances.

CHECKPOINT

Use the CD-ROM to look at the newspapers at the time of the last Budget. What did the Chancellor of the Exchequer do? What comments did people make about his actions?

Unit 3

Risk or certainty?
Case study

A risk or a certainty?

Q1 When Sony and Sinclair developed these products, they each thought that they were onto a winner. Which one was right?

Q2 In what ways were both these products enterprising?

Q3 What would they both have done to attempt to ensure success?

Q4 What reasons can you think of for the success of one and the failure of the other?

The Sony Walkman was launched in the UK in 1980.

In 1985, Sir Clive Sinclair launched the Sinclair C5; a small, light vehicle for one person, powered by an electric motor and pedals.

Unit 4

Big or small?

ENQUIRY 1: IS BIG BETTER?	**120**
Why get big? *Economies of scale*	120
Does it work out cheaper? *Exploring different kinds of economies of scale*	122
Who gains from growth? *External economies and stakeholders*	124

ENQUIRY 2: WHAT MAKES A FIRM GROW?	**126**
Tell them what you do *Promotion, brands and advertising*	126
Designed to grow *Technology and new product development*	128
Joining together *Different kinds of mergers*	130

ENQUIRY 3: IS SMALL BEAUTIFUL?	**132**
When is bigger not better? *Diseconomies of scale*	132
When is it good to talk? *Communication*	134
How do people make a difference? *Leadership and teamwork*	136

ENQUIRY 4: CAN WE CONTROL THE GIANTS?	**138**
What is a monopoly? *Monopoly power*	138
Taming the giants *Government action on monopolies*	140
What is a transnational? *What transnationals can do when they invest*	142
In everyone's interest? *The local impact of a transnational*	144

ENQUIRY 5: WHY BELONG TO THE EUROPEAN UNION?	**146**
Why belong to the European Union? *International trade and the EU*	146
In or out? *The impact of the EU on businesses*	148
Food for Europe *The Common Agricultural Policy*	150
A bigger Europe? *Enlarging the EU*	152

CASE STUDY: A QUESTION OF SCALE	**154**

Unit 4 Big or small?
Enquiry 1: Is big better?

Why get big?

EVIDENCE

THE BIC CRYSTAL

You won't often find an exhibit in a London museum that costs less than a pint of milk. But an ordinary Bic Crystal ballpoint pen is displayed in the Museum of Design. The Crystal is a classic product.

The first ballpoint was developed for pilots in the Second World War, and ballpoints were a hi-tech present for Christmas 1945. They cost £2.75 – about £55.40 in today's money!

The Bic Crystal was the first throwaway pen – but at its UK launch in 1958 it was still an expensive throwaway at 5p, or 60p in 1996 terms. How is it that we can now buy quite a sophisticated piece of technology for so little?

Quite simply, much of the answer lies in the scale of production. Bic produces 14 million Crystals every day, and people lose about 10 million every day! At its giant factory in France, the new 1990s version of the pen pours off production lines that are fully computer controlled and that guarantee constant quality of product.

Q1 Why are Bic Crystals so much cheaper today than they used to be?

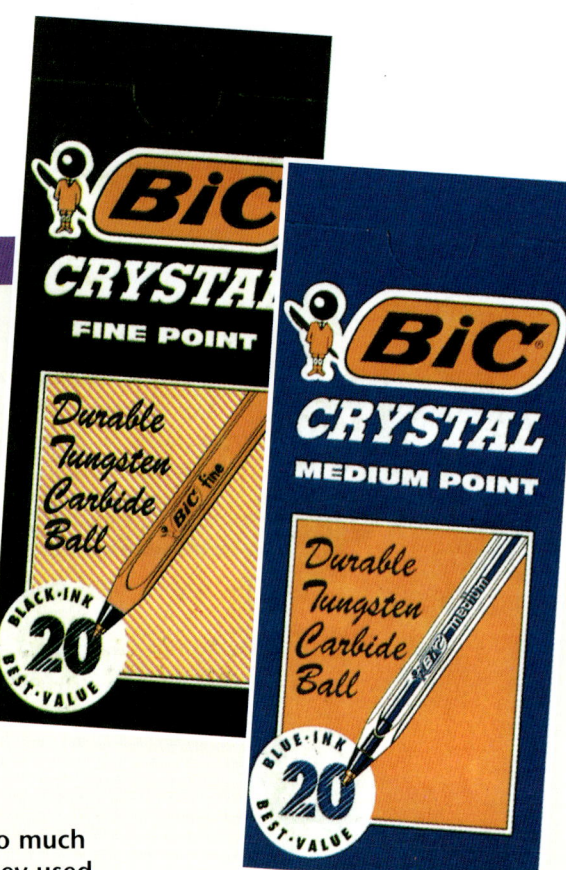

ECONOMIES OF SCALE

If ballpoint pens were produced on a small scale – for instance just for the town where you live – each one would cost the equivalent of what it did in 1945. The same is true for thousands of products that most people use every day. No cars are made in Cumbria, no steel is produced in Suffolk, no light bulbs are made in Leicester. It would be perfectly possible to make most products locally on a small scale, but they would be hugely expensive because it would be impossible to use so much machinery, or to have the benefit of computer control. Costs of production would be much higher, and prices would have to be higher as well. Overall, the standard of living would fall very sharply indeed if all our consumer goods were made locally, because paying higher prices would mean we could all afford less.

When large-scale production is more efficient, we say that there are **economies of scale**. The cost cuts that come from using the biggest and best machines are called **technical economies** of scale. Large machines cost more than small machines, but they are able to produce proportionately more. So the cost of the machine per unit of output is less. And a large firm can make better use of all its equipment: in small firms expensive plant may stand idle. When mass production is practical, the product can be built or assembled in a continuous chain of operations that usually makes good use of new technology.

As the production process becomes more efficient, costs per item fall and the product is likely to be cheaper. Bulk-buying economies are also possible. The business can get discounts when buying larger quantities of its inputs. This means that its costs fall.

CHECKPOINT

Q1 Food, newspapers and other items can be bought in a corner shop, which will usually be a very small business, often run by a sole owner. The same items can also be bought from a gigantic supermarket chain, where prices will often be lower than in the corner shop. Why is this? Although many corner shops have gone out of business, many still survive. How are they able to do this?

Q2 The technology of ballpoints is now well known. Since the Bic Crystal is such a simple design and has been such a worldwide business success, why do you think no one has set up a small business and launched a competing product?

EVIDENCE

REFINING OIL

Oil is so important and valuable that it is sometimes known as 'black gold'. Yet the crude oil that gushes from the head of an oil well has little value in itself. Crude oil cannot be used until it has been distilled in an oil refinery. This involves heating the oil to boiling point and collecting the different types of product (called 'fractions') which condense at different temperatures. The light fractions are used to make petrol and the inputs for chemical manufacturing. The middle fractions make diesel and jet fuel, while the heavy fractions become heating oil and bitumen.

An oil refinery large enough to compete in world markets is huge and costs at least £75 million to build. (If you were to win the biggest prize ever in the National Lottery, you would still be unable to afford to build even a small oil refinery!) Obviously, the larger the refinery, the higher the construction cost. But what about the construction costs *per unit of output*? Will they be lower for a larger refinery?

Figure 1 shows construction costs for different sizes of refinery. The size, or capacity, of the refinery is measured in barrels per day (BPD). Figure 2 measures construction costs per barrel of oil.

Figure 1: Oil refinery: construction cost and capacity (size)

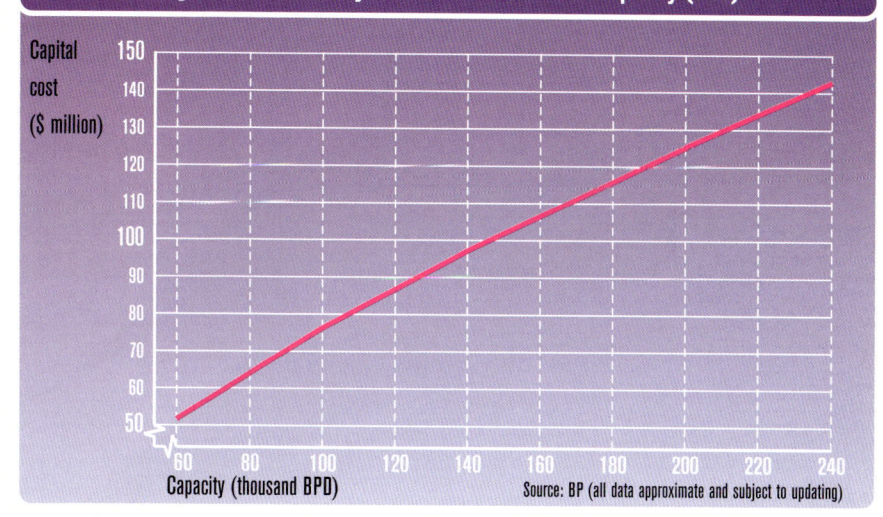

Figure 2: Oil refinery: construction cost per barrel of oil

Q1 Use figure 1 to find the construction cost of refineries with the following capacities:
(a) 60,000 BPD (b) 120,000 BPD
(c) 180,000 BPD (d) 240,000 BPD.

Q2 What happens to the cost of the refinery as its size increases? How does this data explain the shape of the curve in figure 2?

Q3 How can you explain the relationship between the size of the refinery and the construction cost per barrel of oil?

FORUM

If getting bigger can lead to lower costs and lower prices, would you support the merger of large firms such as Tesco and Sainsbury's?

KEY TERMS

Economies of scale are the reasons why the average cost of production may fall with increasing levels of output.

Technical economies can be made when costs are cut because inputs can be used more efficiently as output rises.

Unit 4 Big or small?
Enquiry 1: Is big better?

Does it work out cheaper?

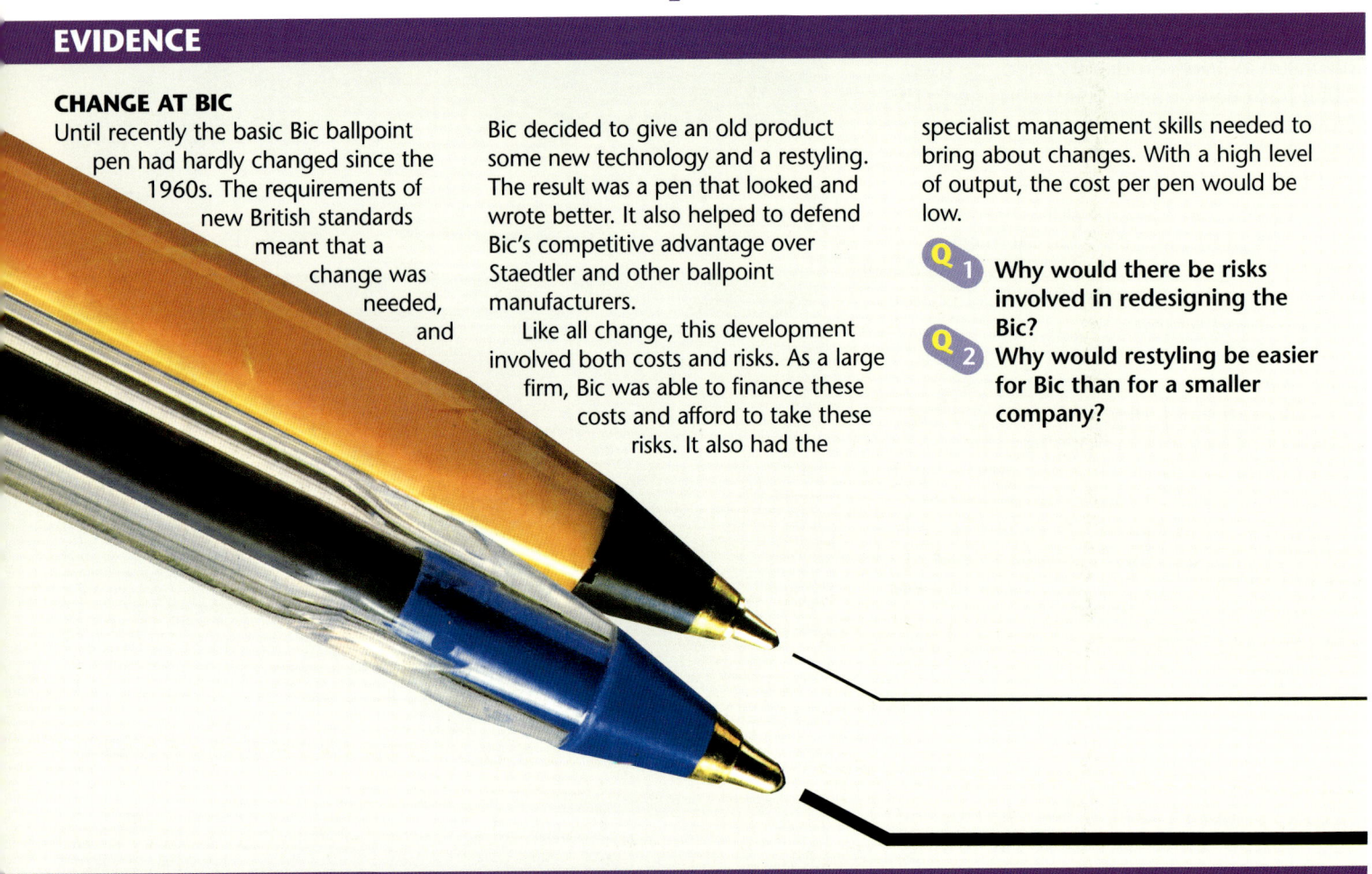

EVIDENCE

CHANGE AT BIC

Until recently the basic Bic ballpoint pen had hardly changed since the 1960s. The requirements of new British standards meant that a change was needed, and Bic decided to give an old product some new technology and a restyling. The result was a pen that looked and wrote better. It also helped to defend Bic's competitive advantage over Staedtler and other ballpoint manufacturers.

Like all change, this development involved both costs and risks. As a large firm, Bic was able to finance these costs and afford to take these risks. It also had the specialist management skills needed to bring about changes. With a high level of output, the cost per pen would be low.

Q1 Why would there be risks involved in redesigning the Bic?

Q2 Why would restyling be easier for Bic than for a smaller company?

MORE ECONOMIES

Can you imagine a small business that extracts and refines oil? Similarly, it is quite difficult to imagine a huge international company running your local hairdressing salon. The secret behind these varied sizes of business lies in economies of scale.

We have already looked at technical economies of scale, but there are others. For example, large firms find it easier than smaller firms to obtain loans from banks. They are thought to be more certain to repay the money at the right time. The interest rate that is charged to larger firms is also likely to be lower. These **financial economies** of scale help to reduce Bic's costs and to hold down prices.

Marketing costs can be spread over a bigger output: in this case there are **marketing economies** of scale. They work through the whole marketing mix. New product development is easier and more likely in large firms than in small ones. Advertising rates are lower. A national sales team becomes possible when market share is high enough. Bulk distribution brings down the costs of delivery.

To take advantage of economies of scale, an enterprise needs effective management. In a very small business, every manager must be able to do the work of everyone else. Managers may often work on the shop floor if there is a rushed order. As the business grows, it is able to employ managers who specialize: for example, in marketing or finance. Specializing further, within the marketing department there may be managers for new product development, for advertising, for sales teams and for distribution. Having specialists on the staff can make the team more effective, bringing **managerial economies**.

Job specialization allows people to become better at their work. This can reduce costs and add to quality in all areas of the business.

Large firms also enjoy advantages in their entrepreneurial or risk-taking role. New and risky projects often require expensive **research and development (R & D)**. Only a large firm has the necessary cash or can borrow the funds. Should the project be a failure, the large firm can cope with the loss because it has other projects that do succeed. In this way it spreads the risks.

EVIDENCE

PORTMEIRION POTTERIES PLC

The company takes its name from the village in North Wales where the pottery began in the 1960s. Its founder, Susan Williams-Ellis, began making her award-winning designs for tableware based on exotic plants and flowers. The business soon transferred to Stoke-on-Trent, the traditional centre of Britain's potteries industry, where it could make use of local businesses that provide specialist services. There are also large numbers of people in Stoke-on-Trent who have the appropriate skills.

Portmeirion has since expanded hugely and become a public company. Sales were worth £27 million in 1995 and profits reached £4.75 million. Strong demand has meant that the company is expanding its output of hand-painted products with an extension to the factory. The chairman adds: 'We are delighted to support and develop this traditional skill that is concentrated in Stoke-on-Trent.'

Source: adapted from Portmeirion Potteries plc, *Report and Accounts*, 1994

Q1 By deciding to locate in Stoke-in-Trent, Portmeirion found itself surrounded by many competitor firms. Why do you think it made this choice?

Q2 How might a good supply of skilled labour affect Portmeirion?

EXTERNAL ECONOMIES

When an industry develops and expands in a particular area, it actually creates special local advantages that benefit every individual firm. These advantages can reduce costs, and may improve quality. They are called **external economies of scale** because they arise from the growth of the industry and are outside, or external to, the particular firm.

One example is specialized skilled labour. The potteries industry has built up a pool of people with skills that would be difficult or impossible to find elsewhere. They are available only to local firms. Firms also benefit from the training available at local colleges.

Stoke's potteries have also attracted a vast range of supporting firms. Other enterprises have clustered around the core potteries industry, varying in business from designers of the transfers used to decorate pottery right through to firms that dispose of toxic waste. Other companies supply kilns and specialized machinery, or provide suitable packaging and transport services.

In addition, the firms in the industry can co-operate through joint research projects and trade associations.

CHECKPOINT

Excelsior plc is an international hotel chain. Senior managers are considering a proposal to build a 100-room extension to the company's recently built 250-room hotel in Torquay. The company accountant expects that this plan would add 30 per cent to the hotel's total annual costs. The hotel can expect some help with advertising from the local tourist board. It will also benefit from the general expansion of tourist and conference facilities in the town.

Q1 What will be the likely change in costs per room?

Q2 What will have to happen if profit is to rise after the extension is built?

Q3 Might there be any other advantages for an expanding hotel in Torquay?

Q4 What other factors should the senior managers consider before making their decision?

KEY TERMS

External economies of scale are those factors that may reduce an individual firm's average costs through the larger size of the industry (rather than the larger size of the firm).

Financial economies allow larger businesses to obtain money for their expansion plans more easily and cheaply.

Managerial economies occur when the business grows large enough to appoint specialists to its management team.

Marketing economies arise when the costs of marketing can be spread over a larger output.

Research and development (R & D) is the process of creating and designing new products, and new methods of production.

Unit 4 Big or small?
Enquiry 1: Is big better?

Who gains from growth?

EVIDENCE

DARTINGTON CRYSTAL LTD

Torrington is a small market town in North Devon. Just 30 years ago most of the people living there were involved in some way in farming. But farming offered work to fewer and fewer people. So the Dartington Trust, a Devon charity, decided to set up a factory to design and manufacture top-quality glassware. Output began in 1967 with fewer than 40 employees, including a group of craftsmen from Denmark and Sweden.

The range of modern but very distinctive glassware found a profitable niche in the market, and sales grew steadily through the 1970s and 1980s. More employees were recruited from the area and trained at the factory. By the mid-1990s, Dartington was the town's biggest employer, with nearly 300 staff. Its success became all the more important when, in 1993, Dairy Crest closed its large Torrington creamery, with 300 redundancies.

Although Dartington is still a fairly small producer of glassware, increasing output has led to greater efficiency. Sales and profits have grown. The company has been able to expand its buildings, facilities and workforce.

Dartington Crystal is also a leading tourist attraction, with over 200,000 visitors each year. There is a factory tour, two large shops, a café and a restaurant.

Today the company is owned by its management team and there are further plans for growth. The old creamery has been bought for the development of warehousing and distribution. There is also a project for opening a moulded glassmaking operation in Plymouth using recycled glass.

Q1 Who are the stakeholder groups for Dartington Crystal?
Q2 Which groups might have gained from the company's growth, and how?

GROWTH AND THE BUSINESS

At Dartington Crystal the directors, management and employees are also shareholders who gain from dividends and growth in the value of their investment. Growth provides management with increased responsibility and higher rewards. The workforce benefits from better wages and much greater security of employment. All these groups of people are stakeholders. They gain from the expansion of the business.

Growth can also bring some economies of scale. These keep costs down and prices competitive. So customers (who are also stakeholders) get value for money and the company can widen its niche in the market. It may be possible to export – helpful when the UK market is in recession.

Increasing output can also mean more business for suppliers. This affects not only the firms that supply raw materials and packaging, but also local firms of builders, cleaners, caterers and providers of many other services. Even a local taxi operator becomes a stakeholder in a major business enterprise.

EVIDENCE

THE TOWN OF TORRINGTON

Torrington is in a remote but beautiful part of North Devon. It has been a market town since medieval times and is built on a hill overlooking the River Torridge. Unfortunately, jobs are scarce and wages are mostly low. Although attractive, the town centre is not prosperous. The local council tries to encourage business development, but there are no government grants available. Transport links are very poor. Many young people find little to do, and petty crime has increased.

In such a small community, the growth of Dartington has been important. Many people are directly or indirectly connected with the firm. Tourists visiting the factory spend money in local shops, restaurants and hotels. If the town centre could be made more appealing, tourist spending could be much increased.

One problem caused by Dartington's growth is increased traffic congestion. Cars, lorries and tourist coaches must follow the winding road from the motorway link and then find their way through the town's old streets to reach the factory.

GROWTH AND THE COMMUNITY

The growth of a business enterprise does not only affect those who are directly involved, such as owners and employees or suppliers and customers. It also carries costs and benefits outside the firm – called **externalities** – that are experienced by the community. Often these effects are positive, as when increased trade is attracted to the area or when public facilities are improved – for example, better transport or town centre upgrading. The local council also benefits from higher receipts of business rates, which can be spent in the community.

However, growth can also carry negative externalities. Levels of environmental pollution may increase, congestion may worsen and the value of some people's houses may be reduced. A locality may also become too dependent on one employer. If the firm closes or relocates, there is not only the loss of jobs, but also the sudden withdrawal of income from a network of suppliers and support services as well as the local council.

The benefits from the growth of a business may not be evenly spread among all the people in the community. Some may gain more than others, some may be unaffected and some may lose.

CHECKPOINT

Cumbrian Chemicals Ltd, wholly owned by international Mogul Enterprise plc, is based in a small town in the northwest of England between the Lake District and the Cumbrian coast. It produces a range of chemicals used by the motor industry on a site between a housing estate and a recreation ground. The firm now plans to double its capacity and will need to take on a further 100 staff in an area suffering from high unemployment.

As a consultant to the local council, what factors would you consider when preparing a report on the proposal?

FORUM

What would be the effect of large-scale business expansion in the area where you live? Who would benefit most? Who or what might be losers?

KEY TERM

Externalities are costs or benefits arising from business activity that are experienced by people or organizations outside the firm.

125

Unit 4: Big or small?

Enquiry 2: What makes a firm grow?

Tell them what you do

EVIDENCE

UNIVERSITIES AND ADVERTISING

Universities have to compete to attract students. The more students that attend a university, the greater the income the university receives from the government. One university that has set out to increase its number of students is DeMontfort, with campuses in Leicester and Milton Keynes. The university has designed a marketing strategy, aimed at 17–19-year-olds, with the plan to raise the profile of the university and create an image that would be understood by interested students. With a budget of £500,000, a campaign of television and cinema adverts, as well as a press campaign, was launched in 1993.

The campaign used images of a killer whale and sealions from the BBC TV programme Trials of Life. Although this appeared to be a strange way of advertising a university, market research had shown that 17–19-year-olds understood the underlying message that life was tough and that you need to be well prepared. The campaign was very successful in raising people's awareness of the university and what it had to offer.

Preparation for Life

Call 0645.454647

De Montfort University The Gateway Leicester LE1 9BH Fax: 0116.255 0307

DE MONTFORT UNIVERSITY
LEICESTER·MILTON KEYNES
BEDFORD·LINCOLN

Q1 If you use the Internet you can access many universities via the World Wide Web. Complete a search for your nearest university and see what image it is presenting to students who might apply.

Q2 Look at the image DeMontfort University has used. Would this persuade you to enquire about the university's courses? What impression of university life do you get by looking at this image?

CREATING AN IMAGE

The Evidence shows how DeMontfort University is trying to create its own **brand image**. This is something that is usually associated with **consumer goods** as manufacturers create ways of persuading customers to continue buying their products. The creation of a brand image is one way in which a business can promote itself.

The university has also targeted its advertising on 17–19-year-olds, most of whom are in school or college. The university attracts a great many students and 17–19-year-olds are only one **segment** of the market. There are also part-time students, day-release students, mature students over 25 and research students. The killer whale and sealions campaign is clearly focused on one sector of the market where it is particularly important to raise awareness of the university and create a distinct brand image. The university could promote itself in different ways to the other sectors of its market. Older students and part-time students may see university life in a different way. The university, just like any other business, is using the marketing mix to ensure that it promotes itself in the best possible way.

PROMOTING A PRODUCT

Businesses grow by promoting themselves and their products. No business can expect to expand if the customers do not know what is on offer. Advertisements are one way to persuade customers to buy, as well as informing them of the nature of the product or service on offer. Successful advertising campaigns also persuade people to buy a second and third time. Kellogg's and some petrol companies have for a long time used gifts as a means of encouraging repeat sales. Other successful strategies to encourage repeat sales

EVIDENCE

MCDONALDS AND POCAHONTAS

McDonalds is well known for the products it sells. Its advertisements also attract a lot of attention, and they are often linked to other products and images. From 13 October to 16 November 1995 McDonalds ran a television campaign for the McChief, designed to coincide with the release of the Walt Disney film, Pocahontas. Obviously McDonalds can promote the new product in its restaurants, but this advertising alone is unlikely to be sufficient to bring it to the notice of large numbers of people.

The idea of a theme, based on the American Indian, allows the promoters to link the new product with the sales of existing products. During the television campaign, McDonalds gave small models of the characters in the Disney film to anyone buying a child's Happy Meal. This was expected to encourage customers to return to the restaurant on further occasions to collect all five models in the set. To be successful, it is important for an advertising campaign to encourage repeat sales as well as raising customer awareness.

Q1 Do you know any other company that uses small gifts, which may be collected as part of a set, to encourage future sales?

Q2 Why do you think this McDonalds campaign lasted for only one month?

---

include giving discounts on larger orders, giving loyalty cards for regular customers, 'buy two, get one free' campaigns, and adapting the product to meet the changing needs of the customers.

Businesses want to grow for a great many reasons. If they can make economies of scale, they can cut costs and perhaps compete on price. They may be able to take a larger share of the market: they then have more power. All parts of the marketing mix can be used to achieve growth. This in turn benefits many stakeholders: employees, managers and shareholders.

FORUM

Could a business grow and continue to grow without advertising its products? What would be the circumstances in which it could do this?

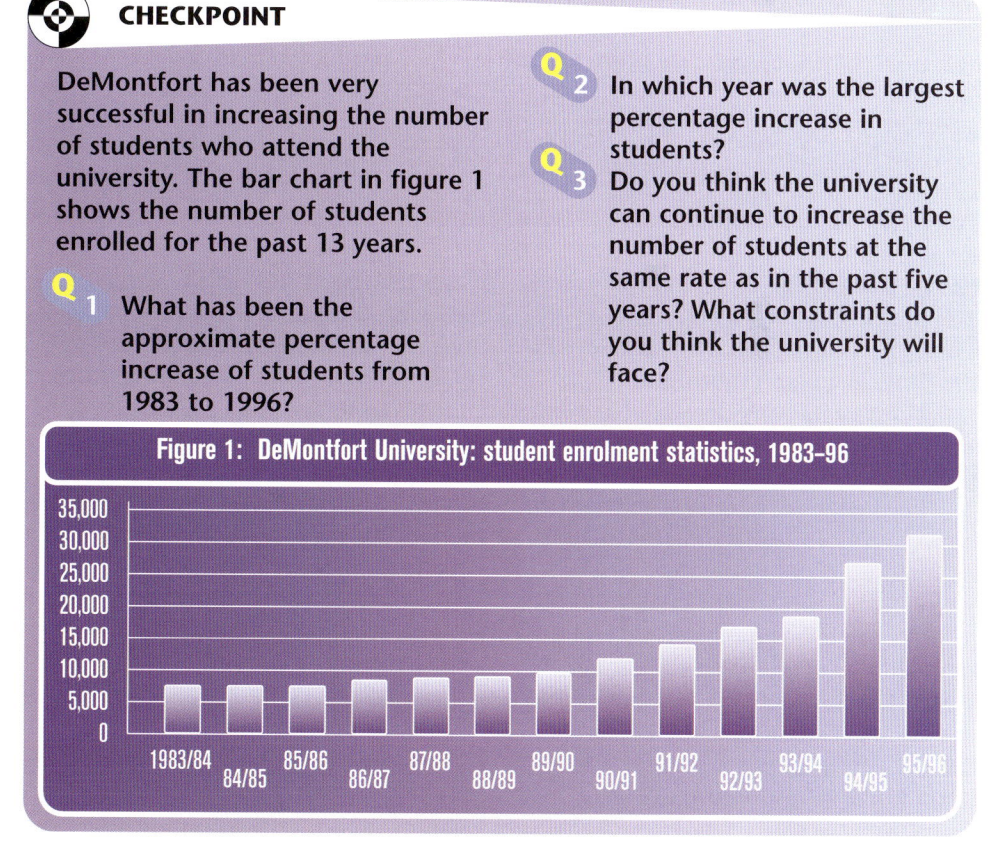

CHECKPOINT

DeMontfort has been very successful in increasing the number of students who attend the university. The bar chart in figure 1 shows the number of students enrolled for the past 13 years.

Q1 What has been the approximate percentage increase of students from 1983 to 1996?

Q2 In which year was the largest percentage increase in students?

Q3 Do you think the university can continue to increase the number of students at the same rate as in the past five years? What constraints do you think the university will face?

Figure 1: DeMontfort University: student enrolment statistics, 1983–96

KEY TERMS

A *brand image* is a way of identifying a product or service. This can vary from using standard colours to a logo, or any means of making recognition easy.

A *market segment* describes a group of customers who have certain things in common, e.g. all those living in the northwest of England, all those under 35 with children, pensioners, and so on.

Consumer goods include any product regularly bought by people for their own personal use.

Unit 4 Big or small?
Enquiry 2: What makes a firm grow?

Designed to grow

EVIDENCE

THE WIND-UP RADIO

Trevor Baylis observed that the cost and availability of batteries in rural parts of Africa were preventing many people from using their radios. He set out to design a new product that would meet the needs of this market, rather than trying to sell a battery-powered radio to people who could not use it. Baylis knew that the market for radios in Africa is different from the market in the UK simply because the batteries are expensive to buy and can be difficult to find in local shops. The clockwork radio, when wound up for 20 seconds, generates enough electricity to keep it operating for 40 minutes. Once the research and development process was complete, Baylis had to find a manufacturer and a marketing team to make his business a success. This all worked out well and the first factory to produce clockwork radios was set up in Cape Town, South Africa, in 1995.

Q1 The radios were launched in the UK in December 1995, retailing at £67.90. Do you think the radios will sell well in the UK? Explain your answer.

Q2 For some people in Africa, the price of the clockwork radio will be the equivalent of nearly three months' income. How well would you expect the radio to sell there?

NEW PRODUCTS

Companies introduce new products all the time. Heinz often brings out variations of its tinned spaghetti, such as hoops, animals, twists and other shapes.

The clockwork radio shows the importance of meeting the needs of the market in designing new products. There is probably a very small market for it in the UK as most people will use electricity to power their radios. What Baylis had discovered was a niche market for his product. Niches can be developed if producers recognize the importance of responding to customers' needs.

Many product markets follow a pattern. At the beginning just a few products may sell. Owners may be proud of their new, different possession. Then more and more people may buy the product until, in time, nearly everyone has one. Later still, sales may drop off. You can see this pattern in the sales of black and white television sets. In the early 1950s they were a luxury. Then sales grew, until eventually people began to buy colour televisions instead. Sometimes changes in technology are involved, or it may be just a matter of fashion.

This pattern is called the **product life cycle** and is shown in figure 1. The product life cycle has four stages:
- A – introduction stage, when sales are slow because the product is new.
- B – growth stage, when sales grow very quickly as the product is accepted.
- C – mature stage, when regular sales are achieved and the product is accepted.
- D – decline stage, when newer, better or more popular competing products are introduced.

The product life cycle for the radio in the UK market has reached the mature stage, but in Africa the clockwork radio is clearly in the introduction stage.

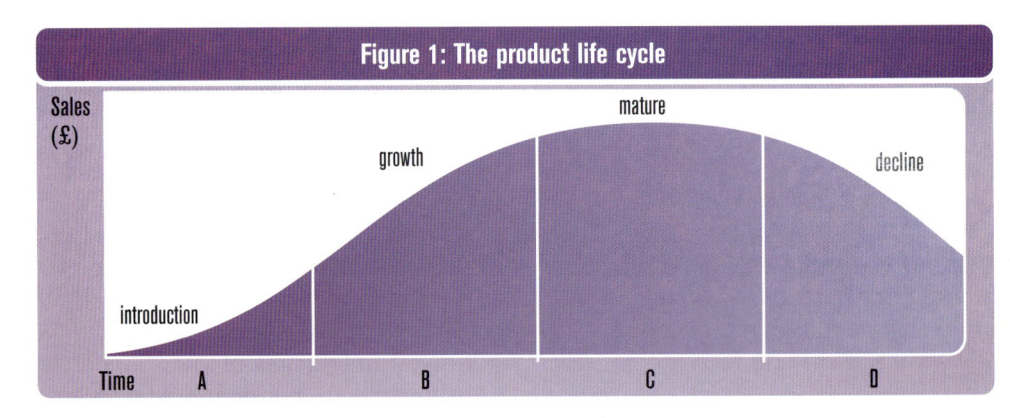

Figure 1: The product life cycle

NEW TECHNOLOGIES

Businesses can expand by developing new products. But designing a new product can take a long time. Businesses have to invest both time and money in research and development to bring their inventions to the market. Money is spent before there is income from sales. Businesses need to be protected from competitors who might take their ideas and use them, otherwise there would be no incentive to take risks and design new products.

Protection is provided by a number of laws. Inventors can apply for a **patent** to safeguard their ideas. The patent will last for 20 years, and only then can competitors use the same ideas. In a similar way designers can safeguard their designs and **logos** to prevent competitors using them.

Sometimes the product stays the same, but the technology used to produce it changes. Costs of production will fall, and perhaps prices as well. Productivity rises. The product will be more competitive. For example, changes have taken place in the telephone system which make it possible to connect people more quickly and at lower cost. The product – a telephone call – has not changed, but the process has.

Businesses try to expand and grow by developing new ideas and using modern technology. But not all developments need new technology and businesses can succeed by using the appropriate technology. When this happens, the business is said to be using **intermediate technology**.

Bicycles use intermediate technology for personal transport. Wheelbarrows do the same, for moving heavy items. Sometimes a new product is designed, using some advanced technology with a simple idea. The wind-up radio is one of these.

EVIDENCE

A NEW TYPE OF VACUUM CLEANER

From an early idea in 1979, James Dyson set out to design a more effective vacuum cleaner. After five years and over 5,000 versions, the private company owned by Dyson launched a vacuum cleaner that did not rely on existing technology. By using a new approach to removing dust and dirt the company proved that invention is important in breaking into existing markets. The Dyson upright became Britain's best-selling vacuum cleaner in February 1995, outselling its two main competitors by 3–1. This success has been achieved despite the fact that the company's products are more expensive than other vacuum cleaners.

Q1 In which stage of the product life cycle is the Dyson vacuum cleaner?

Q2 What would happen to Dyson's sales if other companies used the same technology to make a competing product?

KEY TERMS

Intermediate technology means using the lowest level of technology that is appropriate for the situation.

The *product life cycle* shows the pattern in which sales of a new product first increase, then peak and later go down. It includes the introduction, growth, mature and decline stages.

A *logo* is a sign or symbol that is used to promote the products of a particular business.

A *patent* is the legal protection for exclusive use of a design or idea. It can apply to a product or a way of doing things.

FORUM

Both examples on this page show how new products can be brought to the market. What incentive is there for a well-established business to try to develop new products?

Unit 4 — Big or small?

Enquiry 2: What makes a firm grow?

Joining together

EVIDENCE

KINGFISHER

The Kingfisher group was formed in 1982 and is now made up of a number of well-known businesses: Woolworths, B & Q, Comet, Superdrug, Music Video Club and others. When Kingfisher started, the business consisted of Woolworths. By buying other businesses Kingfisher was able to expand and grow.

Table 1: Kingfisher's acquisitions

Year	Acquisition	Type of business
1983	B & Q	DIY
1984	Comet	Electrical appliances
1987	Superdrug	Discount chemist

Kingfisher has also joined with other businesses rather than buying them. This happened in 1992, when it entered into a joint venture with an American company, Staples, from which the Music and Video Club was developed.

Businesses that merge or work together can pool resources. They get expertise from one another and can share specialist managers: these are managerial economies.

Q1 What do you think are the advantages for Kingfisher of buying up the other businesses?

Q2 Are there any disadvantages for the consumer?

MERGERS

If a business is successful it will expand into new markets and increase its sales. This will allow it to employ more people and to invest in research and development. Few businesses are able to grow quickly: it takes time to build up sales and market share. A business can expand quickly by joining with another company. This can be in the form of either a **merger**, where there is a voluntary agreement to join, or a **takeover**, where one business buys the other. In both situations the business increases its size and the value of its assets rises.

Sometimes the merger or takeover involves businesses in the same industry. This can mean that the amount of choice available to the consumer will be reduced. There will then be less competition. But the new business may find opportunities to save money by sharing various services such as marketing, distribution costs and head office expenses. These are all economies of scale and could lead to lower prices.

Some mergers and takeovers involve completely unrelated businesses. Although there appears to be little benefit in these businesses joining, the managers believe that they can run the businesses more profitably once they are merged. They expect to be able to make managerial economies, so reducing costs.

EVIDENCE

WHO OWNS WHAT?

Many well-known high street retailers are owned by the same company. This means that there is not as much competition as you would expect if they were all independent businesses. All the retailers shown here are fully or partly owned by Sears.

All these businesses are involved with high street fashion. This not only allows the Sears group to have a large influence in the retail fashion trade, but it also saves money because the separate businesses can work together on certain projects. They can co-ordinate their promotion activities and share information about the market. They can carefully select different parts of their marketing mix to target particular groups of people. In this way each shop will cater for a different market segment.

WAREHOUSE

SHOE CITY

Wallis   **CABLE & Co** FINE SHOES   **adams** childrenswear   **RICHARDS**   **Miss Selfridge**

SHOE EXPRESS   **Hush Puppies®**   **dolcis**

Q1 Why doesn't the Sears group simply call all its shops Sears?

Q2 Why would you expect Miss Selfridge and Warehouse (or Shoe Express and Dolcis) to sell different products and have different shop designs and styles?

Q3 For as many of these stores as you can, describe the market segment or segments for which the store is aiming. Briefly describe a typical customer who might visit the store regularly.

MERGERS AND ECONOMIES

Taking over, or merging with, other companies, allows for certain advantages. The larger business is able to take advantage of economies of scale and the new business usually has a larger market share. This may enable it to charge higher prices on some of its products, and make a bigger profit. Another advantage for larger companies is the sharing of risk, because if one of its businesses is doing badly, the chances are that other parts of the company are doing well. This gives larger companies a better chance of surviving difficult trading conditions. In the Kingfisher example described earlier, one of its businesses, Woolworths, suffered falling profits in the 1990s, but the company as a whole had continued to grow.

Even when businesses do not merge, there are opportunities for sharing costs. **Joint ventures** allow businesses to keep their independence at the same time as sharing their expertise. For example, two car manufacturers might decide to share the research and development costs of a new engine. Once the development is complete the two companies can then use the engine in their own cars. Each car manufacturer can then create its own products with its own image and design. The car companies can still compete with each other, but they have saved a considerable amount of money on their research.

There was co-operation of this kind in the 1980s, when Rover made an agreement with Honda. Rover produced cars to Honda's design and the two shared in the manufacture of parts. The agreement lasted until 1994, when Rover was taken over by BMW. This in turn has made other kinds of co-operation possible.

FORUM

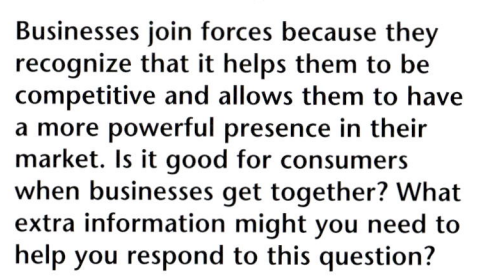

Businesses join forces because they recognize that it helps them to be competitive and allows them to have a more powerful presence in their market. Is it good for consumers when businesses get together? What extra information might you need to help you respond to this question?

KEY TERMS

A *joint venture* means that two businesses work together on a specific project, e.g. Hotpoint and Persil may organize a joint advertising campaign.

A *merger* is when two businesses join together through a voluntary agreement to create one larger company.

A *takeover* is when one company buys the shares of another company, thereby taking ownership of the business.

Unit 4 — Big or small?
Enquiry 3: Is small beautiful?

When is bigger not better?

EVIDENCE

THE STORY OF IBM

International Business Machines (IBM) built its first computer during the Second World War. It was 16 metres long and more than 2 metres wide. By the 1960s IBM was the undisputed market leader in computers. It spent serious money on research and development to enable it to bring out new ranges often. It beat the competition because it paid more attention to customers and aimed to give the best service. During the 1970s IBM made massive profits selling large mainframe computers to businesses, designing the system to meet the precise needs of the company. Its culture and organization were geared to selling expensive and profitable machines.

By the late 1970s, many people were buying personal computers (PCs). They were smaller, cheaper and more adaptable. They were off-the-shelf models and used chips bought in from outside suppliers such as Intel. Prices were kept down by strong competition from many fairly small producers. The big computers' share of the market fell from 80 per cent in 1974 to 30 per cent ten years later.

IBM was slow to react. It was not used to selling large numbers of cheap computers with a small profit margin. Although it did begin to produce personal computers, IBM found the competition very stiff. Smaller companies had an advantage. In the words of Michael Spiro, financial director of Elonex, a London-based manufacturer of PCs: 'We can undercut IBM because our overheads are much lower. In addition, smaller companies are nimble. The bureaucracy at IBM is so much heavier: in our company we can decide on the spend and just do it.'

The ability to remain nimble has become increasingly important as the pace of change has accelerated in the computer business. IBM survived, but it had to make 125,000 employees redundant.

Source: adapted from *The Independent on Sunday*, 24 January 1993

Q1 How did IBM become a world leader in the computer business?
Q2 What were the changes that made IBM less profitable?
Q3 What type of company gained the competitive advantage in the computer business?

DISECONOMIES OF SCALE

As IBM grew, it became less able to adapt to changing circumstances. When the market shifts such firms find it difficult or impossible to respond, and may go under or be forced to make major changes.

When a business grows it may find that its costs of production are falling. Bigger machines can produce more, cheaply. The business benefits from economies of scale. It can compete more easily. But some businesses experience a different outcome, at least after a time. They find that growth leads to problems. If costs of production rise, and the business finds it hard to compete, it is suffering from **diseconomies of scale**.

Diseconomies of scale usually mean that the business has become so big that it is no longer well managed. There are a number of ways in which this may happen. Becoming unable to adapt quickly, as in IBM's case, is just one way. Most of the problems come from difficulties in organizing people effectively.

THE HUMAN DIMENSION

When businesses grow, they take on more people. Some are directly involved with production, but others are not.

Up to a point, employing more people brings benefits. Employing a receptionist means that people on the shop floor do not have to stop work every time the telephone rings or someone walks through the front door. On the other hand, the output of the shop floor workers has to support that receptionist. There is a danger that the number of people not directly involved with production may become too great. If the added value of production workers is not high enough, then the firm may be unable to support its administrative staff and managers.

Once there are large numbers of employees, **communication** becomes more difficult. In a small business, workers are able to talk to the right person whenever they need to. In a larger business, it is often difficult to find out who the right person is. Then it may prove hard to make an appointment to see him or her, by which time it may be too late to do anything about the problem.

Large organizations can be difficult to manage. Workers who are directly involved with production see many other employees who appear only to be creating and moving paper. Sometimes the paperwork itself seems designed to make their jobs harder. Production workers become alienated and produce less. There may be disputes between management and employees. People may feel less motivated to work hard.

Individual departments may be unable to see how they fit into the overall organization. For example, the marketing department may set a target of a 10 per cent increase in sales for the next year, while the production department may be trying to reduce costs in the same period by stopping overtime working. If sales are increased but output is limited, customers will not get their goods on time and may buy from another business. Communication failure will have affected business performance.

CHECKPOINT

Q1 Hairdressing businesses are usually small. There may be one shop, or several. Worthingtons is quite big as hairdressers go. It has four shops in central London. Why do hairdressing businesses never seem to grow very large compared to car or washing machine manufacturers, for example.

Q2 Make a list of products that you think are produced cheaply on a large scale. Then make a second list containing products that are usually produced by small businesses. Don't forget to consider services as well as goods. Compare your list with someone else's. Can you think of any products that can be produced competitively on both a small and a large scale?

Q3 Think about your lists. What reasons can you identify for some kinds of production being best organized on a small scale?

KEY TERMS

Communication is the process by which managers and employees exchange information, opinions and ideas.

Diseconomies of scale occur when an increase in output results in a higher cost of production per unit.

Unit 4 Big or small?
Enquiry 3: Is small beautiful?

When is it good to talk?

EVIDENCE

THE CHARGE OF THE LIGHT BRIGADE

Half a league, half a league,
Half a league onward,
All in the valley of Death
   Rode the six hundred.
'Forward the Light Brigade!
Charge for the gun!' he said:
Into the valley of Death
   Rode the six hundred.

'Forward, the Light Brigade!'
Was there a man dismay'd?
Not tho' the soldier knew
   Someone had blunder'd:
Theirs not to make reply,
Theirs not to reason why,
Theirs but to do and die:
Into the valley of Death
   Rode the six hundred.

Alfred, Lord Tennyson, in *Poems and Plays*, Oxford University Press, 1968

This poem tells the terrible story of the attack by British cavalry against Russian artillery in the Battle of Balaclava in 1854. The details are unclear but it appears that the British commander, Lord Raglan, ordered the Light Brigade to attack the heights around the valley in which they were camped. Disastrously for the Light Brigade, the order was badly worded, and their commander, Lord Cardigan, ordered his force to charge straight up the valley. As the poem says, every soldier knew someone had made a terrible blunder, but they had to obey: 'to do and die'. And that is exactly what happened – for every ten men who started the charge, only six returned.

Was Lord Cardigan being awkward? He disliked Lord Raglan and might have made his own decision. He was a man who believed he could do anything. Whatever the truth, communications definitely broke down.

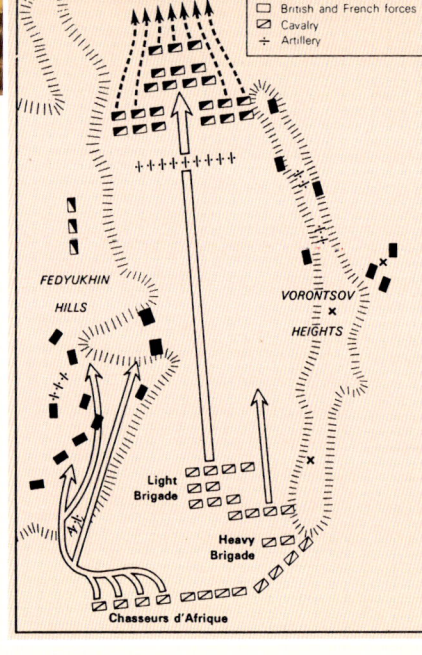

COMMUNICATION

The Charge of the Light Brigade is a classic example of one-way communication and the dangers that ensue. Had Lord Cardigan questioned the orders, or asked for more details, many lives would have been saved.

What has this to do with business today? Well, the market in which firms compete may be compared to a battlefield. Getting the orders wrong may mean the death of a firm. In war, it becomes harder to keep effective communications flowing as more people become involved. In the same way, companies become harder to manage as they grow because communications become more difficult.

There are many ways in which communications can go wrong. The person sending the message may use language, such as technical **jargon**, symbols or diagrams, which may not be understood by the receiver.

People may communicate badly because they do not know one another well. Or the message may have to be passed through a number of different people, and therefore not be received in the way that was intended. As a firm gets larger the barriers to communication increase. This is a diseconomy of scale. What can businesses do to overcome the problem?

First, there are technical improvements. Someone 'in the field', visiting customers to sell the product, no longer needs to feel isolated – cellular phones have seen to that. Fax machines, portable modems, the Internet and other technical breakthroughs have increased our ability to communicate. Importantly, this communication is two-way, so that when an order is issued it can be clarified with the person sending.

Second, firms can ensure that they operate through official **channels of communication**. The so-called 'grapevine' is the name for unofficial channels, which spread rumours of changes; these may be wrong and damaging. For example, a rumour might get around that employees are going to be made redundant. In this instance, the trade union, as the official channel, should be told first so that rumours cannot get started.

The third way of improving communication is to reduce the number of people through whom messages must pass. In an ideal world all management decisions would be sent at once to all the people affected. Many businesses reduce the number of managers with this in mind.

FORUM

Think of two examples of weak communication that you have experienced. What were the results of failure to communicate? How serious were the consequences?

K KEY TERMS

Channels of communication are the ways in which decisions can be passed through an organization. They can be official or unofficial.

Jargon is technical language which is not understood by everyone, e.g. 'economies of scale'.

EVIDENCE

Wensleydale cheese was first made about 900 years ago at Hawes in North Yorkshire. In 1992 the then owners of the Wensleydale factory, Dairy Crest, became concerned. Their accountants, based in Surrey, thought that Dairy Crest had too much factory capacity in northern England and that the Hawes factory should be shut down. This production could easily be transferred to the firm's other northern factory in Longridge, Lancashire. This would reduce overheads, but would also make production more efficient at the Longridge plant because there would be economies of scale.

The management at the Wensleydale plant decided to buy the factory from Dairy Crest rather than see it close down. By December 1995 Wensleydale cheese production had risen from 200 to 850 tons, the number of employees from 13 to 72, and nearly a quarter of a million people had visited the factory and its shop within 18 months. Turnover was rising steadily.

Large companies can employ specialists: this is an economy of scale. In fact, the advantages of employing specialist accountants in this case were more than offset by the fact that they had very little local or detailed knowledge. The Wensleydale factory could have been closed despite being potentially profitable. As Dairy Crest became bigger, communications had weakened so that the full facts were not known.

Q1 What was the percentage increase in production of Wensleydale cheese between 1992 and 1995?

Q2 The accountants in Surrey thought that the Wensleydale factory should be closed. How could they make such a big mistake?

Q3 Why was the Wensleydale factory less successful under Dairy Crest than it is now that its own managers are in charge?

Unit 4 Big or small?
Enquiry 3: Is small beautiful?

How do people make a difference?

EVIDENCE

BP

Every year *The Independent on Sunday* conducts a survey of 122 of Britain's top industrialists. They are asked who they think is the most impressive industrialist of the moment. In 1995 the winner was Sir David Simon of BP. Sir David was appointed to the company as managing director in 1992 when BP's share price was 245p. By early 1996 its share price was over 530p. Quite clearly, leadership makes a difference; however it is measured, BP is a large company and therefore diseconomies of scale are possible. In Sir David's view, poor managers are those who don't listen. 'Telling' he says 'is not enough.' And what is the secret of his leadership style? 'The process of building teams is one of the most important factors in getting performance out of big organizations. Obviously we've got a lot of talented people in BP. The issue is, are they switched on or not?'

Source: *The Independent on Sunday*, Business Section, 31 December 1995

AMSTRAD

One of Britain's best-known entrepreneurs is Alan Sugar. When he brought the first reasonably priced home computer to the UK market in 1984, it sold like hot cakes. Big profits followed. Yet his company, Amstrad, is in one of the riskiest and most competitive lines of business.

Alan Sugar is himself a tough competitor. His style is quite individual. He will close a deal with a short, sharp telephone call, agreeing a price almost before the person on the other end has worked out what is happening. He will walk from department to department or drop into a meeting, asking questions and pushing things along, keeping the whole company alert. He likes to keep control of all aspects of his company's business, and it is clearly through his talent that it has done well.

Of course, he cannot be everywhere at once. And as the company has grown, effective management by one man has become more difficult.

Q1 Is the share price a good way of judging the performance of a firm's managing director?

Q2 Are there other ways of measuring performance?

Q3 What differences can you see in the two styles of leadership shown by Sir David Simon and Alan Sugar?

LEADERSHIP STYLES

Leaders do make a difference. The headteacher affects the performance of a school; Sir Winston Churchill had an impact on the winning of the Second World War; Sir David Simon has clearly changed BP's profitability. Leaders' personal qualities can change the way organizations are run, for better or worse.

Some leaders give orders and expect to be obeyed. That results in speedy decision making, but may lead to a wrong decision. Some businesses take all the decisions at head office, as Dairy Crest did with the Wensleydale cheese factory on the previous page.

Other leaders prefer to discuss matters with their workers. This is more likely to produce decisions which are right and which everyone supports, but taking them is a slow process.

Encouraging people to make decisions about things that directly affect them can speed things up and improve morale. This is called **delegation**. When firms delegate decisions away from the head office it is called **decentralization**.

Sometimes a good leader will be able to see what the best leadership style is in a particular situation. By using the right approach, he or she helps the workforce to give of its best. The pupils in a school are more or less the same, but a different headteacher can motivate both staff and pupils to work harder and more effectively.

EVIDENCE

MILLING FLOUR

At Rank Hovis's flour mill in Selby, North Yorkshire, nearly everyone is multi-skilled, meaning that they are capable of performing more than one task. Almost one-third of the workforce is involved in job rotation, which means that people get the chance to see another part of the factory and learn about other workers' problems. Communications have been improved through having meetings at which all employees can share decisions and thus feel involved in the running of the company. All the staff have benefited from increased training, either in the plant or at the local college. There have been many areas of improvement:

- customer complaints are down 50 per cent
- accidents in the workplace are down 46 per cent
- flour production has increased despite the workforce being halved
- less time is lost due to breakdowns
- the mill won a national training award.

TEAMWORK

A person working as part of a very large organization may feel that his or her contribution doesn't count. However, as part of a small team, an individual may feel more encouraged to work hard, both for the team and for each team member.

The idea of teamwork has come partly from the example of Japan. It involves giving people opportunities to decide how the job should be done. This can help to avoid managerial diseconomies of scale, which cause costs to rise.

One way of encouraging teamwork is to create **quality circles**. This involves employees getting together at regular intervals to discuss how production and the product can be improved. People then feel that they are part of their firm's decision-making process. As a result, everyone in the organization, from managers to office cleaners, can work towards the idea of total quality at every stage. Improvements can be continuous.

CHECKPOINT

At The Mighty Meat Processors factory the employees feel they are ignored in all the big decisions the business makes. They don't understand the changes that are taking place. What effect do you think their lack of involvement will have on the company? What can be done to improve matters?

KEY TERMS

Decentralization means ensuring that decisions are taken at a level as close as possible to the people whom they will affect.

Delegation occurs when a more senior person asks a more junior person to take over a task, while continuing to be responsible for seeing that the task is done well.

Quality circles are groups of employees that get together at regular intervals to discuss how production can be improved.

Unit 4 — Big or small?
Enquiry 4: Can we control the giants?

What is a monopoly?

EVIDENCE

TENSION RISES AS STAGECOACH ROLLS INTO TOWN

Britain's buses, chugging along in the slow lane until the late 1980s, have suddenly hit the accelerator. Since the government encouraged private firms to run bus routes, there have been battles over local routes, soaring profits and takeovers. Some companies have been making money while others have become casualties.

In Darlington, in the northeast of England, up to 200 ageing buses trawl the most popular routes for passengers at rush hour. 'The town centre is not the same as it used to be', says Ray McKay, a local businessman. 'It is difficult for people to cross the roads and the centre is not pleasant to be in. It is not as though the buses are well used.'

The bus war heightened with the influx of even more buses from the UK's biggest bus company, Stagecoach, based in Perth. The company has set up a new operation in Darlington almost overnight and at the same time, one local company, Darlington Transport Company (DTC), has almost collapsed. Neither DTC, with 50 buses, nor the two other local operators, Your Bus with 15 buses and United with 50 buses, have made money from running local services and the fear is that the bigger, richer Stagecoach will force them out of business.

'It is the passengers who get caught in the middle', says Alan Milburn, the local MP. 'This is an example of Stagecoach using its finance to flatten other companies.'

Stagecoach is now running free bus services until it can start full commercial services later in the year. There have been many complaints around the country from small bus operators, who claim that Stagecoach is trying to put them out of business.

Adapted from *The Guardian*, 18 November 1994 and 5 April 1995, and *Evening Standard*, 30 November 1994

WHAT'S FAIR ON THE BUSES?

In the UK, Stagecoach has:

- grown from two staff and three buses to 19,500 staff and 6,500 buses;
- spent a total of £125 million over 18 months buying regional bus companies;
- 12 per cent of the total bus market;
- seen its profit in 1994–5 go up by 72 per cent to £32.6 million.

WHAT ABOUT THE PASSENGERS?

- Passenger journeys have dropped from 5.6 billion to 4.4 billion over the period 1985–95.
- Fares in some areas have risen.
- Bus timetables are complicated and uncertain.
- Travel cards are often no longer valid.

Q1 What do you think passengers in Darlington and elsewhere want from a bus service?

Q2 How has Stagecoach grown?

Q3 By the year 2000, Stagecoach might be one of a few nationwide companies providing bus services and the only company providing services in Darlington. Why might this be a problem?

THE POWER OF MONOPOLY

We have seen the likely advantages of having many firms willing to compete for customers. Such firms try to keep costs down in order to charge a competitive price and often develop new products. Customers have good choices at a reasonable price.

A successful business in a competitive world will want to expand. This can be at the expense of other firms. The end result could be just one large supplier, which has a **monopoly** in that market. The monopoly business could provide all that customers want at a reasonable price because there would be economies of scale to keep down costs. Stagecoach, for example, could buy a large number of new buses at a lower price than a small company would have to pay.

However, a monopoly business might take advantage of its position to charge unreasonable prices or provide a restricted range of products. In some places passengers might find the only routes on offer in the future are the main commuting routes into the city centre. Those living out of the city might have no service or be forced to pay very high fares.

A company can be in a position to abuse its monopoly power when it has a sizeable, but not complete, share of a market. It may charge 'suicidal prices' for a while to get rid of competitors or prevent possible competitors from entering the market. (If the price is low enough, it will not be worth their while to start up in business.) A monopoly may also buy a smaller rival to reduce competition.

MONOPOLIES THAT WORK

In some cases a monopoly supply may be preferred. It would be a waste of resources, for example, to have several different firms lay water pipes to your house when you are only going to use one for your supply.

Governments even create monopolies by giving firms a patent for a new product. This allows the firm to act as the only supplier of that product for a certain number of years. It can recoup costs and make profit from products that are expensive to research and develop. Drugs are a good example. If firms could not get patents they might not develop new ideas.

FORUM

What rules could be created to ensure that a large bus company with a monopoly share of the market operated in the best interests of customers and others in the community?

KEY TERM

A *monopoly* is the only supplier of a product in the market, or a business with a large enough share of a market to control prices or restrict supply.

CHECKPOINT

Ice cream sales in the UK in 1992 were worth about £785 million, 35 per cent of which was intended for immediate consumption ('impulse' ice cream). In the 1970s, Wall's and Lyons Maid shared almost all of this market. Since 1989, Mars has won a 16 per cent share of the impulse market with a new product based on its reputation in the confectionery market.

Mars claims that it has been hard to compete because its rivals, now Bird's Eye, Wall's and Nestlé, have supplied freezer cabinets free to shops in return for exclusive supply agreements. A shop can then only stock that supplier's products in the freezer. Shops can buy their own freezers and negotiate supply prices, or stock several different freezers.

Q1 What action have the big suppliers taken to restrict customers' choice?

Q2 How have customers been affected by this?

Q3 How could Mars have got 16 per cent of the market if Bird's Eye, Wall's and Nestlé were making exclusive supply agreements?

Unit 4 — Big or small?
Enquiry 4: Can we control the giants?

Taming the giants

EVIDENCE

STAGECOACH MUST STAND AND DELIVER

Stagecoach has been ordered to sell its 20 per cent shareholdings in SB Holdings (SBH), a rival Glasgow bus company. Also, Stagecoach must now drop an anti-competitive practice recently agreed with SB Holdings. According to the **Monopolies and Mergers Commission (MMC)**, Stagecoach has been acting against the public interest. The MMC noted that although SBH now had two-thirds of the local bus market after a recent merger, there were still other large operators around the region who provided potential competition.

Source: *The Times*, 28 April 1995

RECORD FIRMS CLEARED OF RIGGING CD PRICES

The Monopolies and Mergers Commission backed away from ordering the music industry to slash compact disc prices after a year's investigation. The report rejects claims that record companies are conspiring to keep the price of discs higher than overseas. An MMC price survey suggests that the difference in prices between the UK and USA is no wider than on a number of other consumer goods. The MMC thinks the price isn't out of line because it depends on how many dollars there are to the pound. They found the difference could also be explained by economies of scale and lower retail costs in the USA.

UK profits of EMI, Polygram, Sony, Warner and BMG, which control 70 per cent of sales between them, were not excessive. The MMC said that record companies' prices had to give a return on their heavy, high-risk investment. It would not make sense for them to sell CDs and cassettes at the same price when consumers think CDs have a higher value.

The MMC spokesperson admitted that it had not asked what profits the record companies made in the USA.

Source: adapted from *The Guardian*, 22 June 1994

THE WATCHDOGS

The Office of Fair Trading (OFT) is a government organization that looks at the anti-competitive practices of business. The OFT can refer cases to the Monopolies and Mergers Commission, which can make recommendations to government ministers. Complaints can be made to the OFT about particular anti-competitive practices. Or a whole industry can be investigated if a business is thought to have a monopoly share (above 25 per cent).

CHECKPOINT

Q1 What sort of 'anti-competitive practices' are the bus companies using?
Q2 What action has been taken against Stagecoach by the MMC?
Q3 Why was the MMC asked to investigate CD prices?
Q4 What evidence did the MMC use to back up its arguments about fair prices?

EVIDENCE

A WATCHDOG WITHOUT TEETH?

An all-party committee of MPs has called for a powerful regulator to stamp out bad behaviour in the bus industry. They claim that the OFT was slow to respond to complaints and by the time it took action, rival companies had been forced to close down. The report said that 'bus wars' have broken out on many city streets, where operators hang on to bus stops to pick up passengers or race to stops that are known to be busy.

The MPs would like a bus regulator to be appointed. A regulator could prevent the registration of predatory services, stop anti-competitive behaviour and apply a price cap to fares in areas where effective monopolies have been established.

Adapted from *The Guardian*, 14 December 1995

Comments from Stephen Locke of The Consumers' Association:

"The toothless watchdog has come up with yet another weak and muddle-headed report. The losers are the consumers who must continue to pay for overpriced CDs.

A simple change in the law would help because then CDs could be imported from the USA. Prices would tumble."

Comments from Gerald Kaufman, Chair of House of Commons Heritage Committee:

"The MMC might as well shut up shop and close down if it can conduct such a lengthy investigation with such incompetence.

It has failed to answer why record companies charged shops £2.50 more for CDs than for cassettes when there was virtually no difference in their manufacturing cost."

Q1 On what grounds did people criticize the two reports?
Q2 Why are some people asking for a bus regulator in place of action by the MMC?
Q3 How might supply and demand be used to explain the difference in price of cassettes and CDs?

HOW THE MMC WORKS

MMC investigations are carried out by a group of independent experts. They have to decide how competitive a market is. They look at how many competitors there are and whether the companies being investigated are keeping out new firms that might want to compete.

The final recommendations of the MMC are based on whether the company is acting '**in the public interest**'. If an activity is seen to have more advantages than disadvantages to the community as a whole, it will be allowed to go ahead. The MMC decided that the music industry was acting 'in the public interest' when the price of CDs was set.

REGULATION

Critics say the MMC is too slow and cautious. Sometimes, though, the possibility of investigation can be enough to prevent hasty actions and put firms off taking advantage of positions of power in order to control a market.

An alternative approach to regulation is used for those industries that have moved from public to private hands yet continue to operate as monopolies. These include gas, electricity, telephone and water companies. The government has appointed **regulators** (for example OFWAT, which regulates the water companies). They are responsible for overseeing the fair operation of the industry. They can set guidelines for prices and act quickly on customer complaints.

KEY TERMS

'*In the public interest*' is the yardstick used by the MMC to decide whether the actions of firms should be allowed to continue. It involves weighing up all the advantages and disadvantages to different groups within the community.

The Monopolies and Mergers Commission (MMC) exists to investigate all cases in which firms are suspected of trying to use monopoly power to raise prices or reduce customer choice.

The Office of Fair Trading (OFT) is the government body responsible for ensuring that businesses act in line with competition law.

Regulators are independent people appointed by the government to oversee the activities of particular industries.

FORUM

The USA monopoly laws expect firms to prove their innocence if accused of fixing prices or of controlling a market.

What difference might this make in the case of Stagecoach's operations or the CD investigation?

Unit 4 — Big or small?

Enquiry 4: Can we control the giants?

What is a transnational?

EVIDENCE

Ford Motor Company has manufacturing facilities located in 22 countries on 5 continents. There are 159 Ford plants worldwide.
Source: *Ford Media Guide*, 1995

SPANNING THE WORLD

Ford makes cars. Its head office is in Detroit, in the USA, but it has factories all over the world. Any firm that has factories, shops or offices in several countries is known as a **transnational**. Many familiar names are, in fact, very large companies that span the world. Unilever, Shell, IBM and Marks & Spencer are examples.

WHAT'S WRONG WITH HOME?

Why doesn't Ford make all its cars in the USA? There are many answers to this question.

Although there are economies of scale in producing many cars in one factory, if the end product is expensive to transport, some cost savings may be lost. So it can be cheaper to make cars near to where you want to sell them.

The USA is an expensive place to make anything. If a company wants to sell in countries where incomes are lower, prices also may have to be lower. It will therefore be better to make cars where labour and other costs are lower, too. Many companies take advantage of the low wages in countries such as the Philippines or Thailand to make things that they want to sell all over the world. Take a look at your T-shirt, baseball cap or trainers – you will probably find that they are made in a country such as this. In the same way, because wages are lower in Europe than in the USA, Ford manufactures cars in Europe for the local markets. In every case, people are specializing in what they do most cheaply.

Many countries, or groups of countries, restrict imports. The European Union (EU) does this. To avoid the problem, companies set up factories within the EU. Nissan and Toyota both have car plants in the UK. They use parts and raw materials that come from countries inside the European Union so that the cars produced can be described as European in origin.

Table 1: A comparison of transnationals' sales and countries' GDP

	Transnationals' sales (US $ million)	Countries' GDP (US $ million)
MITSUBISHI	176,000	
Sweden		166,000
Turkey		156,000
GENERAL MOTORS	155,000	
Indonesia		145,000
FORD	128,000	
Thailand		125,000
South Africa		106,000
EXXON	101,000	
Hong Kong		90,000
TOYOTA	88,000	
Poland		86,000
Portugal		85,000
IBM	64,000	
Greece		63,000
Venezuela		60,000
NISSAN	59,000	
Philippines		54,000
Colombia		54,000

Source: *Fortune*, 7 August 1995, *World Development Report*, Oxford University Press, 1995

EVIDENCE

TAIWAN BRINGS JOBS TO SCOTLAND

Chungwa Picture Tubes, which makes parts for televisions and computer monitors, is setting up a new plant costing £260 million in Motherwell. The new plant will be the most automated and technically advanced in the world, producing 10 million television tubes a year.

The factory will employ over 3,000 people and will supply the whole of Europe. New recruits will be sent to Taiwan or Malaysia for training. Scotland was chosen because it gives direct access to the European market and has a high-quality workforce.

Q1 Almost all the cars made by Ford in the USA are sold there. Why is this?

Q2 Nissan can (a) make cars in Japan and sell them in Europe; (b) make cars in each EU country for the local market; or (c) make cars in the UK and sell them all over the EU. Which is likely to be the cheapest option? Why?

Q3 Motherwell was delighted to welcome Chungwa Picture Tubes' investment there. How might it affect local people?

WHAT'S THE APPEAL?

Since the steel works nearby shut down, unemployment in Motherwell has been high and the town has been very depressed. The arrival of a new employer will bring jobs to people who thought that they might be jobless for the rest of their lives. The local shops will revive as people have more money to spend and the local economy will start to grow again.

Many poor countries also welcome transnationals for the same reasons. They bring employment, incomes and growth. People who are employed in the new industries will receive training and develop new skills. The communications network may be improved because of the need for roads, railways and telephones.

WHAT'S THE DOWNSIDE?

Despite the fact that many governments try to attract transnationals by reducing tax levels and other incentives, this does not always create a 'win-win' situation. The interests of some very large companies may be different from those of the inhabitants of the country in which they are setting up a factory.

- *Profits*: shareholders are looking for a good return on their shares and therefore want the company to make a profit. These profits are therefore returned to the country where the company originates instead of being used to build the economy around where the plant has been built.
- *Power*: on occasion, transnationals have been known to put political pressure on governments in order to make policy changes to suit them. Though this may sound improbable, many transnationals are financially larger than many small countries, so their influence can be powerful. Table 1 compares the worldwide sales of certain transnationals with the **gross domestic product (GDP)** of some countries in which these companies operate. Gross domestic product is a measure of a country's total output.
- *Products*: some companies have sold products in developing countries that they would not be allowed to sell in the developed world. Equally, they may use marketing techniques in ways that might be considered inappropriate. In many countries there are legal restrictions on cigarette advertising, especially to some sections of the population. Sales have fallen in the developed world, and companies have targeted poorer countries in order to expand their markets again.
- *Prices*: in a highly competitive industry, it is important to keep prices down. The search for cheap resources has led companies to set up factories where costs are low. If many firms do this, the country will start to grow richer and wages and other costs will rise. When this happens the search may be on again to find a new location where costs are still low.

FORUM

Who are the stakeholders in a transnational? Do they all have an equal influence on the actions of the company?

If not, make a list that puts them in rank order, starting with the most powerful.

KEY TERMS

GDP (gross domestic product) is a measure of the value of total output from all the businesses in the economy.

Transnational enterprises are those that have business interests in several countries.

Unit 4 Big or small?
Enquiry 4: Can we control the giants?

In everyone's interest?

EVIDENCE

DIGGING IN THE DUNES

On the southern tip of Madagascar, just outside a town called Tolanaro, the sand beneath the rainforest is full of ore containing titanium dioxide. You will find this substance in all sorts of things – from make-up to paint to pills. The mining company QIT, which is part of a transnational mining corporation, is planning to extract 2 billion tonnes of titanium dioxide from three locations near Tolanaro over the next 40 years.

The plans involve building a barrier to keep the sea back, a port and a new town.

A floating dredger will then suck up the sand, remove the titanium dioxide and spit out the rest.

Q1 Who are the stakeholders involved in this plan?

Q2 What needs to be taken into account before a decision is made to go ahead?

RESPONSIBILITY

QIT and its parent company on the other side of the world have a responsibility to their shareholders to produce a profit. By mining the sand dunes of Madagascar, they would be meeting this objective. The decision to go ahead may, however, conflict with the needs and objectives of some people, while providing benefits for others.

The remaining items of Evidence explain some of the issues that need to be taken into account.

MADAGASCAR

This island of Madagascar, in the Indian Ocean, is two and a half times the size of the British Isles. It is among the world's poorest countries and is getting poorer. The population is small but is growing fast. At current rates, it could double in 22 years. Some 40 per cent of the population suffers from chronic malnutrition, and 11 per cent of babies die at birth or soon after.

The southeast corner of the island, where the mining is intended to take place, is the poorest part of a poor country. Average income is about £10 a month.

EVIDENCE

THE ENVIRONMENT

Madagascar has been isolated for millions of years and has developed its own unique array of wildlife. The titanium dioxide is to be found in the sand dunes that lead down to lagoons behind the sea beaches. The coastal forest along these lagoons is unique and is the habitat of a wide range of plants and animals. There are, for example, 60 different species of reptile in the forest. In Britain, there are only six.

The local villagers are, however, destroying the forest themselves. They cut down the trees and undergrowth and burn the remaining vegetation in order to extend their rice fields. If they do not change this practice, in 40 years there will be no forest left.

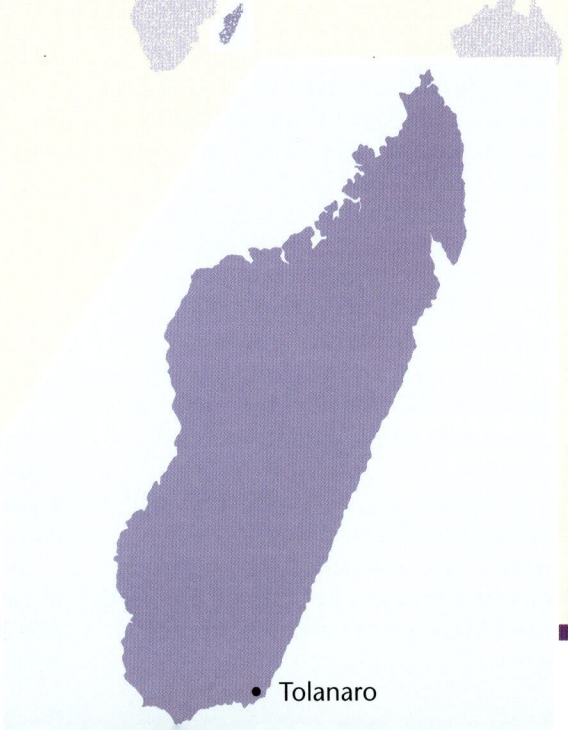

• Tolanaro

144

EVIDENCE

THE BUSINESSMEN

The businessmen in town are in favour of the mine. The developers would have to build roads, install water, power supplies and communications as well as providing a range of social services. They see the benefits of these facilities because it would bring trade and improve access to the area. It takes three days by bush taxi to reach the capital at the moment. The developments would also create jobs and therefore bring in more money. The mine is expected to employ almost 500 local people.

THE FISHERMEN

The fishermen live in villages along the lagoon and they make their living by catching shrimps, prawns and crabs. If a dam were built the level of salt in the lagoon would fall and this could change the nature of the marine life.

The mining project would affect 27 families who fish these waters. Their livelihood comes from selling the catch in the market. As 20 per cent of the fish sold comes from the lagoon, the diet of the local population would also have to change.

RESTORING THE SITE

As mining is completed in each zone, the company will replant the site. The topsoil will have been saved and replaced afterwards to help this process. Forests will be replanted with trees that are grown for their timber. There is, however, some doubt about whether the trees will survive.

ECO TOURISM

An alternative strategy for Madagascar is to attract tourists who are interested in seeing the varied environments the country has to offer. Apart from the ecology, there are miles of sandy beaches and places of historic and cultural interest close at hand.

At present, only 10,000 people a year visit the southeast corner of the island, despite its attractions. This is largely due to the poor communications and lack of facilities in the area. By improving the situation, tourism could become the main source of income for the country as a whole. Already, approximately 1,000 people are employed in the tourist industry in the area.

Q1 Who stands to gain if the mining goes ahead?
Q2 Who stands to lose?

Q3 What questions should the mining company ask itself before it decides to go ahead?

Q4 If you were the Minister for Economic Development, would you allow the development to take place?

THE TRADE-OFF

Madagascar is a country with many economic problems. It owes millions of dollars to other countries and some of its population is hungry, unhealthy and poorly educated. It has to make a decision about whether it should permit this development to take place.

Many countries are put in this position by transnationals that want to set up factories in places where labour is cheap, regulations are few, or there are natural resources to be exploited.

Such companies are often welcomed because they bring economic development by providing jobs for the local population, building roads and providing other forms of communications.

There is, however, often a **trade-off**. In the case of Madagascar, the issues are environmental and social. Some countries have become very dependent on transnationals, so the decisions they make can have serious consequences for the economy.

As a key objective is to find a low-cost location, many firms will move manufacturing to another country if wages start to rise. A company that makes a well-known brand of trainers did just that. The government tried to hold wages down in order to stop the move from taking place.

KEY TERM

A *trade-off* happens when the advantages of an activity are weighed against the disadvantages.

Unit 4 — Big or small?

Enquiry 5: Why belong to the European Union?

Why belong to the European Union?

EVIDENCE

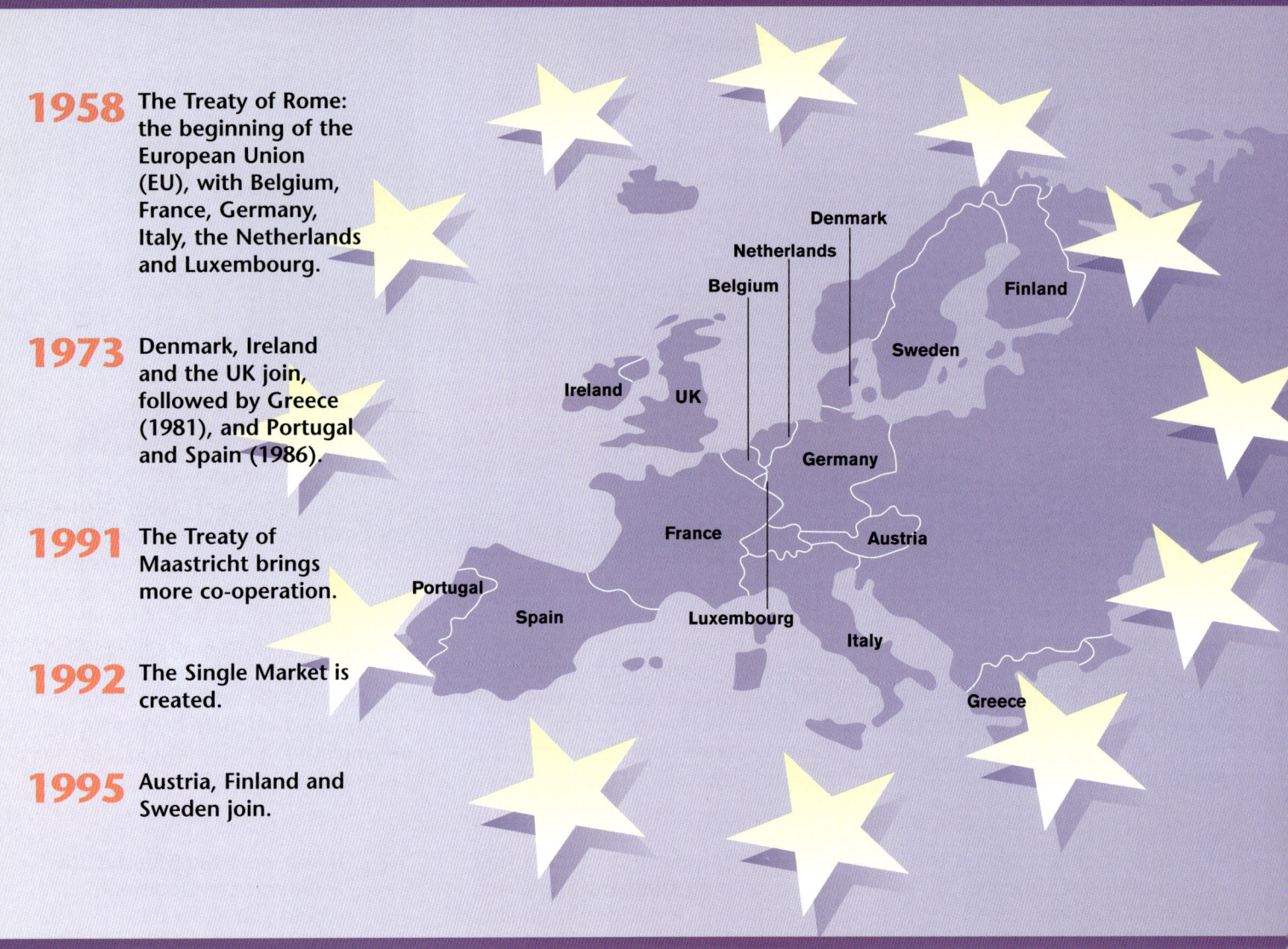

1958 The Treaty of Rome: the beginning of the European Union (EU), with Belgium, France, Germany, Italy, the Netherlands and Luxembourg.

1973 Denmark, Ireland and the UK join, followed by Greece (1981), and Portugal and Spain (1986).

1991 The Treaty of Maastricht brings more co-operation.

1992 The Single Market is created.

1995 Austria, Finland and Sweden join.

WHAT IS THE EUROPEAN UNION?

After the Second World War, many people thought that peace would be ensured if nations would co-operate. In Europe, first a few countries, and then many more, joined together to create the European Union. This allowed each member country to sell its goods freely in any other member country's market. In this way, the member countries have achieved higher real incomes. More specialization and more co-operation have been good for all.

Businesses with larger markets can grow, and can cut costs and prices through economies of scale. But there is more to the European Union than that. Citizens of EU countries can move freely within its borders and can work in any member country.

The EU also encourages governments to work together on common problems such as unemployment.

The administration of the EU is carried out in Brussels. The European Parliament meets in Strasbourg.

CHECKPOINT

Q1 What political party does your Member of the European Parliament (MEP) belong to?

Q2 Explain why a larger market may enable a business to cut costs and prices. What effect is it likely to have on profits?

HOW DOES THE EU WORK?

All countries trade: they sell their **exports** in other countries' markets, and buy **imports** from other countries for their own use. In this way you can get goods and services you might otherwise not have: a banana or a weekend in Paris, for example. (Services, like tourism, are an important part of international trade.)

The European Union is a '**customs union**'. This means that all the member countries can trade without restrictions. They trade 'on a level playing field', so they all face the same rules, regulations and opportunities. There is strong competition on price and quality. The member countries are a single market: they all compete on the same terms.

Trade can involve taxes, known as **customs duties**, paid when the goods move between one country and another. There may be other restrictions, too. Within the EU, there are none. Customs duties are payable only on imports from outside the EU.

The EU has other important features. Standards have been set for a wide variety of products. If you look at the packaging of all sorts of consumer goods, you will find a European Standard number, showing that the contents meet the requirements.

The Common Agricultural Policy (CAP) provides support for farmers in all member countries.

The Social Chapter of the Maastricht Treaty aims to set standards for a wide variety of factors affecting people throughout the Union, including standards relating to the workplace, minimum wages and pension rights. The UK government has so far decided to opt out of these arrangements.

A common currency is an important objective. It is intended to bring unity by obliging all the members to work closely together, both economically and politically. This and other objectives are set out in the Maastricht Treaty. Many people still disagree about this.

EVIDENCE

There are differences in the tastes of consumers and in their buying habits between one region of a country and another, sometimes between one town and another in the same region. Between one country and another these differences are often more noticeable. Each business tries to identify and meet the needs of its customers in different markets.

Marks & Spencer's stores in London, Paris and Madrid will have a very similar appearance. However, a closer look at the items for sale will reveal a careful attempt to select goods from their range that appeal to the different tastes and cultures of their customers. Parisians refused to buy clothes that they could not try on, so Marks & Spencer had to break with tradition and provide changing rooms! The implication is that the businesses that gain most from the European Union are those that make the most effort to understand their customers' needs.

London

Paris

WHAT ABOUT THE OUTSIDERS?

EU restrictions on imports from outside mean that non-member countries have to be more competitive in order to sell there. The insiders have an advantage. The size of this advantage depends on the level of customs duties for the product. This is usually quite high for farm products like sugar or butter, but rather lower for manufactured products like televisions.

Some foreign businesses that want to sell to EU countries invest and set up businesses within the borders of the EU. This makes it easier for them to compete. Chungwa Picture Tubes came to Motherwell for this reason (see page 143).

Of course, there are countries that suffer because they are outside the EU. As their output sells at a higher price inside the EU, because of customs duties, it is more difficult for them to sell there. This also has an impact on EU consumers because it may exclude them from cheaper products that could be bought outside the EU. New Zealand butter would be cheaper in the EU if there were no customs duties payable when it is imported.

FORUM

In what ways do members of your class think they are European? To what extent have you and other members of your class been influenced by other countries and cultures? (Think about the food you eat, for example.)

In what ways do you think tastes and cultures differ between the place you live and another region or country?

KEY TERMS

Customs duties are taxes on imports.

A *customs union* is formed by a group of countries that agree to trade freely with one another while taxing imports from non-member countries.

Exports are goods and services that are sold to other countries.

Imports are goods and services that are bought from other countries.

Unit 4 — Big or small?

Enquiry 5: Why belong to the European Union?

In or out?

EVIDENCE

WE WANT IN

Ericsson is a Swedish transnational company with worldwide interests. Just under half of all its workforce is based in Sweden. Ericsson designs and manufactures mobile phones as part of its product range. A mobile phone is a consumer product that has a number of competitors, so demand is very sensitive to price changes. People buying mobile phones first look at the price and then they compare quality. Until recently, Sweden was not a member of the European Union and had to pay customs duties in order to sell products made in Sweden to consumers within the EU.

Ericsson was pleased that the Swedish people voted to join the EU because one outcome of this has been the reduction in the price of its mobile phones sold in the EU, because there is no customs duty to pay. Of course, Ericsson may now face competition in the Swedish market from EU producers.

Q1 What effect would the customs duty have on demand within the EU for Ericsson's mobile phones?

Q2 If Sweden had not joined the EU, what might Ericsson have had to do to keep up sales?

THREAT OR OPPORTUNITY?

Herman Miller is a US-based transnational designing and making high-quality office furniture. It has factories within the EU in England, Germany and Italy. Competing firms in the furniture industry all use low technology, and similar materials and designs. The result is fierce competition. There are many producers trying to carve out a share of the EU market, which in total is worth over £5 billion. Herman Miller is ranked as the 14th largest, with a market share of 1 per cent.

With no customs duties between member countries, there is even more competition. To survive, Herman Miller must not only meet the local design and styling requirements of each country. It must also provide customers with value for money by giving good customer service and keeping prices in line with those of other producers.

Within the EU single market customs controls have been dismantled. There are now fewer forms to complete and far fewer delays when the lorries cross national borders. The materials and the finished products are delivered more quickly, reliably and cheaply. These lower **distribution costs** allow stock levels to be kept down, and the lead time between receiving an order and completing it can be reduced. Herman Miller passes on most of the savings to its customers.

Q1 Do you think Herman Miller views the EU as a good or a bad thing?

Q2 Why do you think Herman Miller wants to keep its factories going in Europe?

Q3 How does being a member of the EU reduce costs?

Q4 Why does Herman Miller pass on most of the savings to customers rather than keep them?

Q5 What is the impact of the single market on consumers?

Figure 1: Trading sources and destinations

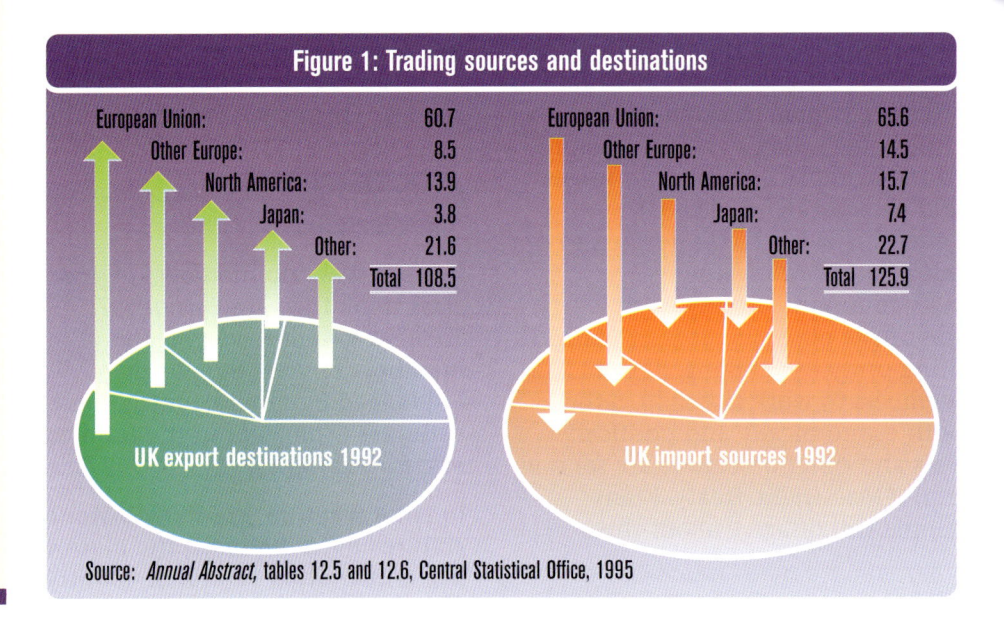

UK export destinations 1992
- European Union: 60.7
- Other Europe: 8.5
- North America: 13.9
- Japan: 3.8
- Other: 21.6
- Total 108.5

UK import sources 1992
- European Union: 65.6
- Other Europe: 14.5
- North America: 15.7
- Japan: 7.4
- Other: 22.7
- Total 125.9

Source: *Annual Abstract*, tables 12.5 and 12.6, Central Statistical Office, 1995

BUSINESS AND THE EU

The European Union has helped increase trade between member countries. Figure 1 shows the extent to which the UK's trade focuses on the EU. Businesses like Herman Miller have seen this as an opportunity to expand, but they must also become more efficient to survive. The increased competition means that cost savings have often been passed on to the consumer in the form of lower prices.

On the other hand, the EU has tried to protect businesses operating within the member countries by imposing customs duties on goods imported into the EU. This affected Ericsson's factories in Sweden before that country became a member. Consumers buying products made outside the EU are paying higher prices than would be the case if there were no customs duties.

To try to ensure the production of quality products that meet standard safety levels, the EU has set up a certificate system. This is a form of regulation that ensures that all producers for the EU market work to the same rules. However, meeting the requirements does increase production costs, particularly for small businesses. One concern to businesses that have gained the certificate is that often little is done to insist that the regulations are met.

Standardization can be useful for quality control and safety, and for cutting costs in large markets. At the same time, member countries have many variations in consumer choice. Many companies, like Herman Miller, see being able to meet these market needs as the most important issue. Different businesses see the EU in different ways. It all depends on how they are affected by having a large market and by having to stay within the regulations.

EVIDENCE

IS IT WORTH THE PAPER IT'S PRINTED ON?

ISO EN 9002 is a certificate awarded to a business that meets a common standard of European quality control. It is a bit harder to get this certificate than a British kite mark, but it is accepted throughout the EU. It is designed to improve the standards of products. Terry, from Bence Coachworks, said that it took his business three years and cost £16,000 to meet the standards. He estimates that it costs an extra £100 a week to do the administration. Terry does not believe that he lost any customers in the EU when the company did not have the qualification, and wonders whether it was worthwhile.

Q1 How much extra does it cost per year for Terry's business to administer the European quality control system?

Q2 Why may Terry be a little frustrated with this regulation?

[Registration Certificate from QMS Quality Management Systems Limited for W.H. Bence (Coachworks) Limited, BS EN ISO 9002:1994, Original Approval: 4th October 1995, Current Certificate: 4th October 1995, Certificate Expiry: 3rd October 1998, Certificate Number: A 0768]

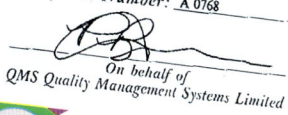

FORUM

Why are more countries wanting to join the EU? What might their concerns be?

CHECKPOINT

Work out ways in which the EU affects people. Remember people are consumers, but they may also have jobs that are affected.

KEY TERMS

Distribution costs are the costs of getting the products from the manufacturer to the customer.

Standardization means designing and making identical products for many different markets.

Unit 4

Big or small?

Enquiry 5: Why belong to the European Union?

Food for Europe

EVIDENCE

TO GROW, OR NOT TO GROW?

Graham Lock owns and manages a farm in Somerset. As a mainly arable farmer, Graham's most important task is to fill in a special EU form giving details of every field he farms, including the field size, what was grown last year and what was grown this year. From this information, the Ministry of Agriculture, Fisheries and Food (MAFF) calculates how much money to give him. This money is called a **subsidy**.

The subsidy scheme pays Graham and other arable farmers so much per hectare for each crop grown. Rates are set for all crops: cereals, vegetables or oilseeds. In exchange Graham must agree not to farm some of his fields. This is known as 'set aside'.

At present Graham feels that arable farms are fairly profitable, but funding for set aside may last only two or three years. He is very uncertain about the future.

Q1 Why are subsidy payments important to farmers like Graham?

Q2 Why might the EU pay farmers not to grow food?

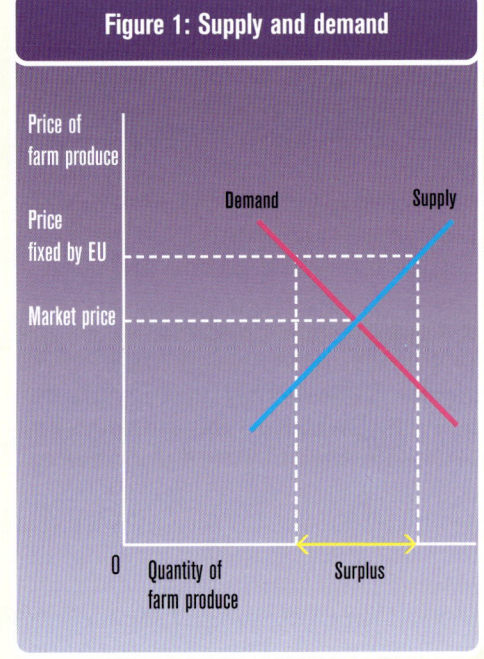

Figure 1: Supply and demand

LAKES AND MOUNTAINS

From its very beginning until the late 1980s, the European Union believed that agriculture should be supported, for two reasons. One was to increase output, reducing the need for imports. The other was to increase farmers' incomes. The way it did this was through the Common Agricultural Policy (CAP).

The CAP guaranteed EU farmers high prices for their products. This was combined with customs duties on food imports. Together, these measures brought high food prices for consumers, but helped many poor, small farms to survive.

The CAP encouraged large, efficient farms to invest heavily in order to produce more. The high prices made it worth farmers' while to increase output as much as they could. Productivity increased, leading to huge crops of grains and quantities of butter and meat. The CAP authorities bought and stored the unsold farm output. These surpluses came to be known as 'grain and butter mountains' and 'wine lakes'. In the late 1980s the EU began to try to match supply and demand in order to reduce the lakes and mountains. A quota system for milk production was introduced to cut the butter mountain. This limited the amount of milk that any farmer could produce. Set aside is used to control the grain mountains and other products of arable farming. The amount of land that farmers are expected to set aside varies according to the demand and supply situation. In 1993–4 it was 15 per cent. In 1994–5 it fell to 10 per cent as the grain mountain was reduced by poor world harvests and increased demand for grain from Eastern Asia.

EVIDENCE

THE FARMERS' FUTURE

What does the future hold for farmers in the EU? In the opening Evidence, Graham Lock said that the future is very uncertain. First, other countries have persuaded the EU to reduce trade restrictions on farm products, to give their exporters more of a chance in EU markets. Second, the expansion of the EU to include Eastern European countries (see pages 152–3) whose inefficient farms will require support, will result in the available money being spread more thinly.

One choice would be to reduce the protection given by customs duties and force farmers in the EU to compete on the world market. This would mean more large farms, possibly with problems in Southern Europe as small family farms would disappear. Consumers would benefit from lower prices, but the countryside might become less attractive as hedgerows could be ripped up to improve farm efficiency.

An alternative choice might be to give farmers money to improve the environment for both wildlife and recreation. Increasing farm output is now less important to most governments than it used to be.

HAY BARN OR CLUBHOUSE?

Cumberwell Farm in Wiltshire is run by the James family. The land farmed was originally 400 hectares, about the size of 400 football pitches. The main business was milk and butter production. In the late 1980s the amount of milk the farm was allowed to produce was restricted by the EU. This meant that sales were lower and the profits were squeezed. The family decided that they needed to **diversify** and in 1988 they converted part of the farm into a landfill site for topsoil and debris from the local road builders and housing developers. The project proved a success, so the family diversified further. They opened up a golf course in 1994 covering 100 hectares and centred around a new luxury clubhouse, built to look like an old barn. The farm is now less than half its original size. The final twist is that plans to build a road that would cut through the golf course were to have been partly funded by the EU. These plans were shelved in the 1995 budget. Good for the golf side of the business, but bad for the landfill site.

CHECKPOINT

Q1 Why did farm output in the EU grow so fast?
Q2 What effect does a system of high food prices have on consumers?
Q3 Why do you think it might be important to have some support for farmers?
Q4 Why does EU policy lead to uncertainty for farmers?

FORUM

What do you think would be the advantages and disadvantages of the two choices put forward in the text above?

KEY TERMS

To *diversify* means to produce other things in order to spread the risk.

A *subsidy* is a payment made by the government, usually to encourage a particular type of production.

Unit 4 Big or small?

Enquiry 5: Why belong to the European Union?

A bigger Europe?

EVIDENCE

HOW MUCH BIGGER?

Q1 Approximately how much bigger might the new Europe be?

Q2 What opportunities will this provide for industry in the pre-1996 member countries?

Q3 What threats might there be to the future of these industries?

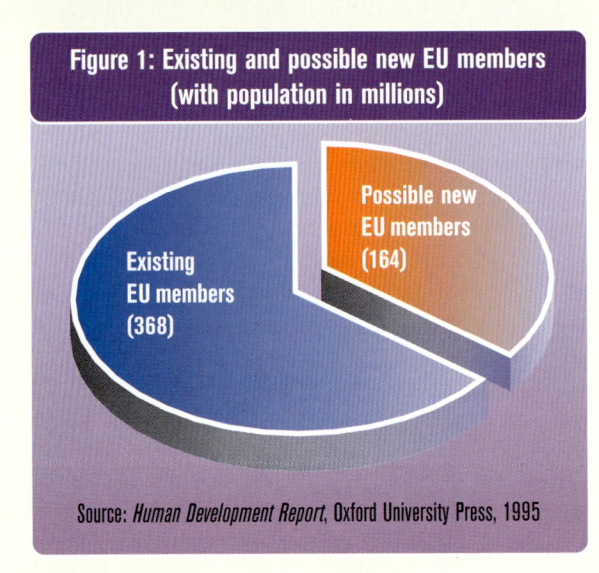

Figure 1: Existing and possible new EU members (with population in millions)

- Existing EU members (368)
- Possible new EU members (164)

Source: *Human Development Report*, Oxford University Press, 1995

Table 1: Possible new EU member countries

Turkey
Cyprus
Malta
Estonia
Latvia
Lithuania
Romania
Bulgaria
Poland
Slovakia
Hungary
Czech Republic

NEW OPPORTUNITIES

The new Europe could have a much larger total population than the 1996 version. Many companies are looking upon this as an opportunity to sell their products into a new market. Some of these countries are growing fast, but others have economic problems that will make them less likely to provide the source of demand that businesses are looking for.

The Polish economy has been growing at a rate of 6 per cent per year. That means that the standard of living of the average Polish family has been improving. However, there is still a long way to go before it compares with that of the average British family.

Until 1989, the countries of Eastern Europe had communist economic systems. That meant that the government took all the decisions about production and prices. After the fall of the Berlin Wall, these countries shifted to a system in which markets were allowed to operate. So production decisions could be made on the basis of what would make a profit. Prices could be set to cover costs and attract customers. The changes were painful, but could lead to growth in the future.

Since the decline of communism, industry has been keen to invest in Eastern Europe in order to make the most of this growing market. In Unit 1, the Cadbury factory that has been set up in Poland was used as an example (see page 5). Many other big companies have done the same thing.

Western products are given high status in much of Eastern Europe. The newspaper advert from a Russian paper shows clearly how western brand names have great appeal.

EVIDENCE

Q1 What sort of goods are being sold in this advertisement?

Q2 What is the most powerful attraction for customers?

Q3 Would the same products be advertised in the same way in papers in the UK?

152

EVIDENCE

ANOTHER VIEW

"For the farmers here, the European Union means that we can't sell any of our milk or fruit in Warsaw any more. It's full of imported produce. The price of milk means that it is not worth keeping a cow any more. In this whole area, there are only two cows left."

Slawomir Laskowski, aged 28, farmer from Brzesce near Warsaw, Poland

The sort of small holding Mr Laskowski manages would look familiar to an English farmer of the 17th century. His five hectares, just below the national average, are broken into three narrow strips up to a mile apart. He rotates the crops around the strips, leaving one fallow each year. Mr Laskowski has the use of an old tractor, but many farmers further away from the towns use only horse-drawn carts and ploughs.

Source: *The Guardian*, 16 March 1994

Q1 Why do you think that the people of Warsaw, the capital of Poland, buy imported milk?

Q2 How does the above method of farming compare with the farms described on pages 150–1?

Q3 What effect do you think these differences have on the costs of production?

WINNERS ON BOTH SIDES

Polish industry is adapting fast and ensuring that output meets the standard required in the EU market. Many Polish products can already be found on shelves of shops in the UK. Krosno Glass, which used old-fashioned techniques and made glasses that no one wanted, now has a successful business selling to the consumers of Western Europe (some is sold through Habitat).

WHAT ARE THE THREATS?

The increased size of the EU provides challenges for both existing and new members. The farmer in the Evidence shows the problems that arise in trying to unite two very different systems. Many Polish farms are still very small and inefficient. As a result, their costs tend to be high. The agricultural policy of the EU was designed to protect small farmers, so they might benefit considerably if the rules stay the same.

It has been estimated that under the existing system, EU expenditure would be increased by 20 per cent if Poland were included. Income, however, would rise by only 1 or 2 per cent.

Another threat exists because countries such as Poland could in time produce vast quantities of farm products. They will modernize their farms, invest in more equipment and increase productivity. If farm prices are kept high, the lakes and mountains could get larger again.

Poland is just one example of the countries that may want to join the EU. Many of the others are in a similar economic and industrial position. Some have been more successful than others in adapting to change. If the EU is to expand in this way, there will have to be changes made to some laws and regulations because of the very different nature of some of the new members.

FORUM

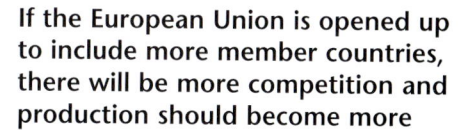

If the European Union is opened up to include more member countries, there will be more competition and production should become more efficient.

Who will gain? Who will lose? Should there be rules to protect those who lose?

153

Unit 4 Big or small?
Case study

A question of scale

Q1 Which meal would cost more to produce and why?

Q2 Why might people be willing to pay more for a meal cooked by an expert chef than for a packaged meal?

Q3 Can you think of any other products which can be produced on both a small and a large scale? Would the costs and prices vary in the same way?

Gary Rhodes prepares a meal on the BBC's *Rhodes Around Britain* series.

School dinners are produced in large quantities.

Unit 5

Create or destroy?

ENQUIRY 1: WHAT MAKES PEOPLE RICHER?	**156**
What is growth?	156
Exploring the nature of growth	
Going for growth?	158
The impact of investment	
The missing millions	160
How to interpret the figures	
What's the whole story?	162
Standards of living and insecurity	

ENQUIRY 2: CAN THERE BE MORE AND MORE?	**164**
What's the spin-off?	164
Growth and externalities	
Who pays the price?	166
Gains and losses	
Will the gas run out?	168
Energy and resources	

ENQUIRY 3: WASTE NOT – WANT NOT?	**170**
What is sustainability?	170
Sustainable growth	
Going green	172
What businesses and governments can do	
Could we be doing better?	174
Recycling: new technologies	

ENQUIRY 4: HOW SHOULD FIRMS BEHAVE?	**176**
Can firms be 'good'?	176
Ethical responsibility	
Next-door neighbours?	178
Business in the community	
Will it cost the earth?	180
Business and the environment	
Putting on the pressure?	182
Pressure groups	

ENQUIRY 5: SHOULD THE GOVERNMENT INTERFERE?	**184**
What price pollution?	184
Taxes and subsidies as incentives	
Rules and regulations	186
Controlling the impact on the environment	
Cleaning up	188
Costs and benefits for governments	

CASE STUDY: POWER STATIONS	**190**

Unit 5

Create or destroy?

Enquiry 1: What makes people richer?

What is growth?

WHAT DOES GROWTH REALLY MEAN?

How does the way you live differ from the way your great grandparents, or even your grandparents lived? Do you think their lifestyle was much simpler when they were your age? The pictures in the Evidence give clues as to how people's lives have changed over recent centuries. As the economy has grown, the **standard of living** has improved beyond all imagination.

As industry, commerce and governments invest in machines and people, the country can produce more. Incomes rise, giving us more to spend. Our increased spending encourages firms to produce more, so the economy continues to grow.

In the UK we have to look back in time to see the changes. We can also look around the world to see differences. In table 1 the countries at the top of the list are the ones that have achieved a high standard of living. As you move down the list, you can see how things change.

The standard of living can be measured by looking at the way people live. Almost everyone in the United States has a television. In Sierra Leone there is one to every hundred people, and in Ethiopia there are fewer than one per thousand!

The rate at which the standard of living improves varies between countries. In 1970 Indonesia had one doctor to 26,820 people and only 16 per cent of the population had secondary education. Compare that with the data in table 1. Indonesia has been one of the fastest-growing countries in East Asia, as have Japan, South Korea and the Philippines.

COUNTING UP

An important way of measuring the standard of living is to calculate the size of the economy and how it is changing. All governments work out **national income** statistics. To do this, they calculate the value of:
- all the incomes that are earned in one year
- all the money that is spent in one year
- all that is produced in one year.

Each of these totals should be the same because people spend what they earn and are paid for providing goods and services. (In fact, the amounts are never quite the same, because it is so difficult to make sure that all items are included.)

From the national income data, governments calculate gross domestic product (GDP). This is the main measure of the value of output in the whole economy. By comparing this information from one year to the next we can see how much **growth** has taken place. This gives us a very good indication of the change in the standard of living. Table 2 shows this for the UK.

Of course, in a country that is growing fast, people may still be very poor. When we want to make comparisons between countries, we use GDP per head (that is, per person). Look at table 3, which shows the rate of growth and the GDP per head in a number of countries.

EVIDENCE

Q1 What do the pictures tell you about how people's standard of living has changed over the years?

Q2 What does table 1 tell you about how people's standard of living varies between countries?

Q3 Do you think that the 6 per cent of people in Indonesia who have a television also have secondary education and easy access to a doctor?

Q4 Why do you think some of the data is missing from table 1?

Table 1: Standard of living in various countries

	Population with safe water	Population per doctor	% in secondary education	TVs per 100 people
USA	100	420	90	82
UK	100	560	86	44
Japan	96	610	97	61
Greece	98	580	68	20
Turkey	84	1,260	51	18
Tunisia	70	1,870	46	8
Indonesia	51	7,030	45	6
Nigeria	42	?	20	3
Sierra Leone	39	?	16	1
Ethiopia	18	32,500	12	-

Source: *Human Development Report*, Oxford University Press, 1995; and *Medical Register*, General Medical Council, 1996

Table 2: UK GDP, 1990–5, at 1990 prices

	GDP (£ billion)	Growth rate (%)
1990	478.9	0.6
1991	468.9	-2.0
1992	466.5	-0.5
1993	476.9	2.2
1994	496.8	4.2
1995	505.7	1.8

Source: *National Institute Economic Review*, April 1995

MAKING GROWTH HAPPEN

Achieving economic growth involves many different factors:

- firms building new factories and installing new equipment
- education and training
- modern networks of communication such as roads, railways, telephones
- supplies of energy where they are needed
- governments that invest and also encourage firms to invest
- research and development of new products and ways of producing.

The factors that lead to growth can give a country a competitive advantage. This explains why some countries are more successful than others at selling their output. It involves a combination of entrepreneurial spirit, government encouragement and the range of other factors above.

EVIDENCE

Q1 If you made a league table to show how countries compared, would it matter which column you used out of tables 1 and 3?

Q2 Why is having better water and medical treatment and more education linked to the level of income?

Table 3: GDP and growth, 1992

	Real GDP per head (US$)	Rate of growth (%)
USA	23,760	3.1
Japan	20,520	0.1
UK	17,160	2.1
Greece	8,310	-0.5
Turkey	5,230	7.6
Tunisia	5,160	2.1
Indonesia	2,950	6.5
Nigeria	1,220	2.3
Sierra Leone	880	-2.4
Ethiopia	330	7.7

Source: *Human Development Report*, Oxford University Press, 1995; and *Industrial Development*, Oxford University Press, 1995

EVIDENCE

Q1 Put these four countries in order for their level of national income, with the highest first.

Q2 What do you know about these countries that might explain why there is such a difference in the way people live?

Russia

USA

Ethiopia

The Philippines

FORUM

Growth has generally improved the standard of living for many people. How might it make things worse? Why is it important to look at the effects that growth might have on a country?

KEY TERMS

Growth in an economy is the percentage change in total output from year to year.

National income is the total of all the incomes in the country.

The *standard of living* measures the way people live in terms of what they are able to buy.

157

Unit 5

Create or destroy?
Enquiry 1: What makes people richer?

Going for growth?

EVIDENCE

INVESTING IN MACHINES

NISSAN JOBS BOOST

In the last nine years, Nissan has spent £1.25 billion in Britain. The last £250 million comes from a decision to expand the company's factory in Sunderland, in the north-east of England. This will create 300 new jobs.

The latest investment provides the space and equipment to build the Primera. Nissan said that the project would mean more than £400 million a year of business for European suppliers. Ian Gibson, Nissan's UK chief executive, said that the company had decided to go ahead despite flat demand for cars in the UK. Although the company had been profitable since 1991, it had yet to recover all of its investment from setting up in Britain. But investing in the new car now meant that the factory should be well placed to exploit any increased demand next year.

Source: adapted from *The Guardian*, 19 September 1995

RAILTRACK PLANS £10 BILLION UPGRADE

A £10 billion investment programme for the railway industry was announced by Railtrack 'to deliver a railway network for the 21st century'. Railtrack's chairman, Bob Horton, says it gives the business the freedom to look ahead not just for two or three years, but for ten years or longer. Railtrack intends to replace 2,900 miles of sleepers and 1,400 miles of rails by 2004, renew dozens of bridges, and upgrade stations and depots. Further improvements will be made to signalling and control equipment, some of which is 40 years old.

Industry sources suggest that once Railtrack is sold to the private sector, there would be no guarantee that the plans would be realized.

Source: *The Guardian*, 18 December 1995

Q1 What is Nissan buying with its £250 million investment spending? Who is benefiting from this investment spending? Why is the company spending money now when cars are not selling well?

Q2 Who will benefit from Railtrack's spending? Why would it be difficult for a private sector firm to guarantee a ten-year programme?

Q3 Why do firms invest?

WHY SPEND THE MONEY?

Companies spend money on goods and services to keep their production going, day by day, month by month. They also need to ensure that they have the means to produce goods and services in the years to come. New models have to be researched, designed and made, machines have to be replaced, and new factories have to be built.

This sort of spending is known as **capital investment**. Without such spending, a company will find that its costs begin to rise as outdated machinery breaks down and the business loses competitiveness. Sometimes investment replaces worn-out machinery. At other times it allows production to increase. Often, investment involves using new and better technology. This increases productivity.

Investment spending can be seen be the 'powerhouse' behind growth economic and business activity. If people are earning more, they will more to spend. This will mean mor income for others and they, too, w increase their spending. People wil

EVIDENCE

Q1 What evidence is there in table 1 of links between investment spending and growth in an economy?

Q2 Why might you expect there to be close links between the two?

Table 1: Investment and growth

Annual growth rates

	USA	Japan	UK	France	China
1980	-0.2	4.3	-2.5	1.6	5.7
1984	6.8	5.1	2.6	1.4	14.7
1988	3.9	6.2	5.0	4.5	10.7
1992	2.0	1.3	-0.5	1.4	13.2

Gross domestic investment as % of GDP

	USA	Japan	UK	France	China
1980	19.9	32.2	12.5	24.2	32.2
1984	21.2	28.0	12.6	19.0	32.3
1988	18.4	30.6	17.0	21.1	39.5
1992	15.5	31.1	15.1	19.6	47.5

Source: *World tables and economic trends*, 1993-4; IMF *World Economic Outlook*, 1993

EVIDENCE

INVESTING IN PEOPLE: THE BOOTS WAY

Boots decided that providing a quality service was a key to staying ahead of competitors. The company increased its spending on management and staff training to provide a new approach in the stores. This is what they did:

- a new company code offering a commitment to customers was established;
- 'quality teams' would monitor and research customer needs;
- all store assistants were given training leading to National Vocational Qualifications;
- staff appraisal was linked with performance targets;
- new business planning strategies were introduced.

The company's performance has improved in the following ways:

- in the last five years, profit has more than doubled;
- customer complaints have fallen compared to customer praise;
- staff surveys show increased motivation;
- a 1 per cent drop in labour turnover saves the business £1 million.

Source: *The Benefits of being an Investor in People*, Investors in People, 1995

---

more taxes, and there will be more available to spend on education and health. Whether you are employed by a big company or by the government, or are running your own business, your income will depend on how much is being earned in the whole economy. After all, the amount that is earned is the same as the amount that everyone has to spend.

Not everyone wins from new investment. Sometimes new equipment may mean that the firm needs to employ fewer people because the machinery does the work more efficiently. If someone has a skill that can now be carried out by a machine, that person may find that he or she no longer has a job.

HUMAN CAPITAL

Investment in the education and training of employees at all levels of a company can lead to better working practices, which increase success and profitability.

Some business observers believe that in times of rapidly changing technology, a well-educated and well-trained workforce is the best way to ensure survival for individual companies and for countries as a whole. Investment in training creates **human capital**.

CHECKPOINT

Q1 How has Boots invested in people?

Q2 How might a worker at Boots benefit from the training programme?

Q3 Why does the company believe such investment is value for money?

Q4 What is likely to happen to an economy where little is spent on the education and training of workers?

KEY TERMS

Capital investment is spending on new equipment and machinery for future production.

Human capital involves spending on education and training of workers for future production.

Unit 5: Create or destroy?

Enquiry 1: What makes people richer?

The missing millions

EVIDENCE

WHAT COUNTS?

'I can't live on my wages from the pub – so I do a bit of cleaning in the mornings. At least the tax man doesn't know about it.'

'... but how much would it cost if I paid cash?'

'Do you think I watch the telly all day? How do you think the clothes get washed, the house gets cleaned and the food reaches the table?'

Q1 Why do some people accept a smaller payment if it's offered in cash?

Q2 Do you think these people pay less tax than they should? If so, how are they doing this?

The total amount of work that people do is shown by the value of the gross domestic product:
- gross, because it is the total;
- domestic, because it is within the UK rather than abroad;
- product, because it shows the amount of output.

The figure that the government puts out each year, when it publishes the annual accounts for the country, is thought to be considerably lower than the total amount of output.

OUTSIDE THE LAW

The examples in the Evidence show a variety of ways in which work that is carried out is not included. All sorts of work are not declared to the 'tax man' – or, more correctly, the **Inland Revenue**. Some of this work is legal, but some is not. For example, many people employ cleaners without informing the Inland Revenue.

The building trade is well known for doing work for cash. Anyone paid in cash can pocket the money, which never appears in the accounts. As a result, reported profits are lower and the tax bill is reduced.

Both these activities can involve tax evasion and are against the law. If the government knows nothing about the work, its value will not be included in the accounts. Total output for the year will appear to be lower.

This is a common problem throughout the world. No one knows exactly how much is involved. If income is undeclared, it is difficult to count accurately. In the UK, estimates vary widely. Some say that the **hidden economy** is just 7 per cent, whereas others claim that it must be closer to 20 per cent. Table 1 shows some data from just one little part of the hidden economy.

Counterfeits are replicas of original recordings – using the same packaging. Pirates are duplicates of originals sold on another label. Bootlegs are made from concerts or broadcasts. All are illegal under copyright law.

Table 1: The UK pirate market

Retail value (£)

	Cassettes	CD	Total
Bootleg	750,000	22,500,000	23,250,000
Counterfeit	6,000,000	6,000,000	12,000,000
Pirate	750,000	2,000,000	2,750,000
TOTAL	7,500,000	30,500,000	38,000,000

Source: BPI estimates

WITHIN THE LAW

There are all kinds of work that people do without being paid. Who washes your clothes or cuts the grass? Your mum or dad, or maybe even you! If this work were done in a laundry or by a gardener, someone would be paid. Once a payment is made, the activities would be included in the national accounts. Clearly, there is a lot of work going on which is not counted.

Voluntary work is not counted, either. This ranges from organizing junior football on Sunday mornings to running charity shops. Again, the official figures do not show the full value of all activity.

EVIDENCE

WASTE PLANTS SPREAD KILLER FUMES

Levels of cancer-causing dioxins up to 300 times the government safety limits are pouring out from ageing waste incinerators in towns across Britain.

The revelations will fuel public concern over toxic chemicals, which are produced whenever chlorine-based products such as plastics are burned. They persist in the environment for hundreds of years.

Even at low levels they are believed to cause cancer and damage unborn babies.

Official figures reveal that all but two of the 21 largest incinerators that produce about a third of Britain's dioxin emissions break the government's standard.

Many of the incinerators are in town centres or near residential areas. The worst, in Stoke-on-Trent, last year emitted dioxin levels 306 times higher than the government's limit.

Dioxins pouring from the chimneys of another plant in Huddersfield, within 500 yards of homes and close to farmland, were recorded at up to 187 times the limit.

Source: adapted from the *Observer*, 12 February 1995

Q1 How are the activities of the incinerator businesses harming other people?
Q2 Who pays for the side-effects of incinerating waste?
Q3 How do these costs affect our view of the size of GDP?

CHECKPOINT

What would happen to the size of GDP if the following were counted?

- The pollution in rivers that is not cleaned up.
- The wages of builders who work for cash.
- The work done by a parent looking after children.

KEY TERMS

The *hidden economy* includes all work that is not recorded in the national income figures.

The *Inland Revenue* is the government department responsible for collecting taxes.

THE FORGOTTEN COSTS

The businesses that produce dioxins are earning money for doing a job – disposing of waste materials. They have to pay for the cost of the factory and all the people that they employ, but they do not pay for the damage caused by the dioxins that escape. These costs are met by the people who breathe the polluted air, and by the government, which has to pay for the extra cost of health care. Meeting these extra costs makes GDP higher than it otherwise would be. The accounts are not, therefore, a true reflection of the value of the output of the economy.

This is just one example. If all the examples were added together, it would have a significant effect on GDP, not just in the UK but throughout the world.

No national income figures are perfectly accurate. There are too many complications. If, however, the figures are produced in a standard way, they are still useful for comparison.

Unit 5 Create or destroy?

Enquiry 1: What makes people richer?

What's the whole story?

EVIDENCE

WHERE WOULD YOU PREFER TO LIVE?

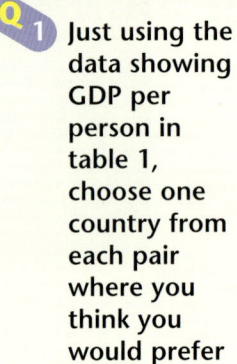

Table 1: Average GDP per person (US$)

Saudi Arabia	10,989
Ireland	10,589
Algeria	3,011
Jamaica	2,979
Sierra Leone	1,086
Ghana	1,016

Source: World Bank, *World Development Report*, Oxford University Press, 1995

Q1 Just using the data showing GDP per person in table 1, choose one country from each pair where you think you would prefer to live.

Table 2: Life expectancy, adult literacy and years of schooling per child

	Life expectancy (years)	Adult literacy (%)	Years of schooling per child
Saudi Arabia	69.7	60.6	3.7
Ireland	75.3	97.4	8.7
Algeria	67.1	57.4	2.6
Jamaica	73.6	93.7	5.3
Sierra Leone	39	28.7	0.8
Ghana	56	60.7	3.5

Source: United Nations, *Human Development Report* and World Bank, *World Development Report*, Oxford University Press, 1995

Q2 What effect does the information in table 2 have on your decisions about table 1?

INTERPRETING THE FIGURES

From table 1 there seems to be little difference between each pair of countries. You would be a little better off financially in one rather than the other – but there is not much in it.

Table 2 tells a very different story. There can be little doubt that life will be of a higher quality in a country where people
- expect to live to 75
- can nearly all read and write
- have nearly nine years of schooling

compared to another where
- people expect to live to 70
- one-third cannot read and write
- people on average have fewer than four years of schooling.

The Evidence shows clearly that have to be very careful in comparing GDP figures. The more information have the better, because any one set figures can be very misleading.

If GDP figures are going to give a helpful picture of how people live, t total must first be converted into dollars so that one country can be compared with another. Then the t must be divided by the population of the country. This data is shown as '**per capita**', or per head, and allows us to compare living standards in countries with large and small populations.

However, in most countries, income is not shared equally between all the population. As a result, even per capita figures do not tell the whole story. In some countries there is a small group of extremely rich people who live in the lap of luxury, while the majority of the population lives in poverty. It takes a much more detailed examination of the situation to make this clear.

IS THERE A BETTER WAY?

In table 2, a range of information was added to the GDP data to give a more detailed picture of life in each country. This is the approach used by the **Human Development Index** produced by the United Nations. It gives us much more information than GDP alone. The actual standard of living for residents of a country can therefore be higher if they have good provision for health and education, even though their income is low. Figure 1 shows how this may vary in a range of richer countries.

The graph shows the difference between the GDP of a country and its Human Development Index (HDI) rating. A positive figure suggests that people's quality of life is above what is shown by the GDP figures. A negative figure shows that their quality of life is lower.

IDENTIFYING INEQUALITY

The Human Development Index can be used to show many kinds of inequalities. If information about gender differences is built in, for example, Japan's score comes out much lower. Women in Japan are less likely to receive higher education and their opportunities are therefore restricted.

The HDI can also be used to show the extent to which minority groups are disadvantaged. In the United States, whites have a quality of life as good as any in the world, but Blacks and Hispanics will find themselves much less well off as regards access to health and education as well as income. Measuring the quality of life involves taking many different factors into account.

The HDI compares the quality of life in terms of people's role in society, but there are other ways in which standard of living can be assessed. In the long run, government data will need to make allowance for the side-effects of industry, because of the environmental problems outlined on the last two pages.

FORUM

DIY HDI
What factors do you think should be taken into account in weighing up the quality of life in different countries? Put the items in order of priority. If you have a total of 10 points to give to your selection, how much would each factor be worth?

KEY TERMS

The *Human Development Index* compares the quality of life in different countries by using a range of factors, such as education and health care, as well as GDP.

Per capita income is the average income for each person and is found by dividing GDP by the population figure.

Figure 1: Difference between GDP and HDI

(Bar chart showing GDP minus HDI for countries, x-axis from -6 to 14)

- Australia
- UK
- Canada
- The Netherlands
- France
- Spain
- USA
- Japan
- Sweden
- Switzerland
- Germany
- Italy
- Denmark

GDP minus HDI

Source: United Nations, *Human Development Report*, Oxford University Press, 1995

Unit 5 Create or destroy?
Enquiry 2: Can there be more and more?

What's the spin-off?

EVIDENCE

PAIN OR PLEASURE?

The continual loud playing of Country and Western music forced a family in West Yorkshire to sell up and move.

A Teesside woman was fined £500 for the torture she inflicted on her neighbours by the repeated playing of Dolly Parton records.

A Whitney Houston fan was jailed for playing 'I will always love you' for hours on end.

Source: *The Times*, 20 April 1994

Q1 Do you think anything should be done to control the noise from someone's ghetto blaster or from noisy neighbours?

Q2 Can you think of any other situations where the actions of one person or a group of people affect others?

FOR BETTER OR WORSE?

How often have someone else's actions got in the way of what you wanted to do? The boy playing his kind of music may irritate some people, but others might enjoy it. How would you feel if you hated cricket and your neighbours were fanatics, and played the test match commentary loudly outside on a sunny afternoon?

These side-effects are known as **externalities** because they all have an external effect on someone else. They may be positive, if you like the music, or negative if you don't!

EVIDENCE

FLOODING

Tony Nicholls lives in a residential area with a high number of car owners. Over the past 15 years Tony has noticed that many households in his street have converted their front gardens into hard surfaces for driveways and parking areas. Rainwater that used to be soaked up by the garden soil now runs directly down the driveways on both sides of the street and eventually into High Street. The same thing is happening in other streets nearby. Some shop cellars in High Street are regularly flooded after heavy rain and as a result cannot be used for storage.

The problem remains, despite new drains being put in by the council. The council is now refusing to give planning permission for households who wish to lay hard surfacing in their front gardens.

Q1 Why does the council have an important role to play?

Q2 What should be done by the people who have already laid down drives? Should they be forced to dig them up, or to pay compensation to the shops that have been affected by their actions?

BUT I DIDN'T MEAN IT TO HAPPEN...

Externalities can have a much more serious impact than just annoying the neighbours. The actions of individuals or organizations to improve their own or others' lives can make some people worse off. They can also have bad effects on the local environment. The house owners in Tony's town would not have dreamed that the building of their driveways would have such an impact on their community further downhill.

Externalities can have unexpected effects. Some have been caused by ignorance, as in the early use of asbestos in the Evidence. Some come about through accidents. Accidents can be unavoidable, but this is not always the case. For example, accidental leakages from factories that result from using old and poorly maintained equipment can be prevented. Are these factories to blame for the leakage? Should a lorry carrying a dangerous chemical be encouraged to use rail or be banned from passing areas of housing, even though this raises the cost of the transport?

Attempts have been made to reduce negative externalities. For example, in Tony's town the local council will not give permission for people to put in driveways. It is possible to pay compensation to those affected, but that's not much good to the woman in the Evidence, who died as a result of cleaning her husband's asbestos-covered overalls. She would have preferred not to contract the disease in the first place. In her case the laws were not strong enough.

CHECKPOINT

Q1 What is meant by an externality?
Q2 In what ways can negative externalities be reduced?
Q3 What examples of negative externalities can you identify in your local community? Are there any positive ones?

EVIDENCE

DEATHLY FIBRES

- Two elderly women who made gas masks during World War II claim that their long and painful illnesses were caused by using blue asbestos. 'I didn't know of the dangers and the company didn't tell you anything about it', said Doris. The company argues that it was unaware of the risks at the time.

- Peter, a 60-year-old carpenter, has only a few months to live. 'My job on the building site was to put asbestos-based boards on the underside of roofs. They used to crumble when cut. I couldn't avoid breathing it in.'

- A woman who washed her husband's overalls died after contracting asbestosis. She never worked with asbestos herself, but her husband used to come home with his clothes covered in the fine dust when he worked at a shipyard.

- Laws were passed in the 1960s to protect factory workers who used asbestos from the dangers of exposure to asbestos dust. However, at the time, these laws were never applied to shipyards, railways and building sites.

Source: adapted from articles in *The Times*, 1994

This factory was closed because of high levels of asbestos

Q1 When asbestos was first used, no one knew there were problems with it. Do you think that companies should be held responsible now for side-effects that they could not have foreseen?

Q2 Shipbuilders did not have to obey the asbestos regulations that were passed in the 1960s, but they must have been aware of the effects of working with blue asbestos dust. Do you think they were at fault?

FORUM

Quite often a factory will be releasing air pollution into the area. At the same time it will provide many local people with jobs. How do you think local people will feel about the situation? What do you think should be done?

KEY TERM

Externalities are the side-effects that result from the actions of an individual, firm or government. If they give benefits, they are positive. If they cause problems or cost people money, they are negative.

Unit 5 — Create or destroy?
Enquiry 2: Can there be more and more?

Who pays the price?

EVIDENCE

The Yangtze River, China, at the Three Gorges

The Three Gorges Dam under construction

THINK BIG AND ACT BIG

The average family in the UK uses a hundred times more electricity than the average Chinese family. At the moment China is short of the power stations needed to produce more electricity. As the country is growing fast, it needs extra energy to power new factories, offices and homes.

One solution has been to go for large-scale hydro-electric power projects. These have an advantage over other forms of energy since they can produce cheap electricity in enough quantities to keep up with the increasing demand for power. Super-dams hold back vast amounts of water, which is then allowed to flow through turbines to generate electricity.

The Three Gorges Dam on the Yangtze River in China will provide all these things to a highly populated area. The 185m-high super-dam, which is due to be finished in 2008, will generate 1,800 megawatts, provide irrigation and prevent devastating floods, which in the past have cost many lives.

However, it will create a lake over 600 km long and change the river scenery and wildlife for ever. It will also mean that 1.3 million people will have to be moved from farms and towns as the level of the lake rises. Three cities will be flooded. The people who are moved are meant to receive compensation so that they are not worse off than before. The dam may also increase the risk of earthquakes.

Q1 Why does the Chinese government want to build this dam?
Q2 What will be the impact of the dam on the local environment?
Q3 Which people will gain from the dam? Which people will lose?

TRADE-OFFS

Every year, more than 4.5 million people have to move from sites where dams are being built. These dams, alongside other large-scale projects such as major road programmes, are national projects often supported by governments and built by private businesses. For example, in India roughly 14 per cent of public expenditure has been spent on super-dams in recent years.

Experiences from previous projects can provide valuable lessons about possible externalities. In the Three Gorges project nearly one-third of the cost goes towards resettling people. Re-siting towns and villages and providing good quality farmland for over one million people is not an easy task. The social effects of forcibly moving people are great.

Much of the power from the Three Gorges project will go towards providing energy for factories producing goods for sale all over the world. Consumer demands are causing environmental and social pressures both within our communities and in distant countries.

Local, national and international environmental organizations, such as Greenpeace, will try to prevent or reduce some developments, but the desire for prosperity makes it difficult for businesses and, in particular, the governments of poorer countries to agree with them.

In China, the government can make such decisions. It is unlikely that the UK government would ever be able to displace such large numbers of people as protests would be too great. But there are many other kinds of negative externalities which can be seen in countries that are much richer than China.

EVIDENCE

NOT ON OUR DOORSTEP, PLEASE

Every day 35,000 vehicles use the A4 through Batheaston village near Bath, splitting the community, endangering lives and shaking the walls of historic buildings. A by-pass would end the misery of many villagers.

Not everybody agreed. The new £75 million by-pass went ahead despite protesters arguing that the new road would affect an Iron Age fort at Solsbury Hill.

PAYING YOUR WAY

More and more people want to drive cars, but more and more roads have their costs. The examples in the Evidence show the type of problems that can arise when new routes for either road or rail are planned. The external effects of both the by-pass and the rail link to the Channel Tunnel are clear.

Even without new roads, motorists do not pay their way. David Pearce, who is a professor of environmental economics, claims that another £500 a year on road tax would just about cover all the external costs they create.

Table 1: The annual cost of motoring in the UK (£ billion)

Traffic accidents	4.7
Air pollution leading to ill health	2.8
Air pollution damaging crops, trees and buildings	1.3
Congestion	13.5
Damage to the roads	1.3
Other costs	2.1
Total cost	25.7
Income from car tax and fuel tax	14.7

Source: *The Times*, 24 January 1994

EVIDENCE

- Concerns over the exact route of the Channel Tunnel rail link have led house prices to fall, sometimes down to half their original value. Many people are trapped in houses that no one wants to buy.

- Manchester's Metrolink is a supertram system that now carries over 13 million passengers a year. Its chief success has been to attract people who previously used their cars.

- In Greece, Athens is to force people to stagger their working hours in summer, ban cars carrying fewer than three people from the city centre, and introduce pollution tests on cars. This is all in an attempt to reduce pollution.

FORUM

How would you feel if, for the sake of a new road, the area where you live were developed so that you would have to move?

How would you feel if road congestion meant that it took an extra day to get your products to the docks for export?

How would you decide whether or not a project should go ahead?

CHECKPOINT

Q1 How much do drivers cost the country?

Q2 What might happen to the number of car drivers if road tax were to rise from £130 to over £600?

Q3 What effect would this have on: (a) the car industry, (b) the petrol industry and (c) public transport?

Q4 How can road traffic be reduced other than by charging higher road taxes?

Unit 5 Create or destroy?
Enquiry 2: Can there be more and more?

Will the gas run out?

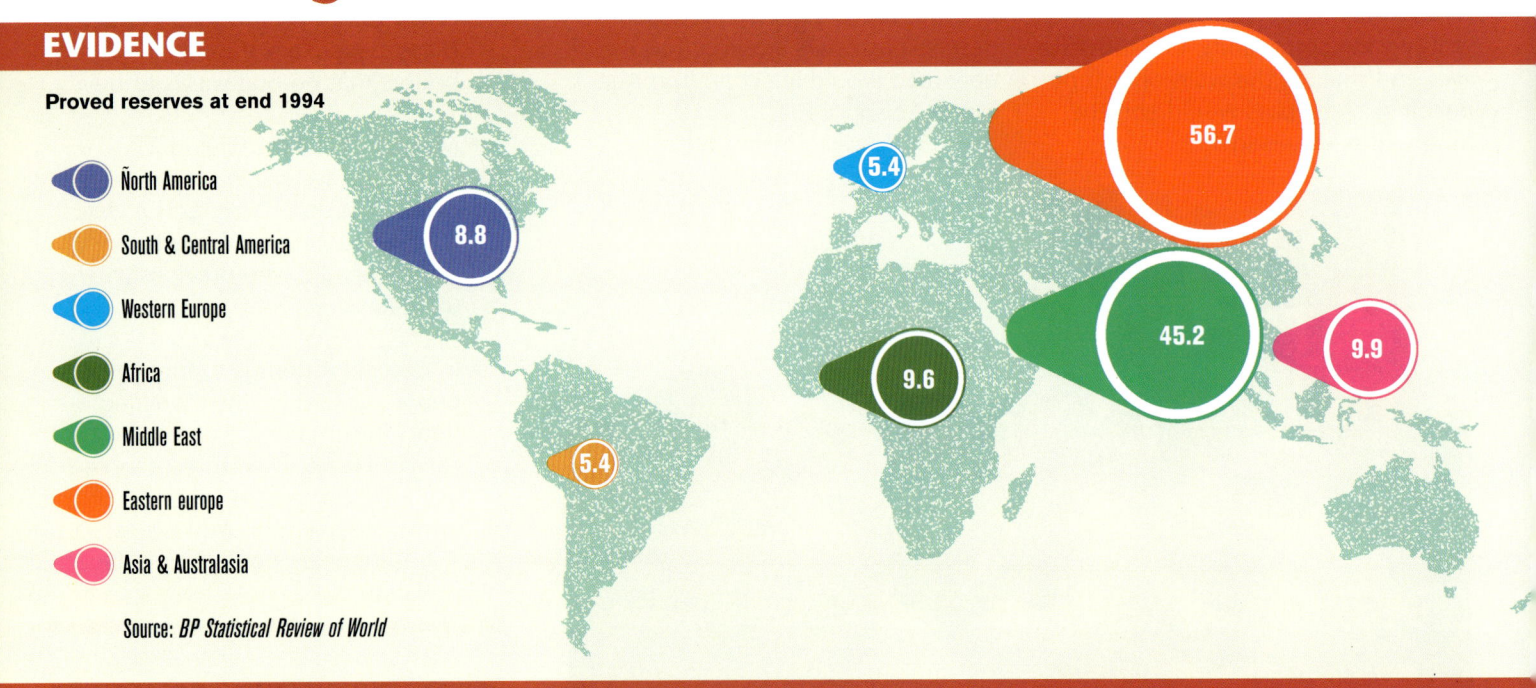

EVIDENCE

Proved reserves at end 1994

- North America
- South & Central America
- Western Europe
- Africa
- Middle East
- Eastern europe
- Asia & Australasia

Source: *BP Statistical Review of World*

Map values:
- Western Europe: 5.4
- North America: 8.8
- Eastern Europe: 56.7
- Africa: 9.6
- Middle East: 45.2
- Asia & Australasia: 9.9
- South & Central America: 5.4

HOW MUCH IS THERE?

The amount of gas under the Earth's surface is fixed. If we use it up, there will be no more left and we will have to look for other fuels to run our central heating and gas cookers. Gas is known as a **non-renewable resource**. Coal and oil are just the same. All three are fossil fuels, formed millions of years ago.

The supply of these fuels is limited, so it is important to know how much there is. Companies spend a great deal of money on exploration to find this out.

The world map shows how many cubic metres of gas there are in each region. This information measures only the gas that is worth extracting at the moment.

- If the price of gas goes up, it becomes possible to drill wells in more difficult places. At the moment these wells would be too expensive.
- If the cost of drilling wells falls, the more expensive sites could start to be developed.

Not all fuels are non-renewable. The hydro-electric power to be produced on the Yangtze River in China is renewable because the water continues to flow. Tides, wind and the sun also provide renewable energy.

WILL FOSSIL FUELS RUN OUT?

Although the obvious answer is 'yes', the real answer to this question is, 'it depends'. In fact, it depends on a variety of things.

- What happens to the price? If people continue to want to use gas, but the supply is running short, they will have to pay more for it.

CHECKPOINT

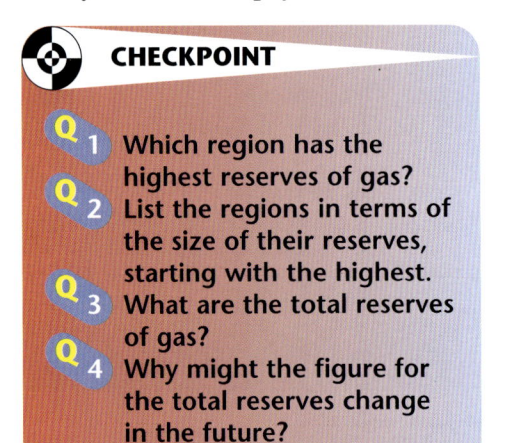

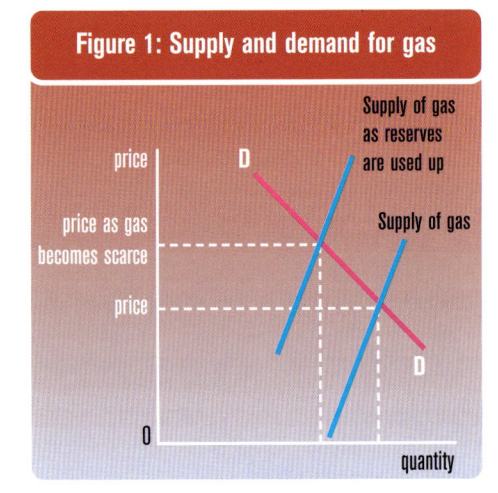

Q1 Which region has the highest reserves of gas?
Q2 List the regions in terms of the size of their reserves, starting with the highest.
Q3 What are the total reserves of gas?
Q4 Why might the figure for the total reserves change in the future?

Figure 1: Supply and demand for gas

Figure 1 shows that as the supply of gas falls, the price will rise. This will make gas less competitive with other sources of energy, so people will start to look at alternatives.

- What are the alternative sources of energy? We will need to consider them if all the fossil fuels become dearer.

The advert from British Nuclear Fuels (BNFL) tells us that nuclear power is a possible alternative source of energy. It will not run out, or pollute the air. But the costs involved in disposing of nuclear waste would need to be taken into account, as well as the radiation risks. The size of these risks is still uncertain. Many people feel that the uncertainty makes the risks too high.

Renewable energy is clean. It does not pollute the air in the way that burning fossil fuels does. But at the present time some of the sources of energy that could be used are still expensive, and some cause other kinds of changes to the environment. Tidal barrages change the waterside environment. Wind farms that provide enough power to be useful cover many hectares of ground.

WILL THINGS CHANGE?

If and when the price of fossil fuels rises, it will become more attractive to search for alternatives. The Evidence shows how a house and car can be powered completely by solar energy. This removes any need for fossil fuels. Although the technology for solar power is still expensive, the price is falling steadily. As firms see opportunities for new products, they will be prepared to invest the necessary resources in their development.

Energy can be conserved as well. The higher the price of fuel, the more sense it makes to insulate roofs and install double glazing. Industry may reuse heat that comes from the production process. Cars can be designed to run on less petrol. Less energy is used and less pollution is created. In these ways, new technologies can often be developed to use energy more efficiently. Some of them exist already.

We could change our lifestyles, too. We could wear warmer clothes and turn down the heating. We could make fewer car journeys and travel on trains. Many other lifestyle changes are possible.

FORUM

Should we panic? At the moment, we rely on fossil fuels because they are cheaper than most of the alternatives. As they become more scarce, what will happen? What alternatives might we then think about? Should we change our lifestyles?

EVIDENCE

AND WHAT OF FOSSIL FUELS?

As the majority of our power comes from burning them, can we afford to stop? We're going to have to conserve our fossil fuels because they won't last forever and they are not being replaced.

Dams, windmills and tidal barrages are beginning to be taken more seriously, although a wind farm the size of Manchester would be needed to replace a single power station.

Fortunately, we do already have a clean source of energy for the future.

NUCLEAR POWER

At BNFL, we believe that it has an important role to play in a balanced energy policy for this country. Not only that, it has an important role to play in the environment.

In France and Belgium, for example, they generate more than two-thirds of their electricity from nuclear power. Are others offering really workable alternatives?

Naturally, we'd expect you to weigh up the arguments for and against.

An extract from a BNFL advert

EVIDENCE

THE LIGHT FANTASTIC

Is the sun trying to tell us something? Should we be moving towards a solar-powered society? Architect Susan Roafe certainly thinks so – her Oxford home is the first in Britain to be entirely powered by solar energy.

From the road, it looks like an ordinary suburban house. But the 48 panels on the garden side will produce enough electricity for the household's entire annual needs. When the sun is brightest, the system exports surplus power into the grid; on cloudy days, it imports. As a result, Susan expects her electricity bill to be about 58p a year. Yet the house has a TV, video, dishwasher, even an electric car, which is also powered from the roof.

At £25,000 the solar roof was costly. But if total construction and running costs of this super-insulated building are spread over 20 years, the price looks more reasonable.

Source: *The Guardian*, 16 August 1995

KEY TERM

Non-renewable resources are natural resources which are in limited supply. Once they have been used up, they cannot be replaced.

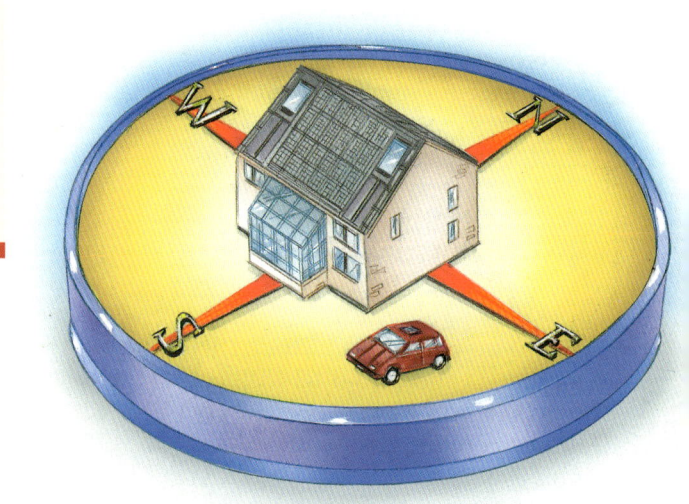

Unit 5: Create or destroy?

Enquiry 3: Waste not – want not?

What is sustainability?

EVIDENCE

ENERGY

Table 1: Energy use, 1993

	Use of energy per person (kilos of oil equivalent)	Income per person (US$)
Zambia	146	380
Brazil	666	8,512
UK	3,718	18,060
USA	7,918	24,740

Source: World Bank, *World Development Report*, 1995

Q1 How is energy use linked to income levels?

PEOPLE

In 1983, the population of Africa south of the Sahara desert was 245 million. Ten years later in 1993 it had grown to 559 million. In many parts of Africa wood is cut to make fires for cooking. As more is cut, by more people, soil erosion worsens because the roots of the trees are no longer there to hold the ground in place. Soil erosion reduces the quality of the soil and makes food production more difficult. With more people to feed, African countries find it difficult to stop standards of living from falling.

Q2 Why might a population increase cause soil erosion problems?

WHAT'S HAPPENING TO THE WORLD?

Table 1 shows how high incomes and a high standard of living can use up large quantities of resources. The story of the search for firewood in parts of Africa shows how people who are trying hard to provide for themselves may destroy natural resources. In both ways damage is done to the global environment.

When there is economic growth there is an increase in gross domestic product (GDP). Usually this enables people to raise their standard of living. Economic growth has allowed people to buy things their grandparents never dreamed of, such as computers and colour televisions. Also people now have access to better health care, more education and a shorter working week. But these benefits have not been without some costs to society.

If incomes rise too fast, the increase in pollution and other environmental problems could actually in time reduce the standard of living. **Sustainable growth** means growth that can continue because care is taken to ensure that the environment is not destroyed. Unsustainable growth cannot be continued without damage to the environment. It may mean that the quality of life goes down, even though incomes seem to be rising.

'Tropical and other forests are disappearing; land is being badly cultivated; many species of animals and plants are being lost; deserts are spreading. Coal, oil and gas are being used up. Increased consumption generates more waste, which in turn causes disposal problems. We need to manage natural resources better and to waste less.'

Source: *Wake Up To What You Can Do For The Environment*, Department of the Environment

SUSTAINABLE GROWTH

Sustainability means economies can continue to grow without creating difficulties for future generations by polluting the world or using up all the scarce resources. There is a trade-off between allowing economies to expand and expanding too fast in an unsustainable way. Finding the right balance is important.

All economies grow by using resources, either natural or human. But sustainable growth is possible. One way to achieve it is to increase productivity. This means finding ways to increase output while using the same resources more efficiently.

In fact, many problems can be approached in imaginative ways which save on scarce resources. Sometimes technology helps us to find new materials so that scarce or dangerous materials are no longer needed. Machines can be designed to use less energy. Technology can also change the way people work.

Altogether there are many different ways of moving towards sustainable growth. One is to improve standards of living in ways which are good rather than bad for the environment. Another is to stop producing products that are harmful and find alternatives. Examples of three ways forward are given in the Evidence.

CHECKPOINT

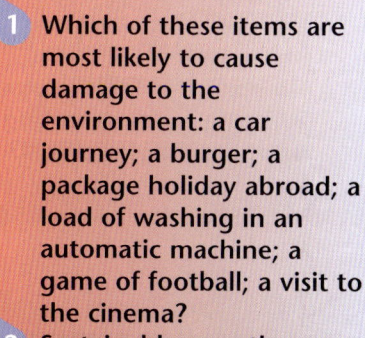

Q1 Which of these items are most likely to cause damage to the environment: a car journey; a burger; a package holiday abroad; a load of washing in an automatic machine; a game of football; a visit to the cinema?

Q2 Sustainable growth may require us to change our lifestyles. In what ways might lifestyles change in your community in the future so that growth can continue without damage to the environment?

FORUM

'In 1984 the rich consumed 80 per cent of the world's global resources; 75 per cent of the world's population who live in the poor South share the 20 per cent of resources that are left.'
Source: adapted from *New Internationalist*, January 1990

What can be done to make the majority of the world's population better off without destroying resources?

EVIDENCE

SOLUTIONS

- Teleworking can make economic growth more sustainable. Fewer car journeys are needed and there will be less pollution and congestion. Many people, such as accountants, writers, translators, data input workers and publishers, can work at home and maintain contact with their employers by using the phone, fax and modems.
- For many years, the towns around Britain's coast used to get rid of sewage by emptying it into the sea. The result of this was that many beaches were dirty. During the early 1990s, most UK water companies had to do something about this, because of new EU regulations. They had to build treatment plants. This cost money – in fact, it increased GDP. To pay for it, many people had higher bills from their water companies. But it meant that the sea and the beaches would remain cleaner in the future, with benefits to both wildlife and people.
- During the late 1980s, scientists realized that CFCs (chlorofluorocarbons), the gases used in making fridges, were damaging the atmosphere. After some time, many countries agreed to ban the use of CFCs after 1995. It didn't take very long for the experts to come up with an alternative, although it is more expensive. There are still a lot of problems: not all manufacturers comply with the agreement, but a solution is in sight

Q1 Explain why teleworking, cleaning up beaches and finding new ways to make fridges are examples of sustainable growth.

Q2 Which of the following could be part of a sustainable growth process?
- spending on new railway carriages
- increased spending on clothes
- eating more meat
- spending on research and development

KEY TERM

Sustainable growth is an increase in incomes that does not cause environmental problems for future generations.

171

Unit 5 – Create or destroy?

Enquiry 3: Waste not – want not?

Going green

SATISFYING GREEN CUSTOMERS

Many companies, such as Big Table, have seen that environmental concerns and 'green issues' are important to their customers. Businesses are able to use these concerns to develop new products that meet the demand. They can add environmentally friendly products to their ranges. Many businesses have developed such goods, for example:

- cleaning materials which cause less damage
- pump-action sprays on hair products, rather than aerosols
- cosmetics and other products that are not tested on animals
- recycled paper products

Concerned consumers provide a market for businesses and '**green issues**' have become an important element in the marketing mix of companies that sell their goods to the general public. New businesses have also been set up to meet consumers' wants (see 'Out of This World' on page 93).

Firms are demonstrating sound business sense by considering 'green issues'. They are aware of the importance of meeting the customers' needs and the dangers of not providing **environmentally friendly** products. Even when it is expensive to use different raw materials or change the production systems, the costs of not doing so, in terms of sales, may be high.

DOES EVERYONE WANT GREEN PRODUCTS?

Environmentally friendly products are often more expensive than those sold by businesses that compete on price. Organic food, which is produced without fertilizers or pesticides, involves no harm to wildlife and does not reduce the quality of the soil. But it costs more to produce. Can people pay the extra?

EVIDENCE

REFORESTATION

Many businesses are aware of the need to conserve natural resources. Big Table, a manufacturing and retailing co-operative in London, uses raw materials that are part of a reforestation programme. There are advantages to the business in this approach because consumers prefer to buy products that use recycled materials, and therefore using wood from forests that are being replanted will increase the co-operative's sales. In addition, the reforestation process is beneficial to society. This seems to be a situation where everyone wins.

Some people do choose to pay more for organic food. This may be easy for them if their incomes are rising. People on lower incomes have a difficult choice. They may want to pay the extra but be unable to afford a bearable standard of living without buying the cheapest.

DO ALL BUSINESSES REALLY MEAN IT?

Many businesses have made a real effort to reduce the environmental effects of their products. Others have made very minor changes and then advertised their products as 'green'. It is not always easy to tell whether the product is really improved, or whether it just exchanges one kind of environmental problem for another. Sometimes it is very unclear whether the business has acted really responsibly, or has just given the appearance of doing so.

The National Consumer Council carried out a survey of claims that firms make to show that they are

At Big Table we have been making beds by hand for over a decade. In our West London workshops we put this experience into practice every day of the week by making bed frames and mattresses out of the very best materials available. The result is top quality beds at affordable prices.

Q1 If forests are managed on a sustainable basis, there has to be a replanting programme. How will this affect the price of the wood?

Q2 How will Big Table's prices compare with competing furniture makers' prices?

EVIDENCE

LOGOS WORTH LOOKING OUT FOR

Soil Association: A mark of organic products protected by EU regulation and UK law.

UK Ecolabel: The EU label of environmental friendliness.

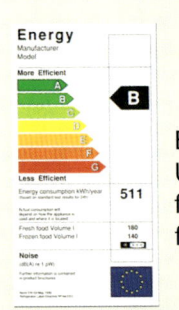

Energy label: Used on all fridges and freezers.

Source: *Evening Standard*, 15 March 1996

172

What was agreed at Rio ...

- Treaty on climate change to curb emissions of greenhouse gases
- Statement of principles on forests: non-binding agreement to conserve forests
- Bio-diversity treaty to preserve flora and fauna. US refused to sign
- Agenda 21: action plan covering all aspects of environment. Non-binding, but a yardstick against which to measure government actions

... and what was not

- Treaty on forests: dropped because of Third World opposition
- Earth Charter: too simple to meet complex international requirements

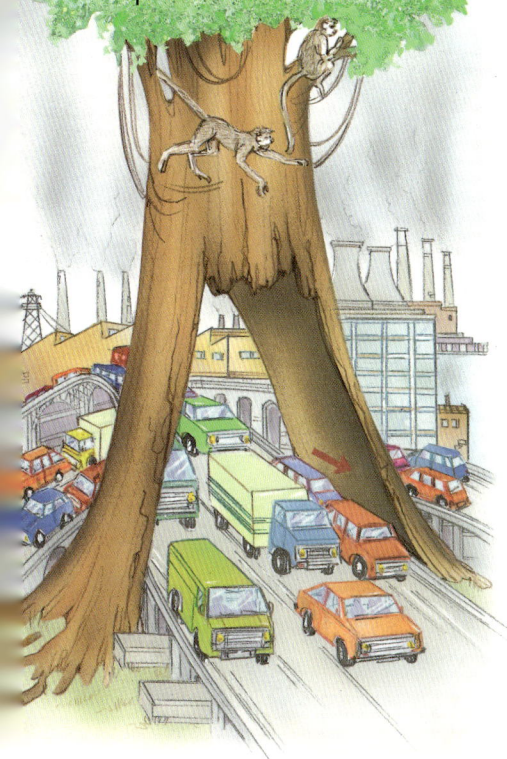

being environmentally friendly. Their comments can be found in the Evidence. There is a need for agreement about how products should be labelled so that consumers can be better informed. If products show the logos in the next Evidence, you can rely on the claims that are being made.

WHAT IS THE WORLD DOING?

Damage to the environment is a world problem. The actions of individual countries are beneficial, but unless everyone works together global warming and acid rain will continue.

International agreements have been made on a variety of issues. The Earth Summit in Rio de Janeiro in 1992 was an important moment in environmental history, when 103 world leaders gathered together to try to overcome the world's problems. Of course, this proved much more difficult than was expected because people want to protect their own interests.

Some developing countries would not sign the Treaty on the Forests because they felt that it took away their powers over an important national resource. The United States would not sign a bio-diversity treaty because it would limit the rights of industry to own new strains of plants and animals that are developed.

Despite this, important agreements were made. Agenda 21 set out objectives for all countries to meet. The UK government and many others produced statements showing what they were doing to meet these objectives.

FORUM

Do you buy products that damage the environment? How far do you feel able to go in avoiding them and buying 'green' products?

EVIDENCE

THE GREAT GREEN MYTH

- Sainsbury's Green Care range: 'specially formulated with priority given to the environment. Wherever possible we use biodegradable materials from renewable resources'.

National Consumer Council (NCC) comment: 'An extremely common form of claim. It is woolly, unverifiable, and means absolutely nothing.'

- Tesco can of tuna: 'steel recyclable' and 'dolphin friendly'.

NCC comment: 'Nothing special about the first. The second is unverifiable. What methods are used to catch the tuna?'

Source: *Evening Standard*, 15 March 1996

KEY TERMS

Environmentally friendly products are designed so that they cause a minimum of damage to the environment, in the process of production or when they are used or thrown away.

'Green issues' involve questions about the environmental effects of particular activities.

CHECKPOINT

Q1 Why have businesses been able to use environmental friendliness as a selling point?

Q2 How can customers be sure that what they are getting is really environmentally friendly?

Q3 Why is it difficult for countries to agree on ways of protecting the environment?

Q4 Why is it important for countries to work together?

Q5 How does an international standard for labelling products help?

Unit 5 — Create or destroy?

Enquiry 3: Waste not – want not?

Could we be doing better?

EVIDENCE

Although bottle banks and save-a-can centres are now found in many places in the UK, we are not **recycling** as much as other European countries are. For example, less than 1 per cent of all plastic in the UK is recycled. Domestic waste is only part of the scene, as commercial and industrial users are responsible for much of the waste produced in the UK. **Pressure groups** such as Friends of the Earth would like everyone to use fewer materials as this would reduce the amount of waste that needs disposal. Looking at figure 1, it is clear that much of what is thrown away by consumers can be reprocessed and reused.

Q1 Do you recycle any of your rubbish?

Q2 Would you recycle more of your rubbish if your community made it possible? What kinds of recycling facilities would you welcome?

Q3 Why do people sometimes not recycle their rubbish when they could?

Figure 1: The nation's dustbin

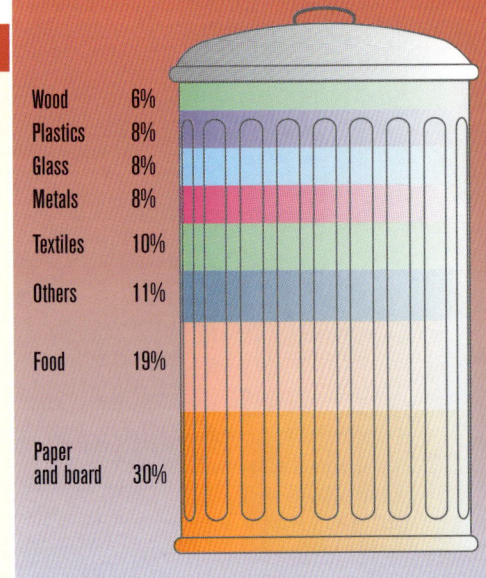

Wood	6%
Plastics	8%
Glass	8%
Metals	8%
Textiles	10%
Others	11%
Food	19%
Paper and board	30%

Source: *The Guardian*, 15 July 1995

RECYCLING

Most of us could be recycling more than we do. This would reduce the amount of waste and reduce pollution from incinerators and landfill sites. It would also save on the use of natural resources, such as wood. But recycling has costs and benefits. Collection, sorting and reuse may be more costly than disposal in a landfill site. In each case, people, communities and businesses need to look at the costs and the benefits of the individual situation.

The actual cost of recycling depends on the price that is paid for the waste products. If that price is lower than the cost of sorting and processing the waste, then recycling will be an expensive solution. Even so, communities may choose to recycle because that way there will be less harm to the environment.

EVIDENCE

WASTE AS BUSINESS!

Milton Keynes is home to the largest recycling project in the country. The local council has built a factory to recycle its waste, which the council collects and sorts. This waste is then sold to businesses that can use it as an input for their production process. Waste can provide a cheap source of raw material. Paper, plastic and glass can all be reused and this allows the Milton Keynes project to be profitable. In addition it saves natural resources and creates benefits for society.

Source: adapted from *The Guardian*, 15 July 1995; information sheets from Milton Keynes Borough Council

Q1 What are the benefits to society of this recycling project?

Q2 Would the users of waste materials continue to buy them from the council if the price went up?

Q3 If the supply of waste materials increases, what will happen to the price? Try drawing a supply and demand diagram to illustrate your answer.

TECHNOLOGY

There was a time when it was difficult to recycle much. Now recycling has become easier because new technologies are being used to sort and process the waste.

New technologies can help in other ways. For example, there are **biodegradable** packaging materials, and detergents are put in plastic bags instead of bottles. New ways have been found to use waste, such as making cloth from plastic bottles and making better quality recycled paper. In general, changes in technology have great possibilities for helping us to move towards sustainable growth.

Sometimes new technologies bring about change in a quite different way, by helping people to create less waste in the first place.

ELECTRONIC MAIL

More and more people are using computers for work, entertainment and education. Use of electronic mail, the Internet and the World Wide Web grows at an ever faster rate each year. These are all ways in which communications can proceed directly from one computer screen to another. They are much faster than the post or even fax messages.

Many businesses have used this technology to increase the efficiency of their operations. In the same way that companies replaced typewriters with word processors and manual bookkeeping systems with spreadsheets, electronic mail is now replacing letters and memos as a means of communication between employees. Only occasionally will people need to use paper to communicate. With fewer memos and letters, a business can adopt an environmentally friendly approach to saving resources.

EVIDENCE

THE PAPERLESS OFFICE

Oticon is based on the outskirts of Copenhagen in Denmark and manufactures hearing aids. As a small business it needed to find new ways of competing with larger companies in the world market. One of its solutions was to create a paperless office at its headquarters. In the mail room all letters and documents are scanned and saved on the computer. All relevant information is then distributed to the people who need it via their computers. Unwanted material is shredded in the mail room. The company believes that this improves productivity as staff do not waste time with unwanted letters, and it encourages staff to talk to each other rather than sending memos. As well as improving the efficiency of the business, the policy is good for the environment.

Figure 2: Number of Internet users

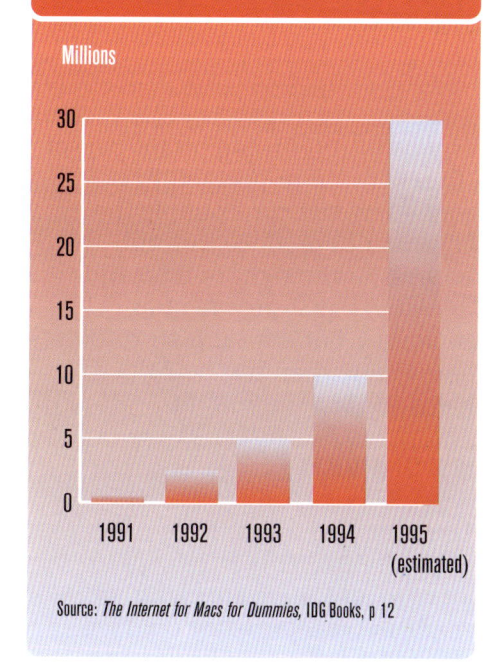

Source: *The Internet for Macs for Dummies*, IDG Books, p 12

"EXCUSE ME – IS ANYONE HERE NOT TALKING ABOUT THE INTERNET?"

FORUM

What do you feel are the world's biggest environmental problems? What is being done about them? What do you think could be done?

KEY TERMS

Biodegradable items will break down naturally when disposed of and are harmless to the environment.

Pressure groups are organizations that have been set up so that groups of people with a particular interest may persuade members of the public, businesses or the government of the importance of making changes.

Recycling means reusing waste materials in production so that fewer resources are needed to maintain output.

Unit 5: Create or destroy?

Enquiry 4: How should firms behave?

Can firms be 'good'?

EVIDENCE

GOOD BANKING IS GOOD BUSINESS?

Most people expect their bank to be honest. But they do not usually expect to find that their bank refuses to deal with certain companies.

Yet this is exactly what the Co-operative Bank did when it launched its 'ethical policy' in 1992. It avoids any contact with firms that supply weapons to governments that do not respect human rights, or that test cosmetics on animals, or that use unpleasant methods of factory farming.

The policy has been a huge business success, with only a few accounts lost and many more gained. (Remember the Evidence on page 102?)

Q1 Think of as many different reasons as you can why a customer might regard his or her bank as 'good'. Which would be the most important to you?

Q2 Is there a difference between a firm that is honest and a firm that is 'good'?

This is the daughter — *The Hills sent to law school* — *Using savings they kept in their bank* — *Which their bank had invested* — *Abroad in a country* — *That denies most of its people* — *Legal rights.*

The CO-OPERATIVE BANK

DIFFERENT VIEWPOINTS

Most people know the difference between 'good' and 'bad', between behaving well and behaving badly. When a company is formed it becomes a 'legal person'. Can it, too, behave well or badly?

Although a company is not really a person, it is made up of people and those people make decisions that affect other people – both inside and outside the firm.

Whether an action seems good or bad often depends on how you are affected. For instance, a firm might decide that its trucks could avoid traffic congestion by re-routing through a housing estate. This would probably be perfectly legal. From the firm's angle it would be a 'good' decision because it cuts journey times and transport costs. But from the local residents' angle it is clearly 'bad', increasing pollution and the risk of accidents.

Morals are general rules about right and wrong. The duty to do right rather than wrong is called **ethical responsibility**. An important part of a firm's ethical responsibility is required by law, for example the obligation to produce truthful accounts or the right of men and women to equal treatment as employees. But ethical responsibility means more than just being 'legal': that is the bare minimum.

RESPONSIBILITY

To whom does a firm have responsibility? This is a tough question and there are plenty of people in business who could get very angry indeed while arguing about the answer. Some would say that the answer is obvious: the firm has a responsibility to owners or shareholders. They have put up the money for the enterprise and have employed managers to win rewards in the form of profit. Others would say that the answer is less obvious. A firm is responsible to all those with a stake in the success of the business: in other words, the stakeholders. That means it is responsible to the community in which it operates, as well as to the people actually involved in the business.

While people argue about these matters, the stakeholder view is becoming more common, particularly among large firms. Ethical responsibility is at the heart of the issue. Once a firm accepts that it has ethical duties to meet the needs of stakeholder groups, then ethics becomes more than a matter of obeying the law. Instead, ethics must influence all business decisions.

Many firms have found that a strong sense of ethical responsibility is also good for business. A reputation for honesty and fair dealing can give a competitive edge in the marketing mix. It can add value to brands. In contrast, if something goes wrong, even one lawsuit against a company can be extremely expensive in legal fees and damages. For example, if faulty goods cause accidents, people who were hurt must be compensated and the firm may find that its reputation is wrecked.

EVIDENCE

The Promise from SmithKline Beecham

At SmithKline Beecham, health care – prevention, diagnosis, treatment and cure – is our purpose. Through scientific excellence and commercial expertise we provide products and services throughout the world that promote health and well-being.

The source of our competitive advantage is the energy and ideas of our people; our strength lies in what we value: customers, innovation, integrity, people and performance.

At SmithKline Beecham, we are people with purpose, working together to make the lives of people everywhere better, striving in everything we do to become the 'Simply Better' health care company as judged by all those we serve: customers, shareholders, employees and the global community.

Source: SmithKline Beecham, *Annual Report and Accounts*, 1994

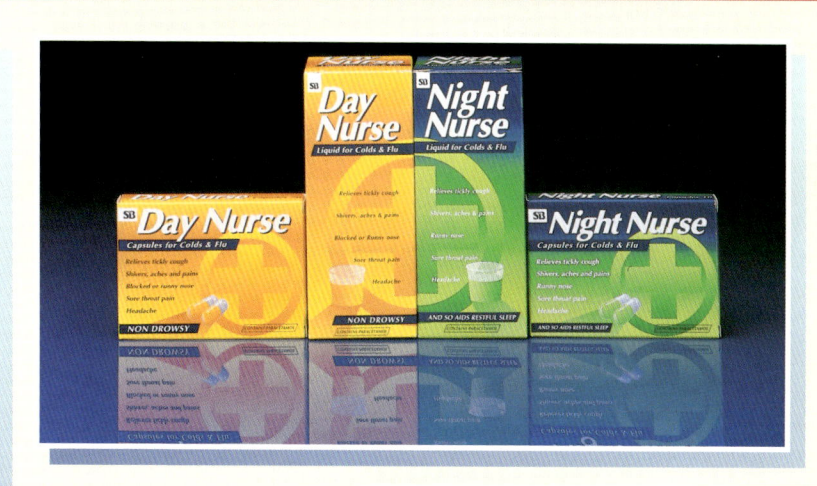

Q1 What does SmithKline Beecham claim to provide for customers, shareholders, employees and other members of the community?

Q2 How does this make sense if the company wants to improve its return on capital employed (ROCE)?

CHECKPOINT

Pear Tree Farm is in peaceful countryside near Canterbury. The owner has a herd of Guernsey cows and some orchards. Now he has applied to the council for permission to grub up the orchards and build concrete platforms for intensive chicken-rearing units. The birds will be sold to a large company that supplies supermarkets.

In a normally quiet village an angry campaign by residents opposes the plan. They argue that heavy lorries will need access along winding lanes, while the noise and smell will be intolerable for homes nearby. Some also add that factory farming is cruel and unethical anyway.

Q1 Who are the stakeholders in this case and why?
Q2 What arguments can be used to support the action of the owner of Pear Tree Farm?
Q3 If you were a councillor in Kent, what information would you want to help you decide on the planning proposal?

FORUM

'Business is not about being good – it's about being profitable.'

What do you think?

KEY TERM

Ethical responsibility is a sense of moral duty; in a firm this may mean duty towards any or all of the stakeholder groups.

Unit 5 – Create or destroy?

Enquiry 4: How should firms behave?

Next-door neighbours?

EVIDENCE

POWER STATION AT COCKENZIE, LOTHIAN

Cockenzie is a large village on the Lothian coast about 23 miles from Edinburgh. It has 4,330 inhabitants and an oil-fired power station owned by National Power. Originally built in the 1960s, the power station provides work for 250 people and for a number of local contractors. It also generates electricity for thousands of homes and firms in Scotland.

Q1 When the power station was built, what might have happened to the value of the houses in the picture?

Q2 In what ways might the power station be helpful to the people of Cockenzie?

COMMUNITIES AS STAKEHOLDERS

Everyone knows that neighbours can be difficult. Normally we are talking about other residents in our road. But firms are also 'resident' in villages, towns and cities. Like other neighbours, they can be friendly, co-operative and generous, or they can be noisy, difficult and interested only in themselves.

It is often said that with wealth and power comes increased responsibility. Some firms make very wealthy and powerful neighbours. Yet their success is built on the work and needs of ordinary families. Business cannot be separated from the community.

Put another way, the community is a key stakeholder in business. Employees are drawn from the community. Customers may be in the local community or in communities elsewhere. In return, the community is deeply affected by the decisions of business. A new supermarket may open, owned by a national chain. Its tills will take thousands of pounds every day, and perhaps local grocers or butchers or chemists will be forced to close. But what does the supermarket put back into the community?

When firms decide to expand or close down their operations, they m[ay] be acting in the interests of society [as a] whole. On a local level, however, th[eir] actions can hugely affect a whole to[wn.] The effects may be either for the be[tter] or for the worse. When a new facto[ry] opens it can create many jobs and bring prosperity. But if it closes a reverse chain reaction is triggered. J[obs] are lost and families have much less [to] spend with local shops and services. This in turn cuts more local spendi[ng] and a downward spiral of decline h[as] begun.

EVIDENCE

GRAND METROPOLITAN PLC

Grand Metropolitan (GrandMet) is one of the world's leading consumer goods companies, specializing in branded food and drinks. Worldwide turnover in 1995 amounted to over £8 billion.

'Corporate responsibility is not a fringe activity. Increasingly, business people are realizing that their prosperity is directly linked to the prosperity of the whole community. The community is the source of their customers, their employees, their suppliers and, with the wider spread of share ownership, their investors.'

George Bull, Group Chief Executive

COMMUNITY VISION

'Grand Metropolitan will contribute actively to the prosperity of the communities in which it operates, and will seek to play a leadership role in helping others to help themselves.

'Customers are looking through the front door of the companies they buy from. If they do not like what they see in terms of social responsibility, community involvement and equality of opportunity, they won't go in.'

Lord Sheppard, Chairman

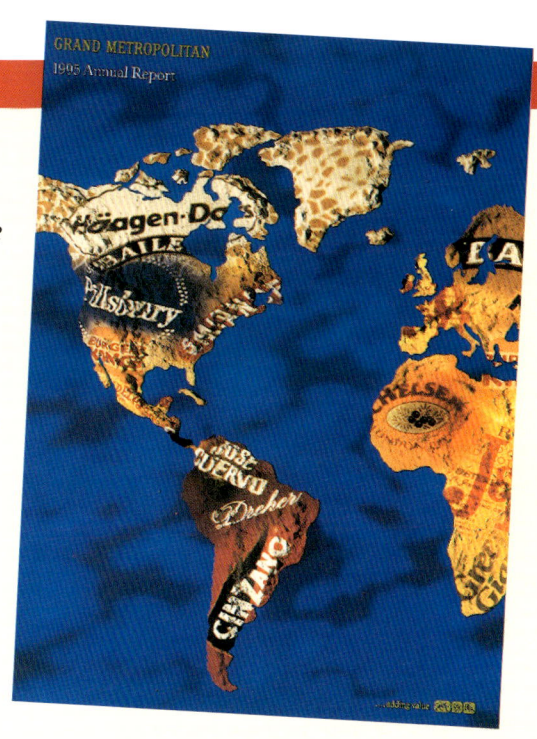

Q1 GrandMet spends large sums of money on community causes. Why should it want to do this?

Q2 How might spending on the community be good for business?

CORPORATE GIVING

Many large companies accept that they should give some support to the community and to charities. This is known as **corporate giving**. The scale of this spending varies widely. GrandMet contributes about 1.8 per cent of its profits after interest payments, or £17 million out of £920 million profit. Marks & Spencer gives 0.9 per cent. Others give far less.

GrandMet is unusual in its approach to community needs, but its senior managers see **social responsibility** as playing an important part in the company's business success. For example, GrandMet has become part of a partnership with the housing charity, Shelter, and several housing associations. GrandMet provides funds for the partnership to build and run hostels for homeless young people. There they are given training and help in finding jobs and permanent homes.

A reputation for being honest and for showing goodwill towards the community is a source of competitive advantage. This is particularly important for national brands. Like many other companies, GrandMet wants its brands to be seen as long lasting, desirable, honest – and socially responsible. Large firms may also aim to keep ahead of new laws that require higher standards in the relationship with stakeholder groups – including the community. In the long run, firms themselves have a stake in community well-being.

Table 1: Corporate giving

Company	Business	Profit (£ million)	Giving (£ million)
United Biscuits	Snack foods	179	0.68
Land Securities	Property	245	0.13
SmithKline Beecham	Health care	691	8.06
Kingfisher	Retailing	309	1.78
RTZ	Mining	922	1.66

Source: company reports, 1994, 1995

FORUM

All large firms could be required by law to spend at least 1 per cent of their profits on local community projects. As very few give anywhere near 1 per cent at present, this would make a real impact on social problems. Would you agree with this proposal? Can you test the reaction of one or more firms?

KEY TERMS

Corporate giving means payments by a company to trusts, charities or community organizations in support of causes outside its line of business.

Social responsibility is the idea that business organizations are to some extent responsible to society for the effects of their operations.

Unit 5

Create or destroy?

Enquiry 4: How should firms behave?

Will it cost the Earth?

EVIDENCE

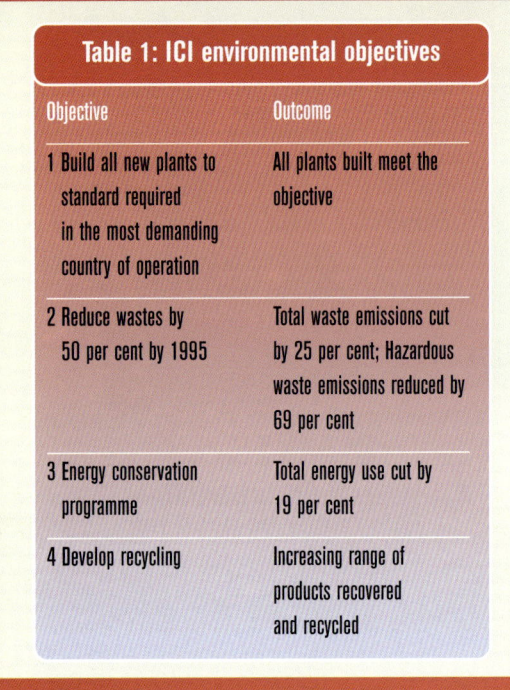

Table 1: ICI environmental objectives

Objective	Outcome
1 Build all new plants to standard required in the most demanding country of operation	All plants built meet the objective
2 Reduce wastes by 50 per cent by 1995	Total waste emissions cut by 25 per cent; Hazardous waste emissions reduced by 69 per cent
3 Energy conservation programme	Total energy use cut by 19 per cent
4 Develop recycling	Increasing range of products recovered and recycled

ICI is a world leader in the production of chemicals, paints, materials and explosives. With 64,000 employees, its turnover in 1995 was £10,269 million, including profit at £951 million.

In the early 1990s, ICI recognised that its environmental performance no longer met public expectations. It therefore launched its first set of environmental objectives to be achieved by 1995. ICI was also criticised for producing ozone-destroying chemicals and for releasing poisonous chlorides into rivers.

Q1 What difference will ICI objectives make to the environment?
Q2 ICI operates in some very poor countries. Why, then, is the first objective important?
Q3 Why might the second objective not have been achieved?

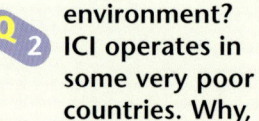

PRODUCTION AND THE ENVIRONMENT

Your environment means, literally, your surroundings. Business activity affects human surroundings in many ways. Production makes use of raw materials drawn from the natural environment. Most production processes yield wastes that are discharged in the sea, on the land or in the air. Many goods and services require energy in production or use. Energy is itself a scarce resource which creates waste products. All manufactured products have a limited lifespan and are eventually thrown away somewhere in the environment. Figure 1 shows the links between the firm and the environment.

In the years of fast economic growth following the Second World War, most people assumed that natural resources were limitless and that the environment could be used as a dustbin. Then doubts began to grow. Campaigns to protect the environment were launched in the 1970s. However, it was not until the 1990s that widespread public concern caused many businesses to consider environmental questions.

An important milestone was the Earth Summit of world leaders at Rio de Janeiro, Brazil, in 1992. This meeting set agreed goals for governments which would help to tackle problems such as global warming and the widening hole in the ozone layer.

Figure 1: The firm and the environment

180

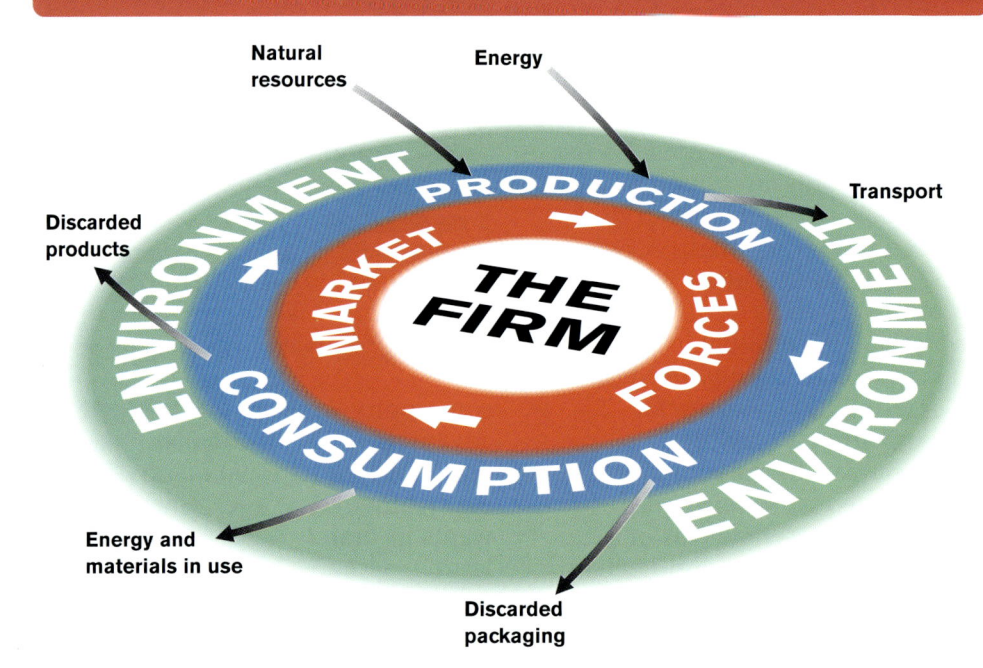

'Volvo stands for reliability, safety, respect for people and the environment in which we live. These core values are integral to our organization, our products and the way we act.'

'We are currently a long way away from establishing environment as the third Volvo cornerstone in the UK. So how do we get there?'

Volvo Cars UK Ltd commits itself to minimizing the environmental impact of its overall business operations by adopting a clear, open and 'cradle-to-the-grave' approach to its products and processes. We must therefore:

1. Be aware of the total effect of all that we are doing.
2. Measure these effects accurately.
3. Formulate action plans that minimize our environmental impact.
4. Continuously improve our environmental performance on a year-by-year basis.
5. Inform our staff, customers, legislators and the wider world what we are doing and why we are doing it.

EVIDENCE

THE THIRD CORNERSTONE?

These statements from Volvo mean that the company will consider the impact of its products on people from the time when production begins, to the time when the car is disposed of at the end of its useful life.

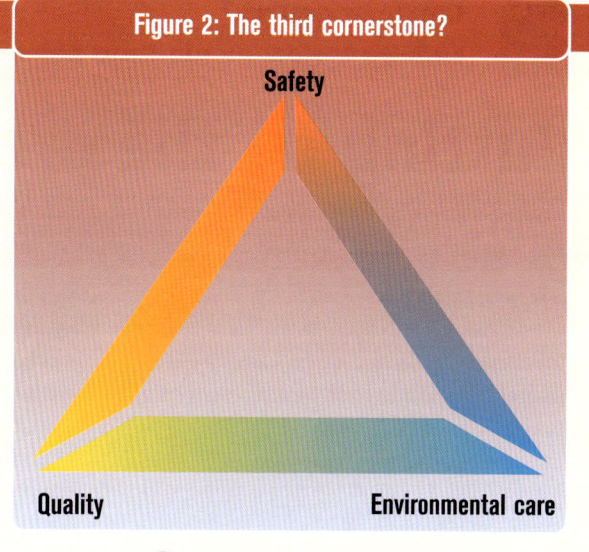

Figure 2: The third cornerstone?
(Triangle with vertices: Safety, Quality, Environmental care)

Q1 Why might Volvo believe that 'reliability, safety, respect for people and the environment' are so important?

Q2 Why is Volvo doing this? Explain (a) from the point of view of the company's directors, and (b) from the point of view of a critic of the company.

EXTERNALITIES

It could be said that every product has behind it an 'environmental shadow'. This would be the invisible costs of damage to the natural and human environment caused by the production and use of the goods or services concerned. These are externalities: the hidden costs of products which cause damage.

Many firms are now trying to improve their environmental performance. This is partly driven by the law. Regulations from the European Union and the Environmental Protection Act, 1990, have set tougher environmental standards that must be met. But a growing number of leading companies are getting tough on their own environmental performance.

An effective environmental policy needs backing from top management and must influence what happens in the organization at every level. When a detailed measurement of a firm's environmental performance takes place, it is called an **environmental audit**. This involves practical targets and a regular check on progress. Shell, ICI, British Airways and Body Shop International have all pioneered environmental auditing.

Environmental problems are also business opportunities. An environmental audit often leads to cost savings from cutting waste, recycling materials and marketing by-products. There may be new product developments such as filters that remove toxic wastes from water or smoke.

During the 1990s many consumer product brands have made environmental quality a source of competitive advantage. For instance, Varta, the German battery manufacturer, made its reduction of toxic chemicals a top priority in the marketing mix and gained ground on competitors. But although major firms want to be seen as environmentally friendly, many large companies still show little care or concern for the environment.

FORUM

Some environmental costs are not paid by the producer, but by the people who suffer from the environmental damage. If all the costs were paid by the producer, the price of the product would rise. What changes might then take place in (a) the level of sales, (b) the design of products?

CHECKPOINT

A manufacturer produces batteries in packs of four with a selling price of £3.00. A 'green' version of the batteries is then developed with no mercury or other heavy metals, but the price has to increase by 50p. The company relaunches the product with special 'green' packaging and advertisements explaining the improvements.

Q1 How do you think consumers will respond to these changes? Do you think they will all respond in the same way? Explain.

Q2 How do you think other battery manufacturers will respond?

KEY TERM

Environmental audit means the detailed inspection and measurement of a firm's performance in limiting its unfavourable impact on the environment.

Unit 5

Create or destroy?

Enquiry 4: How should firms behave?

Putting on the pressure?

EVIDENCE

SUGAR-FREE?

Sugar-free Ribena was launched with a poster campaign that featured just four words:

SUGAR-FREE OUT NOW

But this was enough to make the food **pressure group** Action and Information on Sugars (AIS) complain to the Advertising Standards Authority (ASA). Their letter says that 'sugar-free' Ribena actually contains 3 grammes of sugar per 100 ml, and the chairman of AIS called the posters 'the most blatant example of untruthful advertising which AIS has ever seen'.

A representative of SmithKline Beecham, which owns the Ribena brand, responded: 'Our view is that our advertising complies with all applicable and proposed legislation. We do not believe the current advertising is misleading.'

At that time there was no ruling in the UK regarding the amount of sugar a product could contain and still be called 'sugar-free'.

Source: *Campaign*, 17 September 1993

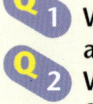

The description 'Sugar-free' has since been withdrawn.

Q1 What do you think is the main aim of the pressure group AIS?
Q2 What does AIS want SmithKline Beecham to do?
Q3 How far do you think SmithKline Beecham's view is (a) truthful and (b) ethical?

PRESSURE GROUPS

The Evidence shows how one group acted on behalf of consumers. AIS tries to improve the information available about the contents of the foods we buy. Other pressure groups also work in the consumer interest. The best known is the Consumers' Association, which publishes the magazine *Which?* Another group, Action on Smoking and Health (ASH), focuses on the tobacco industry.

There are now many other different kinds of pressure group that aim to influence business. Friends of the Earth fights all kinds of environmental threats and has been very active in opposing new road schemes, which are often backed by business. Many small groups oppose the development of industry in areas that they wish to be kept as they are. Some groups exist mainly to influence government.

About 9 million people in employment choose to belong to trade unions, which represent their interests and negotiate with firms. Trade unions are important in pressing for improved conditions and legal rights for employees, as well as protecting individuals.

All these pressure groups try to bring people together so that they can have more influence than they would have if they acted just as individuals. Where one person might be powerless, a group can make itself heard. Imagine what would happen if a major chemicals firm near your home applied to the council for permission to build storage tanks so that highly poisonous wastes could be reprocessed. You and others would wonder what would happen if there was a leak or a fire. On your own it would be difficult to change the company's plans. But if you formed an 'action group' with other local people, then the company could come under real pressure.

Even the directors in companies are represented by the Institute of Directors, while many senior managers belong to the Institute of British Management and their companies to the Confederation of British Industry (CBI). Then there are local Chambers of Commerce and many associations of small businesses. All of these organizations provide professional advice to members and 'push' their interests in the media and with government.

Through pressure groups, all stakeholders can be represented and have a collective voice.

HAVING INFLUENCE

Shareholders in companies can vote on decisions at the annual general meeting (AGM). They are also represented by the elected directors of the company. So, in theory, shareholders have a voice. However, only around 10 per cent of the shares in large companies are owned by private individuals. The rest are owned by banks, insurance companies and pension funds. In real life small shareholders have very little power. As a result there has been growth in shareholder pressure groups, such as the UK Shareholders' Association.

Some people buy shares in order to campaign for environmental or ethical causes. During the 1990s groups have organized demonstrations at company AGMs, gaining publicity for their cause. For example, Campaign Against the Arms Trade encourages members to buy a

EVIDENCE

GAS PRESSURE?

It was one of the rowdiest AGMs ever known. On 31 May 1995 the British Gas AGM was attended by over 4,500 shareholders. Richard Giordano, the chairman, and Cedric Brown, the chief executive, posed for photographs before what they hoped would be an orderly meeting. But uproar soon developed. Small shareholders were furious and for five hours attacked the directors over big pay increases, poor standards of service and other complaints.

Cedric Brown's 71 per cent pay rise had put him on £850,000 a year. Small shareholders ignored the opinions of the board and voted overwhelmingly to reduce his and others' pay.

Meanwhile, an unusual appearance at a company AGM was made by a 20-stone British saddleback pig named Cedric. A representative of the GMB trade union that had brought the pig shouted: 'This is Cedric. Our members have been losing their jobs. His snout is in the trough…'

In the end, the banks, insurance companies and pension funds voted to support the British Gas board of directors. The small shareholders were defeated.

Q1 Small shareholders in large companies can feel very frustrated. Why?

Q2 What effect might this AGM have had on the British Gas directors?

---

single share in companies such as British Aerospace and then to attend the AGM and speak against the selling of arms abroad. Animal rights activists may campaign in the same way against companies that test their products on animals.

Pressure groups can influence businesses, and sometimes also the government. The corporate affairs director for the British Airports Authority observes: 'There has been a professionalism developing among pressure groups. Companies have realized that they are not just dealing with unreasonable fanatics.'

FORUM

The High Street in the village of Combe is very congested. Traffic often slows to a halt. Many local people want a by-pass. This would have to be built through an ancient woodland of great beauty. A group of protestors has formed to oppose the by-pass. It has put pressure on the local council, which will be taking a decision. Is it fair that an unelected pressure group, which may represent a small minority, can influence decisions that then affect the great majority?

KEY TERM

Pressure groups are organizations that aim to change the beliefs, values or decisions of other organizations, including companies and the government.

Unit 5 Create or destroy?

Enquiry 5: Should the government interfere?

What price pollution?

EVIDENCE

In 1983 a government report said that lead in the atmosphere was dangerous to children. Following this it was decided to introduce different rates of tax paid on leaded and unleaded petrol. At first the difference was only 2.5 per cent and there was little change in petrol sales, but as subsequent budgets increased the gap, more and more people switched to unleaded fuel. At the same time, the government started a publicity campaign on the advantages of unleaded fuel. It explained how cheap conversions could be made to most cars to allow them to run on unleaded petrol. The petrol companies were persuaded that consumers would switch, and so started to offer unleaded fuel in their filling stations.

By late 1995 the average price of a litre of four-star leaded petrol was 57.9p, of which tax accounted for 36.1p. Unleaded was priced at 52.1p, of which 31.3p was tax.

Q1 What did the government do to encourage people to change to unleaded petrol?

Q2 Which of its policies do you think was the most important? Why?

Q3 What would the price of a litre of leaded and unleaded petrol be without the tax?

Q4 Could the process of switching to unleaded petrol be carried further?

DEPARTMENTS OF ENVIRONMENT AND TRANSPORT

ADJUST TO UNLEADED

Figure 1: Unleaded petrol sales, 1987-94

Source: BP

WHAT SHOULD THE PRICE BE?

The price of petrol that consumers pay at the garage forecourt includes the price to the petrol company, and the tax. Petrol is an attractive product for governments to tax because it is a good way of raising tax revenue. Also, because the tax is a large part of the cost of the fuel, governments can have a big impact upon the market itself, and can alter demand.

Different governments have different policies. In the United States, for example, most people want a car, public transport is poor and there are large distances to cover. Only about 30 per cent of the final price of petrol is tax, whereas in the UK it is about 70 per cent. By contrast, France taxes petrol more heavily than the UK.

Raising the final price of petrol reduces fuel consumption overall. Raising the tax on leaded fuel more than the tax on unleaded gave people an **incentive** to switch to the more environmentally friendly product.

CREATING INCENTIVES

Incentives do not apply only to individuals. Businesses pay petrol taxes too, and for some they may be a major part of their costs. Governments can create other incentives which encourage businesses to use roads less.

Some products such as coal and chemicals are bulky or heavy. In the past, these products all used to be transported by freight trains. Now, many companies find it cheaper just to put them on lorries. Building a

184

EVIDENCE

FREIGHT GRANTS

Tunstead Quarry is just outside Buxton, Derbyshire, in an area of great natural beauty. It cost £4 million to build a railway terminal at the quarry itself. However, the government gave a 'freight grant' of £2.6 million towards the cost. This subsidy left the owners of the quarry, Buxton Lime Industries, with very much less to pay. It created a real incentive to build the railway line, rather than to put the stone onto lorries.

The rail terminal at the quarry is reckoned to have saved 45,000 lorry journeys per year. Overall, since 1979, the UK government has given out £100 million in freight grants, spread over 150 schemes.

---

railway line right up to the chemical plant or the quarry is very costly.

Only when you begin to look at the environmental costs of putting more lorries on the roads does the picture change. Congestion can end in demands for more roads. Pollution is an externality, which can spoil the quality of life for many people. The total cost of road transport may make it worth looking at the alternatives.

How can companies be encouraged to make better use of the railways, which are clean and cheap to run once they are in place? They need incentives. The Evidence shows how a **subsidy** can be used to create the incentive. A subsidy is like a reverse tax: a payment by the government. By reducing the price of railway use, subsidies make railways more competitive with roads.

IS IT ENOUGH?

Although many people welcome subsidies for rail transport as a step in the right direction, much more could be done. Some European countries, such as Switzerland and the Netherlands, provide much larger subsidies to their rail systems. This means that both freight charges and passenger fares can be reduced. Railways are then better able to compete with road travel, and congestion and pollution are reduced.

Governments can change market conditions so that prices and incentives automatically adjust. Usually people buy or use less of the product that causes damage, because it has become more expensive. This is just one way in which environmental problems can be tackled.

Sometimes, governments use what is called a carrot and stick approach. The 'carrot' takes the form of the change in price incentives just described. The 'stick' part of the approach brings in laws that actually prevent people from doing something. We turn to this on the next page.

FORUM

Should the UK government be spending more money on railways?

CHECKPOINT

Q1 What would happen if the government doubled petrol taxes?

Q2 Make a list of all the ways in which a government might reduce traffic congestion. What problems does each method have?

Q3 What products other than petrol does the government tax? What effects do these taxes have?

KEY TERMS

An *incentive* encourages people to decide in favour of a particular course of action.

A *subsidy* is a payment from the government which covers part of the cost of the item and allows it to be sold at a lower price.

Unit 5: Create or destroy?

Enquiry 5: Should the government interfere?

Rules and regulations

EVIDENCE

TOUGH POLLUTION CURBS

Factories may be forced to switch to cleaner fuels, car parking charges could soar, and drivers of dirty vehicles could face immediate fines under anti-pollution measures made law yesterday.

Under the Environment Act, local authorities must carry out surveys detailing pollution hot spots, which are expected to include many city centres.

Areas that fail national and European health limits for air pollutants will be required to draft anti-pollution plans showing how they will meet tough new targets by 2005.

John Gummer, Environment Secretary, will review each local authority's plan before approving it. Local authorities that seek powers to shut down roads on high pollution days are likely to be disappointed. Those opting for pedestrianization schemes, cycle routes and higher parking charges are likely to win support.

The department said it would also back on-the-spot fines for vehicles failing emission tests. Planners are also expected to curb out-of-town shopping developments.

Source: adapted from *The Times*, 21 July 1995

Q1 What does the 1995 Environment Act require local councils to do?
Q2 What changes do you think we are likely to notice as a result of the Act?
Q3 How would you expect businesses to be affected by the changes?
Q4 Do you think there will be public support for these changes?

MAKING NEW RULES

One way to reduce pollution is to set limits on the amount that will be allowed. This means passing laws and regulations that force people and businesses to stop polluting activities. If time is allowed for adjustment, many changes that seemed impossible can be made. So governments increasingly use these direct controls as a way of responding to environmental problems.

Just passing a law may mean long battles with polluting companies, which have to be prosecuted for breaking the law. Court cases are expensive, so in a number of countries alternatives to fixed limits are being tried out. Systems are being created that are flexible yet give businesses a real incentive to clean up their production processes.

Power stations that generate electricity have been guilty of pollution which is thought to have caused acid rain. This can have a very bad effect on plant life far away from the place where the power station is located. Pollution from UK power stations is falling on the forests of Germany, Norway and Sweden. So finding good ways to stop power stations from polluting the atmosphere is important.

Since 1990 in the United States, power stations have been permitted only a certain level of pollution emissions. After 1993, they had to buy their 'pollution credits' from the Environmental Protection Agency of the US government. These credits state exactly how much pollution the power station is allowed to create. If it in fact manages to pollute less than the amount to which it has bought the right, it can sell the pollution credits to other electricity companies.

EVIDENCE

TOO MUCH FISHING, NOT ENOUGH FISH

Almost everywhere in the world there is overfishing. Modern technology allows more fish to be caught more often, so there is a real danger that some species may decline and perhaps become extinct. On the other hand, the livelihoods of many families depend on fishing. In New Zealand things are no different, except that the government there believes it may have found an answer to the problem. Under a system introduced in 1986, every fishing boat was given a certain number – a quota – of fish that it was allowed to catch. The total was determined by what had been caught in the past. This would not reduce the number of fish caught, of course, so after a time the government bought some of the quotas from the fishing fleet and kept them so that the total catch was reduced. Any New Zealand fisherman who does not use his quota can resell it to another, so new boats are allowed to enter the industry, but the total catch is gradually reduced. This gives fish stocks time to recover.

Of course, quotas are not always popular with the fishing industry. They can also pose problems when boats from different countries are trying to catch fish in the same waters. In 1995 Spanish boats fishing off the coast of Canada were said to be catching small fish, which is not permitted under the Canadian fishing regulations. After much dispute, the Canadian government sent out government patrol boats with orders to board the European fishing boats. In time, the European Union (on behalf of the Spanish fishing industry) and the Canadian government made more effort to agree on what should be done.

Q1 What would happen to the incomes of fishermen if overfishing is allowed to continue?

Q2 What will happen to the incomes of fishermen who are given quotas and not permitted to catch more than that amount of fish?

Q3 How can quotas be used to increase fish stocks?

This is what is known as a system of **tradeable permits**.

Over time, the number of pollution permits available to companies can be gradually reduced. As the permits become scarcer, their price will rise. The higher the price of the pollution permit, the bigger the incentive the business has to find ways of polluting less. Tradeable permits can be quite a powerful method of control and can be applied to very different situations, as the above Evidence shows.

CHECKPOINT

Q1 If polluting companies have to pay for a permit in order to continue polluting the atmosphere, what happens to the prices they charge for their products?

Q2 How can a system of tradeable permits ensure that businesses have an incentive to find ways of not polluting?

FORUM

Paint is produced by the chemicals industry. The processes involved in producing it used to cause pollution. That situation is now much improved, although the new processes that are used have added to the price of paint. Is it worth paying a bit extra for products that have been made without causing pollution? How much extra do you think people will be prepared to pay?

KEY TERM

Tradeable permits allow businesses that pollute to carry on doing so, but they are set at a price that gives these businesses an incentive to curb pollution. If businesses reduce the amount of pollution below the level permitted, they can sell all or part of their permit.

Unit 5
Create or destroy?
Enquiry 5: Should the government interfere?

Cleaning up

EVIDENCE

The Sea Empress

Environment

Make or break

THE Labour MP for Pembroke, Nick Ainger, claimed last night that the government was directly responsible for the massive oil spill from the tanker Sea Empress. This is because the government has failed to provide enough powerful tugs for the salvage operations that are needed.

A report written in 1994 recommended that the government should set up a system so that powerful tugs would always be available. Mr Ainger went on to say: 'It is quite clear that the recommendations have been flagrantly ignored by the government.

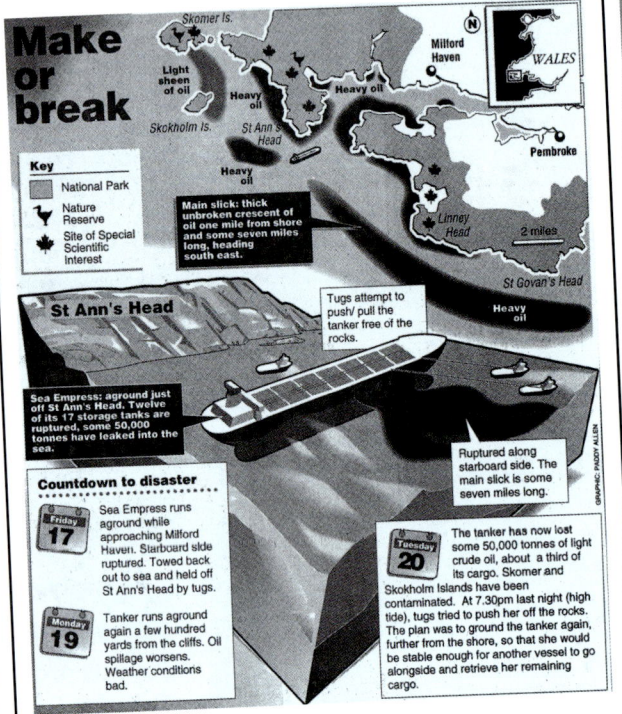

Because of its complacency, one of the most environmentally sensitive habitats in the world is now threatened by a massive oil spillage.'

The government said that it had sufficient resources to tackle the salvage operation as well as the pollution clean-up.

Key: National Park; Nature Reserve; Site of Special Scientific Interest

Main slick: thick unbroken crescent of oil one mile from shore and some seven miles long, heading south east.

Tugs attempt to push/pull the tanker free of the rocks.

Sea Empress: aground just off St Ann's Head. Twelve of its 17 storage tanks are ruptured, some 50,000 tonnes have leaked into the sea.

Ruptured along starboard side. The main slick is some seven miles long.

Countdown to disaster

Friday 17 — Sea Empress runs aground while approaching Milford Haven. Starboard side ruptured. Towed back out to sea and held off St Ann's Head by tugs.

Monday 19 — Tanker runs aground again a few hundred yards from the cliffs. Oil spillage worsens. Weather conditions bad.

Tuesday 20 — The tanker has now lost some 50,000 tonnes of light crude oil, about a third of its cargo. Skomer and Skokholm Islands have been contaminated. At 7.30pm last night (high tide), tugs tried to push her off the rocks. The plan was to ground the tanker again, further from the shore, so that she would be stable enough for another vessel to go alongside and retrieve her remaining cargo.

GRAPHIC PADDY ALLEN

Source: *The Guardian*, 21 February 1996

Q1 What problems are caused by oil spills?

Q2 What would happen if the owners of the oil paid for the clean-up?

Q3 What are the reasons for and against the government providing bigger tugs?

RIGHT AND WRONG

Although many of us might agree about what is right and what is wrong, we would be unlikely to see things exactly the same way all the time. So our **ethical codes** will vary. However, when many people agree, and can use their influence on the government, laws will be passed. These laws will require us to behave in particular ways.

Businesses are a little different. Firms exist to make a profit, but, as we have seen, they also have a responsibility to other stakeholders, which includes society as a whole. As with individuals, however, businesses have very different ethical codes. So, on the one hand, there are organizations such as the Body Shop and the Co-operative Bank, which make it very clear that they regard a strong concern for society as central to their operations. Meanwhile, other businesses continue to pollute rivers, poison the air and destroy wildlife – in fact, to do anything that they believe they can get away with.

Governments have for some time been passing laws that impose ethical codes on the less responsible businesses. Consumer protection, equal opportunities laws and environmental controls have all grown up in order to force firms to maintain certain standards of behaviour.

Unfortunately, however, governments do not always do enough. Although they hear many pressure groups telling them to do more to make businesses responsible, they also hear other pressure groups telling them to leave businesses as free as possible. So environmental controls are not always as strong as they might be. Some businesses can still be quite irresponsible.

Governments can themselves do a good deal to clean up the environment. The Evidence shows that there are many ways in which governments have been trying to

EVIDENCE

RECYCLING IN GERMANY ...

'Green' pressure groups in Germany have been strong for some time, and the German government has responded with stronger laws than most. Businesses are required to be responsible for the recycling of all of their products when they reach the end of their life. This has brought about massive changes in the packaging and disposal of products.

... AND IN TORONTO ...

The City government gives every household in Toronto a blue box. Every week, products that can be recycled (glass, plastic, aluminium, paper) are separated from the rest of the rubbish, put in the blue box and left for collection.

Also, if you want one, you can have a wormery. This is a bin with worms living in it, into which kitchen waste is emptied. The worms eat the waste, converting it into fertilizer – very useful for people with gardens.

These measures depend on people co-operating. In Toronto, almost everyone co-operates. In fact, many places with good recycling arrangements can count on co-operation.

... AND IN THE UK

Some local councils now have 'Waste for Fuel' projects. Rubbish is burnt, creating heat which can be used to heat buildings such as schools and hospitals. This disposes of the rubbish and saves on energy costs.

Q1 What efforts has your local council made to improve your environment?

Q2 What else would you like to see done?

improve matters, both by changing the law and by acting themselves. Many people still think that not enough is being done.

COSTS AND BENEFITS

One reason why governments sometimes do not do more is that they are trying to save money. Many of the things that governments could do to improve the environment are costly. Air pollution measurement stations need to be built and monitored. There must be inspectors to ensure that industry is obeying the law. Recycling products can be more expensive than disposing of them.

Another reason why governments do not always act is that they do not want to displease too many people. They often want to please people who are in business, who in turn want to make a profit. Not everyone agrees about the need for measures to improve the environment, especially if it means the costs of production will rise, and perhaps also prices.

One way of approaching this problem is to study the costs and benefits of environmental measures carefully, before deciding which are the most important. Another useful approach is to spend money on **research and development** of new technologies. We have seen many times that new technologies have produced solutions to difficult problems. Often they can reduce the cost of improvements. Governments can help by providing money for research.

FORUM

Should governments be spending more money on the environment? Where would the money come from?

KEY TERMS

An *ethical code* sets out everything that a person or a business believes is important for responsible behaviour.

Research and development means finding out more about the scientific background to problems and looking for new ways to solve them.

Unit 5 — Create or destroy?
Case study

Power stations

Q1 What would life be like for both firms and individuals if there were no power stations?

Q2 If economies continue to grow, what happens to the demand for power?

Q3 If the production of power were limited, what decisions would countries have to make?

Q4 Find out how these methods of producing electricity compare in economic and environmental terms.

A coal-fired power station

A wind farm

A hydroelectric pumping station

Unit 6

Winners or losers?

ENQUIRY 1: WHO ARE THE WINNERS AND LOSERS?	192

A wealth of difference — 192
Inequality worldwide

Who are winners and losers? — 194
Pay, jobs and working conditions

Down the slippery slope — 196
Poverty the world over

ENQUIRY 2: WHAT MAKES A WINNER?	198

Simply the best? — 198
Competitive advantage and corporate culture

Windows of opportunity? — 200
Flexibility and market orientation

Playing to win? — 202
Competing for jobs

Do winners mean losers? — 204
Possible gains and losses

ENQUIRY 3: IS THERE HELP AT HAND?	206

What incentives exist? — 206
People and unemployment measures

What does the government spend? — 208
The welfare state

Government spending and taxation — 210
Revenue, spending and borrowing

What are your rights? — 212
Consumer law

ENQUIRY 4: WHO TRADES WINS?	214

What are the benefits and costs of trade? — 214
Specialization, trade and growth

How do we stay competitive? — 216
The effect of the exchange rate

Making gains happen — 218
Export marketing

Keeping trade going — 220
Trade restrictions and agreements

ENQUIRY 5: RICHER COUNTRY – RICHER PEOPLE?	222

Win some – lose some — 222
Growth and change

The business of growth — 224
Investment, growth and enterprise

Can business make a difference? — 226
Business responsibility across the world

Stakeholders' rights and responsibilities — 228
All the links between the stakeholders

CASE STUDY: A WINNER OR A LOSER?	230

Unit 6

Winners or losers?

Enquiry 1: Who are the winners and losers?

A wealth of difference

EVIDENCE

£1.80 PER WEEK

Pappathy earns just 30p a day for picking coffee. Even in southern India this is not enough to feed her family of five. She tried to get a place for Amudha, her eldest daughter, at the Goodwill Village, a charity where she could be looked after and could continue her education. Unhappily, the village had already turned down 800 children that month, so there was no place for Amudha. The only solution was for her to join her mother on the plantation.

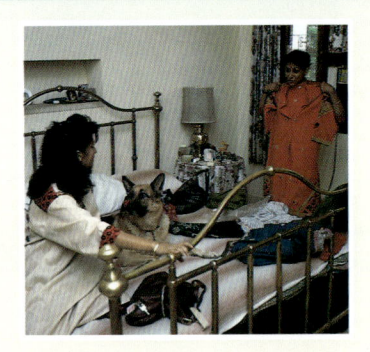

WE'LL BE LATE FOR THE PARTY

I think the blue one suits you better – but do hurry up, the chauffeur will be here to collect us any minute. We don't want to be late for the party. Have you forgotten that Imran wants to take us to the polo match in his new helicopter this afternoon?

Q1 Suppose each of these people were given an extra £100. What do you think they would spend it on?

A DOLLAR OR TWO

Josh can't claim benefits any more. He hadn't found a job in the time allowed, so there's no more help. He spends his days wandering the streets of New York picking up Coke and other cans. When he's got enough, he can trade them in for a few dollars.

Q2 How would it affect the work they do?

$5 MILLION + + + +

Bill Gates, the founder of Microsoft, receives $5 million a week plus earnings from his shares in the company – which could be much more. How does he spend his money? He's building a house costing around $40 million. Its reception hall will hold 150 people, the garage has room for 20 cars, and there are video walls that can be programmed with art. When Bill gets home, computers will alert the bathroom, the library and the trampoline room so that the climate is perfectly adjusted to his needs.

Q3 How would the way they spend the £100 affect other people living near them?

RICH WORLD, POOR WORLD?

People are rich throughout the world. People are poor throughout the world. The Evidence above shows the extremes. Pappathy earns so little that she can barely survive. The Prince has money to play with.

Bill Gates and Josh have little in common apart from the country they live in. Bill is rich beyond imagination, while Josh scarcely survives. Throughout the world, there are people living at both extremes.

Some people seem to earn more beacause of where they live. But this is not the only factor. As people become more highly skilled, they tend to earn more. The engineers of Bogota, for example, earn more than the textile workers of Frankfurt. This overlap can be seen between almost all the countries on the graph in figure 2

From figure 1 it is clear that income levels round the world vary greatly, between countries and between types of work. Unskilled workers in the **developed world** receive higher pay than skilled workers in the **developing world.** This explains why manufacturing industries are growing fast in countries like South Korea and the Philippines: lower wages help them to compete.

THE UK PATTERN

The general pattern linking skills with pay is the same in the UK as it is in the rest of the world. As the level of skill and qualifications increases, so does pay. Some people break out of this pattern and have high pay without having passed many exams. They may have bright ideas and an enterprising approach.

Table 1 shows income levels for the whole population, including those without jobs. The data divides the population into fifths and identifies the percentage of total income that is earned by each fifth.

EVIDENCE

Figure 1: International wages, 1992

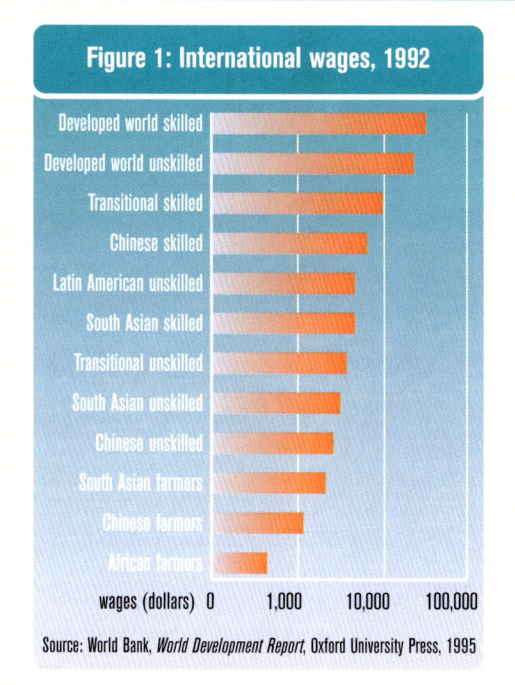

Wages (dollars), from highest to lowest:
- Developed world skilled
- Developed world unskilled
- Transitional skilled
- Chinese skilled
- Latin American unskilled
- South Asian skilled
- Transitional unskilled
- South Asian unskilled
- Chinese unskilled
- South Asian farmers
- Chinese farmers
- African farmers

wages (dollars) 0, 1,000, 10,000, 100,000

Source: World Bank, *World Development Report*, Oxford University Press, 1995

Figure 2: Wages for five groups in different countries

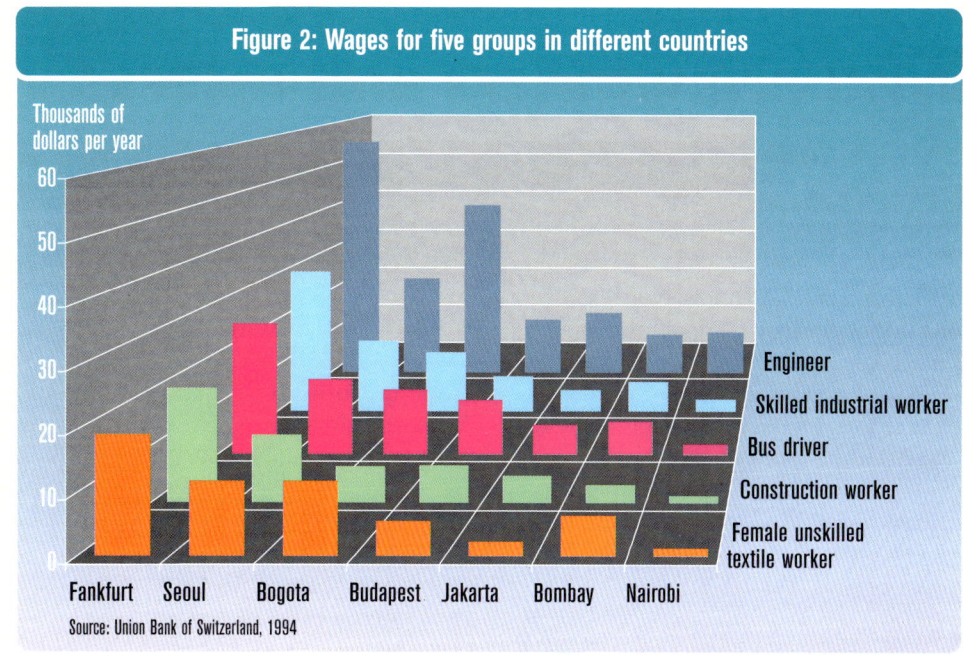

Thousands of dollars per year (0–60)

Cities: Fankfurt, Seoul, Bogota, Budapest, Jakarta, Bombay, Nairobi

Groups: Engineer, Skilled industrial worker, Bus driver, Construction worker, Female unskilled textile worker

Source: Union Bank of Switzerland, 1994

THE WAGES MOUNTAIN

Q1 Which group of workers is the lowest paid?

Q2 Where do the best paid workers live?

Q3 List the lowest paid to the highest paid in terms of (a) what they do; (b) where they live.

A CLOSER LOOK

Q1 In which country is each of the cities?

Q2 Where would you want to live, and which job would you do, if you wanted the highest possible standard of living?

Q3 Which job, in which city, offers the lowest standard of living?

Q4 Can you think of reasons for these differences?

EVIDENCE

Table 1: How is income shared?

Percentage of total income earned

Year	Bottom fifth	Next fifth	Middle fifth	Next fifth	Top fifth	Total
1979	10	14	18	23	35	100
1981	9	14	18	23	36	100
1987	8	12	17	23	40	100
1989	7	12	17	23	41	100
1992	6	11	17	23	43	100

Source: Central Statistical Office, *Social Trends*, HMSO, 1995

Q1 What has happened to the bottom fifth's share of income between 1979 and 1992?

Q2 What has happened to the top fifth's share of income between 1979 and 1992?

Q3 What about the groups in the middle?

Q4 Most of the people in the bottom fifth are on state benefits. What does the table tell you about the level of benefits compared with other forms of income?

FORUM

The information tells us that the world is a very unequal place. Do we want to make it more equal? What do you think would happen if it became more equal? What might help to make it more equal?

KEY TERMS

The *developed world* consists of those countries where manufacturing and services are the main economic activity, and incomes are on average fairly high by world standards.

The *developing world* includes all those countries which have low or middle incomes and can be expected to become more industrialized in the future.

Unit 6 Winners or losers?

Enquiry 1: Who are the winners and losers?

Who are winners and losers?

EVIDENCE

DRINKING TEA

The UK tea market is now worth £650 million a year. Four companies supply three-quarters of the tea we drink:
- Brooke Bond, a subsidiary of Unilever, has led the market for nearly 40 years. It has 30 per cent of the market.
- Tetley's share has risen to 25 per cent.
- Hillsdown, which produces Typhoo, Fresh Brew and some supermarket own brands, has 10 per cent.
- Co-operative Wholesale Society has a 10 per cent share.

A PROFITABLE BREW
Sales = £1,068 million
Trading profit = £87 million
Although 1994 was a difficult year for most food-based manufacturing companies, our sales have improved by some 10 per cent. The UK drinks market is very competitive and we have sold some of our coffee businesses. There has been intense price discounting and promotional activity, but we have held on to our brand leader position. A £5 million advertising campaign for tea granules has been well received.

Source: Lyons-Tetley report to staff, 1994

Q1 What evidence is there that tea is a popular drink in the UK?
Q2 What choices of product do consumers have when buying tea?
Q3 What evidence is there for saying UK companies benefit from tea production? Who benefits from the profits made by companies like Lyons-Tetley?

Figure 1: Drinks for all in the UK

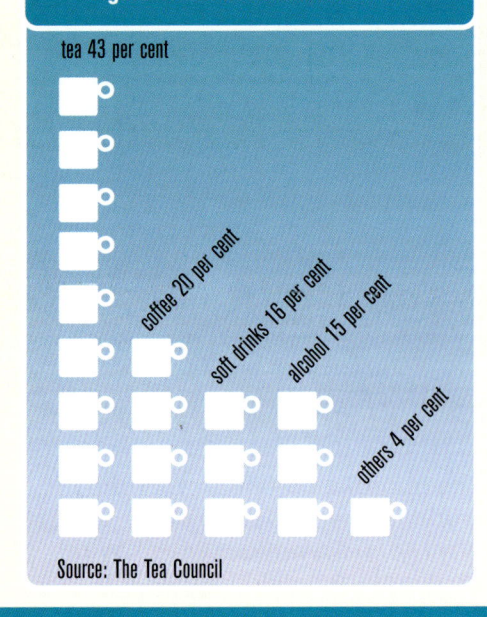

tea 43 per cent
coffee 20 per cent
soft drinks 16 per cent
alcohol 15 per cent
others 4 per cent

Source: The Tea Council

Figure 2: Tea consumption around the world (cups per person per year), 1993

UK, USA, Denmark, Poland, USSR (before break-up), Australia, New Zealand

Source: The Tea Council

PRODUCING AND CONSUMING

In some countries people drink an amazing quantity of tea. It is cheap and it is part of a way of life for many people. There is a large market for it. In this way, tea drinkers create jobs for people who produce tea.

You might decide from the Evidence above that there would be money in tea. If you did, you would be right. But who benefits? The Evidence on the next page is about the people who grow tea.

WHO ARE THE STAKEHOLDERS?

A feature of our modern business world is the interdependence not only between consumers and companies, but also between countries. The decisions of UK consumers directly influence the future success of a tea bag factory in north-east England. The price paid by tea-buyers in London auctions affects the future of thousands of tea-pickers, tea-dryers, and tea-blenders and packers in Kenya, India, Sri Lanka and elsewhere. Production on an international basis can provide income and wealth for individuals, groups, companies and countries.

The winners and losers from these production activities are to some extent determined by circumstances beyond our control. Extreme weather conditions, for example, may damage the crop, so the pickers earn less and tea drinkers pay more for their cup of tea.

If consumers of tea and shareholders of tea companies insisted that workers abroad experience good working conditions and reasonable pay, the balance might change.

EVIDENCE

EARNING A LIVING FROM TEA

- Tea is grown on plantations.
- People are more important than machines.
- Wages and working conditions are often poor.
- Pesticides are used frequently.

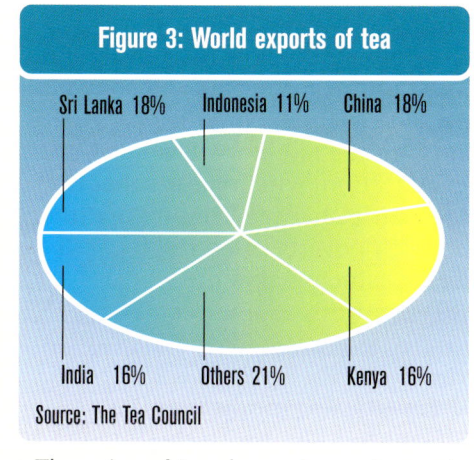

Figure 3: World exports of tea

Sri Lanka 18%, Indonesia 11%, China 18%, India 16%, Others 21%, Kenya 16%

Source: The Tea Council

- The price of tea depends on demand and supply.
- Tea-growing countries receive income from taxes and duties paid by growers and buyers.
- Countries receive payment in other currencies from the sale of tea. This helps them to buy imports.

A RISKY BUSINESS

The tea crop was poor in 1995. No one was sure when the rain would come. As a result, some parts of India have gone for quality rather than quantity, and prices are high in the tea markets of Calcutta. This is a relief to growers, as the price of tea has tended to fall in recent years.

IN BANGLADESH...

There may be six adults and as many children living together in a one-room hut with no door and a leaky thatched roof. The combination of a poor diet and mosquito attacks leaves people weak and unable to resist common diseases such as 'flu.

Fewer than 3 per cent of women on the estate could read or write. There is a school, but few can afford to send their children to it because the family cannot survive without the extra wages.

IN INDIA...

Many plantation workers live in purpose-built accommodation with proper sanitation, electricity and water. There is a crèche on each estate and children are cared for by trained nurses. All children receive regular health checks, so the infant mortality rate on the Brooke Bond estates is now half the national average.

Q1 What are the benefits of tea-growing for a farmer in India or Bangladesh?

Q2 How do tea-workers benefit from foreign firms owning the plantations? How could the working conditions of tea-workers be improved?

EVIDENCE

TETLEY PUTS THE TEA IN TEA-SIDE

The world's biggest tea bag factory is to be built in the north-east of England. Tetley will move all of its UK production to the Teesside plant and invest in new equipment. It means jobs all round at the Eaglescliffe factory, with an extra 30 posts added to the 180-strong workforce. The current output of 120 million tea bags a week will rise sharply. Tetley will stop making tea bags at a second factory in Greenford near London, where 30 jobs will go.

Source: *Financial Times*, 30 June 1995

Q1 Choose two pieces of evidence from these pages which you think can be linked to Tetley's decision to build a new plant.

Q2 Is Tetley making a good decision? Why?

Q3 Who are the winners and who are the losers as a result of Tetley's decision?

FORUM

Design a marketing campaign for a tea product that would ensure a greater benefit for tea-pickers abroad. UK consumers may have to pay more for this product than for other tea. How much more do you think they might be willing to pay?

195

Unit 6: Winners or losers?

Enquiry 1: Who are the winners and losers?

Down the slippery slope

EVIDENCE

THE TRAP

You have probably never been really hungry. That is, you've probably never felt that stomach cramping, hurting hunger day after day. Pappathy knows all about it. She works on the coffee plantation, earning much less than it takes to keep her family alive. She used to rely on her parents for help with her four children. This way she could keep them at school. Recently her father died and her mother went blind. She has no one to help her now.

In India, the government can just about afford to provide free education. There is no money left for social security. Her only option is to take her eldest child onto the coffee plantation and make her work. Without education or training her daughter will never escape poverty.

UK POVERTY

Sandra is a single parent who has ended up living in bed and breakfast accommodation, paid for by the council. She shares one damp room with her two children. There are two gas rings on the landing where she tries to cook. She wants to feed her family well, but how can she provide nourishing meals for growing children in such conditions? The younger one has asthma and misses a lot of school. He cannot really read, although he's nearly eight.

Friends cannot come home for tea when home is just one room. Anyway, the landlord gets mad if there's too much noise. The old telly keeps breaking down, so Sandra and her children feel left out as they cannot even follow the soaps.

Q1 What evidence is there to suggest that Pappathy lives in absolute poverty?

Q2 What evidence is there to suggest that Sandra lives in relative poverty?

Q3 What do Pappathy and Sandra have in common?

Q4 Why is it difficult for Pappathy and Sandra to escape from situations like these?

POVERTY AND POVERTY

Pappathy lives in misery. Not only does she not have enough to eat, but she has to watch her children miss out on the opportunities that would help them to improve their standard of living.

Anyone who cannot afford the basic necessities of life is living in **absolute poverty**. Compared with Pappathy, Sandra lives in luxury. She has enough food to keep her and her children from hunger, a roof over their heads and clothes to wear, even if they are second-hand. However, compared with most people in the UK, Sandra lives in poverty. This is **relative poverty**.

Being on or below the **poverty line** does not just mean that someone's diet is inadequate. Both Pappathy's and Sandra's families are missing out on education, which means that they stand little chance of improving their lot. Such poverty often results in ill health, which makes the whole situation worse. Some people see poverty as a cause for the increase in crime.

Poverty also means that it is difficult to join in with the things that other people do. People become cut off and feel excluded, and it becomes increasingly difficult for them to get a job.

In later Enquiries we will see how life might be improved for people living in poverty. Some may benefit from employment opportunities, while others may be helped by government schemes to provide them with some income.

POVERTY AND CHILDREN

In places where many people are poor, children may become victims of attempts by other people to make some money. They may be unable to get an education because their families need income. The work they do may be very hard and there may

EVIDENCE

CARPET BOYS

The children of richer families in northern India can be sold into bondage with a carpet maker at the age of ten. If the child comes from a poorer family, it may happen at four. The children then work a 14-hour day and may be dragged from bed to do overtime. If they fall asleep or make a mistake in the pattern, they are punished.

Campaigners try to put a stop to it all – but there is another side to the story. Robin Garland runs a charity that provides education for children in the carpet industry. His opinion is that 'in an ideal world there should be no child weavers, but chasing them off the looms takes incomes away from poor families and does not give children back their childhood. They are simply driven into even more hazardous employment'.

BURKINA FASO: WEST AFRICA

GUIRO MAHAMA, VILLAGE PRESIDENT:

'Years ago the land around our village was forest. There were many wild animals – lions, panthers, buffalo, elephant, antelope and a lot more. But now there are very few animals and almost no trees.'

HAMADOU NAMOUDOU:

'My father had a huge herd of animals. We were particularly rich in cows and I knew nothing but the taste of milk and meat. Today I have forgotten the taste of that life as all those animals are dead.'

Source: Burkina Faso: *New life for the Sahel*, Oxfam, 1990

Q1 What changes have taken place in the lives of Guiro and Hamadou?
Q2 How is the environment responsible for the plight of people in Burkina Faso?
Q3 Is there anything that can be done to help people in this type of situation?

---

be no chance for them to break away from the cycle of poverty.

POVERTY AND THE ENVIRONMENT

Some people have been made poor by environmental changes. This happened to Guiro and Hamadou (see the above Evidence on Burkino Faso). In the part of West Africa where they live, the climate has become drier. Trees cannot grow so easily. At the same time the population living in the area has grown. This means that people need more firewood for cooking. These two trends have led to the destruction of their environment. As trees were cut down, the ground became less stable and erosion started. This made farming much more difficult, so that people became poorer.

KEY TERMS

People who live in *absolute poverty* do not have the food, clothing or shelter needed to keep them alive.

People who live in *relative poverty* are poor compared to the society in which they live.

FORUM

Banning child labour sounds like the right thing to do, but if it makes life worse rather than better, what should be done?

The *poverty line* defines a level of income below which standards of living are too low to be acceptable.

Unit 6

Winners or losers?

Enquiry 2: What makes a winner?

Simply the best?

EVIDENCE

KWIK-FIT

Kwik-Fit was founded in 1971 by Tom Farmer, then aged 30. He is still the chairman and chief executive of Britain's largest 'drive-in, while you wait' supplier of products such as tyres, exhausts, brakes, batteries, suspension and in-car safety equipment. There are now over 500 Kwik-Fit centres in Britain, plus major operations in Holland and Belgium.

THE KWIK-FIT PHILOSOPHY BY TOM FARMER:

'At Kwik-Fit, the most important person is the customer, and it must be the aim of us all to give 100 per cent satisfaction 100 per cent of the time. Our continued success depends on the loyalty of our customers. We are committed to a policy of offering them the best value for money with a fast, courteous and professional service. We offer the highest quality products and guarantees.

We at Kwik-Fit recognize that our people are our most valuable asset. The Kwik-Fit people in our centres are the all-important contact with the customers and they are the key to success.'

Kwik-Fit
Our Aim is 100% Customer Satisfaction *Delight*

Q1 What does Kwik-Fit claim to provide for its customers?

Q2 What other information would you need in order to decide if Kwik-Fit is offering 'the best value for money'?

COMPETITIVE ADVANTAGE

Firms are competing for every moment that their products are in the market. As a British Airways slogan used to say, 'We always remember that you have a choice'. When a customer looks at a range of different but competing products, the one chosen for purchase is a winner – and so is the firm that made it ... if it can keep winning.

Regular winning means having a competitive advantage. This is most simply explained as the best value for money. The idea of value for money splits into two key issues: price and quality. We saw in Unit 1 (page 23) that there are two broad approaches to gaining a competitive advantage: reasonable quality at a low price, or high quality at a reasonable price. Some firms successfully aim for a third position: above-average quality at a below-average price. In every case the firm must watch cost and quality.

The low-cost route to market success is easiest for large firms that can exploit the economies of scale. But small firms may also gain a cost advantage by keeping down fixed costs – for example, by working out of a simple office in a cheap location. Increasingly today, however, the focus is on quality. Customers are becoming more demanding and want products to meet their personal tastes and needs.

It is important to remember the difference between quality and luxury. Quality is about a product being fully fit for its purpose and meeting – or exceeding – the expectations of the customer. A recent slogan at Safeway supermarkets was 'And a little bit more ...'. Often that 'little bit more' is the basis for competitive advantage – if it's real! Quality can push up costs and therefore price. But winning firms often find that total quality throughout the business saves waste and increases the motivation of the staff. The real winning line is more quality for less cost – or value for money.

CORPORATE CULTURE

Do you see the glass as half empty or half full? Positive thinking combined with creativity and teamwork are vital springs of competitive advantage. More and more the key source of added value in business is people – their skills, their commitment and their ideas. A firm that is pushing at the frontiers of cost and quality will be restless, curious, 'fizzy' in its atmosphere. People will not just 'do the job they are paid to do', but will always be wondering how it might be done better or differently.

Like families, firms develop ways of doing things and seeing the world: this is what is called a **corporate culture**. A creative culture quite closely resembles the thinking patterns of the entrepreneur that were explained at the beginning of this book. In a very creative firm everyone becomes like an entrepreneur, seeing their own job as a real enterprise. In such firms managers involve all staff in the effort to reduce costs and to improve quality. All ideas are taken seriously and there are rewards for the most promising. Far from it being a crime 'to rock the boat', staff are encouraged to ask awkward questions. They are also allowed to make mistakes and do not fear the consequences if they – and everyone else – can learn from what went wrong.

Work in a creative firm may even feel less like work and more like fun. In the words of leading American business writer, Tom Peters: 'Joy of life. That's what an ordinary day at work ought to be about. Why not?' Certainly people who manage to enjoy their work are often good at it and are more likely to be creative. Their achievement of quality and the originality of their ideas may be rich sources of competitive advantage. A recent article in *The New York Times* said of the most famous software designer: 'Microsoft's only factory asset is the human imagination'.

EVIDENCE

GOLDENEYE

Eon Productions Ltd. is a London-based family firm founded in 1962 by an American – Albert R. 'Cubby' Broccoli – and still owned by his family. Producer of all 17 James Bond movies, Eon has never failed to offer extraordinary story lines and unforgettable special effects. The company has about 12 full-time staff at its offices in London and Los Angeles. It has a culture in which creative flair has been given every opportunity to grow, and originality is strongly encouraged.

CHECKPOINT

Q1 What is meant by a firm that aims 'to exceed customer expectations'? Give an example of what this might mean for a restaurant chain.

Q2 Can you think why a firm might deliberately increase its costs and prices in order to give its customers better value for money?

FORUM

It is obvious that having a competitive advantage benefits the business. How does it benefit the consumer?

How might a firm lose its competitive advantage? How would this affect the consumer?

KEY TERM

Corporate culture describes the particular way that events are understood and things are done within an organization.

Unit 6 — Winners or losers?
Enquiry 2: What makes a winner?

Windows of opportunity?

EVIDENCE

THE NEXT MISSION

'To be the natural choice retailer in the UK for fashion-aware men and women who expect style, distinction and quality from their clothing.'

Back in 1990, when Next was nearly bankrupt and its shares were down to 6½p, there were those who said it was a 1980s success story and a 1990s disaster. Against all the odds, Next made a spectacular recovery: by 1996 its operating profit was £100 million and those same shares were trading at 530p each.

The company offers one brand in 'Next' and two methods of shopping – through its High Street stores or through the Next Directory, which is a computerized mail order system.

Clothing represents 95 per cent of all sales at Next. The stock in the stores – over 300 in the UK and Ireland – is changed completely twice a year for the Spring/Summer and Autumn/Winter collections. In addition, there is a stock injection every eight weeks in response to changing weather conditions.

Fashion retailing always carries the risk of getting it wrong. Next needs the most detailed and accurate understanding of what the customer wants in order to get it right.

Q1 What is special about Next's products?
Q2 How does Next try to keep ahead of its rivals?

ADAPTING TO THE MARKET

Marketing is about linking producer and consumer. The market-oriented firm receives and collects information about consumer wants, shapes its products accordingly, and targets them into the correct market segments through a flexible marketing mix. 'Keeping your eye on the ball' in business is about watching the market. In a sense, every source of competitive advantage is only temporary. It is achieved at a point in time, but is immediately threatened not only by competition, but also by the market moving on (see page 35).

Markets are a moving target. They change in different ways. First, there are certain broad trends that affect the whole market. For example, more people use cars to do the shopping, which changes the way they shop. Then, over time, segments and niches change in complicated ways. Competitors may spring up in a niche that the business used to have to itself – Body Shop now faces competition from chains like Boots. Then a segment may shrink or break up. For example, if the number of babies born falls, Mothercare gets less business, while the market for pop singles has become smaller and divided into sub-sections.

Markets are tending to change faster than they used to. This means that firms must be sensitive to their customers' wants. As Tom Peters says, the windows of market opportunity open and close with little warning, and firms must be in a state of instant readiness to seize their chance.

Of course, there are times when a business can keep a market to itself, and then it may be less sensitive to consumer demand. It all depends on how much competition there is.

ORGANIZING THE BUSINESS

The need to change direction rapidly and readily makes flexibility in a firm a vital source of competitive advantage. Flexibility means a production system that can be adjusted and adapted at short notice. It also means that the staff are likely to be **multi-skilled** – to take on new challenges and to learn new ways of working. Change becomes normal. Indeed, some highly innovative companies argue that change should be celebrated, even 'loved'.

Naturally there must be flexibility in the marketing mix. Just as the firm tracks its market opportunities, so it constantly refocuses its mix as the target market moves. Product development and modifications, new packaging and advertising, new channels of distribution: there is no pause for the opportunity-hungry firm.

The flexible firm cannot easily work with a rigid structure. This is why the traditional **pyramid style of organization** has 'flattened', with fewer layers of management and with staff more trusted to think and act for themselves. Some firms are even moving away from a pyramid structure altogether and are organizing their activity in a kind of web or network.

Figure 1: The end of the pyramids?

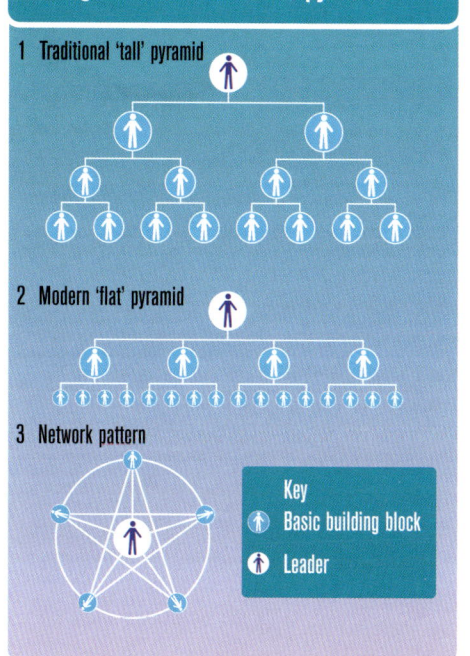

1 Traditional 'tall' pyramid
2 Modern 'flat' pyramid
3 Network pattern

Key
- Basic building block
- Leader

EVIDENCE

PSION PLC

Psion makes palmtop computers. Founded in 1980 by its present chairman and chief executive, David Potter, the company designs, manufactures and markets its own products. The Series 3 Psion range has been an international success, with over 500,000 units now sold. Growth of the enterprise has been spectacular, with sales expanding annually at an average rate of 35 per cent.

Flexible computer-assisted design and manufacturing allows Psion to keep ahead of a market driven by new technology as well as changing customer demand. The firm has over 200 staff but no organizational pyramid or traditional layers of management. Staff work in self-managed teams for particular projects, which then change their purpose and pattern according to evolving needs.

CHECKPOINT

Choice Chocolates makes luxury assortments of traditional English chocolates, which it sells through small retailers and department stores. The firm's competitive advantage is based on high-quality chocolates and distinctive old-fashioned packaging, including a hand-tied ribbon around each box. Unfortunately, sales growth has slowed to zero and the marketing manager is now concerned by two emerging trends. First, there is a swing in public taste towards Belgian chocolates, with an emphasis on truffles. Second, the age profile of Choice Chocolates' consumers has risen quite sharply, as table 1 shows.

What steps would you recommend?

Table 1: Age profile of Choice Chocolates' consumers

Percentages of sales in the UK

Age range	1991	1996
Over 60	45	63
40–59	34	28
20–39	16	7
Under 20	5	2

FORUM

Do businesses always respond to customer demand? Why do some firms get caught with a shrinking market? What will happen to their employees?

KEY TERMS

Multi-skilling is the ability of a worker or a workforce to use a range of skills with flexibility according to need.

The *pyramid style of organization* describes the organization of a firm where managers are arranged in many layers, each layer having control of the next one down. The lower the level in the organization, the larger the number of people.

Unit 6 Winners or losers?
Enquiry 2: What makes a winner?

Playing to win?

EVIDENCE

NOT TAKING 'NO' FOR AN ANSWER

Andrew Shore was determined to join an advertising agency. Soon his CV and letter of application were landing in filing baskets – and wastepaper baskets. 'No vacancies' was the message.

Carefully dressed and with a portfolio of his best ideas, Andrew went uninvited to a major agency. 'I'm sorry, but Mr Porter [the managing director] is far too busy to see you. With the best will in the world, you're wasting your time. We have no vacancies.' Andrew sat down on a chair in the foyer. 'I've got the best will in the world and plenty of time,' he said cheerfully. 'I'll wait.' It took six and a half hours for Mr Porter to emerge. 'I'll give you five minutes,' he said.

Half an hour later Andrew was waiting for the bus. 'Only a three months' trial, remember.' The words came back to him. He'd make sure they *were* three months to remember.

PEOPLE AND VALUE

We have seen that for many firms a large element of added value comes from people. For a rising proportion of firms, people are the key to competitive advantage. This is particularly true of hi-tech and service industries. Meanwhile, more and more unskilled or low-skilled jobs – in offices as well as factories – are disappearing as computer-based systems are introduced. The result is a competitive jobs market where firms are keen to find well-qualified and hard-working people.

Fewer jobs are now neatly defined 'slots' waiting to be filled. In the past, businesses had to advertise and even search for a given number of workers: for example, fitters, welders, machine operators, clerks and typists. Often anyone with the minimum level of qualifications was given a job. In many cases it was not necessary for employees to understand the firm's business or to worry about customers. In return for doing a repetitive job to the proper rules, the firm would pay a standard wage every week. There are many people who still have employment of this type. But their numbers are falling as they are replaced by new technologies. Some full-time jobs have been replaced by part-time or short-contract labour.

People as well as firms are now facing a competitive market. Every individual has a special mix of qualifications, skills and personal qualities. Each person, each mix has value and is able to add value. Again, the person is like a firm. You have a set of useful resources but you need to turn them into a product for which there is a market. 'Me plc' is one way of describing the individual who wants to earn a living. You are your own managing director and you are in charge of marketing, production and finance! It is not enough to be 'adequate'. Winners have that vital extra quality called competitive advantage.

PEOPLE AND IDEAS

Look back in this Enquiry to find some sources of competitive advantage for firms. Since these are mostly dependent on people, it is not surprising that they are also the seeds of competitive advantage for individuals. Quality arises from people who are talented, well qualified and reliable. Creativity flows from individuals who are lively, curious and original, with a readiness to try new ideas and to learn from mistakes. Flexibility comes with education and skills such as the ability to communicate well and to

EVIDENCE

ARTPLACE

Amanda Metcalf lives with her family near Portsmouth. Back in 1991 she was an art teacher, but then a serious illness forced her to give up her job and cope with a series of operations at a London hospital. It took two worrying years to recover – and to get an idea…

Why were so many hospitals dismal and even depressing in the way they looked? Excellent staff seemed to work in surroundings that did little or nothing to make patients feel better. So would it be possible to use art and design to make hospitals more welcoming, reassuring and inspiring places to be?

This was the creative idea for Artplace, now a small business run by Amanda that puts new paintings, murals and interior designs into hospitals. The system of National Health Service Trusts, which gives hospitals more independence in using their budget, has helped. Doctors and administrators have been keen to improve the environment for patients and staff. And Amanda recently had the satisfaction of meeting the same doctors who operated on her, although this time it was to plan the interior design of their new hospital!

work in a team. Dynamism is a state of mind and depends on energy, positive thinking – and a good sense of humour.

This is a long list. No one will have all these strengths, but everyone probably has some. These will then need to be demonstrated to employers, the buyers for the person's skills. Each individual can develop his or her own 'marketing mix'. And, like a firm, being a winner is about the right product well communicated in the right place – and at a price the market will pay.

Competition for jobs means that people who are not well qualified are in a weak position. They are likely to spend more than the average amount of time looking for work. They may need help in order to improve their positions.

CHECKPOINT

A successful leisure centre needs a new manager. As human resources manager for the company that owns the complex, what qualities would you be looking for in the successful candidate? Why?

FORUM

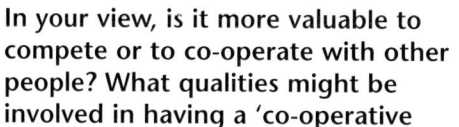

In your view, is it more valuable to compete or to co-operate with other people? What qualities might be involved in having a 'co-operative advantage'?

Unit 6 Winners or losers?
Enquiry 2: What makes a winner?

Do winners mean losers?

EVIDENCE

TIME OFF

Keeping a competitive advantage at Time Off has been winning for the firm and winning for its stakeholders. Founded in 1967, this small package tour operator pioneered the idea of 'short-break' holidays in city centres across Europe. At first it was a small niche market, but during the 1980s the competition caught up and some big companies moved into the city break business.

However, Time Off kept its competitive edge and has managed to expand. Quality has always been important. Hotels are carefully selected; brochures are tastefully designed; clients are well looked after and given unexpected extras. The prices are not the cheapest, but they do give value for money.

Staff need to be committed and willing to work hard. In the open-plan office everyone is expected to co-operate and work well in a team. Flexibility is important in meeting clients' exact needs, often on late bookings.

TIME OFF City Selection
1996 2ND EDITION
A PLEASURE OF CITIES
Voted the Best Travel Company in the 1995 Observer Travel Awards

Q1 How does Time Off manage to survive when large firms such as Thomsons and British Airways also offer city centre holidays?

Q2 Will Time Off be able to put pressure on a hotel to ensure that it offers a good service? How could the hotel benefit?

MAKING WINNERS

The greater a firm's competitive advantage in the market, the more likely it is to earn above-average profits. Return on capital employed (ROCE) will rise compared to other firms in the industry. Both dividends and retained profits can be higher, and the shares may rise in value. All this is a success story for the owners and managers of the business. But is it good news for the other stakeholders?

For employees there may be winners and losers. Profits often lead to expansion, helping to pay for new equipment. Some new jobs will be created. Employment at Time Off has expanded, but in other cases job losses are possible as costs are reduced and the product mix changes. Older and less-skilled employees may be at risk. Other staff might feel driven to work long hours in order to keep their jobs. Most suppliers should be winners. Order sizes are likely to increase and to be more secure. Obviously, the quality of what is supplied affects the quality of the final product. So the supplier may be expected to improve quality. Equally, suppliers may be asked to cut prices and that could mean lower profits for them. Customers may win. Competitive advantage for the firm normally means better value for money. Either prices are lower or quality is better. The customers' needs are more likely to be met.

Customers can also lose. Sometimes the firm's main advantage is lack of competition. A monopolist is able to charge high prices while giving poor value for money. Or there may be competition, but consumers are being misled by an advertising campaign which is not based on real product advantages. There is no doubt that some advertising is used to market products that are of less value than competing products. You can probably think of products which are very similar, and which use costly advertising to keep up sales.

EVIDENCE

WILL THE TOWN LOSE ITS HEART?

Ludlow in Shropshire has been the scene of a battle. On one side is the council and others who support an application from Tesco to build a new supermarket on the derelict cattle market. Against them are people who say the plan will put small shops out of business and spoil the character of an historic town.

There is a strong tourist trade in Ludlow. Its streets have many buildings dating back to Tudor times and earlier. The council argues that Tesco will actually encourage people to shop in town, but opponents say that trade will be sucked out of the historic heart, leaving behind a gift-shop economy and boarded-up old buildings.

Q1 Why might shoppers choose Tesco rather than an older, smaller shop?

Q2 If people do switch to Tesco, why should anyone object?

SUCCESSES AND FAILURES

Successful firms in the community should mean more jobs and investment. There may also be **positive externalities** as other quality firms are attracted into the area. But the need to be flexible may mean rapid change in the types of jobs available and the exact skills required. The competitive success of one large firm may mean the competitive failure of others. Sometimes this reduces choice and alters the way of life in the community. **Negative externalities** can also arise. For example, Ludlow has an important tourist industry that depends in part on the appeal of the town's small shops.

Firms with a strong competitive advantage may be more likely to protect the environment. But there is the risk that cost-cutting might tempt a firm to ignore pollution. Successful firms can also be greedy for land as they look for **green-field sites**, often on the edge of towns. Supermarkets and retail warehouses are obvious examples, but manufacturers of winning products are also often drawn to an undeveloped site. One result can be a 'doughnut effect' on towns and cities as they are ringed by firms that are winning, leaving a business 'hole' in the older centre where firms are losing ground.

CHECKPOINT

A successful pizza restaurant chain has people queuing outside its branch in a seaside town for the three-course menu at £5.95 all inclusive. An application has now been made to the council for a major extension. Up to 20 new jobs will be created in a town where unemployment runs at 15 per cent. Critics say that the seafront building will be an eyesore, parking will be impossible and other restaurants will be driven out of business.

Who might win and who might lose in this situation?

FORUM

Who is most likely to win and lose in the drive for competitive advantage? Should we protect stakeholders who may lose? How might this be possible?

KEY TERMS

Green-field sites are undeveloped land with no previous history of industrial use.

Negative externalities are the damaging effects of business activity that are not included in the company's costs.

Positive externalities are the beneficial effects of business activity for which no charge is made.

Unit 6 Winners or losers?

Enquiry 3: Is there help at hand?

What incentives exist?

EVIDENCE

TRAINING FOR WORK

Michelle Hanger had had periods of unemployment since leaving school in 1991. She had tried a variety of jobs, but none of them really fitted what she wanted to do and she kept finding herself out of work after very short periods of employment. Then the local job centre suggested that, as she was over 18, she could follow a Training for Work programme. This enabled Michelle to find work experience in a garage where she had hoped to get a job. The scheme also gave her an additional £10 per week on top of her usual benefits. These schemes are organized by the Training and Enterprise Councils working with local employers. Although there was only an extra £10 per week, the scheme did allow Michelle to gain relevant work experience and receive training at the same time. Even though Michelle's placement lasted six months and did not lead to a job with that garage, it did make it possible for her to include the relevant experience on her curriculum vitae when she applied for other jobs.

Q1 What advantages are there for Michelle in taking this work experience programme? What are the disadvantages?

Q2 What advantages are there for society in a scheme of this kind?

HELPING PEOPLE

We have already seen that there are many reasons why people can find themselves in a weak position. They may be made redundant, or be unable to find a job in the first place. They may lack the skills and personal qualities that help to get jobs. They may be unable to work because of health problems or accidents. They may be working, but on such low rates of pay that they cannot live a decent life. The fact is that a culture of business success can leave some people behind, struggling to compete.

In the UK the government has provided a large range of solutions to these problems. Even so, there are still many people without work or on low pay. Their standard of living is much lower than they or anyone else would like. This Enquiry looks at what has been done to help, so far.

People who want a job but cannot get one receive benefits. However, simply offering people benefits does not solve the problem. There are schemes designed to help people get more skills and also to help them to set up their own businesses.

PRACTICAL SOLUTIONS

Unemployment costs the government, and therefore the taxpayers, a great deal of money. It is in everyone's interest to help people find employment. As well as bringing the individual higher earnings and personal satisfaction, there are benefits for the whole economy. A larger number of people in work means that tax rates can be lower. A better trained workforce allows the UK to compete more effectively with other countries.

Schemes that encourage people to find employment or to become self-employed include practical advice on applying for jobs, computer matching of skills with job vacancies, schemes to gain work experience, and retraining courses.

At the same time, the government aims to give people incentives to find work. If people do not search very hard for a job they may lose their benefits. So there is a 'carrot and stick' approach: help is available, but people are also expected to help themselves.

Even though the number of 16- and 17-year-olds looking for work in the UK has fallen because more are staying in further and higher education, this age range still needs incentives to seek employment. Without incentives to obtain training, many of the unemployed 16–24-year-olds will remain unemployed for some time. There is a danger that they will never become used to regular work.

EVIDENCE

HELPING OURSELVES

Help is provided by some charities, for example the Prince's Trust (see page 92), and the National Lottery. Both help people to help themselves.

THE PRINCE'S TRUST

The charity, set up in 1976 to help disadvantaged young people, now relies on 7,000 volunteers, who help individuals set up their own businesses. In 1996 another 4,000 businesses will be supported, making the charity the largest source of **venture capital** for young businesses in the UK. The schemes have proved to be successful, with over 60 per cent of businesses still in operation three years after they were started.

THE NATIONAL LOTTERY

The National Lottery allocates some of the money it receives to 'good causes'. In the first year of operation £1.22 billion was allocated to the five groups that benefit. The five groups are: charity; the Millennium Fund (set up to celebrate the year 2000); sports; the arts; and national heritage. Money from these funds will create jobs and new developments all over the UK.

EVIDENCE

DIFFERENT PLACES

Regions with high unemployment are defined as **assisted areas**, which means that they get some extra help from the government. Figure 1 shows which regions qualify for help. Some businesses in those areas can get grants towards the cost of their investment. The regions shaded darker on the map receive more money than those in a lighter shade.

Figure 1: Map of assisted areas

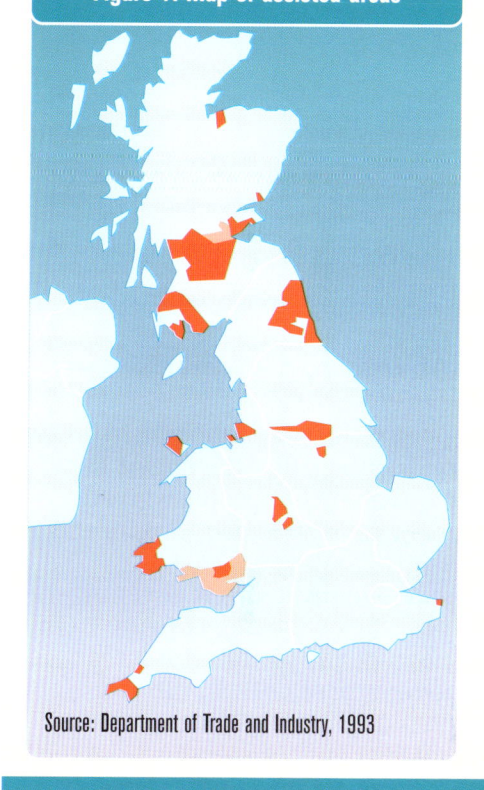

Source: Department of Trade and Industry, 1993

FORUM

A group of libraries in Stockport has been allocated £73,000 from the National Lottery. The money will be spent on improving an old library to provide access for the disabled, developing a meeting place and giving the front of the building a facelift. Do you think this sort of work should have to rely on a grant from the National Lottery?

Source: reported in the *Assistant Librarian*, March 1996

CHECKPOINT

Use the data on pages 69 and 73 to help you answer these questions:

Q1 How does the percentage of younger people unemployed compare with that of the rest of the working population?

Q2 Which regions suffer most from unemployment?

FORUM

Do you think more could be done to help people find work?

KEY TERMS

Assisted areas are those places that get extra help from the government for the development of industry.

Venture capital provides finance to support new businesses or existing small companies which might have difficulty finding funds through the usual channels.

207

Unit 6

Winners or losers?

Enquiry 3: Is there help at hand?

What does the government spend?

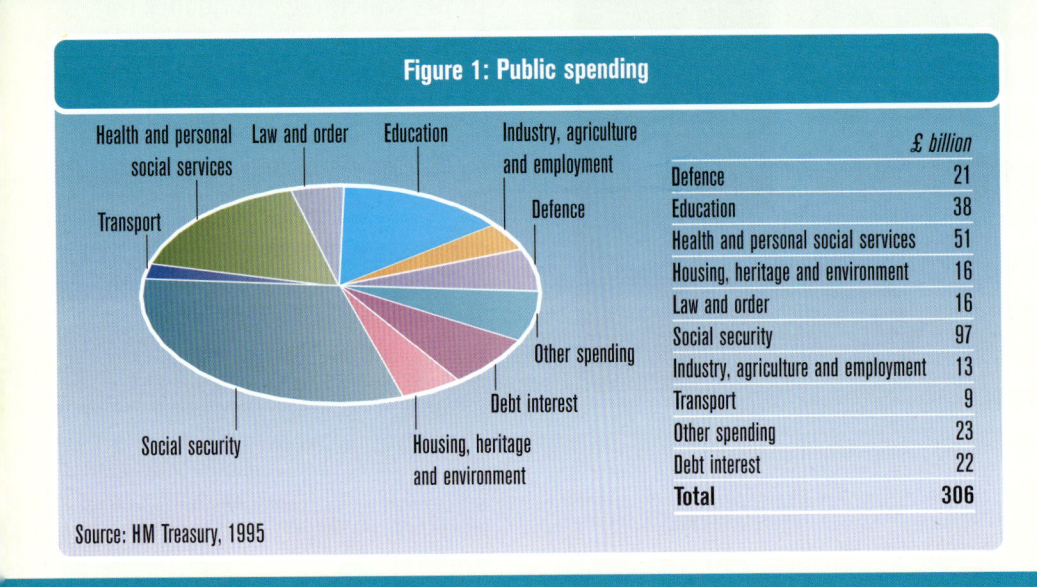

EVIDENCE

Figure 1: Public spending

	£ billion
Defence	21
Education	38
Health and personal social services	51
Housing, heritage and environment	16
Law and order	16
Social security	97
Industry, agriculture and employment	13
Transport	9
Other spending	23
Debt interest	22
Total	**306**

Source: HM Treasury, 1995

Q1 Explain how spending on social security, health and personal social services, education and housing helps people who are in need.

Q2 What percentage of total spending goes on each of these:
(a) social security,
(b) health and personal social services,
(c) education and
(d) defence?

LOOKING TO THE GOVERNMENT

Social security spending includes all kinds of benefits. The largest items are payments to people who are unemployed and pensions for the elderly. You can see that unemployment affects government spending by looking at figure 2. This shows public spending as a percentage of GDP. In the years 1990–2 unemployment was rising and government spending rose too.

There are many other benefits that can help to protect people from need. They are listed in the picture. They are all part of the **welfare state**, which provides a safety net for people who have low levels of income or other special needs. Some of these benefits are universal, which means that everyone who qualifies receives the benefit. For example, child benefit goes to everyone with a child. Other benefits are given according to how much money someone has. These are called **means-tested benefits** and are aimed at people with particular needs, such as student grants and Family Credit.

Many benefits are targeted at particular groups of people. The

Figure 2: Government spending, 1985–96

Percentage of GDP

Source: HM Treasury, 1995

Evidence on the next page shows how the welfare state tries to help people with disabilities, many of whom have a hard time finding jobs even though they are capable of working.

Sometimes the government tries hard to save money on benefits. This means that the value of benefits may be reduced. This in turn means that some people who are unable to earn good incomes face reduced standards of living. There is less money for those who need it.

FORUM

Students who go to university sometimes receive a grant from their local education authority (LEA). This grant comes from the money paid by taxpayers. Do you think it is right that people who do not go to university should have to pay, through their taxes, for the education of students?

K KEY TERMS

An Act of Parliament makes a change in the law in the UK. A proposal is considered by the House of Commons and the House of Lords. When it is approved it is legally binding on everyone.

Means-tested benefits are payments made by the government only to people whose incomes are below a certain level.

The welfare state is a system of government-funded support for people in the UK. It includes the National Health Service, education, and the benefits provided to people on low incomes.

EVIDENCE

People with disabilities face higher rates of unemployment. This may be because some employers have a negative attitude towards disability, adopt stereotypes or set unreasonable standards that are not necessary. In addition, society has made it difficult for some people with disabilities to enter buildings, gain access to public transport or participate fully in their community. These barriers mean that the work done by people with disabilities differs from the jobs held by other members of society. They are more likely to work part-time or be self-employed. This allows people with disabilities more opportunity to control what is expected from them in the world of work.

There are various benefits available to people with disabilities. These are designed to provide financial help for mobility and personal care. This is an important part of the welfare state as it allows everyone, regardless of physical ability, to have a stake in their own community. In addition, a new Act of Parliament in 1996, the Disability Discrimination Act, requires employers and people who provide goods and services to the public to take reasonable measures to make sure that they are not discriminating against people with disabilities.

Figure 3: Economic activity rates, 1995

Source: *Labour Market and Skill Trends 1996/97* Department for Education and Employment, March 1996

Q1 Why do you think people with disabilities find it more difficult to gain employment?

Q2 Why does it make sense to find ways of involving people with disabilities in the everyday life of the community?

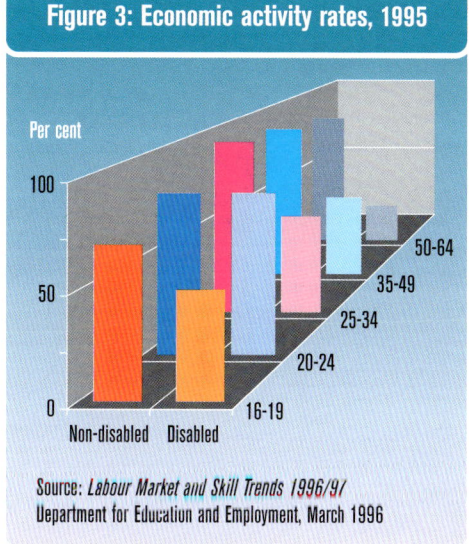

WHICH BENEFITS?
Can anyone get help?

Housing Benefit for people who need help to pay their rent

Income Support for those who are not working or who are working part-time for low wages

One-Parent Benefit

Invalid Care Allowance for people of working age who look after a severely disabled person

Retirement Pension

Child Benefit

Student Grant depending on parents' income, this is given to students in higher education

Industrial Injuries Benefit

Disability Working Allowance for working people whose disability restricts their earning ability

Disability Living Allowance for people who need help with personal care or getting around

Maternity Allowance for women expecting a baby, provided they do not get any benefits from their employer

Family Credit for families with children when their income is low

Job Seekers' Allowance given during the first six months of unemployment

Unit 6 — Winners or losers?

Enquiry 3: Is there help at hand?

Government spending and taxation

EVIDENCE

SCOTTISH FILM COUNCIL

The public sector provides money and services through local authorities, the national government and the European Union. The Scottish Film Council is the national body for promoting film, television and video in Scotland, and has benefited from public sector finance. The Council aims to provide:

- public access to a wide range of films;
- the development of film studies;
- assistance for film producers in Scotland;
- the collection and preservation of Scottish films.

Some of the more recent films that have been helped by the Scottish Film Council are Braveheart and Loch Ness. These films bring jobs and income to the areas of Scotland where the films are made.

Q1 Do you think this is a good way to use taxpayers' money?

Q2 What are the opportunity costs of funding these projects?

Figure 1: Scottish Film Council: sources of funding in 1994

£ (thousands): Private funding, Self-generated funding, Public funding (approx 1,000)

Source: *Scottish Screen Data Digest*, 1994

GOVERNMENT FUNDS

Governments use the income they raise from taxation to help the economy. This income may be spent supporting industry and business, giving assistance to certain regions in the UK, providing benefits and perhaps training to individuals, and meeting many other needs.

Money for public spending is raised from taxes. Some of these taxes are direct taxes on the income earned by individuals and businesses. Others are indirect taxes, which are based on the spending of individuals and businesses. However, tax revenue is not usually enough to cover spending plans. The government will then borrow some of the money it spends. This makes sense if some of the spending is an investment, which will bring in income in the future.

The details of taxes and spending for the year are set out by the Chancellor of the Exchequer each November in the Budget (see page 117).

BORROWING

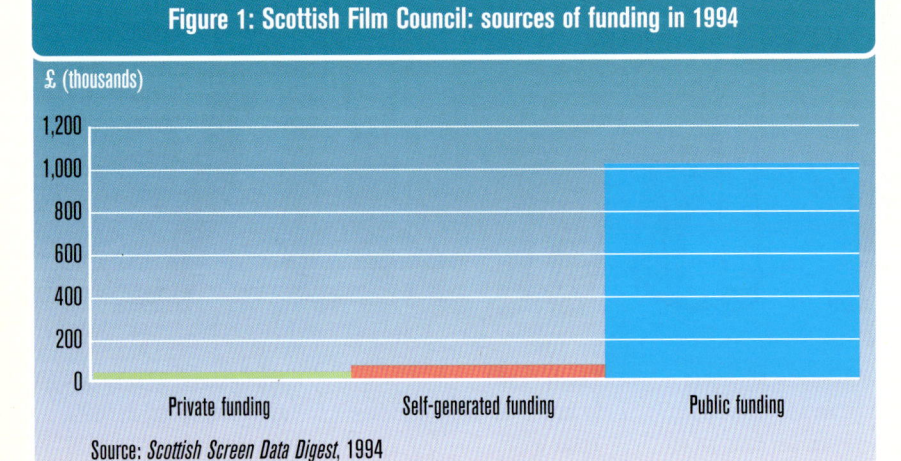

At the time of the Budget, the government predicts how much money, if any, it will have to borrow to pay for its spending. The gap between spending and income is called the **public sector borrowing requirement (PSBR)**.

In years when the economy is successful there are more people at work and businesses are making higher profits. Incomes are higher and the government can collect more money. The public sector borrowing requirement may then be very low.

Figure 3 shows that from 1987 to 1990 the government was able to pay back some of its previous loans.

EVIDENCE

DIFFERENT TAXES

Income tax is paid by individuals. Corporation tax is paid by businesses. They are the **direct taxes**. Value-added tax (VAT) and excise taxes are paid on the goods and services we buy. They are the **indirect taxes**. Social security contributions are paid by everyone who works more than just a few hours a week.

Q1 What percentage of the government's money came from income tax in 1995?

Q2 Which raises more money, direct or indirect taxes?

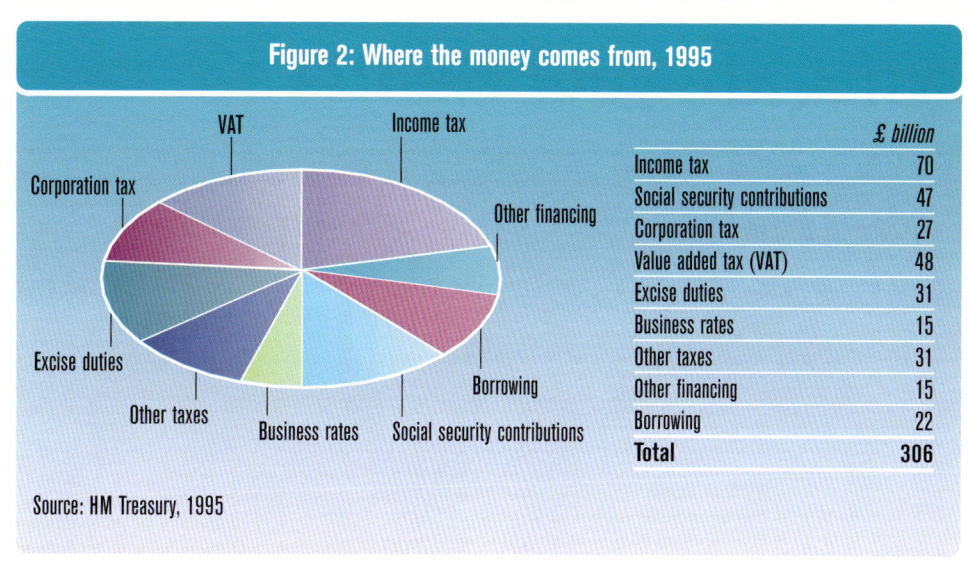

Figure 2: Where the money comes from, 1995

	£ billion
Income tax	70
Social security contributions	47
Corporation tax	27
Value added tax (VAT)	48
Excise duties	31
Business rates	15
Other taxes	31
Other financing	15
Borrowing	22
Total	**306**

Source: HM Treasury, 1995

GOVERNMENT POLICY

The government can affect the whole economy by changing the amount of money it collects in taxes or spends on projects. This is called **fiscal policy** and is an important way for the government to influence businesses and consumers. By spending more money the government can create extra jobs in society. More spending on the National Health Service means more jobs. Investment in road improvements or in education means the same. When there are more jobs people have higher incomes.

Sometimes governments are very careful about spending more money because they do not want to raise taxes or to encourage inflation. Inflation increases if the people with valuable skills become scarce, so that employers want to pay higher wages and raise prices.

If taxes are increased then consumers have less money to spend and the economy may not expand so quickly. Politicians argue about taxes. They fear that if they raise them they will lose the next election.

COULD WE DO MORE TO HELP THE LOSERS?

We could always do more. Benefits could be more generous. There could be more training opportunities. There are many possibilities. But they are costly. Either taxes would rise, or borrowing.

Governments are cautious about borrowing too much. The money has to be paid back later. This in turn means that governments often want to control the level of spending. Because benefits are one of the largest items in the list of government spending, they are not generous.

FORUM

Could the government spend more on helping people in need? If people voted for a government that would do more to help, what might happen?

KEY TERMS

Direct taxation includes any tax based on income, e.g. income tax, corporation tax.

Fiscal policy is about the amount of money the government spends or collects in taxation. If the policy is tight then the government is not spending very much money. If it is slack, then the government is spending a lot of money.

Indirect taxation includes any tax that is based on spending, e.g. value-added tax (VAT), excise duty.

The *public sector borrowing requirement (PSBR)* is the amount of money the government has to borrow each year to make sure it has enough money to meet its spending plans announced in the Budget.

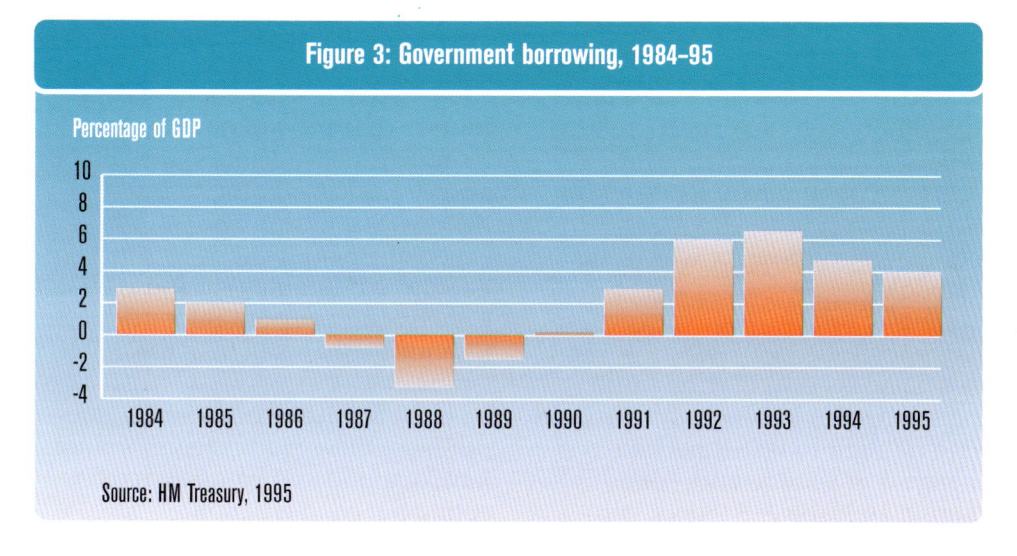

Figure 3: Government borrowing, 1984–95

Source: HM Treasury, 1995

Unit 6

Winners or losers?
Enquiry 3: Is there help at hand?

What are your rights?

EVIDENCE

CONSUMER PROBLEMS

Mr Edwards purchased a jumper from the local shop. After wearing it for one week, he washed it following the manufacturer's instructions. When he removed the jumper from the washing machine he found that it had shrunk, so he took it back to the shop to complain. At the shop he is told that there have been a lot of problems with this type of jumper and that he should write to the manufacturer. Does the shop have to give him a refund?

Ian purchased a Blur compact disc from the local record store. When he tried to play the disc at home, he discovered that it was damaged and would not play properly. He took the disc back to the shop to complain. Does the shop have to give him a refund?

Q1 Are these three people right to ask for a refund?

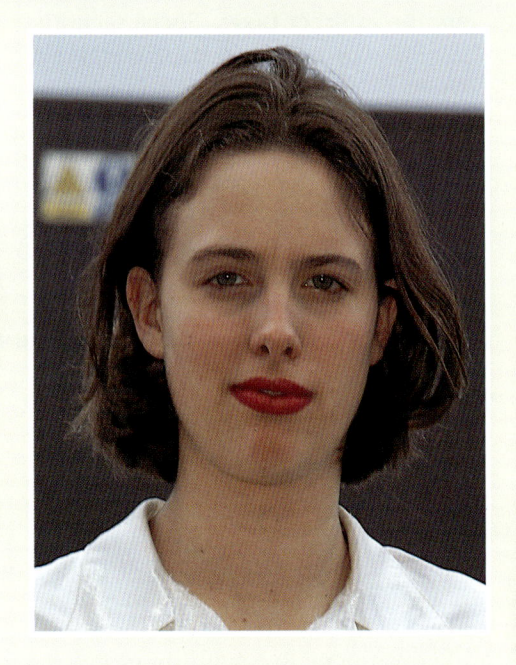

Michelle is persuaded by her friend to buy a fashionable pair of fake crocodile skin shoes. By the time she gets home she realizes that she has made a mistake and that she does not really want them. She returns the shoes to the shop to ask for a refund. Does the shop have to give her a refund?

Q2 What are the differences between the three cases?

CONSUMER RIGHTS

When you buy something from a retailer, you have **consumer rights**. These rights protect consumers against being sold faulty goods or receiving a poor-quality service. If your rights are infringed then you are entitled to have a refund of the money that you have paid.

When you buy from a shop you can expect the products to be in good condition and to do the job for which they were sold. A cassette player must be able to play cassettes, for example. In addition, you can expect products to be described accurately. These rights can be summarized as follows. Products must be:

- fit for the purpose for which they are sold;
- of merchantable quality;
- as described.

If there is nothing wrong with something you have bought then you have no right to take it back to change it or get a refund. Some shops, like Marks & Spencer, will allow you to do this if you make a mistake, but they do not have to.

You also have rights when you buy a service, such as going to the hairdressers. In this case you can expect the hairdresser:

- to use **reasonable** care and skill;
- charge a reasonable amount;
- complete the work in a reasonable time.

If the service – the haircut – does not meet these requirements, you can have a refund and you may receive additional compensation.

WHEN THINGS GO WRONG

If things go wrong and your purchases are faulty, you can get help. Some shops give excuses and say it is not their fault, or that they do not give refunds. You do not have to accept this. It is the retailer's responsibility to give a refund. You may decide to have the items repaired, exchanged for something else, or take a credit note, but you do not have to do this. Retailers also know that the law requires them to give refunds and most shops will do so without any problems. This is also good for customer relations, as shops do not wish to lose a customer.

If you buy something privately, not from a shop, then you do not have as many rights. In these cases you can expect the seller not to mislead you and for the goods to be described correctly, but that is all. The rule is 'buyer beware', so if you are buying something privately, you need to check your purchase carefully and take a friend along as a witness.

If you cannot get any satisfaction at the shop you can get extra help from any of the following:

- the local trading standards department, which will investigate your complaint;
- the Citizens' Advice Bureau, which will offer advice;
- a trade association, to which the shop belongs – for example, the Association of British Travel Agents (ABTA).

THE BUSINESS VIEW

It is important for retailers to know what rights their customers have. They can then ensure that the law is obeyed and create a good impression. For some companies, like Marks & Spencer, allowing customers to return items that they do not like in exchange for a refund is an important part of the company's marketing policy. It encourages customers to buy with confidence.

To make sure that the customers' rights are met, businesses have to ensure that all their staff are properly trained and know how to respond to customer complaints about faulty products or poor service. Although there are costs involved in training the staff, these are very small compared to the cost of not training staff, since the business could lose the customer for ever and face a legal case.

FORUM

When you look at holiday brochures, you always see lots of 'small print' on the back pages. These are extra conditions affecting your holiday which allow the company to change things. An example is 'We reserve the right to cancel your holiday for any reason'. Why do you think holiday companies put this in the brochure? Why do you think people wanting holidays accept these conditions?

KEY TERMS

Reasonable is a legal term that means you must compare things with the 'normal' standard that applies in the situation, e.g. what you would usually expect from a hairdresser.

Consumer rights are legally enforceable entitlements. For example, you have the right to expect your new CD player to work properly.

Unit 6 — Winners or losers?
Enquiry 4: Who trades wins?

What are the benefits and costs of trade?

EVIDENCE

In 1957 Mr Laxmishanker Patak arrived in England with £5 in his pocket, and started selling samosas and pickles to the local community. His business was moderately successful. In 1970, one of his sons, Kirit Patak, joined the firm. Kirit had been studying for a business degree, but he left the course to help run the business. He quickly identified a number of markets in the UK for the firm's bottled spices, including a large number of Indian restaurants and food stores.

In 1978 Kirit moved the firm to Wigan, because the damp climate in Lancashire is ideal for the wooden barrels in which pickles from around the world are stored. By 1995 the firm had sales of around £30 million, profits of £2.5 million, two production units, one in Lancashire and the other in Scotland, and sales in 24 countries. It employs 250 people in the UK and around 1,000 more, mainly spice growers and shippers, overseas. The firm is still owned by the Patak family and Kirit spends half the year travelling the world buying ingredients. He gets tomatoes from Greece; mangoes from Nigeria; cumin seeds from Iran; garlic from China; limes and ginger from Brazil; and, of course, a range of spices from India. Indeed, he buys in any country that will supply the best raw materials at the most reasonable price.

Q1 What were the important decisions that led to Patak's success?

Q2 Explain why being able to import and export is important to the company.

THE BENEFITS OF INTERNATIONAL TRADE

We can easily take the benefits of international trade for granted. You can see in the supermarket how much we rely on imports. Look at the fruit and vegetables. Whatever the time of year a huge variety is available. We can have bananas and oranges at reasonable prices. It would be almost impossible for us to grow them in the UK without building very expensive glasshouses. It is much cheaper to import them. Trade gives consumers the benefit of a great variety of reasonably priced goods.

Trade in fact does much more than that. An overseas supplier of grapefruit who sells in the UK market can specialize and expand, and benefit from economies of scale. This in turn will lower the price and attract still more people to buy. It may be possible to invest in research leading to a naturally sweeter grapefruit, so widening the market even more.

More trade means more specialization and exchange. People specialize in the products they can produce most effectively.

CHECKPOINT

Q1 A Spanish orange grower has been selling oranges in Spain and is now planning to sell them in the UK. What extra costs will the grower have to meet?

Q2 Unlike oranges, apples can be grown in the UK very easily. Why, then, are supermarket shelves full of apples grown in other parts of the world?

Q3 How do consumers benefit from trade?

EVIDENCE

In 1991 the Patak family decided to expand the business worldwide. They appointed David Page and a team of people to specialize in sales and marketing. Mr Page took two important decisions, which were very large gambles. The first was to re-package and re-label the pickles and spices to make them instantly recognizable. The second was to have a TV advertising campaign, which is unusual for a relatively small company. Both gambles paid off. In 1993 the Patak's brand grew by 92 per cent, becoming the fastest-growing consumer good in the UK. This provided the base for exports.

Now Patak's brands are sold in 24 countries with labels printed in local languages, giving recipe information and serving suggestions. A factory is planned in India. The company found that it was buying raw materials there, sending them to the UK for processing, and exporting them back to Asian markets.

Q1 Why were the two decisions made by Mr Page such gambles?

Q2 Why do you think there are recipes on the labels of Patak's jars?

EVIDENCE

COAL

In the 1940s, just under 900,000 people were employed in the UK coal industry. Table 1 shows what has happened between 1973 and 1993. The fall in employment is partly because the demand for coal has gone down as gas has become cheaper. It is also partly because imports have grown, from almost none to about 40 per cent of total supply. A third reason for the fall in employment is that far more machinery is now used.

What has happened to all those miners? Some, sadly, remain unemployed, but others have retrained or found new jobs. Some have gone into business for themselves. Many have just retired.

Coal can be extracted more cheaply abroad. People who were coal miners in the UK can move to safer and more productive jobs doing other things, perhaps for export. Unfortunately, of course, what may be good for everyone in the long run may cause a great deal of personal pain in the short term.

Table 1: Output and employment in the coal industry, 1973-93

	1973	1983	1988	1993
Output (million tons)	99	90	86	42
Number employed (thousands)	298	256	120	36

Source: Central Statistical Office, Annual Abstract of Statistics, 1986, 1995

INTERNATIONAL TRADE AND GROWTH

The developments at Patak's since 1991 show how international trade encourages employment and growth. The factory in India will employ local people who might otherwise not have a job, because the firm has the ability to add value to raw materials from all around the world.

Figure 1 shows the close connection between trade and economic growth. The people in India from whom Patak's buys spices have money they would otherwise not have had. They can use it to buy goods and services they could not afford before. They might well buy goods produced abroad that are cheaper than those produced at home. So trade goes on.

Of course, more international trade is not good news for everyone. It may involve structural changes such as those we investigated in Unit 2. People have to be prepared to change jobs as these changes take effect. Not everyone who is made redundant will find it easy to get another job. The Evidence above on coal shows what may happen.

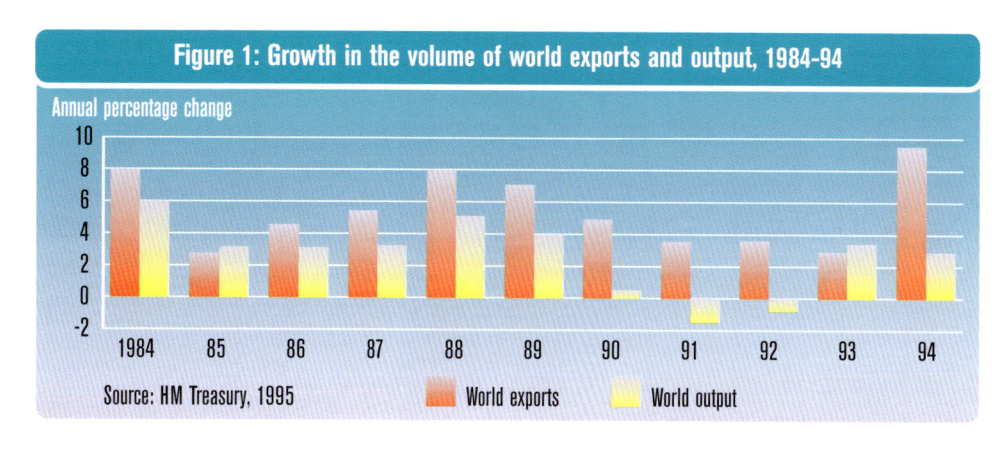

Figure 1: Growth in the volume of world exports and output, 1984-94

Source: HM Treasury, 1995 — World exports, World output

FORUM

What happens when increasing numbers of businesses find it difficult to compete internationally? What happens to the people involved? What can be done to deal with the difficulties? Which stakeholders win and which lose?

Unit 6 — Winners or losers?
Enquiry 4: Who trades wins?

How do we stay competitive?

EVIDENCE

Elms Marketing is a Stockport-based, family-owned, T-shirt company. Having sewn up 70 per cent of the London souvenir T-shirt market, it is now targeting Germany as its next success story.

Export manager Joanne Elms decided to make a similar range for Germany. Prices on the firm's products are very competitive compared to German suppliers. This factor, combined with fast delivery times and a high level of service, has led to a solid customer base.

Agents come up with ideas and send in local pictures and postcards with suggestions for designs, which are then created back in Stockport. Mostly these are local crests and coats of arms or traditional scenes. The cheeky Blackpool-style T-shirts do not find favour in the German market.

Looking ahead, Joanne comments: 'Sales in 1996 have been much higher than expected. We are expecting a big increase in export turnover – possibly as high as 40 per cent.' The firm has 38 staff and a £7 million turnover, of which 5 per cent is for export. But that is set to grow.

Source: *Manchester Evening News*, 18 March 1996

Q1 List all the factors that make Elms Marketing's T-shirts competitive in the German market.

Q2 What effect do fast delivery and personal service as selling points have on costs?

COMPETITIVENESS

Being able to compete can be complicated. Price may be important. But so is quality and sometimes design. Reliability may be a major factor for mechanical products. The service that comes with the product can be critical. Together, these decide whether the consumer thinks the product gives value for money.

How do some businesses manage to produce things more cheaply than others? One reason is often that their costs are lower than those of their competitors. We have seen that very many factors can affect costs. Wage rates, the way machines are used, the efficiency of management and the technology used can all play a part. One reason for Elms Marketing's success is that wage rates are usually lower in the UK than in Germany. But this is not all.

THE EXCHANGE RATE

When an exporter receives sales revenue it will be in **foreign currency**. Currency is the money used in the country where the goods were sold. It will have to be sold by the exporter, on the foreign exchange market, in order to get pounds. These can then be used to pay the costs of production. Table 1 shows what prices in pounds will be at different **exchange rates**.

When Elms Marketing sells a £10 T-shirt in Germany, it gets German marks (Deutsche marks, or DM) for it.

Table 1: Prices and exchange rates

Price in pounds	£1 = DM2.25	£1 = DM2.50	£1 = DM3.00
	£10 = DM22.50	£10 = DM25.00	£10 = DM30.00

If the exchange rate is £1 = DM2.25, it will get about DM22.50. This means that its prices are low compared to those of most German suppliers. The company's prices in

EVIDENCE

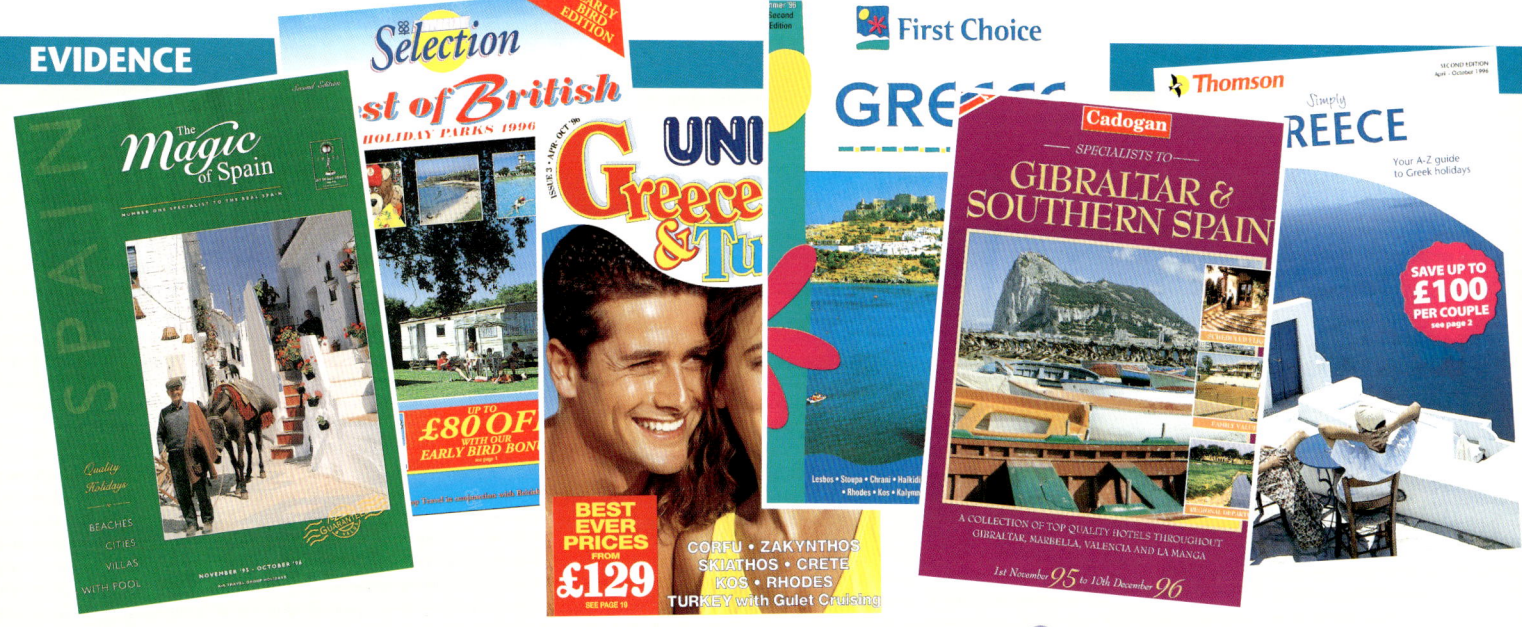

DECIDING ON A HOLIDAY

In winter and early spring, newspapers and magazines are full of adverts for holidays. Should you go to Greece or Spain? Or should you go to Blackpool or Bournemouth?

Sarah and her friend decided to go to Spain. They arranged a holiday and saved £100 each for spending money. At the exchange rate of 190 pesetas to the pound, they each had 19,000 pesetas to spend.

About a month before they were due to go, the pound went down to 170 pesetas. But Sarah and her friend still only had £100 each for spending money.

The next year the two friends thought it might be better to go to Blackpool.

Foreign holidays are imports of services from abroad: you buy tourist services from another country.

Q1 After the change in the exchange rate, how many pesetas would Sarah and her friend each have for spending money?

Q2 What effect will a fall in the exchange rate have on the prices of imports in general?

Q3 If the exchange rate next year had changed to £1 = 220 pesetas, would the friends change their minds about going to Blackpool?

---

pounds, when converted into marks, look reasonable.

One important reason for this is that it has been able to get a good exchange rate. If the exchange rate rose, would the company's prices look so good in Germany? Table 1 shows what would happen to the price of a £10 product selling in Germany at £1 = DM2.50. The rise in the exchange rate makes the price in foreign currency go up.

If the exchange rate rises, then UK exports become more expensive and therefore harder to sell abroad (i.e. less competitive). The reverse is also true – a fall in the exchange rate will make exports cheaper. Exporting will be easier. Exchange rates can be a very important influence on competitiveness.

CHECKPOINT

Q1 Write down all the ways you can think of in which a business might keep its costs down.

Q2 Find out the current exchange rate for the German mark. At the time when Elms Marketing was planning its export effort, the exchange rate was £1 = DM2.25. Has the exchange rate changed since then? If so, what effect will the change have had?

Q3 What would happen to T-shirt prices if the company had to pay a wage increase?

EXCHANGE RATES AND THE EU

Since 1992, it has been possible for the pound to rise or fall against other currencies. That could change if the UK joined a European Monetary Union (EMU). Then EU countries would use the same currency, the euro. It would be impossible to make exports cheaper by letting the exchange rate fall. Businesses would compete in other ways, just as UK businesses compete with one another now on price, quality and so on.

KEY TERMS

An *exchange rate* gives the value of one currency in terms of another. You can find out the value of £1 in terms of German marks, French francs or US dollars, for example.

Foreign currency refers to the money used in another country.

Unit 6 Winners or losers?
Enquiry 4: Who trades wins?

Making gains happen

EVIDENCE

MATCHING PROMOTION TO PEOPLE

"Pukka People Pick a Pot of Patak's"

"Véritable Saveur des Indes"

"Patak's: The true taste of India, the new taste for America"

The words that are used to market Patak's spices around the world are subtly different. In Britain the word 'pukka', although not used much these days, is known by enough people to make it effective as an advertising slogan. It comes from the Hindi *pakka*, meaning cooked or ripe, but it came to be translated by the British to mean 'first-class'. Using such a word in America would make no sense at all; instead, marketing there has to concentrate on the exotic image of India, and the potential excitement of a 'new taste' for Americans.

Q1 Why do you think the slogans have to be short?

Q2 How is advertising for food different from advertising for perfume, say, or any other consumer good?

THE EXPORT MARKETING MIX

The marketing mix includes Price, Promotion, Place and Product. Businesses place a different emphasis on different parts of the mix for each product. One may have a competitive price, another will advertise a great deal, while a third will ensure speed and reliability in getting its products to the customer.

The same is true when firms export, although in some ways it is more complicated. The firm may compete on price in one country, but be forced to compete on delivery in another. So, not only is there a different emphasis within the mix, but there are also differences between countries to be taken into account.

PRICE

The price of the product will vary depending on the exchange rate. A rise in the exchange rate will make exports more expensive in the overseas market. Because of local competition, however, some companies may prefer to keep the price the same and take a smaller profit.

A jar of relish might sell for £1.50, or 12 French francs (FF), if £1 = FF8. What happens if the exchange rate rises to £1 = FF10? Now the exporter has a choice. The price could be raised to FF15. If the cost of production were £1, or FF10, the profit would be 50p, or FF5, as before. But at that price it is possible that sales will fall. It might be better to leave the price at FF12. Profits per jar would be less, but sales would be higher.

The decision will depend on the demand for relish at different prices in the individual country. It may also be important to consider whether sales depend on a marketing image or on a competitive price.

PRODUCT

It may seem straightforward to sell an identical product in different markets, but it is not. In the United States and Japan, car models almost always have names; in Europe they often have numbers, which tell us the engine size, number of doors, whether the car runs on petrol or diesel, and so on. This reflects a different car culture. Thus the Volkswagen Golf was renamed the

Figure 1: Promoting block merchandising

The key benefits of block merchandising are:

1. Generates sales by product association.
2. Improves profitability of the fixture.
3. Assists customers who are shopping for the complete meal.
4. Offers excellent promotional opportunities.
5. Enables retailers more easily to manage the Indian Food Product Category.

Source: Patak's Foods USA

EVIDENCE

PROMOTING AN IMAGE

An alternative approach has been used by the French bottled water company, Perrier. Its advertising campaign depends upon English speakers knowing how to pronounce the French word for water (eau). By knowing this they appear more sophisticated, and this carries over into the image of the product itself.

Q1 Have you seen any other advertisements that use foreign words as a way of selling, as Perrier does?

SLEAU LUNCH

Rabbit in America because it was targeted at a different group of consumers.

There may be local regulations that have to be met before a product can be sold. In the UK we impose safety requirements on soft toys and fire regulations on furniture that imports have to meet before they are allowed in, even though they may be perfectly acceptable in their country of origin.

PROMOTION

Some countries, such as the UK, North America and Australia, have well-developed and sophisticated retailing sectors. In these markets, products such as those made by Patak's can be promoted using the concept of 'block merchandising', which means putting all of one type of food together to encourage buyers who want a 'meal occasion'.

Such promotion would be impossible in countries with less sophisticated retailing sectors, and so it would need to be modified. In the same way, advertising on television is only effective if the target market can afford, or has access to, a television set.

The exact style of the advertising may need to be fitted to the individual country. When Pathak's was planning its adverts for the Australian market, it decided that it must allow for the fact that Australians have in the past eaten much less Indian food than people in the UK. They know less about it. So the adverts there concentrate on advice about preparation.

PLACE

Getting the product to the customer is as important as any of the other aspects of marketing. One of the most serious problems facing Russia at the moment is the lack of developed distribution channels, so that although customers may order goods, they do not always arrive at the right place at the right time.

Next time you are in your local supermarket look at the number of items in one aisle and imagine what is involved in getting all those products from all over the world into one place convenient to you.

CHECKPOINT

Q1 How will an exporting business decide the price at which its product should be sold in each country?
Q2 What are the benefits to the business of giving attention to export marketing?
Q3 How do rising exports affect the stakeholders in the business?

Unit 6

Winners or losers?

Enquiry 4: Who trades wins?

Keeping trade going

EVIDENCE

HOW MANY CARS? HOW MUCH STEEL?

USA and European Union restrict imports of Japanese cars

JAPAN RESTRICTS BEEF IMPORTS

USA limits imports of European steel

European Union limits imports of bananas from Guatemala, Honduras, Mexico and the USA

Usually, the reasons for restricting trade are to do with helping businesses that have to compete with imports. Quite often, people in the car or the steel industry will argue that imports are leading to competition, which causes job losses. Restrictions on imports mean that the price of the product will rise. This makes it easier for home producers to compete.

Q1 What effect do you think these restrictions have had on prices? Give reasons.

Q2 How do higher prices affect consumers?

Q3 How do higher prices affect competing producers?

RESTRICTING IMPORTS

In Unit 4, Enquiry 5, 'Why belong to the European Union?', we looked at the effects of import duties. These are taxes on imports, which make imports more expensive and so discourage people from buying them. If other countries tax our exports, they will be harder to sell in that country because the tax will make them less competitive. That reduces the level of demand for our products.

Quotas have a similar effect. A quota sets a fixed limit on supplies of a particular import, and allows retailers to charge a higher price. That means that the product takes a larger share of the buyer's income, and leaves them with less to spend on other things. Figure 1 shows how restricting imports raises prices.

Import duties, quotas and any other restriction on trade will reduce the amounts that countries can sell to one another. Markets are smaller than they would have been. This reduces economic growth – the increase in incomes that allows standards of living to rise. Because of this, groups of countries have got together and agreed rules that make it harder for individual governments to restrict trade.

Trade can lead to job losses, but without trade, consumers may find some products are more expensive.

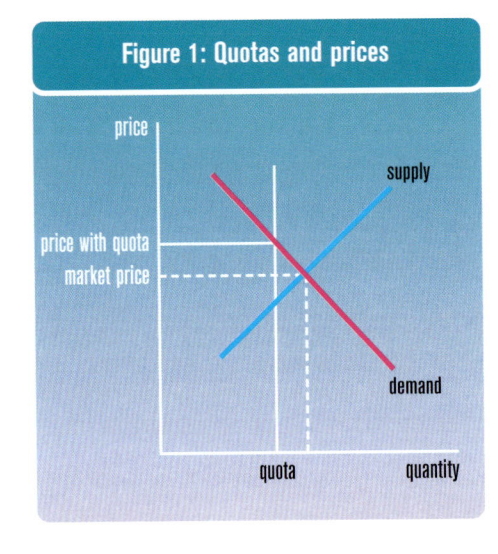

Figure 1: Quotas and prices

THE EUROPEAN UNION

Trade is free for most products inside the European Union (EU). There is strong competition between businesses in all member countries. This means that businesses are forced to become more competitive: if they do not become so, they are unlikely to survive. A more efficient business will force them out of the market.

Along with most countries, the EU has reduced trade barriers against imports from the rest of the world in recent years, but many still remain.

THE WORLD TRADE ORGANIZATION

At the end of 1995, 112 of the world's nations belonged to the **World Trade Organization** (WTO). Together, they are responsible for 90 per cent of world trade. When countries join the WTO, they agree to reduce restrictions on one another's exports. The WTO has helped member countries to agree on rules that allow trade to grow. But countries cannot join until their trade is more or less in line with WTO rules.

Many of the countries that do not already belong to the WTO have applied to join. Applicants include China and Russia, and a number of developing countries. At the end of 1995, there were 28 applicants. Most existing member governments think this enlargement will help to promote trade, and therefore exports, for everyone.

The WTO works to encourage free trade: that is a situation in which people and businesses can buy what they want, where they want, at the price charged by the seller. It discourages member governments from using quotas. This should mean that people can buy imports as cheaply as possible. This helps to create larger markets for businesses. Although many trade restrictions still exist, there are many fewer than there used to be. Trade is comparatively free.

WTO

World Trade Organization

EVIDENCE

WHAT DOES THE WTO ACTUALLY DO?

Where were your clothes made? What about your shoes? The WTO has persuaded member countries to reduce import duties on clothing. This means that your clothes are costing less. Spending on clothes now takes up less of most people's incomes than it used to. Cheap imports make it easy for us to find reasonably priced items.

COPYRIGHT LAWS

WTO members undertake to respect and enforce copyright laws. This means that in these countries it is illegal, for example, to copy a CD or a video and sell it in competition with those of the company that made the original recording. (Illegal copies are sometimes called pirate recordings.) In the same way, WTO members must protect companies with brand names from fake competitors selling cheap imitations of the real thing. You may have seen some cheap branded perfume for sale and wondered whether it was real: it may not have been.

FOOD PRICES

Many governments protect farmers by paying high prices for their food and keeping out cheap imports. This makes food dearer. Since everyone eats, it can make many people less well off. The WTO discourages restrictions on food imports. However, it has not yet been very successful in getting them reduced.

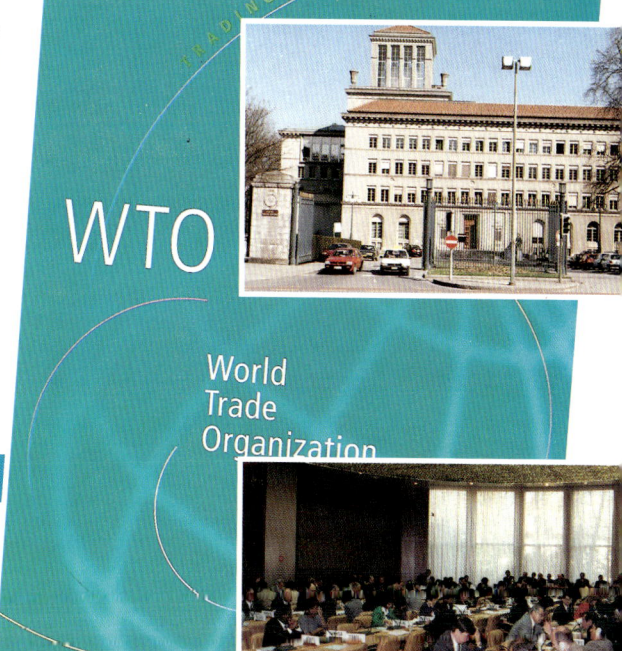

Before new trade rules can be agreed, many governments must negotiate the terms

INSURANCE

The UK sells insurance to people and businesses all over the world. Until recently, it was very difficult to sell insurance in Japan. Under new rules, WTO members must ensure that it is possible for other countries to export services to them. This has helped to open up the Japanese insurance market to UK companies.

Q1 How can reducing restrictions on imports of clothes make people better off?
Q2 How can selling insurance in Japan make people in the UK better off?

FORUM

What would happen if most governments decided on a free trade policy and agreed to remove restrictions on all imports that are not a danger to health and safety?

KEY TERMS

Quotas limit the quantity of a particular product that can be imported.

The *World Trade Organization* provides governments with a framework for making rules about trade. Usually these rules are used to make exporting easier.

221

Unit 6 Winners or losers?

Enquiry 5: Richer country – richer people?

Win some – lose some

EVIDENCE

FOR BETTER – FOR WORSE?

I was born in Mauritius in 1978 and lived there until 1993, when I went to England with my mother. Even in 1993 Mauritius was very different from the country I knew when I was very young. I remember many sugar cane plantations and many families living in rural areas working on the plantations. There were only a small number of cars and lorries on the roads, the beaches were beautiful and quiet, there were very few visitors to the island.

By the time I left, shopping centres were being built in the main towns and investment was taking place in hotel development. The shopping centres were very impressive buildings and housed shops ranging from household essentials to luxuries such as music. Everyone wanted to visit the centres. Although this reduced unemployment it also encouraged Mauritians to spend more than they could really afford. Small businesses had also been encouraged to establish and to grow.

Tourism has grown very quickly. There are hotels springing up everywhere and the Tourist Authority has run some huge campaigns. In 1992, about 300,000 visitors arrived, three times as many as the year before.

Kentucky Fried Chicken was there before I left. My aunt, who still lives there, tells me that Pizza Hut has also made an appearance. The main towns on the island house many of the business names that you would find in large towns throughout the developed world! On average, economic growth in recent years has been approximately 6 per cent each year.

The hotels and eating houses are the biggest buyers of food on the island. This means that Mauritians are finding it harder to buy locally produced supplies, especially seafood. Any spare land is being used to build bungalows and apartments for personal use and for renting. Land near the beaches is at a premium, and is bought for hotels and restaurants. The peace and tranquillity of days gone by has been replaced by the busy-ness of commercial life.

Owning a car is a status symbol and many families are borrowing money to buy one, and are getting themselves into debt. Most families now live in houses with two floors, and children receive free education. There are health care facilities and other social services which did not exist some years ago. These have to be paid for out of taxes raised by the government.

The government set up an Export Processing Zone (EPZ) to encourage firms to process the country's raw materials. As a result clothing has become one of the island's leading exports. Sugar is also an important contributor to GDP.

There is very low unemployment, about 2 per cent, but inflation has been quite high at around 5 per cent.

Source: Karen, a 17-year-old student of Economics and Business

Q1 How does Karen feel about the changes that have taken place in Mauritius?

Q2 What does the data in table 1 tell you about the changes that have taken place in Mauritius between 1960 and 1992?

Q3 How might growth affect lifestyles in a country like Mauritius?

Q4 What problems might a country face when it relies on tourism as its main source of income?

Table 1: Winning or losing in Mauritius

GDP per head ($)	1960	2,113	1992	11,700
Life expectancy (years)	1960	59.2	1992	70.2
Urban population (%)	1960	33	1992	41
Infant mortality (per 1,000)	1970	60	1992	17
Secondary education (%)	1970	30	1992	54

Source: World Bank, *World Development Report*, Oxford University Press, 1995; *Human Development Report*, Oxford University Press, 1995

CHECKPOINT

Q1 What changes have taken place in the sort of work that people are doing?

Q2 How does this fit with the Evidence from Karen?

Q3 What sort of jobs are being created in the service industries?

Table 2: Where do people work in Mauritius?

% of labour force in	1965	1992
Agriculture	37	16
Industry	25	30
Services	38	54

Source: World Bank, *World Development Report*, Oxford University Press, 1995

A CULTURAL CHANGE

Many developing countries experience changes that alter the lifestyles of the population. When farmland is used for development, farm workers find themselves out of work. Investment in new infrastructure, hotels and leisure facilities may create opportunities for employment in the construction industry for unskilled and semi-skilled workers. Further employment may be created in the new hotels, shops and restaurants, for example. Much of the employment is seasonal.

These changes are likely to alter the distribution of income. Some people will become much better off, while others may experience little change in their standard of living. Some may feel that their quality of life is reduced.

Fishing villages can become transformed into tourist towns – hotels and apartment blocks seem to spring up everywhere. Los Gigantes in Tenerife, once a small village, is now a huge resort. The old way of life gives way to the new, and the whole culture and traditions of a country can change.

THE UPSIDE

Economic growth has its upside. People live longer, have better education and health care, and the standard of living generally rises. It certainly puts more income into the economy. By providing opportunities for education, there is greater potential for future development, and so for the process of economic growth.

However, it often takes quite a long time for these effects to work through to the whole population. One reason for the difference between Karen's views and the data is that the growth that has taken place in Mauritius is not evenly spread across the population.

The people taking the new jobs in the new industries notice the difference first, but it may take a long time for the improvements to work through to people who are still working on the land. This means that the distribution of income can be very uneven.

KEY TERM

Distribution of income shows the proportion of income that is paid to different sectors of the population.

Unit 6

Winners or losers?
Enquiry 5: Richer country – richer people?

The business of growth

EVIDENCE

PAINTING THE CITIES OF INDIA

ICI, the makers of Dulux paint, has recently built a plant at Thane, 40 km north of Bombay in India. It produces 20 million litres of paint a year, enough to coat much of the new housing that is being built around India's towns. The country's high growth rate has led to more and more people moving to the towns and cities, which has created a demand for housing. ICI has seen this as an opportunity to extend its market.

The company is committed to its policy of maintaining the highest global standards in quality, process control, safety, health and the environment.

Q1 Why has ICI decided to expand into India?
Q2 What effect might its plant have on the economy of the surrounding area?
Q3 What effect might its commitment to global standards have on local people?

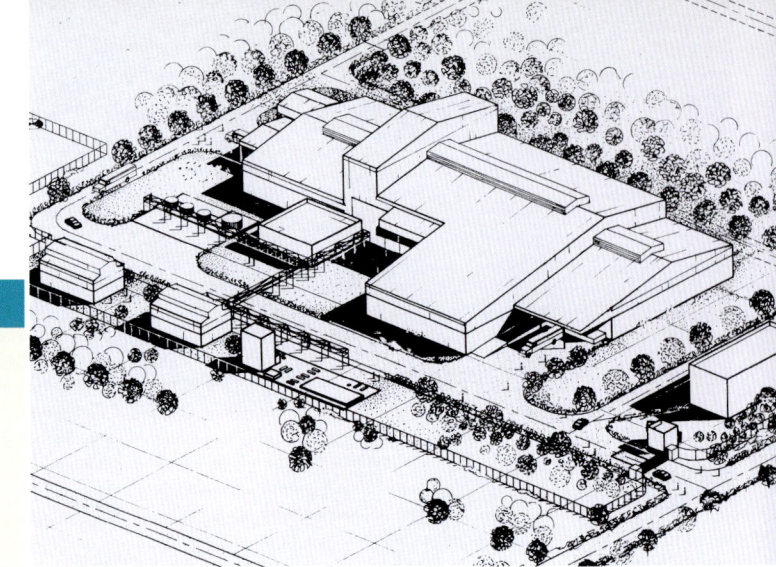

INVESTMENT AND INCOMES

As countries develop, businesses start up. Jobs are created and people's incomes may rise. There is little doubt that new industry helps a whole economy to grow. The process of building a factory employs people. Once built, it will need staffing. All these people will be paid and will spend their money in the local community. The factory will need raw materials, overalls, office stationery, computers – the list could go on. Some of these things will be bought locally, others will need to be imported. Overall, the growth of demand for products of all kinds is likely to make it possible to pay employees a better wage.

In order to set up the factory ICI will have to train people, which again adds to the potential of both the individual and the country. Investment in human resources is just as important as investment in capital equipment.

LOCAL ENTERPRISE

Enterprise in the developing world is often on a small scale. Muraj is showing great enterprise for a 14-year-old. By recycling waste he is one of many poor people in Bombay who contribute to the informal economy. His activities generate income, which means that he has money to spend in the local community, just like the employees of ICI.

He sounds like a survivor, but his lack of education and having to live in a poor environment that is a

CHECKPOINT

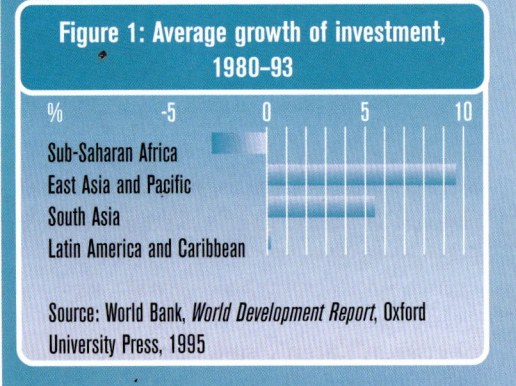

Figure 1: Average growth of investment, 1980–93

% | -5 | 0 | 5 | 10
Sub-Saharan Africa
East Asia and Pacific
South Asia
Latin America and Caribbean

Source: World Bank, *World Development Report*, Oxford University Press, 1995

Q1 List the regions according to the amount of investment that has taken place.
Q2 List the regions according to the growth of real wages.
Q3 How do the two lists compare? Is there always a connection between rising investment and real wages?

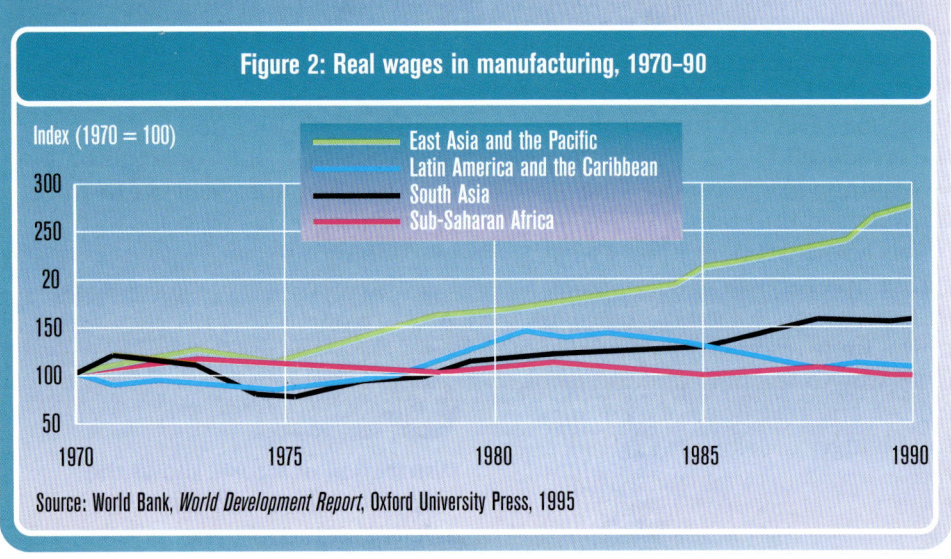

Figure 2: Real wages in manufacturing, 1970–90

Index (1970 = 100)
— East Asia and the Pacific
— Latin America and the Caribbean
— South Asia
— Sub-Saharan Africa

Source: World Bank, *World Development Report*, Oxford University Press, 1995

EVIDENCE

PRODUCTS FOR A BETTER WORLD

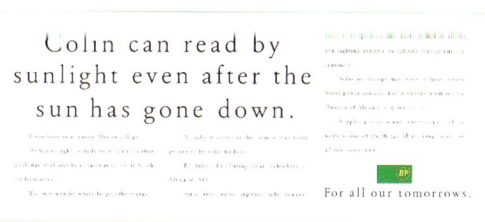

The development of products that improve the quality of life can add value in many ways. In the past, Colin could never have studied after dark, and night sets in early where he lives. The invention of solar cells changed all that. Not only did it help Colin and other students, it also allowed hospitals to work more effectively.

The development of new products for the market can lead to advances that add value. If more students can go to school or college, if more people are cured or avoid diseases that might leave them unable to work, the workforce will be more productive.

All companies are interested in the profit to be made from a product, and when this can be combined with gains to the community, the needs of many stakeholders can be met.

Colin can read by sunlight even after the sun has gone down.

EVIDENCE

THE BEGINNINGS OF BUSINESS?

My name is Muraj and I'm a homeless 14-year-old street kid living and sleeping by the pavement shelter slums of Bombay. I cannot read and write, and I haven't any parents. I used to beg – then I started to collect and sift through rubbish like paper and plastics, and sold these for a few rupees. After a while I got together with some other boys to form a team. We now collect rubbish from offices and we sell all sorts of it to a scrap dealer. The extra money has allowed us to get a friend to cook us a breakfast every morning in her one-roomed house. Everyone around here is busy trying to make a living. There are brush makers, potters, sewers and small shops all within 50 m of where we meet to sort our rubbish.

Q1 How did Muraj increase his spending power?

Q2 How does his activity contribute to the local economy?

Q3 What might prevent Muraj from becoming a great entrepreneur?

---

breeding ground for disease must affect his chances of success. Who knows, if he can organize people like this when he is only 14, with better opportunities, he might have turned into a great entrepreneur by the time he is 20! Would he have been a winner or a loser if he had been born in Britain or Canada?

He is surrounded by many small enterprises. The growth of small businesses can be effective in the process of development. In fact, there are advantages to such growth. It is often more firmly rooted in the country and the profits that are made stay in the country instead of being used to pay dividends to shareholders elsewhere.

NATIONAL ENTERPRISE

At the other end of the scale, governments can be responsible for encouraging industry to move in. Many of the countries of East Asia have grown quickly because of government planning. The Chinese government, for example, is responsible for the Three Gorges development that will bring much needed power to remote but densely populated parts of China (see page 166). It is hoped that new firms will move in because transport will be much easier and electricity should be readily available and cheap.

As firms expand, they need more water, power, transport and other services. The ability of industry to grow will therefore depend on the **infrastructure** of the country. It is generally the role of government to help the development of such services.

FORUM

Small firms, large firms and the government all have different things to offer a developing country. What are they?

KEY TERM

Infrastructure includes roads, railways, water and telecommunications. It provides a basic framework for economic development.

225

Unit 6 Winners or losers?
Enquiry 5: Richer country – richer people?

Can business make a difference?

EVIDENCE

THE DESERT BLOOMS WITH BUSINESS

The Nanhu Indians from the Mexquital Valley, north of Mexico City, have been selling sisal bath scrubs to the Body Shop since 1993. With the help of the company, they set up a co-operative to organize production. The key raw material is the maguey cactus, one of the few plants that grows in the area.

BUSINESS TO BUSINESS

The Body Shop has a very distinctive mission, which includes helping people in developing countries to help themselves. By helping them set up in business, they can start to make a living.

Before the Body Shop starts to work with any organization, it has to be convinced that the business will be commercially viable. There is no point in investing in any activity that will never make a profit.

A second concern is that the process is environmentally sustainable. All projects are investigated carefully to check that they do no harm – and hopefully offer benefits to the environment.

Q1 What were the objectives of the Body Shop in its work to develop trading links with the Nanhu Indians?

Q2 How did the Nanhu Indians benefit from the link?

'RICHER, MELLOWER AND DISTINCTLY LESS BITTER'

Cafédirect is not just talking about the taste of its coffee brand, but also the farmers who grow the beans. The company was set up by Oxfam, Traidcraft, Twin Trading and Equal Exchange Trading.

> 'Cafédirect is a great initiative that has made a real impact on the standard of living of small-scale coffee producers in Peru.'
>
> Luis Ocupa Cruz, with a producer organisation in Peru

> 'Cafédirect has generated a lot of hope for small producers in Uganda. For the first time they are building partnerships which might assure equal terms as compared to the traditional coffee farmers who exploit them.'
>
> Patrick Muyiyi of the Bugisu Co-op Union, Uganda

The brand started life in 1991 when it was available only through mail order and Fair Trade outlets. Gradually, by word of mouth, recommendation and support from church organisations, sales began to rise and the supermarkets took notice (led by Safeway in Scotland).

Cafédirect guarantees to pay farmers' co-operatives a minimum of 10 per cent above the world coffee price, and never to pay less than an agreed fair minimum price, no matter how low the world price drops. Cafédirect is also unusual in producing pre-payments for up to 60 per cent of a delivery, so that the growers can cut out middlemen who often offer a lower price.

The growers use the extra money for a wide variety of needs, including health care and education. The long-term basis of Cafédirect's trading relationships offers some financial security for farmers, enabling them to make plans for the future rather than survive from one harvest to the next.

Growers benefit from fair treatment. They can do business with the 'outside world' with dignity and pride.

Cafédirect coffee is more expensive than many other coffee brands, but it aims to sell to customers who are prepared to pay more for a product that is traded fairly.

Q1 What was the objective of the charities involved in setting up Cafédirect?

Q2 Does this objective differ from that of the Body Shop?

Q3 Is the outcome different?

EVIDENCE

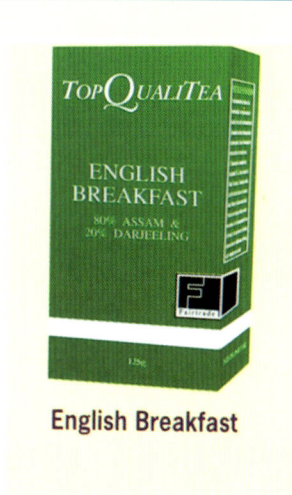

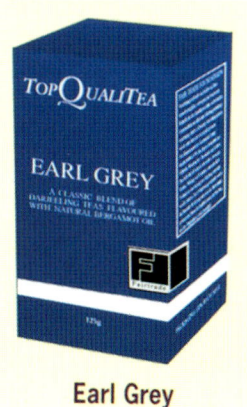

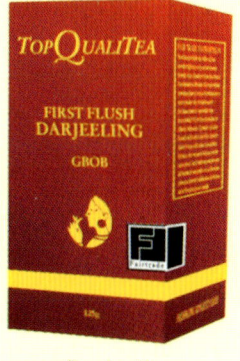

English Breakfast

Earl Grey

Darjeeling

Guarantees a **better deal** for Third World Producers — Fairtrade

COMPANIES FIND ETHICS MAKE COMMERCIAL SENSE

The Fair Trade Foundation is an organization dedicated to do for fair trade what the ecolabelling scheme is supposed to do for environmentally friendly consumer goods.

The Foundation will award fair trade marks to products judged to offer a fairer deal for Third World producers. The aim is to improve the lot of poorer workers by encouraging UK companies to import goods which are produced by people who have fair working conditions.

The market could be big. In the Netherlands, Belgium and Switzerland, such labels have boosted sales by 3 per cent. It is estimated to have yielded an extra £5 million for Latin American coffee growers.

Source: *The Guardian*, 27 April 1993

CHECKPOINT

Q1 In what ways are companies like Cafédirect and the Body Shop trying to help poorer countries?

Q2 What are the advantages and disadvantages of such 'fair trade' campaigns for (a) the companies and (b) the countries involved?

FORUM

In your view, are the actions of the Body Shop, the Co-op Bank and other organizations that have a distinct ethical policy just another way of marketing their products?

RESPONSIBILITY

Some businesses have little regard for the environment in which they operate. The 'bottom line' is to make profit for the owners. The welfare of the local community is of secondary concern. Other companies are quick to recognize the need to have a 'licence to operate' from the local community. If a business wishes to have a long-term presence requiring workers, suppliers, access to sites and materials, then it needs a good working relationship with a neighbourhood, region or country.

This has in the past led companies from wealthier countries to offer a little welfare in return for access to raw materials or a new market. But businesses with an eye to future customers can see the value of striking deals that represent fair trade rather than aid.

A company that pays workers a fair wage and provides good working conditions retains the loyalty of its workforce. A company that pays a good price to suppliers will have first call on future contracts. A company that pays taxes to a host country is entitled to a stake in local decisions and can expect a good partnership link with a government. Today's higher cost is tomorrow's return on an investment. However, the number of businesses which adopt this type of approach is still quite small.

DEPENDENCY FOREVER?

The Body Shop depends on selling its products to people who are prepared to spend a little more because they believe in the product or want to support the company's social and environmental objectives.

If the Body Shop could no longer continue to work in a particular area, the producers would be in difficulties

EVIDENCE

THE DOWNSIDE

'If the Body Shop withdrew and did not give us more work, the families and communities involved would be in serious trouble.'
A member of the Nanhu

Q1 If Body Shop stopped buying sisal scrubs from the Nanhu, what problems might there be?

Q2 Why can it be dangerous for people to become too dependent on a deal with one company?

unless the business was so well established that other people wanted to buy the output at the current price.

227

Unit 6 — Winners or losers?
Enquiry 5: Richer country – richer people?

Stakeholders: rights and responsibilities

You would never imagine that buying a pot of paint could be so complex and raise so many issues. The people on this page have a variety of choices to make. Their decisions involve both rights and responsibilities. One rarely exists without the other.

RIGHTS

We all have rights, which were laid down by laws that have been passed in the UK or Europe. All stakeholders have some rights. Can you identify the rights of each stakeholder?

SHAREHOLDERS
John owns shares in Regal Paint and they've been doing well. Should he sell them because of their poor reputation?

COMMUNITY
The area needs jobs and the clubhouse is falling down, but should people accept the sports club from Regal Paint?

CENTRAL GOVERNMENT
The government makes laws to protect stakeholders, e.g. customers, the environment, employees.

LOCAL GOVERNMENT
Should local council give planning permission for the Regal factory extensions?

ANNE'S CHOICE
Anne was fed up with her bedroom. It needed a coat of paint. She headed off to the DIY superstore to choose a new colour.

ENVIRONMENT
Ecopaint is the only safe buy – but it is more expensive. Should people pay more? Should Regal Paint expand?

REGALPAINT £5.40

228

DECISION!

THE CONSUMER
What paint should Anne choose?
- Ecopaint protects the environment but costs more.
- In China working conditions can be poor.
- Regal Paint has been fined for pollution.

KANTON PAINT
£4.20
made in China

MANAGEMENT
The paint has been selling well and Regal wants to expand. This will mean that more jobs are created, but the company has a poor record for both worker safety and pollution. It plans to develop goodwill in the local community by building a clubhouse for the sports association.

THE BIG IDEA

The rights and responsibilities of stakeholders have become the big idea of the 1990s. It has, in fact, had a much longer history. The idea first appeared as long ago as the 1930s.

RESPONSIBILITIES

Some responsibilities are laid down in law and therefore have to be met. Others are left to the individual company or government. More and more often, companies see the benefits of acting responsibly. Can you identify the responsibilities of each stakeholder?

EMPLOYEES
Jobs are scarce in the area and Regal is one of the main employers, but wages are low and the company's record on working conditions is poor. It has been involved in several pollution incidents.

ECOPAINT
£5.80

SUPPLIERS
Where should the chemicals come from to make the paint? The site which means digging up the dunes in Madagascar – or the more expensive source which does less harm?

229

Unit 6 Winners or losers?
Case study

A winner or a loser?

Q1 Who wins and who loses from the production and use of these products?

230

Index

absolute poverty 196, **197**
academic qualifications 48, **49**
accountant 96, **97**
accounts 100–1
    balance sheets 96–9
Act of Parliament **209**
added value 20, **21**, 28, 40
advertising 21, 46–7, **105**, 126–7, 182
    brand names 20–21
Advertising Standards Authority (ASA) 182
agriculture 147, 150–1
annual general meeting (AGM) 5, 182–3
aptitude test 51
ASA *see* Advertising Standards Authority
assets **83**, 88–9, 99
    current 96, 97, 98–9
    fixed 96, 97, 98–9
assisted areas **207**

balance sheet 96, **97**, 98–9
bank loan 90, **91**
banks, business accounts 101
benefits 208–9
biodegradable **175**
bonuses 52
boom 110, **111**, 117
brand image 126, **127**
brand names 20, **21**
breakeven point 86, **87**
budget **81**, 83
Budget, the **117**
business cycle 110, **111**, 112–13
business failure 32–3
business planning 81–3

CAP *see* Common Agricultural Policy
capital employed **25**, 98
    see also Return on Capital Employed
capital investment 158, **159**
cash 36–7, **97**, 99
cash flow 36, **37**, 106–7
    forecasts 106, **107**
Chancellor of the Exchequer **117**
channels of communication 135
charities 6, 7
child labour 196–7
children, poverty 196–7
collateral 92, **93**

collective bargaining 64, **65**
commission 52, **53**
Common Agricultural Policy (CAP) 147, 150
communication 54, 55, **133**, 134–5
communism 152
communities 178–9
company registrations **113**
competition 22–3
    profit 18–19
competitive advantage 22, **23**, 179, 198, 204–5
    flexibility 201
    people 202
competitive pricing **85**
competitiveness 22, **23**, 216
    exports 216–17
    maintaining 35
    profit 26
    workforce 28
computers
    environment 175
    shopping 11
consumer goods 126, **127**
consumer rights 212–13
continuous improvement **55**
contract of employment 63
copyright laws 221
corporate culture 198, **199**
corporate giving **179**
corporation tax **94**, 211
cost-plus pricing 84, **85**
costs 16–17
    breakeven chart 86–7
    economies of scale 120–1
    overheads 60–1, 94, 95
    profit 19
credit limits **37**
creditors 30, **31**
    business accounts 101
culture 54, **55**
currency, foreign 216, 217
current assets 96, 97, 98–9
curriculum vitae 50, **51**
customers
    monopolies 138–9
    satisfaction 198
customs duties **147**, 148
customs union **147**

debtors 88, **89**, 97, 99
decentralization 136, **137**

decision taking 27, 31
delegation 136, **137**
demand **13**
    see also supply and demand
    labour 71, 73
    price relationship 12, 113
    shift 34, 35
desk research 103
developed world 192, **193**
developing world 192, **193**
    growth 222–7
differentials 52, **53**
direct taxes **211**
disabled persons, benefits **209**
discrimination **51**
diseconomies of scale 132, 133, 135
distribution costs 148, **149**
distribution of income **223**
diversify **151**
dividends **89**
division of labour 40, **41**

Earth Summit 173, 180
economically inactive **61**
economies, underemployment 77
economies of scale 120, **121**, 122–3, 124
    mergers 131
    monopolies 139
    value for money 198
economy
    business cycle 110–13
    growth 156, **157**
education 63, 159
    government targets 67, 71
    grants 209
    lifetime learning 66–7
employees 159
    added value 28
    business accounts 101
    trade unions 29
employment 42, **43**
    see also jobs; unemployment
    contract of employment 63
    rewards 42–3
    self-employment 43
    structural unemployment 62, **63**
    transnationals 142–3
    women 59
employment laws 64, 65
EMU *see* European Monetary Union
energy 170–1

sources 168–9
enterprise 2,3
entrepreneurship 3
environment 172–5, 180–1, 184–7
    controls 184, 186
    government policy 184–9
    pollution 184–9
    poverty 197
environmental audit **181**
Environmental Protection Act 1990 181
environmentally friendly 172, 173
equal opportunities 51
ethical codes 188, **189**
ethical responsibility 176, **177**
ethics 227
EU *see* European Union
European Monetary Union (EMU) 217
European Union (EU) 146–53
    trade 220
exchange rate 216, **217**
excise taxes 211
expansion *see* growth
exports **147**
    see also European Union
    marketing mix 218–19
external economies of scale **123**
external sources of finance 90, **91**
externalities **125**, 164, **165**, 166–7, 181, 205

Fair Trade Foundation 227
farming *see* agriculture
finance 88–91
financial economies 122, **123**
fiscal policy **211**
fixed assets 96, **97**, 98–9
fixed costs 16, **17**
flexibility 63–4, 66, 200
flexible labour markets **63**
foreign currency 216, **217**
fossil fuels 168–9
fringe benefits 42, **43**, 45
fuels 168–9

gas 168–9
GDP *see* gross domestic product
General National Vocational Qualification (GNVQ) 67
goods 10, **11**
    adding value 20

insurance 108
government
    Act of Parliament 209
    borrowing 210, 211, 215
    business accounts 101
    business cycle 116–17
    education targets 67
    environment 184–9
    funds 210
    public sector enterprise 9
    spending 208–9, 210–11
    training targets 67
    unemployment 76–7
green issues 172, **173**
    see also environment
    recycling 174–5, 189
green-field sites **205**
gross domestic product (GDP) **75**, **143**, 156–7, 160–1, 162–3
    government borrowing 211
    government spending 208
gross profit 25, **94**, 95
growth 124–7, 130–1, 156, 157, 158–9
    developing countries 222–7
    diseconomies of scale 132, 133
    international trade 215
    sustainable 170–1

hidden economy 160, **161**
hire purchase **91**
homeworking 60, **61**
hotdesking 60, **61**
human capital **159**
Human Development Index **163**
human resources 55
hyperinflation 114

imports **147**
    restrictions 220–1
incentives 52, **53**, 184, **185**
income
    developing countries 224
    distribution 223
    national 156–7
    per capita income 163
income tax 211
indirect taxes **211**
industrial relations 29
inflation **111**, 114–16
    government policy 211
infrastructure **225**

Inland Revenue 100, 101, 160, **161**
insurance 108, **109**
    imports 221
insurance policy 108, **109**
interest **37**
interest rates 90, **91**
intermediate technology **129**
internal source of finance 88, **89**
international trade
    benefits 214
    growth 215
interviews 51
inventions, safeguards 129
investment 56, **57**, 158–9
    developing countries 224
investments, capital investment 158, 159
investors, business accounts 101
Investors in People 67

jargon 134, **135**
job description 46, **47**, 50
job enrichment **55**
job fulfilment 45
job interviews 51
job markets, trends 63
job security 29
joint venture 7, 130, **131**

Labour Force Survey 68
labour market 42, **43**, 72, **73**
    changes 58–9
laws
    copyright laws 221
    pollution 186, 187, 188–9
leadership 136–7
liabilities 96, **97**, 99, 108
lifetime learning 66, **67**
limited company 3
limited liability 92
liquidation **107**, 112
liquidity **37**, 88, **89**
loans 90, **91**
    bank loan 90, 91
    long-term loans 97, 99
    short-term loans 97, 99
    local councils 9
logo **129**, 172
long-term loans 97, 99
losses 18, **19**
    see also profit and loss account

machinery 56–7, 158–9
management 54–5
managerial economies 122, **123**, 130
mark-up 84, **85**
market clearing price 12, **13**
market niche **15**
market research 4, **81**, 102–3
market segment 126, **127**
market segmentation 14, **15**
market share 62, **63**
marketing 104–5
marketing economies 122, **123**
marketing mix 82, **83**, 200, 201
   exports 218–19
markets 10–15, **11**
   adapting 200
   pirate markets 160
   shifts in demand 34–5
   targeting 14–15
means-tested benefits **209**
merger 130, **131**
MMC *see* Monopolies and Mergers Commission
money 40, **41**, 44–5, 48–9
   motivation 52–3
Monopolies and Mergers Commission (MMC) 140, **141**
monopoly 138, **139**
   regulators 140–1
morals 176
motivation 42, **43**, 52–3
multi-skilling 201

National Consumer Council 172–3
national income 156, **157**, 161
National Lottery 7
National Vocational Qualification (NVQ) 67
negative externalities **205**
net profit **25**, 32
niche markets 15, 102
non-renewable resources 168, **169**
nuclear power 168–9
NVQ *see* National Vocational Qualification

Office of Fair Trading (OFT) 140, **141**
operating profit **94**, 95
opportunity cost **27**, 31
organizations, pyramid style 201
output 44, **45**, 56, 57
overdraft 37, **91**

overheads 60, **61**, 94, 95
part-time working 58–9
patent **129**
payment *see* wages
per capita income **163**
performance-related pay 52, **53**
person specification 46, **47**
personality questionnaire 51
pirate markets 160
place 82, **83**, 105, 219
plc *see* public limited company
pollution 184–5
   costs 189
   ethical codes 188–9
   rules and regulations 186–7
positive externalities **205**
poverty 196–7
poverty line 196, **197**
power, transnationals 143
premiums 108, **109**
pressure groups 174, **175**, 182, **183**
price 10, **11**, 82, 83, 105, 218
   breakeven chart 86–7
   competitive pricing 85
   competitiveness 22–3
   cost-plus pricing 84, 85
   demand 113
   inflation 114–15
   marketing 12–13
   quality 84
   transnationals 143
   value for money 198
primary research **103**
primary sector 58, **59**
Prince's Youth Business Trust 92
private limited company **5**
private sector 9
product 82, **83**, 105, 219
   promotion 126–7
   transnationals 143
product life cycle 128, **129**
product range **105**
productivity **29**, 56, 57
profit **11**, 19
   balance sheet 97–9
   calculation 18
   competition 18–19
   costs 19
   gross profit **94**
   measuring 24–5
   net profit 25, 32
   operating profit **94**, 95

planning 80–1
   private-sector companies 9
   retained profits 97, 99
   transnationals 143
profit and loss account **94**, 95, 98
profit margin 24, **25**
promotion 82, **83**, 105, 126–7, 218
PSBR *see* public sector borrowing requirement
public interest **141**
public limited company (plc) 5, 89, 92
public sector **9**
   spending 210
public sector borrowing requirement (PSBR) 210, **211**
public spending 208
pyramid style of organization 201

qualifications 48–9, 63
qualitative research **103**
quality
   competitiveness 22–3
   price 84
   value for money 198
quality circles **137**
quality control **55**
   EU standards 149
quantitative research **103**
questionnaires 102
quotas 220, **221**

R & D *see* research and development
Race Relations Act 1976 51
reasonable 212, **213**
receivership 32, **33**
recession 110, **111**, 112–13
   governmental influences 116–17
recruitment, advertisements 46–7
recycling 174, **175**, 189
redundant 63
refunds, consumer rights 212–13
regulators **141**
relative poverty 196, **197**
research and development (R & D) 122, **123**, 189
reserves 98
resources 168–9, 170–1
responsibility 144, 176–9
Retail Price Index (RPI) **115**
retained profits 97, 99
retraining 64, **65**

233

Return on Capital Employed (ROCE) 25, 26, 32, 204
rewards 28, **29**
rewards package 42, **43**
rights 212, **213**
risk 3, 18, 90, **91**, 113
    insurance 108–9
ROCE *see* Return on Capital Employed
RPI *see* Retail Price Index

safety, EU standards 149
salaries *see* wages
sales revenue 18, **19**
scarce skills 48, **49**
secondary sector 58, **59**
security 29, 108
self-employment **43**
service sector, trends 58
services 9, 10, **11**
    adding value 20
    consumer rights 212–13
'set aside' 150
Sex Discrimination Act 1975 51
share price **27**
shareholders **5**, 30, 89, 182–3
    business accounts 101
    private-sector companies 9
shareholders' funds 96, **97**, 99
shares 5, 89
    Stock Exchange 92, 93, 98
shift in demand 34, **35**
short-term loans **97**, 99
side-effects *see* externalities
skills 48–9
slump 110, 111, 112
small businesses 112
    finance 88
social class, unemployment 75
social responsibility 30, **31**, 179
sole owner **3**
specialization 40, **41**
stakeholders 30, **31**, 194
    communities 178–9
    rights and responsibilities 228–9
standard of living 156, **157**, 162–3, 170–1
standardization **149**
start-up capital 92, **93**
stock **97**, 99
    insurance 108
Stock Exchange 92, **93**, 98

structural change 58, **59**
structural unemployment 62, **63**
subsidy 150, **151**, **185**
success 26–7, 205
supply 13
    price relationship 12
supply and demand
    farm produce 150
    gas 168
surplus 6, **7**
sustainable growth 170, **171**

T-Form 96, **97**
takeover 32, **33**, 130, **131**
targeting 14–15
tax evasion 100, 160
taxation 184, 210–11
    corporation tax 94, 211
    customs duties 147, 148
    direct taxes 211
    excise taxes 211
    income tax 211
    indirect taxes 211
    value added tax 211
teamwork 55, 137
technical economies 120, **121**
technology, intermediate 129
TECs *see* Training and Enterprise Councils
teleworking 60, **61**, 171
tertiary sector 58, **59**
total costs 16, **17**
total revenue (TR) 86, **87**
trade
    EU 147, 149, 220
    international 214–15
    restrictions 220
    WTO 221
trade unions **29**, 64–5, 182–3
trade-off **145**, 166–7
tradeable permits **187**
training 55, 159
    government targets 67, 71
    job related 71
    retraining 64, 65
Training and Enterprise Councils (TECs) 66, **67**, 92, 206
Training for Work programme 206
transnational 142, **143**
trustee 6, **7**

underemployment **77**

unemployment 66, 68–77, 206–7
    see also employment
    assisted areas 207
    business cycle 110–11
    consequences 74–5
    reasons for 70–1, 73
    solutions 76–7
unemployment benefits **75**
unemployment figures 68, **69**
unions *see* trade unions
unique selling point (USP) **81**, 82
USP *see* unique selling point

value added tax 211
value for money 198, 204
variable costs 16, **17**
venture capital **207**
vocational qualifications 48, **49**
voluntary work 60, **61**

wages 17, 42–5, 192–3
    average earnings 48
    inflation 114
    labour market 73
    transnationals 142
wealth 192–3
welfare state 208, **209**
women 59
workforce 28–9
    see also employees
working capital 98, **99**
World Trade Organization (WTO) **221**
world-class firms **35**
WTO *see* World Trade Organization